GENETICS AND CHRISTIAN ETHICS

In the immediate future we are likely to witness significant developments in human genetic science. It is therefore of critical importance that Christian ethics engages with the genetics debate, since it does not just affect the way we perceive ourselves and the natural world, but also has wider implications for our society. This book considers ethical issues arising out of specific practices in human genetics, including genetic screening, gene patenting, gene therapy and genetic counselling, as well as feminist concerns. *Genetics and Christian Ethics* argues for a particular theo-ethical approach that derives from a modified version of virtue ethics, drawing particularly on a Thomistic understanding of the virtues, especially prudence, or practical wisdom, and justice. The book demonstrates that a theological voice is highly relevant to contested ethical debates about genetics.

CELIA DEANE-DRUMMOND (FRSA) is Professor in Theology and the Biological Sciences at the University of Chester. She is Director of the Centre for Religion and the Biosciences, and her publications include *Brave New World? Theology, Ethics and the Human Genome* (ed.) (2003) and *The Ethics of Nature* (2004).

Christian ethics has increasingly assumed a central place within academic theology. At the same time the growing power and ambiguity of modern science and the rising dissatisfaction within the social sciences about claims to value-neutrality have prompted renewed interest in ethics within the secular academic world. There is, therefore, a need for studies in Christian ethics which, as well as being concerned with the relevance of Christian ethics to the present day secular debate, are well informed about parallel discussions in recent philosophy, science or social science. *New Studies in Christian Ethics* aims to provide books that do this at the highest intellectual level and demonstrate that Christian ethics can make a distinctive contribution to this debate – either in moral substance or in terms of underlying moral justifications.

New Studies in Christian Ethics

Titles published in the series:

GENETICS AND CHRISTIAN ETHICS

CELIA DEANE-DRUMMOND

University of Chester

CAMBRIDGE
UNIVERSITY PRESS

CAMBRIDGE UNIVERSITY PRESS
Cambridge, New York, Melbourne, Madrid, Cape Town, Singapore, São Paulo

CAMBRIDGE UNIVERSITY PRESS
The Edinburgh Building, Cambridge CB2 2RU, UK

Published in the United States of America by Cambridge University Press, New York

www.cambridge.org
Information on this title: www.cambridge.org/9780521536370

First published 2006

Printed in the United Kingdom at the University Press, Cambridge

A catalogue record for this book is available from the British Library

ISBN-13 978-0-521-82943-4 hardback
ISBN-10 0-521-82943-7 hardback
ISBN-13 978-0-521-53637-0 paperback
ISBN-10 0-521-53637-5 paperback

To my wonderful daughter Sara Elisabeth, who teaches me the meaning of maternal love

Contents

General Editor's preface

This book is the twenty-fourth in the series *New Studies in Christian Ethics*. There are many points of mutual concern between this monograph and others within the series. Like Kieran Cronin's *Rights and Christian Ethics*, Michael Northcott's *The Environment and Christian Ethics*, Stanley Rudman's *Concepts of Person and Christian Ethics* and Susan Parsons' *Feminism and Christian Ethics*, it provides an expert critical overview of a complex area of secular discussion from a well-informed theological perspective. It also makes creative use of another monograph in the series, Stephen Clark's challenging *Biology and Christian Ethics*.

Celia Deane-Drummond's *Genetics and Christian Ethics* is well written, up to date and well informed. It covers a very full range of genetic issues and shows expert knowledge of both British and US developments. Using her own scientific background in this area, she provides detailed discussions of genetic testing and screening, genetic counselling, gene therapies, gene patenting and genetics and the environment. In each of these sub-areas changes are rapid and complex. Doubtless, particular scientific and technological developments will happen in each over the next few years. As she herself shows, the whole area of gene therapies, for example, has changed dramatically over the last decade, with scientists now being considerably more cautious than they were earlier. However, in each of these sub-areas she identifies ethical issues that are likely to abide whatever new developments take place.

A particularly helpful feature of this new monograph is the critical discussion of the distinctively theological principles that have been used by other Christian ethicists engaged in this area. In contrast to many others, Celia Deane-Drummond frames her own analysis in a suitably modest theology based upon virtue ethics. Theologians can all too often appear uncomfortably shrill (especially those without scientific training) when engaging in areas of novel science and technology.

This text will be invaluable to students and professional academics alike. It admirably fulfils the two key aims of the series as a whole – namely, to promote monographs in Christian ethics which engage centrally with the present secular moral debate at the highest possible intellectual level and, secondly, to encourage contributors to demonstrate that Christian ethics can make a distinctive contribution to this debate.

ROBIN GILL

Acknowledgments

First thanks for the genesis of this book goes to Kevin Taylor at Cambridge University Press and the series editor, Professor Robin Gill, who first invited me to contribute to this series in an area relating science and ethics. In the course of our discussions it soon became clear to me that an area of unprecedented significance for our current generation is that of genetic science, with its important social and political ramifications, as well as for its purely scientific issues.

I had the privilege of trying out sections of the chapters on environmental concern and women and genetic technologies in papers given at the Association of Teachers in Moral Theology, in May 2003 and November 2004. I am grateful for the detailed feedback and suggestions offered on both of these occasions. In March 2003 I presented a public lecture to Portsmouth University on 'Human Genetics: Perspectives from the Christian Wisdom Tradition'. I also had the opportunity to give a paper entitled 'Forbidden Knowledge: A Theologian's View' at a conference entitled 'Does the Future Need Us? Christian Faith and the Prospect of Post-Human Evolution' at the Garrett Evangelical Seminary in Evanston, Chicago, in April 2003. I gave a short paper called 'Putting Preimplantation Genetic Diagnosis in its Context: A Christian Ethical Response' at the Science and Religion Forum September 2003 Conference, entitled 'The Place of Humans in the Universe – World Faith Perspectives'. In November 2003 I presented a paper at St Mary's University, Halifax, Canada, entitled 'Fabricated or Fabulous Humans? Human Genetics and the Christian Wisdom Tradition'. In June 2004 I presented a paper at the Manchester University Contextual Theology Seminar entitled 'To Be or Not to Be? A Preliminary Analysis of Media Reporting of Stem Cell Research: A Theologian's Perspective'. In July 2004 I gave a paper entitled 'Fabricated Humans: Human Genetics, Ethics and the Christian Wisdom Tradition' at the Ian Ramsey Centre conference entitled 'Our Posthuman Future'. I am grateful for the invitations to give all these public lectures and also grateful for the feedback and discussions with

xiii

colleagues, both those known to me and those who were members of informed audiences, all of whom have helped to shape my thinking in this area. I am grateful to individuals who have read and commented on different parts of this book, in particular to Julie Clague for her comments relating to the chapter on genetic patenting, and to four anonymous reviewers who commented on the chapters on environmental concern and theological principles. I am also grateful to Gerard Manion for commenting on the chapter on eugenics, and to Neil Messer and Amy Laura Hall for many stimulating conversations. In February 2004, in the course of writing this book, I was co-opted as a member of the Ethics and Law committee of the Human Fertilisation and Embryology Authority (HFEA). While the discussions that have taken place in these meetings have helped to inform my views, the position adopted in this book is entirely my own and should not be taken to represent the views of the committee.

While preparing this book, I edited and published a volume in 2003 entitled *Brave New World? Theology, Ethics and the Human Genome.* This latter book arose out of ideas discussed at a colloquium of contributing authors and other participants held at St Deiniol's Library in March 2002. The current book builds on some of the ideas discussed there, but takes many new directions. I have also had the opportunity to develop and teach a module in 'Medicine and Christian Ethics' at University College Chester (now the University of Chester). I am grateful for discussions with my students and with the Very Revd Professor Gordon McPhate, Dean of Chester Cathedral and Visiting Professor at the University of Chester, who has also contributed to the teaching of this module. I should name my doctoral students working in the field of genetics and ethics, who have all helped to stimulate my thoughts in this area, namely the Revd Stephen Bellamy, Dr Lisa Goodard and Anne Marie Sowerbutts. Anne Marie has also enabled me to spend more time on research through her efficient contribution to the administration of the Centre for Religion and the Biosciences, of which I am Director. In this regard I am especially grateful to the Christendom Trust, who have generously given financial support to the Centre for Religion and the Biosciences since its launch in February 2002. This support has enabled more research to be undertaken in line with the mission of the Centre, including the writing of this book. The public outreach of the Centre was further expanded by its affiliation as a Local Society Initiative, supported by Metanexus in Philadelphia, USA.

St Deiniol's Library remains, as always, a place where I can focus on my reading and research and I am particularly grateful for their support. The University of Chester generously provided me with sabbatical leave in the first semester of 2004–5, which enabled me to complete this volume. I would like to thank Professor Robin Gill, and Dr Kate Brett at Cambridge University Press, for their support and encouragement. I would like to thank Gillian Dadd, assistant editor at Cambridge University Press, and Jo Bramwell, copy-editor, who skilfully contributed to the final form of this book. Finally, I would like to thank my husband, Henry, for his support, and my lovely four-year-old daughter Sara, to whom this book is dedicated; her life has been intimately interlaced with mine in the course of the writing of this book, and without her this book would no doubt have taken a very different course.

Introduction

Perhaps one of the most fascinating facets of genetics is its place in the biological sciences, situated at the boundary of evolutionary biology and molecular biology. Such a juncture immediately raises historical questions about human origins, but also possibilities for further manipulation of human genes. Questions such as 'Where do we come from?' and 'Where are we going to?' are as much theological and philosophical as scientific. Hence, the subject of genetics has opened up swathes of associated debates in the humanities, as well as discussions in a purely scientific context of technical knowledge and possibilities. New scientific research and technological achievements are reported almost daily in the media, reflecting another point: that genetic research is of public and social interest, as well as scientific and ethical interest.

Bioethics has tended to look simply to medicine as a context for its discussion. However, the issues raised by genetics show up the limits of approaches that refer simply to medical frameworks and possibilities, defined by given principles of good practice. There has also been a tendency to split the evolutionary view of the gene, perceived as a discrete unit of inheritance, from more molecular models that are becoming increasingly sanguine about the possibility of defining clearly what the scope of gene function might be. For example, the discovery that humans had only around 20,000–30,000 genes, contrary to expectations, showed that there was more to genetics than simply analysing one-to-one gene function; the expression of these genes and their regulation could also have a profound effect on characteristics of both a species and an individual. Hence, it is not always enough to suggest that we share 98% of our genes with our primate cousins. It only takes a moment's reflection and a dose of common sense to realise that we are far more than 2% different from the apes.

Are specific ethical issues raised by evolutionary research? There are, perhaps, areas of theological concern. The fascinating discovery of *Homo floresiensis*, a new species of human discovered on the island of Flores in

Indonesia, was announced in October 2004.[1] This human species, nick-named 'Hobbit', was smaller than its ancestor, *Homo erectus*, and adapted to the particular living conditions of its island home. The species was only a metre tall when adult, and, according to the fossil record, lived on the island from 70,000 to 18,000 years ago.[2] The point is that these humans were alive well into the time when *Homo sapiens* existed. Hence, mytho-logical stories about yetis or other human-like creatures coexisting with humans may be based on the real possibility of their existence at some time in human history. The discovery certainly challenges a naïve view that humans emerged from the primates in a linear way, with each emerging *Homo* species developing new powers and characteristics.

Does this discovery challenge the idea of human uniqueness? Certainly, our own species *Homo sapiens* was not unique in evolutionary history, but it did clearly out-compete its rivals, even if this happened relatively recently in the geological record. Does such a discovery undermine the meaning of humans as made in the image of God, *imago Dei*? I suggest that the meaning of image-bearing needs to be able to take into account such research, but at the same time it is important to note that the biblical record was never intended to be a scientific document. It was, rather, a mythical narrative about human origins and the relationship of humans to the Creator God, rather than a scientific account of how humans emerged. If we believed the latter, then women would have come from a male rib, and humans simply arrived from dirt, rather than from an evolutionary process. A literalist view is quite simply nonsensical. Hence, it is a some-what naïve approach to theology to presume that such scientific discoveries undermine the validity of human image-bearing, or religious understand-ings of the human.[3] It does, nonetheless, call into question any arrogance about our privileged status as humans.

Human image-bearing has been associated in the Christian tradition with particular abilities, such as reasoning, or with particular functions, such as stewardship of the earth. The former, taken to its extreme, would exclude those who have no reasoning powers, while the latter would exclude those who were not able to fulfil these functions. A more satisfac-tory account of image-bearing is a relational one; that is, those who bear the image are in a special relationship with God through revelation and grace.

---

[1] Gee, 'Flores, God and Cryptozoology'.

[2] These figures are approximate only; they may have lived earlier than this, or somewhat later as well.

[3] Henry Gee, for example, believes that this discovery questions 'the security of some of our deepest beliefs': 'Flores, God and Cryptozoology'. But this is only really the case if Genesis is equated with scientific accounts of evolution, which clearly it should not be.

Did *Homo floresiensis* have such a relationship with God? Such a question is answerable only by God, rather than by us, in much the same way that we cannot claim to know for certain whether other creatures of the world will share an eschatological life with human beings. Some theologians have argued that image-bearing should also be less anthropocentric for this reason, and include other creatures of the earth as well.[4]

Genetics, in looking to our evolutionary origin, has also raised important questions about human behaviour, some of which are linked to primate studies. The evolutionary history of a so-called 'warrior' gene, for example, has now been traced to primates. It is equally clear that complex behaviours such as aggression are the outcomes of much more than simply one-to-one genetic correspondence. However, bearing this in mind, researchers have still been able to identify an allele that predisposes both men and apes to aggressive, often violent behaviour.[5] The genetic variant arose about 25 million years ago in a monkey ancestor, surviving in the population originally because of an enhanced ability to catch prey or detect threats. The molecular chemistry of the gene relates to its ability to code for monoamine oxidase, which breaks down neurotransmitters in the brain. The gene exists in polymorphic form, that is, it has several repeats, leading to more expression the higher the number of repeats. When the gene has fewer of these repeats or is missing altogether, then neurotransmitters such as dopamine and serotonin build up, and this can account for the aggressive behaviour.[6] Men who have the short allele are more likely to commit violent crimes such as rape, robbery and assault, especially if they were mistreated as young boys themselves. In primate ancestors, the gene would be subject to what is known as 'balancing selection', where the two or more forms are maintained in a population. A gene that simply led to extreme violent behaviour would not be favoured in evolutionary terms; as such a male would be unlikely to survive in order to reproduce.

While this gives important insights into the genetic origins of some forms of behaviour, it would be facile to claim that all inappropriate behaviour is simply caused by genetic variants. Rather, it is always the combination of environmental conditioning *and* genetic predisposition. It is also clear that claiming that violence of any kind is 'natural' might give the impression that it is justifiable, or even good. There is, undeniably, evidence that genetic

---

[4] R. Page, 'The Human Genome and the Image of God', in Deane-Drummond (ed.), *Brave New World*, pp. 68–86.

[5] Gibbons, 'Tracking the Evolutionary History of a "Warrior" Gene', pp. 818–19.

[6] The gene is X-linked, and, while women also carry this gene, it is easier to study in males, where there is only one X chromosome.

factors are implicated in such violent behaviour. Yet their evolutionary origin should not at the same time give a warrant to affirm their ethical accept-ability. It is one reason, perhaps, that many feminist writers have objected so strongly to sociobiological explanations about the 'naturalness' of 'rape'. Such tendencies for violence should be seen as a sign of a *disorder* in the human community, one that needs to be tackled at the level of social support, hence addressing the environmental facets of the problem, and perhaps medical intervention where appropriate.

Other heated debates about the so-called 'gay gene' may also be sim-plistic where they give the impression that such behaviour is inevitably tied up with genetics. Researchers have found that women who have homo-sexual sons are more likely to be fertile, which is one explanation why the tendency for homosexuality has survived for so long, against an apparent selective disadvantage.[7] Yet such a discovery should not leave the impres-sion that homosexuality is *inevitable* in such families; rather, there is a genetic component to the expression of homosexuality, alongside cultural and environmental factors. The researchers are also quite ready to admit that their results are only partly successful in giving an explanation, and account for only about one fifth of the cases that they have studied.

Other areas of human behaviour that are reported to have a genetic component are mood-affective disorders, such as depression and obesity.[8] The tendency towards an essentialist understanding of behavioural genetics is a recognisable cultural phenomenon, and it would be as well to be extremely wary of naming human behaviour as too closely related to genetic data. On the other hand, where gene effects have a profound impact on particular disease, especially where that disease is from birth, it could also be argued that in these cases genetics actually shapes that person's experience of life and, arguably, their sense of identity. In navigat-ing the complex issues associated with genetics, it is important to distin-guish between (on the one hand) the use of genetic techniques and the ethical issues associated with this practice, and (on the other) the ethical implications of explaining particular human behaviours through analysis of genetic traits. Both areas have vast scope in terms of intersection with medical, anthropological and evolutionary discourse. Genetics is also much more than simply a discussion of human species, for it reaches out to include all species that carry genetic information from one generation to

---

[7] Hopkin, 'Mother's Genetics Could Influence Sexual Orientation'.
[8] For discussion see Kaplan, *The Limits and Lies of Human Genetic Research*, pp. 122–50.

the next. It is obvious that the scope of a book on all the possible issues in genetics and ethics would be virtually unmanageable.

For this book I have chosen to focus more specifically on ethical issues in human genetics, but this is not intended as a slur on the significance of ethical issues in the wider non-human community.[9] In chapter 9 I attempt to situate a discussion of human genetics in the context of the wider community of creatures. I have also chosen to focus more specifically on ethical issues arising out of current medical practice and debates in bioethics, rather than commenting in detail on current debates in evolutionary psychology. These latter debates are important, but they are perhaps of less immediate concern to medical practitioners and policy-makers. In addition, I try here to set out a case for a particular way of approaching ethical issues in genetics. Such an approach might equally be applied to evolutionary psychology debates in further work; thus the scope of this book is intended to be illustrative, rather than exhaustive.

The first, introductory, chapter reviews the current status of bioethics and the scope of ethics and genetics under discussion. What are the key issues raised by genetic science from a secular and religious perspective? What specific areas might be covered by genethics, or the ethics of genetics? I argue that priority needs to be given to a virtue-ethics approach, compared with other approaches to bioethics, such as those based on principle, utilitarianism or case study. In the past, virtue ethics has contributed to bioethical debates in abortion, euthanasia and the practice of healthcare rather than to genetics as such. I suggest that this lacuna needs to be rectified, as virtue ethics brings with it particular areas of ethical concern that are omitted by the other approaches to the ethics of genetics. In addition, I suggest not only that virtue-ethics is compatible with Christian theology, but also that a modified version of virtue ethics offers a particular contribution to the debates. I suggest that virtues such as prudence, justice, fortitude and temperance are also crucial for a Christian understanding of virtue ethics. Such modifications counter the common criticism of virtue ethics that it suffers from narcissism, or that it is concerned only about self-advancement.

The second chapter argues for the place of theological principles as an important ingredient in discussions of the ethics of genetics. The idea of principles at all might seem incompatible with a virtue-ethic approach that stresses the character of the agents, rather than rules as such. I will argue

---

[9] See, for example, Deane-Drummond, *Theology and Biotechnology*; Deane-Drummond and Szerszynski (eds.), *Re-Ordering Nature*; Deane-Drummond, *The Ethics of Nature*.

that some framework is needed in order to define more clearly what the virtues mean, without succumbing to the temptation to subsume the virtues under a set of principles. I compare and critique the theological underpinning to Christian ethics that is either explicit or implicit in discussions about genetics. Dogmatic ethics, for example, which takes its cues from the theology of Karl Barth, is in sharp contrast with process thinking and the like, which assimilates Christian reflection to scientific practice. A third approach is to run alongside strands in the Christian tradition after prior consideration of scientific concepts. While the first is unlikely to be heard in a secular context, the second and third options might seem to make little practical difference. I suggest that all three approaches suffer from some difficulties. I draw particularly on the work of Michael Banner, Oliver O'Donovan, Philip Hefner, Ted Peters, James Peterson and Thomas Shannon. I argue, instead, for an alternative ethic rooted in wisdom as the *theological* ground for an ethics of virtue.

The third chapter sets out to explore the historical dimensions of theological reflection on genetics, and in particular the way genetics was abused in the practice of eugenics in the last century. I suggest that a historical sense of the uses of genetic technologies gives deeper insights into the temptations before us in the present, though the scope and scale of genetic intervention are much more apparent today. I will also explore some of the social issues that have contributed to the rise and fall of eugenics, in particular following the experience of Nazi Germany. I will examine the way public attitudes to genetic engineering have been shaped as a result of this phase of history. Paul Ramsey's work will be discussed in this context and in the light of the previous discussion on virtue ethics.

The fourth chapter examines the social and political issues associated with genetic screening and the current status of screening practice in the United Kingdom. It explores the medical rationale for screening for genetically inherited diseases. It also explores the ethical issues associated with the testing of children, and screening programmes either *in utero* or prior to implantation. It asks, in particular, how far public policy on genetic screening has taken ethical concern into account. It examines the particular case of the UK biobank, which has been set up by the government in order to monitor environmental and genetic components of disease incidence. This chapter sets the scene for further ethical analysis that will be developed in later chapters.

In the fifth chapter I explore the specific ethical issues associated with genetic counselling following screening for genetic disease or familial

knowledge of propensity for disease. I examine the public perception of
risk in relation to genetic results and offer a critical appraisal of the risks
associated with genetic testing. I will argue for a greater emphasis on a
requirement to welcome those with disabilities from a Christian perspective, to counter other trends in secular practice that tend to associate those
who depart from the norm as 'unfit', even if under the rhetoric of choice.
I explore Hauerwas's concept of suffering presence and argue for a recovery
of the classic notion of prudence in counselling practice.

The sixth chapter summarises the current trends in gene therapy and the
use of genetics in medical science. In particular, pharmacological genetics,
which produces drugs through genetic means, can be distinguished from
somatic ethics, which modifies cells of the body, or from inherited genetic
therapy, which affects the sex cells responsible for the next generation.
What does the drive for all kinds of 'therapies' say about our own valuation
of ourselves as unique individuals, made in the image of God? Is therapy
fostering dreams of self-aggrandisement, or, worse, becoming the means of
controlling others? What might be the limits for genetic interventions?
This chapter argues for a recovery of prudence, justice, fortitude and
temperance in socio-political arenas associated with genetics.

In the seventh chapter I explore the knotty questions associated with
genetic patenting, in particular the legal arguments for patenting and some
examples of the way this has been used to further genetic research. I discuss
the ethical implications of patenting, and ask who are the beneficiaries.
Patenting broadens the remit of genetics into the animal and plant worlds
as well as the human sphere. Justice in the Aristotelian sense means
distribution according to merit. Patent law seems to follow this principle.
I suggest that while aspects are compatible with a Christian understanding
of virtue, some modification of the principle of justice is required. In
particular, a Christian understanding of justice according to virtue ethics
offers advocacy for the underprivileged, hence it is necessary to probe more
deeply into ethical approaches based on this model of justice.

In the eighth chapter, on women and genetic technologies, I explore the
questions associated with the new genetic technologies from a feminist
perspective. I examine particular feminist approaches to ethics, such as an
ethic of caring and postmodern critiques of science practice. I ask how the
challenge of genetics is influencing debates among feminists about science
practice. I explore how far any genetic intervention is compatible with
feminist principles. I argue that a Christian virtue ethic is compatible with
a holistic understanding of ethics and is more realistic compared with other
feminist approaches.

The penultimate chapter explores the broad issues associated with genetic intervention in the community of life. The purpose of this chapter is to situate the discussion in previous chapters, which has largely focused on intervention in the human community, in the wider society of animals and the natural world. This chapter develops this idea further with reference to a communitarian understanding of virtue in the human community. I ask, in particular, how far other creatures can be seen as 'other' in relation to humans, but also an inclusive part of a covenant community. I suggest that friendship is integral to an understanding of Christian virtue ethics, and that a modified understanding of friendship can be extended to include non-human creatures. This leads to consideration of how far genetic intervention in the non-human world expresses the virtues of charity and wisdom. Hence I challenge the idea that virtue ethics is inevitably 'anthropocentric', though it does call to account a deeper understanding of 'human being' as underlying 'human agency'.

The concluding remarks explore the particular implications of a Christian virtue ethic for the practice of genetics in all its ramifications. It draws the different strands of the book together and argues that our future depends on a revaluing of science, not just in terms of its utilitarian benefits, but also in terms of a Christian virtue ethic. In particular, what kind of science can we expect if we focus more on humans as agents, and less on humans as producers of the new technologies?

I am conscious that while the areas discussed in this book are wide-ranging, some readers might have preferred me to discuss areas that have not been included. I have, for example, woven the discourse about stem cells and cloning into the debates, rather than devote specific chapters to these questions. I have also decided not to cover evolutionary psychology and Darwinism in any detail, while referring to key examples where these are relevant to current practice. Nonetheless, my impression is that those areas I have tried to cover in this book have not received sufficient attention by ethicists and theologians, and this volume is an attempt to remedy that gap. My hope is that it will be useful not only for theologians, ministers, teachers and ethicists, but also for medical practitioners and those who are engaged in policy-making.

CHAPTER I

A recovery of virtue for the ethics of genetics

Why is there so much interest in ethical issues in genetics compared with other areas of science? What form does this ethical discussion take, and what might be the contribution of theological ethics to this discussion? This chapter attempts to set out the scope of ethical discussion in genetics, and to offer a commentary on its development in the light of the particular position being argued for in this book, namely the relevance of a theologically informed virtue ethics. Genetics, especially human genetics, intuitively seems to equate with our distinctive nature as individual humans, but it also reaches out beyond this to wider social and political questions. Therefore it is not just relevant for individual ethics, or ethics in a family setting through the new reproductive technologies; it also reaches out to significant issues of public and political concern. In facing such diverse issues, the temptation for medical science is to resort to a case-by-case approach and to rely simply on ethical principles such as patient autonomy and informed choice. Yet it is clear that the practice of medicine is itself being reshaped by the new genetic technologies, changing the ethos of medicine, with social and political repercussions, far beyond the limits of medical science. I will argue in this chapter for a recovery of prudence, or practical wisdom, alongside the other cardinal virtues of justice, fortitude and temperance. I will also suggest that the classical understanding of these terms offers fruitful avenues for exploration in the light of particular issues raised by contested issues in genetics. While I argue that these virtues have relevance for decision making by individuals and communities, in the specific instance of the Christian community they need to be understood as fully integrated with the theological virtues of faith, hope and charity.

WHAT IS GENETHICS?

Biomedical ethics is a field that has grown up and transformed itself from a discipline that was once loosely based in Christian morality to one that is more akin to a specialist science. Biomedical ethics has more often than not looked to the principles of respect for beneficence, autonomy, justice and non-maleficence, bringing in a discussion of the virtues almost as a way to supplement these pre-supposed principles.[1] Genethics overlaps with bioethics in that it raises similar issues connected with the start of life, but it is also even broader than bioethics in that it includes research in genetic science and its practice even prior to clinical applications. The scope of ethical discussion, among theologians at least, has tended to limit the ethical analysis of genetics to those areas connected with reproductive biology, rather than considering in more depth those wider medical practices that rely on genetics that have social and political implications, such as genetic screening, gene patenting and feminist concerns. There is also a tendency to focus on emotionally charged debates about the status of the embryo and avoid considering broader ethical questions. Those who adopt the most conservative stance, equating the beginning of personhood with the moment of conception, view more liberal gradualists as trivialising the dignity of embryos or, worse, as murderers. On the other hand, gradualists who perceive personhood as emerging later in embryonic development view conservatives as judgmental or, worse, as self-righteous and legalistic. Neither caricature need apply, but such undercurrents lead to suspicion and stalemate in ethical discourse. Conversation is no longer possible within such entrenched positions.

The boundary between an ethics of genetics and bioethics is hard to define, and it is certainly not appropriate to draw too rigid a line in delineating the scope of ethical analysis. Broadly speaking, where there is the possibility of a treatment that uses the results of fundamental knowledge in genetics, or where a change is brought about because of a change in genetics, then this could be thought of as relevant for consideration. There are grey areas, such as the ethics of human cloning and of stem-cell research. In these cases, both the replacement of the egg nucleus by a nucleus that has a different complement of genes, as in cloning, and the analysis of environmental influences that lead to a change in gene expression, as in stem-cell research, can be considered as arising out of genetic knowledge. There may be other situations where genetic knowledge might be indirect, but they would not be perceived as falling within the scope of genetics and ethics. There are more obvious cases of ethical issues in genetics, such as deliberately changing the genetic makeup of a living person, or gametes or

---

[1] See Beauchamp and Childress, *Principles of Biomedical Ethics.* I will return to a discussion of principles in chapter 2.

embryos prior to implantation. Julie Clague has suggested that we should use the phrase 'genomorality' in order to draw attention to the wider political issues that are under discussion in the general rubric of genetics.[2] Rather less common is the discussion about the influence of genetics on medical practice itself, so that it becomes a new way of doing medicine. Are such shifts desirable from an ethical point of view? In addition, genethics moves beyond the boundary of medicine in that it covers genetic issues in veterinary practice as well as in agriculture. It is also situated in the context of other discussions about the ethics of biotechnology, and biotechnological progress.

Given the scope of genethics, why has it become an area of such acute concern? One of the reasons is likely to be related to the view that in changing genetics we are changing something fundamental about human nature. Consider the following suggestion by John Harris and Justin Burley at the start of their *Companion to Genethics*:

No branch of science has created more acute or more subtle and interesting ethical dilemmas than genetics. There have been and still are branches of science that create problems of greater moral importance ... But it is genetics that makes us recall, not simply our responsibilities to the world and to one another, but our responsibilities for how people will be in the future. For the first time we can begin to determine not simply who will live and who will die, but what all those in the future will be like.[3]

Have Burley and Harris fallen into the myth that genetics will completely take over the future evolution of the human species? Certainly, this was a myth that informed the early genetic scientists prior to the adoption of a more modest approach that was informed by population genetics, which categorically stated that genetic modification would not have population impacts.[4] In addition, even if 'enhancement' techniques were to be used (which would have wider implications, as they would be more attractive to a greater number of people), the expense of such transformations would inevitably mean that there would be differential access to the technology. Further, to claim that genetics will decide 'what all those in the future will be like' seems to affirm the very fallacy that Harris has previously resisted in arguing in favour of reproductive cloning, namely, genetic determinism.

---

[2] J. Clague, 'Beyond Beneficence: The Emergence of Genomorality and the Common Good', in Deane-Drummond (ed.), *Brave New World*, pp. 189–224.

[3] Burley and Harris, *A Companion to Genethics*, p. 1.

[4] Note that this applies particularly to genes that are heterozygous in a population. While it might be possible, in theory, to screen out homozygous dominant alleles, this is unlikely in practice. For further discussion, see chapter 4.

In other words, in making such a strong case for the significance of the impact of genetics for human evolution, does bioethics, as much as eugenics, share an objectionable genetic determinism?[5] Certainly, where there are overstatements about the importance of genetics on influencing human evolution, and, by association, genethics, there is a failure to raise a critical voice in the discussion that is vitally needed in the midst of heated public discourse. However, there are strong advocates among ethicists against genetic determinism, usually from those who believe that developments in genetics can be useful for human societies.[6] It is also reasonable to suggest that while, on the one hand, genetic science is continuing to make more and more discoveries about the importance of genes for bodily function and disease, it is also qualified by the realisation that environmental influences play a highly significant role in almost all cases under discussion. Genetic counselling aims to help those faced with the prospect of developing a genetically based disease make informed choices about reproduction. Yet it talks in terms of probabilities, rather than of fixed inevitabilities, except in particular instances where the genes are almost certain to be expressed, having a high degree of 'penetrance'. The level of expression in any individual may also vary enormously. Of course, this uncertainty then impacts on the ethics of screening programmes at the prenatal or pre-implantation stage, for in many cases there is no way of knowing in advance, other than in terms of statistical probabilities, which of the individuals who are born are going to be the most severely affected.

Another highly significant issue to consider here is the way medicine itself is shifting in its practice, so that genetics is beginning to inform the way medicine is done. For example, arguably, genetic deterministic attitudes have crept into the way medical practitioners and politicians have thought about health and disease. Such an attitude would be represented by the claim that, once all genetic elements are known, then future health would be predictable, and genetics plays a central role in health and disease incidence. For example, why does a woman who knows she has genes which predispose her to breast cancer, BRCA1 or BRCA2, choose to have prophylactic surgery, even though the probability of disease expression is also influenced by many environmental factors? Although the philosophy that permits such direct action is one of informed choice, is such choice partly guided by a subtle form of genetic determinism? Of course, genetic

---

[5] This point is made by Lewens in 'What is Genethics?', p. 327.
[6] For a theological discussion see, for example, Peters, *Playing God*. For other examples of discussions of genetic determinism, see Almond and Parker (eds.), *Ethical Issues in the New Genetics*.

counselling aims always to present genetic information accurately, but statistical results may be loaded by using language such as 'high risk', which then seem threatening to the patients. According to traditional understanding of medicine, the health of an individual is related to the physiological, functional and phenomenological appearance of disease; that is, persons are sick when they show the symptoms of disease. It is worth asking if there is a new trend to identify the sick with those who have genetic traits, regardless of expression of the disease. Tom Butler argues that gene therapy or screening programmes, where this is considered at the stage prior to the appearance of symptoms, reflects the idea of having the disease even before symptoms arise.[7] Yet, is Butler correct in suggesting that this is an entirely new way of approaching medicine? Certainly, the tradition of *preventative medicine* is one that is well established, even prior to modern genetic technologies.[8] The latter could be seen as a way of reinforcing disease prevention by more 'scientific' means, other than general advice about healthy lifestyles. It seems to me unlikely that a medical clinician would consider individuals 'diseased' if they carry genetic traits predisposing them to contract a given disease. Nonetheless, it is worth asking how far such results are taken up and used in social and political contexts. The use of such information by insurance companies or employers, who have a stake in knowing how far persons are likely to contract diseases, is a significant aspect of this trend towards the use of genetics in preventative medicine. In addition, knowledge of the presence of the gene will be a form of preventative medicine only where adjustments can be made in lifestyle or other drug treatments in order to reduce the likely onset of the disease. If environmental factors cannot be changed, it is worth asking what is the point of such genetic knowledge, which could lead to considerable anxiety, with its concurrent health impacts.

GENETICS AND HUMAN NATURE

Where genetic knowledge is used as a means to prevent the birth of certain types of individuals, usually because there is no 'cure' for a disease, this leads to a form of medical practice that prevents those who are likely to have a disease ever existing. Ethical issues in this case bear on the status of

---

[7] For discussion see T. Butler, 'Genetic Reductionism and the Concepts of Health and Disease', in Almond and Parker (eds.), *Ethical Issues in the New Genetics*, pp. 83–90.

[8] It would be inappropriate to name embryo-screening as a form of preventative medicine, since the embryos in this case are discarded. The term here refers to gene therapy and screening of existing babies, infants, children and adults.

the human embryo or foetus. Yet, we might ask ourselves, what if it were possible to change the genetics of such an embryo so that the disease were no longer present? Would this in effect be changing the person's human identity? Some philosophers have argued that if a faulty gene is no longer present, then the experience of life of that individual is so different from that of the one who would have lived had the faulty gene been allowed to express itself that such changes amount to changes in human identity.[9] In addition, the treatment of a young baby (for instance, a baby of eight or eleven weeks with SCID, severe combined immune deficiency syndrome) with somatic gene therapy would change the way that individual came to perceive himself or herself. Walter Glannon argues that, while there have been wrongful life suits in those cases where children have blamed the parents for bringing them into the world, this would be impossible for inherited genetic modification, for in this case the person's experience of life would have been completely different if the genetic change had not taken place.[10] He therefore proposes that inherited genetic modification (IGM) or somatic gene therapy of very young babies cannot be classed as a type of 'therapy', as the person who exists would have been very different and would have had a different identity had the treatment not taken place. Pilar Ossario makes a similar point in her suggestion that 'the problem is not that we do not know who will be harmed or benefited, it is that we change who will be born'.[11] Of course, this might sound like a form of genetic reductionism, linking identity with genetics, so that changing genetics changes identity. This is not being argued for here. Rather, just as twins share the same genes but have different identities, so each of those with certain profound diseases will have a particular identity associated with that experience. Those diseases that are the most severe, such as Tay-Sachs disease, will lead to a life of suffering that is cut short in infancy. A child born without such a disease would have a different experience of life than the one with the disease, and arguably a different identity. On the other hand, those who have late-onset diseases could be considered to be the same person if the faulty gene was removed prior to birth. Where the identity problem exists, decisions are not easy to make on the basis of benefit for the future child, since arguably this child's identity has changed.

---

[9] W. Glannon, 'Genetic Intervention and Personal Identity', in Almond and Parker (eds.), *Ethical Issues in the New Genetics*, pp. 69–80. Pilar Ossario makes similar arguments in her 'Inheritable Genetic Modifications: Do We Owe Them to Our Children?', in Chapman and Frankel (eds.), *Designing Our Descendants*, pp. 252–71.

[10] Glannon, 'Genetic Intervention and Personal Identity', p. 74.

[11] Ossario, 'Inheritable Genetic Modifications', p. 255.

Yet this form of philosophical reasoning seems counter-intuitive. The alternative approach is to use some form of utilitarian calculus in arriving at decisions, based on the projected future suffering of persons.[12] This form of reasoning also seems problematic, as it is not always clear what harms might arise. In addition, it is equally clear that the notion of harm is dependent on who is making the criteria about what counts as being harmful.

The debates over whether or not it is permissible to screen in favour of deaf foetuses prior to implantation are relevant in this context.[13] John Harris has claimed that deliberately deafening a child is morally the same as selecting a deaf embryo prior to implantation; both choices lead to the same overall result, namely the existence of a deaf child. Yet this argument is faulty both morally and conceptually.[14] The case also illustrates the problems associated with an ethical analysis based on impersonal principles that rely on utilitarian arguments about the sum total of suffering. However, Harris fails to consider the identity problem, namely that if the deaf child *had not* been selected, he or she would not have existed, while if the hearing child had not been deafened, he or she would still have existed. In the case of choosing the embryo for selection, the argument about what is in a child's best interests cannot be used, as the child would not have existed had the choice not been made. Accordingly, Häyry believes that the 'real policy choice must be made between reproductive autonomy and socio-economic considerations' in providing for the special needs of the child.[15] He does not consider the other possible hearing children who would have been born had the decision been made *not* to select a deaf embryo. The parents arguing for parental autonomy in this case also do so on the basis of the welfare of the child, namely that a deaf child so born would then be integrated into the deaf community.

This is an unusual example in that genetic screening has been advocated more often for screening *out* those who are likely to suffer various disabilities, rather than for selecting in their favour. On one level one might argue that if hearing parents were to be given the opportunity to choose, through pre-implantation genetic diagnosis (PGD), a hearing rather than a deaf child, why should this choice not also be given to deaf parents, who desperately want a child who can be integrated into their social and communal life?[16] The suggestion that we should not burden society with

---

[12] Parfit, *Reasons and Persons.*   [13] For further discussion see Dennis, 'Deaf by Design'.
[14] Harris's position is discussed in Häyry, 'There is a Difference', pp. 510–12.
[15] Häyry, 'There is a Difference', p. 511.   [16] Dennis, 'Deaf by Design'.

another deaf child elevates socio-economic considerations above the freedom of choice for the parents. Of course, if the selection works the other way round for hearing parents – that is, deliberately selecting an embryo that is *not* likely to develop into a deaf individual – this might imply that deaf existence was a life not worth living. The 'welfare of the child' argument in favour of screening for a deaf child does not make sense, since if the child had not been selected, it would not have lived. On the other hand, if the capacity were present to genetically alter what might have been a deaf child, this too would change the identity of that child. It seems to me that in this case the mantra of autonomy has overreached itself. In other words, to use PGD either to screen in favour of a deaf child, or to select against a deaf child, is an inappropriate reification of freedom and parental 'rights' for children of their own choosing and an inappropriate use of PGD. In other words, the condition is not sufficiently serious to screen out, and to screen in favour implies parental control over their children, rather than parental acceptance of children as gifts, with all their associated weaknesses and strengths. It is, arguably, a version of liberalism that puts value entirely on freedom of choice, rather than rooting such choices in the virtues with an orientation towards the common good. Hence, it is not so much on the basis of socio-economic gains that such an action needs to be resisted, but rather on the basis that there are some uses of the technology that overreach its intentions as medicine, namely to seek to heal those who are sick. Deaf parents who have hearing children face the same sorts of difficulties as hearing parents with deaf children, but few would dare suggest that deaf children should be screened out prior to birth.

In addition, this example raises issues about the kind of society we are becoming and the human practices that are being condoned through the use of genetic technologies. Rather than being concerned that human nature, or even the identity of a child, might be different if that child were to be given genetic 'therapy', we should be more concerned with broader cultural trends that elevate liberalism to such an extent that children become rights that can be purchased according to parental desires and wishes. The limits of a personalist approach that faces the identity problem, and of more impersonal approaches that lack the ability to identify with those facing the problems at hand, come more clearly into view. The question then becomes: are there ways of viewing ourselves as persons that might help us navigate such difficult territory?

There is a recognisable trend in bioethics, including a discussion of genetics, to become 'thinned out' in such a way that overlapping consensus is arrived at through formal modes of reasoning.[17] Such a development could be viewed as a mixed blessing, for formal reasoning seeks to calculate the most effective way of reaching an end that is assumed to be a good. In the case of deaf selection, the good assumed is that shaped by liberalism, namely that parental choice trumps other considerations. The shift to 'thinner' versions of discourse has been particularly evident in the United States, where genetic advisory commissions were set up apparently in order to avoid the possibility of more stringent regulatory bodies that might interfere with scientific research.[18] The ends that were assumed were respect for persons (that is, autonomy), beneficence, and justice; and bioethics was perceived as simply being about how to arrive at such ends. This may be one reason why healthcare provision has apparently lacked any real reference to virtue ethics,[19] for it has relied on policy-making that has taken up this 'thinner' bioethical discourse.

Given these presumptions, it is not surprising that some of the most critical voices about genetic practice come from outside the discipline of bioethics. Francis Fukuyama has voiced particular concerns about the dangers of genetic engineering in terms of changing our identity as human beings.[20] This is not so much the narrow issue of whether someone who has been genetically changed is the same person or not (as discussed above), but more widely about whether human power over nature has changed the meaning of what it is to be human.[21] Even stronger is the suggestion made by C. S. Lewis in his book *The Abolition of Man*, that humanity's attempt to subjugate nature actually leads to its own subjugation. In other words, when humans are treated as artefacts, those acting cease to be human.[22] Or do they? Certainly, there are those who believe, correctly in my view, that treating humans as 'objects' is wrong, but the border between the artificial and the natural is becoming much more blurred in our present century. Is this invasion of the natural by the artefact necessarily to be resisted? While we need to guard against treating human persons as experimental objects rather than as subjects, some theologians have warmed to the idea that we live in a technological age. In this sense technology becomes the means to express creativity, to become made in the image of God, to find meaning through that technology, rather than in pitting oneself against it.[23] Philip Hefner makes the following proposals:[24]

---

[17] Meilaender, 'The Thinning of Bioethical Discourse'. [18] Evans, *Playing God*.
[19] Messer, 'Health Care Resource Allocation'. [20] Fukuyama, *Our Posthuman Future*.
[21] I will come back to this discussion in chapter 6. [22] Lewis, *The Abolition of Man*.
[23] This is the position advocated by Philip Hefner, see his provocative *Technology and Human Becoming*.
[24] Ibid., p. 88.

(a) Technology is a sacred space.
(b) Technology is a medium of divine action as it involves the freedom of imagination that constitutes self-transcendence.
(c) Technology is 'one of the major places today where religion happens. Technology is the shape of religion, the shape of the cyborg's engagement with God.'
(d) Technology is the place where we wrestle with the God who engages with human cyborgs.

Hence, rather than fear technology, Hefner suggests that we should welcome it as an aspect of our human identity and meaning, a place where God can act. Yet I am uncomfortable with this seemingly blanket endorsement of all things technological. In the first place, it seems to lack ethical analysis, bringing religious language into technology in such a way as to reinforce such goals without asking whether such goals are desirable or not. If bioethics works without proper analysis of goals, then theology's contribution needs to challenge such presumptions and seek a critique of both means and ends. Hefner seems to avoid such critique, other than speaking in vague terms about a 'wrestling' with God. Of course, the advantage of his approach is that it counters some of the unnecessarily hostile accounts that make the opposite presumption that technology, especially genetic technology, is a force for evil. Gerald McKenny, for example, is particularly critical of those religious ethicists who resist genetic engineering out of fear that this might impinge negatively on our self-understanding as *imago Dei*.[25] He argues, correctly in my view, that it is incoherent to locate image-bearing in DNA, as if it were untouchable, for this seems to locate what is normative in what is passed from one generation to the next. Yet, there are other considerations indicating that inherited genetic modification (IGM) may be ill advised – to do with responsibilities for future generations – which he fails to consider.[26] He also believes that to focus exclusively on IGM misses the wider issues raised by other practices, such as selective abortion, which could equally serve to devalue human beings. While this is true, it is also important to be aware of the major part that genetic evaluations are now playing in social and political terms. He argues that an important question to ask is: what is the role that genetic knowledge plays in forming us as subjects, and how does this compare with formation according to a religious tradition? In other words, in what ways is humanity

---

[25] G. P. McKenny, 'Religion and Gene Therapy: The End of One Debate, the Beginning of Another', in Burley and Harris, *A Companion to Genethics*, pp. 287–301.
[26] I will come back to this discussion in chapter 6.

being shaped by new-found genetic knowledge? An exploration of the virtues provides a means of entering this territory.

A VIRTUE APPROACH TO GENETHICS

Why should we recover a virtue approach to ethical issues in genetics? Bioethics, in particular, has tended to discuss particular quandaries in terms of principles of action, or of consequences, with the principled approach being dominated by the four pillars of non-malevolence, beneficence, autonomy, and justice. Ethical issues in genetics, on the other hand, seems to have been captured by a utilitarian concept of the good understood according to liberal politics, with an emphasis on freedom understood as freedom of choice. The combination of values leads to resistance to regulation, which either confines the freedom of the scientist to research in any way he or she might choose, or constricts the autonomy of the patient to choose one treatment over the other. Amid this trend there is increasing disquiet about whether such a 'thin' discussion of bioethics, and of genetics in particular, is altogether satisfactory. Beauchamp and Childress, for example, have argued for a recovery of the virtues that are correlates of the principles; hence we find the virtues of benevolence, non-malevolence, respect, and fairness in correlation with the four principles of beneficence, non-maleficence, autonomy, and justice.[27] Yet the virtues are much richer than this truncated description; the virtues are rather those aspects of character formation that help to provide those human strengths that are needed in seeking what might be the good and in deciding what principles might be needed in areas where such principles and goods are in dispute.[28]

There are other dangers, as well, that one might identify with a strong liberalist approach to ethics and its focus on rights language. James Keenan, for example, believes that many of the so-called principles that are arrived at in bioethical discourse are 'nothing more than the claims of conservatives who have accepted the context of liberalism'.[29] Rights language is so dominant that versions of natural law come to be associated with such rights, and debates emerge over whether such rights exist or not. Such a clash is evident in the heated discussion over reproductive technologies,

---

[27] Beauchamp and Childress, *Principles of Biomedical Ethics*.
[28] William May, 'The Virtues in a Professional Setting', in Fulford, Gillett and Soskice, *Medicine and Moral Reasoning*, pp. 75–90.
[29] Keenan, 'What is Morally New in Genetic Manipulation?', p. 291.

where the rights of parents or of mothers are opposed to the rights of the
foetus, though in law the foetus has no such rights. These debates fail, as
both sides are reliant on the same premises, namely that the discernment of
rights is the proper way to approach moral reasoning. An alternative
approach, which moves away from the almost exclusive focus on rights,
autonomy and conflicts of interests, is represented by virtue ethics. Virtues
look more deeply, not just at the actions of agents, but also at the agents
themselves.[30] In addition, the attempt to respond to this trend by simply
incorporating virtues into a pluralistic ethical method is still flawed, in
that it receives its justification from modern epistemologies and liberal
politics.[31] Modern epistemology is flawed in succumbing to the temptation
to believe that objective reason can be arrived at in a way that is neutral
towards any particular tradition. It is also increasingly unclear how public
obligations can be related to private virtues. Theoretical discussions about
the priority of virtue over obligation and vice versa tend to 'invite a self
characterisation of ahistorical disembodied moral agents who are not
adherents of particular traditions and who are relatively untouched by
specific social, economic and political contexts'.[32] Instead, a richer discourse
is essential if virtue is to be more than simply a 'turn to the subject', and is,
I suggest, particularly significant in the context of debates in genethics.

Alasdair MacIntyre defines virtue as 'an acquired human quality the
possession and exercise of which tends to enable us to achieve those goods
which are internal to practices and the lack of which effectively prevents us
from achieving such goods'.[33] If virtue is acquired, then it can be learned,
and becomes a habit of mind leading to particular patterns of behaviour.
Some might even say that such patterns actually begin to alter the psychological structure of the brain in certain ways, hence reinforcing the patterns
built up through constant practice.[34] The goods are both internal in
character formation, and external in outcomes, leading to particular
actions. Hence, even public virtue is valuable not simply for its instrumental
worth in leading to a particular good, but also because of the internal goods
for leaders in a given community. William May argues that virtues need to be
situated in the context of a discussion about what constitutes principles – for

---

[30] For a review of virtue-ethics approaches see, for example, Crisp (ed.), *How Should One Live? Essays on the Virtues*; Statman (ed.), *Virtue Ethics*; Crisp and Slote (eds.), *Virtue Ethics*; Hursthouse, *On Virtue Ethics*; Darwell (ed.), *Virtue Ethics*.

[31] For discussion see L. G. Jones and R. P. Vance, 'Why the Virtues are not Another Approach to Medical Ethics: Reconceiving the Place of Ethics in Contemporary Medicine', in Camenisch (ed.), *Theology and Medicine*, pp. 203–25.

[32] Jones and Vance, 'Why the Virtues', p. 209.   [33] MacIntyre, *After Virtue*, p. 178.

[34] For more detailed discussion of this aspect, see Deane-Drummond, *The Ethics of Nature*, pp. 136–61.

example, what gratitude might mean – in order to prevent such virtues becoming narcissistic.[35] He is also correct to challenge MacIntyre's pessimism about the possibility of virtues working in large-scale bureaucratic settings, but he fails to spell out how this might be achieved. James Drane does not even attempt to answer this question, but focuses on those moral virtues that it is important to develop at the level of medical practitioners.[36] All authors writing on a recovery of the relevance of virtue in medical ethics challenge any criticism that the virtues might be too subjective to be useful. May does this by suggesting that we still need some principles in order to help us see what the virtues might be like, and Drane does this by looking to psychological theories that give some clear indications of what a moral character might be like in comparison with people with character disturbances.

Another way to consider the importance of the virtues is to reflect on the meaning of *éthos*. *Éthos* once meant the home where a person lived, but later became enlarged to mean one's inner home. *Éthos* becomes the ground of practice, but it later came to mean the acts and habits themselves (*éthos*), rather than the inner ground (*êthos*). Drane comments that 'ethics even for Aristotle and certainly since then has focused more on *éthos* in the sense of external acts, habits and customs, and less on *êthos* as the inner wellspring of human action' (p. 289). This can be compared with *mos*, linked to the word 'morals', which is also external in orientation and refers more to the customs of a community. Drane believes that the Anglo-Saxon preference for ethics as related to law soon demolished any further considerations about character as being relevant to ethics. The Roman Catholic tradition of casuistry could also be viewed in this light, namely as an extension of law-based methods in decisions about the morality of particular acts.

In consideration of the ethical issues in genetics, the particular vices and virtues that are most relevant will also depend on the professional setting. Feminists have been among the strongest advocates of an ethic of care, which might be viewed as another way of turning to the virtue approach for ethical practice.[37] Drane names the particular virtues that are relevant for a medical practitioner as courage, prudence, chastity, hope, truth, commitment, and friendship, and the vices as greed for commercial gain, disrespect,

---

[35] May, 'The Virtues in a Professional Setting', pp. 79–81.
[36] J. F. Drane, 'Character and the Moral Life: A Virtue Approach to Bioethics', in Du Bose, Hamel and O'Connell (eds.), *A Matter of Principles*, pp. 284–309.
[37] See, for example, Gilligan, *In a Different Voice*; Noddings, *Caring*; Sharpe, 'Justice and Care'. For further discussion of this aspect see chapter 8 below, on women and genetic technologies.

pride, love of power, self-centredness, and commitment to self-enhancement (pp. 298–303). He also recognised that, historically, medical practitioners were encouraged to hold as high ideals as priests, both were considered to be 'vocations' or divine callings, both were committed to the service of others. In addition, both had a strong tradition of ethical formation as being necessary in order to fulfil the demanding roles required of priest or doctor. Moral failure, when it is found in either profession, is regarded as shameful even though medical training has lost its original link with religious formation. Such formation cannot come out of sheer willpower; what is needed, rather, is a recognition that growth in character formation takes place in a communal setting, so he can add that 'secular cultures, even humanistic ones, do not provide similar opportunities for character and virtue development, and it shows' (p. 305).

Could a similar list of virtues and associated vices be drawn up for those practitioners in genetics who are less involved with patients? Certainly, a researcher in genetics needs to be committed to the virtues of truth, humility, patience, prudence, fortitude, and justice, and to resist those vices to be avoided by physicians, including greed for commercial gain, disrespect, pride, love of power, and self-centredness. Similar virtues would also be required of those in public office in regulatory bodies, implying a public ethic that is rooted in character of those given such responsibility. One of the reasons the media are so concerned with the so-called private lives of politicians is that the public has an interest in how they conduct their personal affairs. Could someone who is faithless to his or her marriage vows be trusted to make important decisions that affect the lives of millions of people? Of course, where such media interest becomes intrusive, it needs to be resisted, but the expectation is that those who hold public office will also be exemplary in character and have the inner resources for difficult decision-making. The tendency to whitewash the behaviour of politicians as if this did not matter from a public-policy point of view is naïve; sooner or later there will almost inevitably be conflicts of interest.

A RECOVERY OF PRUDENCE

In discussions about the virtues needed for medical practitioners, reference is sometimes made to prudence. However, its treatment is far from satisfactory. Drane, for example, describes prudence as a habit of discernment, requiring experience and the ability to learn from it, and the ability to look ahead to what might be anticipated by a patient (p. 301). William May fairs slightly better in that he recognises that the medievalists were correct in their suggestion that prudence is not just about a fitting means to particular ends, but also includes *memoria*, being true to memory; *docilitas*, that is, openness to the present and to being still, ready to listen; and *solertia*, or readiness for the unexpected. However, he does not go much beyond suggesting that prudence is about being conscious of the past, present and future, and he fails to give prudence a central role in the other virtues. Drawing on the work of medieval scholar Jean Porter, Neil Messer also argues that we need to recover a sense of political prudence in healthcare resource allocation.[38] His attention to virtues in the context of debates about healthcare allocation is timely. However, he seems to assume that political prudence equates with distributive justice. He suggests that those influences that can 'train' members of the Christian community in political prudence include, first, a resistance to idolisation of health; secondly, sharing of goods with those in need; thirdly, a recovery of covenant themes as associated with justice; and fourthly, an honest attitude to tragedy. I welcome Messer's attention to political prudence and the relevance of virtues in wider social contexts, often neglected in a discussion of the virtues. His identification of particular goods also seems entirely appropriate from a perspective informed by a Christian faith. However, it is not immediately clear (a) how the values that he has identified as having an influence on political prudence actually serve to inform that prudential process or even arise from it; (b) why these influences are associated with prudence rather than with some other virtues; and (c) what is the precise relationship between distributive justice and prudence. I do not believe that it is sufficient to collate the two, even though distributive justice clearly requires prudential reasoning. In order to tease out this issue further in the present context, I suggest that we need a much richer discussion of what prudence means, and that this discussion, further, is informed by a deeper appreciation of prudential reasoning found in the thought of Thomas Aquinas.

One of the first myths that need to be overcome in any discussion of prudence is that it amounts to a form of restraint, a conserving of resources for one's own use. This version of prudence is a far cry from the medieval concept that is associated with a proactive concern with the good. In this tradition, all virtue is prudent, all virtues are informed by prudential reasoning, and prudence supplies a way of thinking about virtue that assists in assessing what it means to be just, to have temperance, to show charity and so on. May's suggestion that virtues need principles seems to miss the

---

[38] Messer, 'Health Care Resource Allocation'.

point that the very process of applying principles to situations requires a virtue, namely prudence. Prudence, in other words, will allow someone to judge whether some action or other is just, or courageous, or humble. In this way one might reckon that sins are always in opposition to prudence; it 'helps the other virtues and works through them all', and it is only by *participating* in prudence that a virtuous action can be considered virtuous at all.[39] Josef Pieper argues that prudence is not simply an optional extra; rather, it serves to express what it means to be human, for 'the intrinsic goodness of man, and that is the same as saying, his true humanness, consists in this, that "reason perfected in the cognition of truth" shall inwardly shape and imprint his volition and action'.[40] Yet it would be succumbing to the temptation of the Enlightenment if we assumed that reason simply meant rational understanding; rather, Pieper argues that reason needs to be thought of in this context as 'regard for and openness to reality' and 'acceptance of reality'. This is a helpful way of regarding reason, as it allows a definition of the human without specifying it simply in terms of measurable intelligence. In addition, truth is the unveiling and revelation of reality, so that reason perfected in the knowledge of the truth means 'the receptivity of the human spirit, to which the revelation of reality, both natural and supernatural reality, has given substance' (p. 17).

Prudence does not operate in detachment from principles, but these principles are set in the first place by *synderēsis*, which in turn arises from natural law, the most general and naturally understood principles of ethical conduct.[41] Pieper also equates prudence with conscience, so that he suggests that 'the word conscience is intimately related to and well nigh interchangeable with the word prudence' (p. 21). I am less comfortable with this aspect of his interpretation, quite apart from the weakening of our current understanding of conscience to mean individual preferences. A judgment that is made about the most appropriate means of acting in a prudential decision is what Aquinas would term the act of conscience.[42] Daniel Westberg has put this more strongly:

The equation of prudence with conscience is still faulty: conscience becomes the voice of reason, and the role of prudence is reduced to the perfection of the judgment of conscience. This does not necessarily result in good actions if the

---

[39] Aquinas, *Summa Theologiae*, 2a2ae q. 47.5.   [40] Pieper, *Prudence*, p. 16.

[41] For further deliberations on the place of natural law in ethical decision-making in this context see Deane-Drummond, *The Ethics of Nature*.

[42] I am grateful to Rudolf Heim for a discussion on the place of conscience in the context of prudential decision-making in the thought of Thomas Aquinas.

agent's will is contrary ... the agent may not actually follow his conscience, and so not carry out his best judgment.[43]

Hence, it is far too limiting to *reduce* prudence to conscience, even if conscience is enlarged; it does not follow through with the moral act that is an integral aspect of prudential thinking.[44] Prudence does not just include knowledge and judgment, but also follows through with action.[45] Hence, prudence has both an inner and outer dimension; it is insufficient to see it merely as related to right judgments.

It is helpful to tease out more fully the different elements of prudence.[46] Pieper has named these 'prerequisites' for the execution of prudence (p. 25). Jean Porter has called such elements 'component parts' of prudence.[47] While we need to recognise the varieties of interpretations of Aquinas,[48] it is important to find out whether such components were an integral aspect of Aquinas' discussion of prudence, since it seems that other writers have not paid such aspects much attention in their discussion of prudence in Aquinas.[49] It is also clear that, even though Porter lists these facets of prudence, they do not serve to inform in detail her discussion of what prudence might mean. While an understanding of prudence as setting the mean of a virtue – in other words, characterising what it is to be virtuous – is essential in understanding prudence, I suggest that the specific elements of prudence are helpful in demonstrating more precisely what it means to act in a prudent way. Aquinas' discussion of prudence in the *Summa Theologiae* includes two questions dedicated to (a) a consideration of parts of prudence (which is a discussion of philosophical interpretations of what prudence might mean) and (b) the components of prudence (which comprise his own list drawn up from a combination of different philosophical schools)

---

[43] Westberg, *Right Practical Reason*, pp. 7–8.
[44] For further development of the discussion on conscience, see C. Deane-Drummond, 'Freedom, Conscience and Virtue: Theological Perspectives on the Ethics of Inherited Genetic Modification', in Cole-Turner (ed.), *Design and Destiny*.
[45] Pieper was aware of this, and for this reason his apparent equation of conscience with prudence seems to be inconsistent with the rest of his thinking on prudence.
[46] For further discussion on prudence, especially the different forms of imprudence, see Deane-Drummond, *The Ethics of Nature*, pp. 10–15.
[47] Porter, *Moral Action and Christian Ethics*, p. 151.
[48] F. Kerr, 'The Varieties of Interpreting Aquinas', in Kerr (ed.), *Contemplating Aquinas*, pp. 1–40.
[49] See Thomas Deman's French translation of *Somme théologique*, where he considers all the questions associated with prudence, that is, questions 47–56: Thomas Aquinas, *Somme théologique, La prudence, 2a2ae questions 47–56*. Deman's appendix discusses prudence's origin in philosophical and biblical texts, the place of prudence in the moral life, the meaning of prudence and the relationship between conscience and prudence. However, he pays relatively little attention to the component parts of prudence arising from question 48 and 49 in the *Summa*.

(2a2ae qq. 48, 49). In thinking through what it might mean to act in a prudent way, it is perhaps surprising that relatively little attention has been paid to commentary on these component parts. Is such a list too complex? I suggest that these components are not complex when taken one at a time, and that they form a helpful grid which provides criteria for what it might mean to act prudently in any given situation.

Prudence, for Aquinas, has eight elements, namely memory, insight, teachableness, acumen, reasoned judgment, foresight, circumspection, and caution (2a2ae q. 49). Prudence in the mode of cognition has three elements, namely *memoria*, *docilitas*, and *solertia*. *Memoria* is more than just the natural capacity for recollection. Rather, it is a memory that is 'true to being', which means that 'it contains in itself real things and events as they really are and were'.[50] This task is one that shapes the historical mind, where memory reaches back into history even further than individual experiences. If such recollections are falsified in some way, then prudence is no longer possible, as error insidiously establishes itself in a way that is hard to eradicate. Of course, some might say that such an ideal is impossible to attain, and that we can never really know what happened because of the distance between past events and present ones. However, the importance of this element is the attempt at least to aim as far as possible to recall truthfully what happened, without embellishments or omissions and shifts of accent. A second element of prudence is *docilitas* (teachableness), or open-mindedness. Such a desire is essential if prudential decisions are to be made. Those who refuse to listen to advice, or assume that they know it all, will not be able to make prudential decisions. This characteristic also secures the communal element in prudential decision-making; it is never just about my own decisions in detachment from the views of others. The third element of perfection in cognition is *solertia* (acumen), that is, the ability to act clearly and well in the face of the unexpected. Such actions are not rash judgments, but are informed by *docilitas* and *memoria* in such a way that prompt decisions are possible. Irresoluteness (that is, the inability to act, or taking rash and fickle actions) does not show the quality of *solertia*. It is, as it were, the obverse of *docilitas*, which includes an element of stillness and contemplation. *Solertia* draws on this experience and is able to act rightly even though the time for such deliberation is no longer present. It goes without saying that acts that require *solertia* are not the norm, but are a result of an unexpected event. Aquinas also includes

---

[50] Pieper, *Prudence*, p. 26.

insight and *reasoned judgment* in his list of components of prudence related
to cognition.

What might be the elements of prudence as imperative? The first
element here is *foresight*, which Aquinas links with providence. Foresight
is the ability to know whether certain actions will lead to a desired goal.
Aquinas believes that this element is one of the key characteristics of
prudence, for it always points in some sense to the future. Yet the judgments of prudence are not fixed or certain in ways that might be the case if
it were simply an application of rules or principles. Rather, 'because the
subject matter of prudence is composed of contingent individual incidents,
which form the setting for human acts, the certitude of prudence is not
such as to remove entirely all uneasiness of mind' (2a2ae q. 47.9). Aquinas
also includes *circumspection* and *caution* in the list of those components
of prudence that are concerned with putting knowledge into action.
Circumspection is the ability to understand the nature of events as they
are now, while *foresight* is the ability to understand events as they might be
in the future. Caution has to do with imprudent acts that are too hasty in
their execution, and with avoiding obstacles to sound judgments (though
clearly a form of caution that leads to inaction is not what Aquinas had in
mind). In addition, Aquinas also recognises the place of *gnōmē*, that is, the
wit to judge when a departure from principles is called for in a given
situation.

Aquinas was clear that while the moral virtues on their own will incline
themselves towards right action, this inclination is not sufficient; which is
why prudence is so important for all the moral virtues, for 'the bent of
moral virtue towards the mean is instinctive. Yet because the mean as such
is not found after the same manner in every situation, the bent of nature
which works uniformly is not enough, and requires to be complemented by
the reasoning of prudence' (2a2ae q. 47.7). Hence, prudence helps us to
recognise those subtle differences that lead to a different course of action in
given circumstances.

Prudence as setting the mean of the moral virtues has more to do
with individual prudential decisions. Aquinas also wanted to extend the
consideration of prudence not simply to individual acts, but beyond this to
political governance. While Aquinas' discussion of prudence bears some
relationship to that in Aristotle, in this respect it is different, for Aristotle
confined his attention to individual prudence. Aquinas' view of political
prudence relates to justice, but is certainly not identical with it, so he can
claim that 'such prudence bears the same relation to legal justice that
ordinary prudence does to moral virtue' (2a2ae q. 47.10). In other words,

political prudence helps to situate what it means to demonstrate legal
justice in given situations, with reference to the various elements of
prudence discussed above. Aquinas is also ready to admit that there are
varieties of prudence appropriate for the good ends fitting for domestic
care of the family, 'monastic' care of an individual in a monastery, and the
common good of the state (2a2ae q. 47.11). He names these as prudence, as
applied to individuals; economic prudence, as applied to families or house-
holds; and political prudence, as applied to the state. He suggests that there
is a certain hierarchy, so that where individual prudence clashes with
economic or state prudence, then the former must give way to the latter.
Hence, 'the good of the individual is subordinate to the good of the
people . . . the virtue engaged with the furthest end is the superior and
commands the other virtues' (2a2ae q. 47.11). He argues that there are two
kinds of political prudence: one that is appropriate for rulers, and one that
is appropriate for subjects. He was living in a monarchical society, and
regnative prudence was appropriate in such a context. Jean Porter
believes that in a democracy 'there will clearly be more scope for all the
citizens of the community to participate in framing laws as well as carrying
them out'.[51]

Porter suggests that 'the very substance of distributive justice is so
intimately linked with the determinations proper to political prudence
that it would seem that political prudence and distributive justice are in
effect two components of one virtue by which rulers govern wisely and
well' (p. 104). Yet, if this was the case, why did Aquinas argue specifically
for political prudence to be included in considerations of prudence, unlike
Aristotle, who believed that prudence was confined to individual decision-
making? While political prudence will clearly set the way distributive
justice is executed, I suggest that, just as moral virtues on their own do
not have the capacity for knowing how to act well, so distributive justice
alone lacks the elements in prudence that are required for that justice to be
realised effectively and well. In other words, just as individual prudence sets
the mean for the moral virtues, so political prudence sets the mean for
distributive justice. Distributive justice is that which is concerned with
the relationship between the whole and individuals, but what this distributive justice might mean is not self-evident in all cases, and needs to be
supplemented by political prudence, in much the same way as correct
decision-making for the moral virtues must be supplemented by individual
prudence. In addition, there are other branches of justice that it is relevant

to consider in relation to political prudence. Legal or general justice, for example, concerns the relationship between the individual and the social whole.[52] Commutative justice, which concerns the relationships between individuals, is arguably associated more with individual prudence; but it is important to see the various forms of prudence working in a holistic way, in much the same way as the various forms of justice intersect and connect with each other. It seems to me that this is a crucial point, for, if political prudence is simply equated with distributive justice, then prudential reasoning as such is no longer allowed into the political and public forum. Political prudence is one way of helping to heal both the rift between public and private morality, and the false divide between a 'subjective' virtue ethic, which is concerned with individuals, and principled 'objective' approaches that are more often concerned with wider social contexts.

Aquinas also departed from Aristotle in that he situated the good attained by prudence in the context of the Divine Law. In addition, prudence could be acquired by learning, but he also insisted that it could be received or infused by divine grace. These give qualities to prudence which are not simply those arrived at through innate capacities. For 'the prudence of grace, however, is caused by God's imparting' (2a2ae q. 47.14). This allows Aquinas to argue that prudence is present in children and in those whose reasoning is impaired. However, he is also ready to admit that prudence can be spoiled in all kinds of ways, and where truths are forgotten, prudence no longer flowers into action, and becomes 'blocked' (2a2ae q. 47.16). Hence, the virtue of charity in one sense trumps even that of prudence, for without charity prudential decision-making becomes disconnected from its source in the love of God and of neighbour.

JUSTICE, FORTITUDE AND TEMPERANCE AMONG THE VIRTUES

Contemporary writers on the importance of justice in ethical decision-making usually want to make universal claims without relying on meta-physical or religious support.[53] Such a shift includes those who support a rehabilitation of natural-law theory, minimising its original association with religious certainties.[54] The classical tradition of viewing justice as a virtue or a habit of mind is lost in such analysis, as is evidenced in John Rawls's

---

[52] For further discussion of justice in Aquinas see Deane-Drummond, *The Ethics of Nature*, pp. 95–100. This form of justice is also known as contributive justice in contemporary discourse.

[53] See, for example, discussion in O'Neill, *Towards Justice and Virtue*, pp. 11–12.

[54] George (ed.), *Natural Law Theory*.

influential theory of justice.[55] Those critical of Rawls's position believe that his concept of justice is too 'thin'; rather, we need a return to the virtues that offer more particularist accounts that are rooted in specific situations and communities. On the other side is the argument that such virtues fail to offer an adequate treatment of complex socio-political issues. But what if we were to take the more radical step of recovering the notion of justice as virtue? Such an account would be particularist, in that it would refer to the individual's ability to act justly, but would also reach beyond this in its scope, to socio-political realities, as when prudence is enlarged to include domestic and political prudence, discussed above.

For Aquinas, 'justice is the habit whereby a person with a lasting and constant will renders to each his due' (2a2ae q. 58.1).[56] Justice is about governance of behaviour towards others, implying 'a certain balance of equality'; yet knowing what a just deed might be is 'prescribed' not so much by justice itself as by prudence (2a2ae q. 57.1). In addition, Aquinas believes that justice that presupposes 'positive right', expressed in laws, needed to conform with what would be anticipated through natural law, for 'if anything conflicts with natural right, human will cannot make it just' (2a2ae q. 57.2). He also believes in a form of universal law, so that 'that which natural reason constitutes between all men and is observed by all people is called the *jus gentium*' (2a2ae q. 57.3). The latter is necessarily a human construct, for 'only men share in it among themselves'. In this way he avoids both the difficulties associated with simply focusing on particularist issues at the expense of wider social contexts, and the problems associated with a 'thinning' of the discourse through a reliance on universal principles agreed across pluralist communities. Aquinas was also clear that justice was a more 'detached' virtue compared with others, and was rooted in the human will to do good (2a2ae q. 58.3). Justice as virtue also goes beyond merely keeping the law, in that the demands of justice may be morally binding according to that which is honourable or seemly, over and beyond what is legally binding through given laws. Any impression, however, that natural law presents an unalterable fixity should be discounted, for while the first principles to do good and to avoid evil are unalterable, secondary precepts can be changed 'on some particular and

---

[55] Rawls, *A Theory of Justice*.

[56] This definition also raises the issue of how we know what is due and to whom, traditionally the brief of rights. Human rights, from a theological perspective, exist by reason of human existence as creaturely being. Something may become due because of contractual agreements, or because of natural right, according to natural law. Determining what is appropriate as a human right is the task of prudence.

rare occasions ... because of some special cause preventing their unqualified observance' (1a2ae q. 94.5). In addition, human law is in place in order to forbid those vices that 'the average man can avoid' (1a2ae q. 96.2). This point is important, for what can be expected to be followed in a Christian community cannot then be read off directly into human laws. It is further limited by the fact that 'human law cannot forbid all that natural law forbids', so that 'natural law is a kind of sharing by us in the Eternal Law from which human law falls short'. Of course, contemporary writers generally want to remove any reference to Eternal Law altogether. However, if we qualify human law by stating that it is not inevitably coincident with natural law, then we avoid any uncomfortable notions of a universal theocracy, while retaining the original sense that Aquinas desired, namely an integration of natural law with the spiritual life.[57]

How might law, which expresses justice in a community, be related to the other virtues? Aquinas is realistic in this respect as well, for he recognises that 'human law does not enjoin every act of every virtue, but those acts only which serve the common good, either immediately, as when the social order is involved from the nature of things, or mediately, as when measures of good discipline are passed by the legislator to train citizens to maintain justice and peace in the community' (1a2ae q. 96.3). He also recognises that the law needs to be flexible enough to respond to emergencies, equating with the human quality of *gnōmē* mentioned above. Justice as virtue is relevant not simply when considering the relationship between the individual and the social whole, as expressed in legal (general) justice, but also between individuals among themselves, or commutative justice. Prudence helps to set the mean for legal justice and commutative justice, whereas political prudence helps to set the mean for distributive justice, as discussed above.

If the orientation towards the good is achieved through justice acting in accordance with prudence, then fortitude and temperance create the inner basis for carrying this out. They are, in this sense, virtues supplementary to prudence and justice. Fortitude is not feckless bravery, but more the willingness to suffer for the good, both the individual good and the common good. While justice works in the will, fortitude and temperance work in the emotions or 'sense appetites', and fortitude specifically in the contending emotions.[58] If prudence sets out what justice might mean, then fortitude as a virtue is necessary in order to bring such justice into execution. The

---

[57] Jean Porter also argues strongly for natural law to be understood in its theological context. For more discussion on this issue, see Deane-Drummond, *The Ethics of Nature*, pp. 38–41.

[58] See Cessario, *Introduction to Moral Theology*, pp. 129, 197.

ultimate definition of fortitude was in terms of Christian sacrifice of one's own life for the sake of the greater good. Such fortitude endured the evil inherent in a situation where suffering was required, accepting this for the sake of the greater good, in patient expectation. Endurance and patience are therefore virtues associated with fortitude, though there is also an allowance for wrath, where this is specifically directed against evil. For such a sacrifice to be possible, the virtue of fortitude needed to be infused by divine grace.[59] However, while St Bonaventure believed that the infused virtue of fortitude (and temperance) could come only from a transformed will, Aquinas believed that divine grace acted so as to transform human passions, rather than simply restrain them.[60]

Temperance as a virtue, like prudence, has a somewhat truncated meaning in modern parlance, so that it comes to be associated merely with not taking more than one's due. However, the classical meaning of temperance is much more positive than this, affirming both a sense of ordered unity and a serenity of spirit that recognises ordering within the human person. Intemperance arises where the natural forces for self-preservation get out of hand and degenerate into selfishness, as expressed in unchastity, pride, uncontrolled fury and a disordered lust for knowledge or *curiositas*.[61] The primordial form of temperance is chastity. For where there is an uncontrolled urge towards sensual enjoyment, intemperance takes root. This does not mean that Aquinas was hostile towards sexual pleasures where they were expressed in the appropriate context, namely marriage.[62] In this sense it is fair to suggest that 'lack of sensuality is not chastity, and incapacity for wrath has nothing to do with gentleness'.[63] We also find humility associated with temperance, and pride with intemperance, for humility amounts to a correct estimation of oneself according to the truth. Temperance includes the ability to show self-restraint in the face of the impulse emotions, but such self-restraint is not simply a matter of willpower, but reaches down to

---

[59] Aquinas distinguishes three levels of perfection in fortitude. First, there is the political fortitude that is an aspect of the common life; then purgatorial fortitude or 'dark night', where there is a struggle to arrive at perfection; then finally there is a fortitude of the purified spirit, which is equivalent to the beginning of eternal life. Josef Pieper suggests that the three forms of fortitude are pre-moral, ethical and mystical: Pieper, *Fortitude and Temperance*, p. 45. The problem of this classification is that it seems to associate the ethical with the interior life, rather than with the political life, and to separate the mystical from it altogether. I would prefer to see the three varieties of prudence working together, even if some distinctions can be drawn.

[60] Cessario, *Introduction to Moral Theology*, p. 203.   [61] Pieper, *The Four Cardinal Virtues*, p. 151.

[62] He also argued that fornication is wrong only in as much as it does not sufficiently take into account the welfare of the child arising out of such liaison. See, for example, Aquinas, *Summa Theologiae*, 2a2ae q. 154.2.

[63] Pieper, *Fortitude and Temperance*, p. 114.

a transformation of emotions themselves. In this way temperance is associated with gentleness and mildness, whereas intemperance is associated with anger that has got out of hand in uncontrolled rage.

Finally, and perhaps particularly relevant to present concerns, temperance is concerned with careful pursuit of knowledge. However, such a pursuit has the potential to generate into a form of lust or indulgence of sensual perception arising from the knowledge of the world, expressed in the vice of *curiositas*. In Aquinas' time this *curiositas* was associated with magic, and Pieper in particular wants to distance himself from any association of this vice with secular science (pp. 117–22). However, he allows for the fact that the vice is associated with the pleasure of seeing, a concupiscence of the eyes, arising out of an inner restlessness and sadness of heart that are associated with unbelief. It seems entirely plausible to me that such concupiscence could be found in any form of searching after knowledge in the arts, humanities or sciences. Hence, it is a mistake on Pieper's part to exclude secular science from its threat, while at the same time being ready to admit that to confine such an activity to science would also be mistaken. Pieper is also correct to suggest that temperance in this area is vital in order for the subject to regain a sense of true knowledge according to a relationship with God; hence

It is in such an asceticism of cognition alone that he may preserve or regain that which actually constitutes man's vital existence: the perception of the reality of God and his creation, and the possibility of shaping himself and the world according to this truth, which reveals itself only in silence. (p. 122)

But how might we begin to reach such a strong position in fortitude and temperance, in order to express adequately the virtues of justice through prudence? For this the theological virtues of faith, hope and charity are necessary prerequisites for all of the infused virtues. Gifts come through the working of the Holy Spirit, and, as Romano Cessario suggests, 'the gifts of the Holy Spirit complete the practice of Christian moral theology, for they ensure that each virtuous action of the believer conforms perfectly to the will of God' (p. 211). While Aquinas lists the *affective* gifts as fortitude, piety, and fear of the Lord, the *intellectual* gifts are wisdom, understanding, knowledge, and counsel. The gifts are associated with virtues, so that fortitude is linked with the virtue, piety with justice, and fear of the Lord with hope and temperance. The virtue of charity is associated with wisdom; the virtue of faith is associated with understanding and knowledge; and the virtue of prudence is associated with the gift of counsel. How helpful are these associations? In the first place, they are reminders that the life of virtue is not simply about straining to reach a goal in independence of God or of faith in Christ. In order to be perfect, a life of virtue flows from the experience of a graced existence that enables the believer to attain a higher level of goodness than would otherwise be the case. Stanley Hauerwas has criticised Aquinas in as much as he believes that the latter does not sufficiently appreciate the *choice* that one has to make in living out the good life. He criticises Aquinas for his view that the virtues form a unity, suggesting that both Aquinas and Aristotle 'failed to see that we often find ourselves involved in ways of life that require certain virtues to go undeveloped or be essentially transformed'.[64] Yet, like Aquinas, he recognised that the virtues could be sustained only by the action of God; but he resisted spelling out in detail how the virtues and gifts might be interrelated. Yet one might argue that, even though Aquinas argues for the unity of the virtues, he gives higher priority to some than to others. Hauerwas does no less in his suggestion that the virtues of hope and patience should be given primacy (p. 127).

I suggest that the associations that Aquinas makes between the gifts and the virtues are helpful pointers, but they should not be understood as operating in a rigid way. It makes sense, then, to link piety as gift with justice, for piety is about an ordered relationship with God, and justice is about ordered relationships between members of the human community.[65] The fear of the Lord is a gift that is a necessary prelude to having hope. Without deep acknowledgment of the lordship of God over creaturely existence, hope becomes very difficult. The fear of the Lord is also necessary in order to permit the flourishing of temperance, for a right perception of oneself in relation to one's true needs arises out of an acknowledgment of covenant relationships with God. The gift of counsel as associated with prudence also makes sense in the context of prudence as encompassing *docilitas*.[66] The Holy Spirit, as divine counsellor, still preserves the freedom of the individual. Faith as associated with understanding and knowledge is also reminiscent of faith seeking understanding as the task of theology. While Aquinas had theological understanding in mind in this context, it also applies to scientific understanding in the sense that understanding is possible only when there is a degree of commitment.[67]

---

[64] Hauerwas, *A Community of Character*, p. 143.

[65] In chapter 9 I will argue that justice should be extended to other creatures as well, but in the first instance it applies to human societies themselves.

[66] For further discussion of the relationship between prudence and the gift of counsel see Deane-Drummond, *The Ethics of Nature*, p. 13.

[67] I will enlarge this discussion to include Aquinas' concept of a gift of science in the final chapter.

Wisdom as gift will issue in the virtue of charity, though the relationship is somewhat circular, for without charity wisdom becomes dysfunctional. Aquinas also gives charity primacy over faith and hope, even though he recognises that faith precedes hope and charity 'in the sequence of coming to be'. He also believes that hope as act is prior to an act of charity, but 'in the precedence of value, however, charity comes before faith and hope, because both faith and hope come active through charity, and reserve from charity their full stature as virtues. For thus charity is the mother and root of all virtues, inasmuch as it is the form of them all' (1a2ae q. 62.4). Hence the kind of linkages between gifts and virtues is just one strand of the relationships between virtues and their expression in particular acts. It is clear that charity is a fundamental virtue that informs the other virtues, including the four cardinal virtues discussed above. Yet the correlations suggested above also seem to coalesce in wisdom, for 'piety makes wisdom manifest, too, and because of that we can say that piety is wisdom, and for the same reason also is fear. If a man fears and worships God he shows he has a right judgment about divine things' (2a2ae q. 45.1).

CONCLUSIONS

This chapter has tried to set out in summary form some key aspects of the debates in bioethics and their engagement with a discussion of the virtues. I have outlined the scope of those areas in genetics that can be subsumed under a title of 'ethics and genetics' and offered some possible reasons for the intense interest in this field connected with the possible impacts of genetics on our self-understanding as human beings. I have illustrated the range of areas under discussion by reference to a few select examples, in order to give a flavour of the kinds of issues that are ripe for discussion in the chapters that follow. I have argued that bioethics has leaned towards a thin account of ethics, reliant on presupposed goods according to liberalist ideals. Yet we also find some theologians arguing strongly in favour of genetic interventions. Given the complexity of the field, I have argued that it is not so much a matter of dispensing with the ghosts of genetic determinism, as a matter of developing those traits of character that will guide us as to which elements of genetic knowledge may be incorporated into our own individual and communal narratives. I have argued for the particular relevance of prudence, or practical wisdom, in such a context, drawing particularly on the work of Thomas Aquinas. In addition, a virtue ethic needs to be bold enough to enter the territory of social politics and policy-making if it is to make a real difference to the way genetic issues are embedded in society. Such a task is by no means an easy one to define, though the possibility of political prudence, alongside legal, commutative and distributive forms of justice, is a start in this direction. I have also suggested that the scope of the virtues needs to be enlarged to include virtues such as fortitude and temperance, with associated virtues of hope and chastity. In addition, such ideals would be impossible to attain without a strong sense of gifts of the Holy Spirit, and the idea that virtues are both learned and infused by the grace of God. How might such a grace-filled life impinge on the practice of the virtues? In other words, what particular theological principles are presupposed in the form of virtue ethics that I am expounding here? The following chapter seeks not so much to answer this question directly as to put forward a possible form in which such principles might emerge. While these principles will be most relevant in the context of a Christian community, I will argue that an honest approach requires such acknowledgment, while reserving a certain modesty as to the applicability of these principles to specific instances of decision-making in secular contexts.

CHAPTER 2

Theological principles

Men ought not to play God before they learn to be men, and after they have learned to be men they will not play God.[1]

This oft-cited remark from Paul Ramsey's book, *Fabricated Man*, published over twenty years ago, puts theology in the position of interrogator of genetic science rather than conversation partner. He was one of the first ethicists to enter the debate over genetics. Nonetheless, the quotation needs to be set in the context of his argument as a whole, namely that theologians were placid in the face of overreaching claims of biologists, whose goal seemed to Ramsey to take the form of an unregulated religious fanaticism, beyond even the more modest hopes of humanism. The theologians he criticised were not just 'techno-theologians', but Roman Catholics such as Karl Rahner, who, he suggests, 'clings to the belief that men are wise enough to invent themselves' (p. 140). For Ramsey, the critical issue is not so much the future of religion, but the future of humanism. Hence, 'It is not Christianity alone but man as well that the revolutionary biologists have left behind in their flights of grasping after godhead' (p. 146).[2] Moreover, for him, human dignity is not just ensuring that those who come after us are better than we are.[3]

---

[1] Ramsey, *Fabricated Man*, p. 138.

[2] Rahner does have some highly critical comments to make about genetic engineering, even though he resisted blanket condemnation of genetic research. He also, for example, recognised that the 'faith instinct' would be inclined to reject genetic manipulation altogether. While it is fair that in this case 'genetic manipulation' seemed primarily to refer to the new reproductive technologies, there is no reason why it could not also be applied to other contexts where human genetics was controlled. While he seems to open up the theoretical possibility of openness in his strong discussion of freedom, his practical ethics remains highly conservative, failing to follow through on his earlier statements: Rahner, 'The Problem of Genetic Manipulation', in *Theological Investigations* IX, pp. 225–52. This issue is taken up further in C. Deane-Drummond, 'Freedom, Conscience and Virtue', in Cole-Turner (ed.), *Design and Destiny*.

[3] P. Ramsey, 'Moral and Religious Implications of Genetic Control', in Roslansky (ed.), *Genetics and the Future of Man*, p. 139. One of the main alternatives to Ramsey's approach was the situation-ethics

This seems very far from the way the term 'playing God' has come to be used, according to Ted Peters: 'The acerbic rhetoric that usually employs the phrase "playing God" is aimed at inhibiting if not shutting down certain forms of scientific research and medical therapy.'[4] Peters cites Ramsey as the one who pioneered the idea of 'playing God' in posing theological limits to genetic intervention. However, Ramsey is not just critiquing the limits of science (that is, the view that anything that can be done must be done), but also questioning the kind of people we are becoming (that is, a theological anthropology), as well as tackling the question of divine agency, for God created the universe as good.[5] For Peters, by contrast, the correct way of perceiving genetic science, of 'playing God', is through considering ourselves as in some sense co-creators with God (pp. 14–16). He believes that theology supports genetic intervention, within responsible limits, as a creative exercise in which we become partners in God's intentions.

This debate illustrates how two contrasting ethical prerogatives arise from a single phrase, the idea of 'playing God'. It betrays the fact that behind the common language are very different narratives of who God is and how our relationship with God is to be construed. It also leads to opposite ethical outcomes. Both authors assume that theology has a place in ethics, but both arrive at very different positions. In order to delineate more clearly how this might be the case, it is necessary to search a little more deeply into the theological principles underlying Christian approaches to the ethics of genetics. Of course, there are other Christian ethicists who would deny that theological principles are relevant at all, affirming rather that we need a more 'softly-softly' approach to ethical decisions that impinge on policy-making. A Christian ethicist, in this view, might hold strong theological principles, but maintain that these principles make little sense in a public context. They are therefore obscured from view, and a robust philosophical anthropology is put in its place. Robin Gill contrasts these alternatives in the following way, arguing that 'the religious ethicist engaged in the genetics debate within the public forum may simply have to choose either (a) to use explicitly religious arguments and, in the process, inform their religious communities but be ignored by society at large or (b) to represent the virtues of social concern and justice

---

stance taken by Joseph Fletcher, who argued, for example, in favour of artificial reproductive genetic techniques as opposed to the 'roulette' arising from sexual reproduction. Control for him is positive, the essence of rationality. Fletcher, *The Ethics of Genetic Control.*

[4] Peters, *Playing God*, p. 144.

[5] Peters seems to miss this point in his criticism of Ramsey: Peters, *Playing God*, p. 202 n. 5.

derived from their communities while largely eschewing public discussion of theological metaethics'.[6] In the last chapter I summarized arguments in favour of developing a theological approach to the ethics of genetics that drew particularly on the virtue of prudence, or practical wisdom, but that could also be enlarged to include justice, fortitude and temperance. But how might this compare with other possible, specifically theological, alternatives that claim to situate ethics in the context of Christian theology? What might be the place of theological principles in such ethical discourse, which relies on virtues, many of which resonate strongly with secular versions as in Aristotelian ethics? The intent of this chapter is to provide a brief overview of the theological alternatives as a way of situating the particular discussion on prudence or practical wisdom that will be developed in the following chapters.[7] I intend to clarify a specific role and interpretation of wisdom in the context of theological discussions about ethics, alongside its relationship to prudence, that could be considered as correlative of the secular debates on virtues, discussed in the first chapter.

There is an enormous variety of possible approaches to Christian ethics in general. Different possibilities include, for example, natural-law, virtue, gender, liberation theology or pluralist approaches.[8] The purpose of this chapter is not so much to survey all these approaches in relation to their possible cogency for an ethics of genetics. Rather, I hope to ask a different question: about the extent to which theologians concerned especially with ethical issues in technology and genetic intervention are grounding their ethics in specific theological frameworks. The discussion that follows is intended to be illustrative rather than exhaustive, drawing particularly on the work of the more conservative British theologians Michael Banner and Oliver O'Donovan and the more liberal American theologians Philip Hefner, Ted Peters, James Peterson and Thomas Shannon. I will argue, further, that a version of virtue ethics, which takes its bearings from the thought of Thomas Aquinas, includes insights from the former theologies

---

[6] Gill, 'Review: Unprecedented Choices'. Gill names Stanley Hauerwas and Oliver O'Donovan in the first camp, and James Childress and himself in the second. Robin Gill, in *Health Care and Christian Ethics* (Cambridge: Cambridge University Press, forthcoming), makes a distinction between theological purists and theological realists, locating himself as among the latter. He also makes extensive use of the Synoptic Gospels' healing stories to identify four theological virtues – compassion, care, faith, and humility – which, he argues, are particularly relevant to healthcare ethics today.

[7] I am conscious that the theological discussion developed here may not be of interest to readers who are more inclined to be concerned with ethical issues from a secular perspective. I am also aware that the depth of analysis of the authors I have cited could be developed further. However, I suggest that this would represent another work altogether.

[8] See, for example, Gill (ed.), *The Cambridge Companion to Christian Ethics*, pp. 75–168.

rooted in dogmatics and process theology. Furthermore, I shall also suggest that the motif of wisdom is grounded in a wisdom theology. It is thoroughly affirmative of creation, yet offers the kind of resources that are needed in tackling complex issues in genetics.

MICHAEL BANNER'S DOGMATIC ETHIC

Ever since Paul Ramsey's publication of *Basic Christian Ethics*, the concept of Christian ethics as rooted in scripture and in the covenant between God and humanity has served to claim the importance of basic Christian doctrines for ethics.[9] His approach is an ethic of love, but one rooted in the love of God, coming from the righteousness of God, and in love for neighbour. He was keen to move away from fixed concepts of natural law that formed the basis of much Roman Catholic moral theology.[10] Rather, love transformed natural law.

While, in the past, Karl Barth's ethics has been somewhat neglected, he is becoming, perhaps, one of the most influential writers for those who adhere to Protestant dogmatic ethics.[11] Michael Banner is a prominent theologian who identifies strongly with Barthian thought. Following Barth, he argues that Christian ethics is 'a task of the doctrine of God'.[12] Moreover, it 'invalidates' other forms of ethics based on knowledge of good and evil, so that it is incorrect to build on secular knowledge, even in the realm of 'apologetics' (pp. 6–8). Alternatively, to suggest that theological ethics is just one of a number of valid options through a form of *diastasis* is also a view that cannot be tolerated, as to do so amounts to a form of 'esoteric ethics', a failure of nerve, a failure really to believe in what it claims, that is, the universal grace of God (pp. 9–10). Likewise, although Barth admits that Roman Catholic approaches fall into neither of these traps, they fail because, for him, grace can never emerge from nature. For Banner, the task of dogmatic ethics is one that explicates the ethical content of the fundamental dogmas of God as Creator, Reconciler and Redeemer (p. 13). He is positively scathing about the works of liberal theologians,

for when the self-professed Christian ethicist who has learnt his ethics from the world returns to the world from writing his most recent book or paper on some

---

[9] S. Hauerwas and D. S. Long, Foreword, in Ramsey, *Basic Christian Ethics*, p. xiii.

[10] It might be debated how 'fixed' natural law really is, but Ramsey believed, with some justification, that natural law in the Roman Catholic tradition had become linked with versions of casuistry that were restrictive rather than open.

[11] See, for example, Biggar, *Hastening that Waits*. [12] Banner, *Christian Ethics*, p. 4.

aspect of Christian ethics, he finds to his great satisfaction that he can congratulate himself and his colleagues on the quite remarkable influence they have exerted over contemporary life and thought, quite oblivious to the fact that the world's agreement with him is in reality founded on his agreement with the world. (p. 15)

Banner also finds that Stanley Hauerwas, a Christian virtue ethicist, is not sufficiently dogmatic, and suggests that he has lost touch with the initial idea of creation by his focus on the eschaton.[13]

Banner addresses the question of whether dogmatic ethics can be said to be 'sectarian' (pp. 26–35). In the first place, he suggests that those who object to dogmatic ethics do so because they are committed to apologetic ethics, a public ethic that draws on public criteria, in some sense resembling the natural-law argument for politics. Yet Banner is forceful in his argument that the fact that dogmatic ethics builds on dogmas of the Christian faith does not mean that it has to be divorced from public discussion. Indeed, he has put his own views into practice by being influential on various public committees, including one that outlined the principles for animal welfare.[14] Nonetheless, it is significant that the precise principles of the Banner report are arrived at through consideration of an amalgam of existing legislation in the United Kingdom. He fails, in other words, to live out his earlier commitment in an obvious way, that is, to place theological discourse at the heart of his ethical discussion. Instead, his theology becomes strangely obscured from view, surfacing in the final few paragraphs through consideration of the motif of the *Sabbath* (*Christian Ethics*, pp. 204–24). 'Barth begins here for the simple reason that the Christian moral life is to be understood, in virtue of the facts of creation and redemption, as first of all a life of freedom, signified by the rest of the sabbath day' (p. 223). As the notion of Sabbath is taken from Barth's corpus, it could be said in a very loose way to follow from Barthian premises. Nature, as created, culminates in the Sabbath rest, a time that is blessed by God. While this is clearly distinct from cost-benefit analysis or other more consequentialist positions, the extent to which his discussion really flows from a dogmatics centred on Christ in any consistent way is somewhat puzzling. In fact, the ideal of the Sabbath would be more consistent with natural-law approaches, which he is keen to eschew.

---

[13] As I mentioned in the previous chapter, Stanley Hauerwas is one of the leading voices advocating a Christian virtue ethic. However, his focus has been on ethical issues directly relating to the human community, and his concern is not broader than this. The extent to which his theology connects in any rigorous way with his discussion of the virtues has also been the subject of critique. See Kotva, *The Christian Case for Virtue Ethics*, pp. 50–3.

[14] Banner, *Report of the Committee to Consider the Ethical Implications*.

Banner develops the idea of the Sabbath further in more recent work on genetic intervention.[15] He contrasts this idea with the secular concept of the sublime found in philosophical writing on the limits of human intervention in the natural world. He affirms the basic Barthian view on creation, namely:

Creation is for the sake of Christ and the church; this God creates, as another god may or may not, out of love for humankind ... We should think instead that this is an order, which, existing for our own good, is one which we should first of all love and cherish. We should think that our proper and authentic engagement with the created order is that which is learnt by our responding to God's invitation to share in his Sabbath rest, a rest in which, in contemplation of this creation, and in utter conviction as to God's loving purpose in its ordering, we may put away anxiety, fear, dread or awe and learn instead a simple enjoyment of this order in its complexity, vitality, beauty and magnificence. (p. 75)

The Sabbath ideal, then, seems for Banner to point back to an original ordering of creation, but it is love springing from the 'religion of Jesus Christ'. Such a view suggests an almost quietist response to the natural order, namely that it is just *there*. Indeed, while Banner would probably wish to resist the claim, it echoes something of the idea of natural law that he, via Barth, is anxious to reject. Bernard Häring, for example, is a prominent Roman Catholic moral theologian who uses the idea of the Sabbath to speak, not so much of passivity in the face of the natural order, but of the repose needed in order for humanity to act as co-creators. He suggests that 'the fundamental condition for being truly free while acting as manipulators of the world around is our sabbath, our repose before God. Only if man transcends himself and recognises the gratuity of all creation and of his own call to be co-creator, can he submit the earth to his own dignity.'[16]

Oliver O'Donovan also writes as a theologian committed to exemplifying the truths of the Christian faith as explicit in his ethics. However, his understanding of the Sabbath seems to be more specifically eschatological compared with Banner's interpretation, and draws heavily on an Augustinian understanding of the eighth day of creation, pointing to future fulfilment. There is a sense of a dynamic unfolding of a future creation, to be caught up in the fulfilment in Christ. The Sabbath is a sign

---

[15] M. Banner, 'Burke, Barth and Biotechnology: On Preferring the Sabbath to the Sublime: Some Preliminary Thoughts', in Deane-Drummond and Szerszynski (eds.), *Re-Ordering Nature*, pp. 68–76.

[16] Häring, *The Ethics of Manipulation*, p. 50.

that looks forward to the end of history. In the letter to the Hebrews we are instructed to enter into the Sabbath rest, so that 'historical fulfilment means our entry into a completeness which is already present in the universe. Our sabbath rest is, as it were, a catching up with God's.'[17] Yet he contrasts the completeness of God's work in creation with the incompleteness of this work in history. Accordingly, creation is 'a condition of history's movement', which contrasts with historicism's view of creation as another name for history, where evil has no definite characterisation against the criterion of a good natural order (pp. 62–3). O'Donovan also manages to combine his understanding of the centrality of Christ with an affirmation of creation in terms of divine order. For him, it is precisely the ordering in creation that is vindicated in the resurrection of Christ. He comments incisively on the idea of ordering in the natural world:

Any attempt to think about morality must make a decision early in its course, overt or covert, about these forms of order which we seem to discern in the world. Either they are there, or they are not. This decision, which will shape the character of the whole moral philosophical enterprise, forces itself as much upon secular as upon Christian thought. (p. 35)

For theologically informed ethics, this ordering is present and must relate in some sense to belief in Jesus Christ and the significance of his resurrection. If that ordering is rejected, as found in moral philosophers who claim that order is imposed by the human will-to-order, it leads to a completely different view and ultimately to the loss of all ordered relationships. This is one reason why O'Donovan, unlike Michael Banner, can speak in favour of a 'natural ethic', sharing some affinity with the concept of natural law. O'Donovan rejects Hegelian idealism, which tried to steer a middle path between the two extremes, as a 'manifestation of the irresistible thrust of historical necessity' (p. 36). Human freedom consists first of all in responding to this given order, 'in conformity or disconformity, with obedience or with rebellion' (p. 37). In addition, he argues that we are in an unfortunate position between having to choose an ethic that is revealed and has no ontological grounding, and one that is based on creation and is naturally known. He argues, instead, for an intermediate position, one that begins from revelation, while not excluding 'natural knowledge' (p. 19).

Such a view might suggest some lines of continuity between those Roman Catholics following natural-law ethical traditions, and Barthian

---

[17] O'Donovan, *Resurrection and Moral Order*, p. 62.

ethics.[18] Nigel Biggar has commented on the lines of continuity and discontinuity.[19] For a Barthian, it is only once we know about the grace of God in Jesus Christ that the created order can be perceived. Furthermore, it is human propensity to sin that qualifies any sense of ordering that we can observe in the natural world. Yet Barth does seem to allow for the givenness of created nature in human beings, which leads to responsibilities to God, to fellow humans, and to life that are set within time restraints of our own unique history (p. 166).

Nonetheless, Biggar is much more sanguine than Banner about the limitations of a Barthian view of ethics. He suggests that the understanding of reason in Barth and in Grisez's theory of natural law underlies some of the misunderstanding between the two respective positions. For Barth, reason is the modernist aspiration to moral autonomy, while for Grisez it is the grasp of real, irreducible human goods (p. 169). The Protestant scepticism towards the ability of sinners to grasp moral truth leads to a mistrust of reason that is far less pronounced in Roman Catholic moral theory. However, this is only part of the explanation for the difference; Barth was profoundly affected by his experience of the First World War, which, he considered, exposed the hollow pretensions of modernity. For him, the human good is primarily conceived as freedom, yet is it freedom under the Word of God. Biggar suggests that Barth was mistaken to treat the Word of God as the sole source of moral knowledge. I suggest that the implications of Biggar's analysis for Banner's discussion of the ethics of genetic intervention are clear, namely that Barth's schema cannot easily be pressed into the service of an ethics of genetics without seriously moving away from Barth's original testimony. In fact, the degree to which Banner seems to add Barthian reflection of the Sabbath on to his discussion of secular alternatives implies that Barth's dogmatics is failing to deliver what he hoped it would provide, namely a dogmatic ethics for nature. In this respect Oliver O'Donovan's position is far more successful, since it tends towards a strong affirmation of the natural order while insisting on the distinctive contribution of theology. In particular, he argues that there are clear limits to human responsibility with regard to the future of the human species, preferring to resist forms of artifice in areas such as the new reproductive technologies, but for reasons that are distinct from

---

[18] Alister McGrath has, similarly, written rather more positively about the possible accommodation of natural law, perceiving in this tradition the reformed idea of 'natural grace'. For discussion see McGrath, *A Scientific Theology*, II: *Reality*, p. 96.

[19] N. Biggar, 'Karl Barth and Germain Grisez on the Human Good: An Ecumenical Rapprochement', in Biggar and Black (eds.), *The Revival of Natural Law*, pp. 164–83, esp. pp. 165–6.

natural-law theory, which informs more conservative Roman Catholic positions on this issue.[20]

PROCESS ETHICAL ALTERNATIVES

What might be an alternative to the dogmatic approach outlined above? Theologians influenced by process theology who are concerned about ethical issues in genetics have a strong following in the United States. While dogmatic ethics following Barth is the theological counterpart to deontological approaches in philosophy, process ethics is the theological counterpart to consequentialism. Of course, as I will argue below, there is no reason why dogmatic ethics *has* to be deontological; it could just as easily be consequentialist if it stressed eschatology as inclusive of creation, rather than creation as the backdrop to human history, which is closer to O'Donovan's position. On the other hand, process ethics is necessarily consequentialist in that the idea of becoming is at the heart of its theological interpretation of the relationship between God and the world.

For Philip Hefner, science is not so much that which is challenged by the Word of God as that which challenges and enriches our understanding of who God is.[21] It is perhaps more correct to see Hefner as presenting a theological version of evolutionary ethics; for him, freedom emerges through the evolutionary processes and 'is rooted in the genetically controlled adaptive plasticity of the human genotype' (p. 30). We have now reached a 'new stage of freedom', in which, with God's blessing, we are enabled to participate in the intentional fulfilment of God's purposes (p. 32). For Hefner, God is simply that which is ultimate, but God is related in a profound way to the 'way things really are' and 'what really is' (pp. 32–3). Humans are 'created co-creators' in that it is through human freedom and agency that the future is birthed. Such a future must be 'wholesome for the nature that has birthed us – the nature that is not only our

---

[20] O'Donovan argues, in *Begotten or Made?*, that techniques such as IVF are subject to laws of production rather than to 'laws of natural procreation', and in this he seems to affirm the natural as good, though it is good apparently because of its contingency in opposition to being the object of human willing and making. While his contrast between making and begetting might usefully be applied in some contexts, such as human cloning, it seems to me that it is inappropriate in this case, for IVF is still replete with contingency; even the choice of sperm through newer injection techniques is made on the basis of motility rather than on known characteristics that might ensue. Thus, while his insistence on a theological basis for ethics is defensible, it does not necessarily lead to the very conservative outcomes that he argues for in this book. O'Donovan, *Begotten or Made?*, pp. 13, 70–5.

[21] Hefner, *The Human Factor*, p. 9.

genetic heritage, but also the entire community and the evolutionary and ecological reality in which and to which we belong' (p. 27).[22] In other words, our vocation is to shape the future of the planet, and this is known as God's will for humans.

It is not clear in what sense the future shaping of the world by humanity can be 'wholesome' for nature. Nor is it clear how God, who seems to be related to the natural order as the 'profoundest dimension' of reality, can in any way adjudicate in the matter of what nature is to become through humans. Humans, it seems, serve the process of the Creator, but in such a way that they cannot take credit for this themselves, so 'they cannot be said to be morally superior or inferior to any other species or entity in the same ecosystem' (p. 36). Hefner's consideration of the moral status of humans is ambiguous here. On the one hand, humanity is not superior on account of the process of evolution, but, on the other hand, humanity is given freedom to be co-creator, which marks out the distinctive contribution of human agency in the world. Hefner is not shy about finding value in the processes of nature, for any required human response to these structures is 'teleonomic', that is, it represents a 'credible correlate to structures and processes that are innate in the human being' (p. 39). Indeed, the biological process is intimately connected with God's intention, so that 'the will of God is that the creation should fulfil its God-grounded purposes out of its own intentionality' (p. 46). Nonetheless, the new possibilities for the earth also emerge in Hefner's scheme through culture, for it can 'stretch genes and ecosystem in order to fulfil what seem from the cultural perspective to be desirable and useful novel ends' (pp. 47–8). Technology, including genetic technology, becomes one of the phases of cultural evolution.

Hefner's positive evaluation of human freedom is suggestive of a naturalistic ethic. This naturalism in the form of evolutionary ethics is so deeply embedded in his thought that sin now amounts to 'contaminating, if not derailing, our evolutionary futures'.[23] For him, the moral imperative for humans is to work for the 'most desirable future that our genetic and environmental context as a whole can enjoy'.[24] Yet how are we to tell what is desirable? By what criteria do we measure what is acceptable for the human race? For him, this is related to a destiny given by God; but, as we

---

[22] Ronald Cole-Turner also argues for the idea of humanity as a co-creator and likens God to a 'first gardener' elsewhere. See Cole-Turner, *The New Genesis*; Deane-Drummond, *Biology and Theology Today*, pp. 97–101.

[23] P. Hefner, 'Determinism, Freedom and Moral Failure', in Peters (ed.), *Genetics: Issues of Social Justice*, pp. 111–21 (p. 111).

[24] Ibid., p. 118.

saw earlier, God seems to be just the 'ultimate' in reality. Any idea of a fixed ordering in the beginning is inimical to Hefner's view. Thus he has to reinterpret the doctrine of original sin as that which relates to our *evolutionary* origin. It is 'the dissonance between the pre-human information that we carry in our genome and the distinctively human, the dissonance between societal culture and the individual "selfish" human nature; and the innate fallibility and vulnerability that mark our character as humans' ('Determinism', p. 120).

While Ted Peters is not a self-professed process theologian, his negative assessment of traditional categories and his affirmation of elements of process theology, along with a positive attitude to evolution, ally his thought with process ethics. For example, his understanding of original sin is estrangement from God, rather than disobedience to divine law.[25] Accordingly, he welcomes the process metaphysics of Alfred North Whitehead, which relates everything to everything else. Original sin is now re-described in terms of our relationship to our genes and our environment. In other words, our *biological* origin carries with it a propensity to sin that precedes free will (p. 89). However, original sin also carries the connotation of our own socially conditioned existence, so that ultimately it is through nurture than sin is passed on to the next generation. For Peters, we find ourselves in an ambiguous present creation. On the one hand, our ability to reason and to envision justice and beauty promises a better world; on the other hand, if we 'surrender to certain genetic and social determinants we have inherited', science and technology will be used to foster the interest of the few (p. 93).

Overall, he is keen to resist any notion of genetic determinism by his emphasis on the concept of human freedom. In looking at human culture, he finds, with Tillich, spiritual meaning that he extends to the natural sciences. A secularised version of predestination is the concept of biological determinism. But Peters' theology of freedom seeks to move beyond any such restriction; affirmation of the power of God does not need to go hand in hand with a rejection of human freedom; rather, 'God's creative and redeeming work imparts power to the world' (p. 159). Similarly, genetic determinism, such as it is, does not amount to a loss of human freedom, for human beings are greater than the sum of their genes. We can be both free and determined at the same time. Freedom becomes 'self-actualisation', arising from the ability to choose, even though our genes produce the conditions of that choosing. Since our freedom is God-given, Peters

---

[25] Peters, *Playing God*, p. 88.

suggests that while we should not 'play God' in the Promethean sense, 'we should play human in the imago Dei sense – that is, we should understand ourselves as created co-creators and press our scientific and technological creativity into the service of neighbour love, of beneficence' (p. 161). The true nature of liberation, for Peters, is not through liberation from our nature, from our genes, but from the past, so that the future is open. Does this abdicate responsibility? Peters suggests it does not, for 'we can exert creativity within the ongoing processes of creation; and as creative beings we are called by God to exert our creativity in responsible fashion. Responsible creativity is playing human as God intends us to' (p. 162). The elements of process theology in his thinking come out clearly in the following:

The goodness of nature should be seen as a dynamic goodness, as belonging to a history of nature in which the pursuit of the good is a divinely inspired process. Rather than see nature alone as the ontological source of the good, we need to see God as the source of the good bestowed in a redeeming and creative way. Rather than seek liberation from nature, the created co-creator seeks to be responsible within nature for the future of nature. (pp. 162–3)

Yet responsibility, for Peters, seems, following Tillich, to be individually based: 'Because actions that result from deliberation and decision are determined neither by something outside the person nor by any part within the person, the centred whole or self shoulders responsibility for such actions' (p. 168). More significant still is his idea that we are becoming human, so that 'the history and future of nature participate in this defining process, a process that is not yet complete. Our destiny contributes to the future defining process' (p. 169). What is the place of God in all this? We learn simply that 'God will have a hand in this future destiny' (p. 169). This entails an interpretation of divine imaging in terms of human futures; we are on the way to becoming what is intended. Yet Peters seems to stop short of a thorough process interpretation of eschatology, for 'that the advent of the new will be due to divine action and not the continuation of evolutionary progress marks the discontinuity' (p. 171). It is this understanding of the new breaking into history from ahead that bears some resemblance to Jürgen Moltmann's theology.[26] Peters suggests that such a view of eschatology accounts for his 'proleptic ethics' (p. 174). This future in God includes a divinely established justice and the elimination of pain, a new creation. However, such a vision results in a particular ethical

---

[26] See, for example, Moltmann, *The Future of Creation*, pp. 29–31, 45–8.

framework that is also dependent on the core idea of human freedom that Peters wishes to instate. Hence:

This is a form of ethical thinking and moral action that does not seek primarily to conform itself to a set of laws or commandments, although there will be some value in this. Nor does it pursue a higher life of virtue, wherein we cultivate within ourselves greater sensitivity and appreciation for values such as beauty, truth and justice (although there is great value in this too). Rather, proleptic ethics tends towards seeking the most practical way to love the neighbor in light of a vision of a better future. Because it is orientated towards the new, proleptic practice does not attribute sanctity to previously established norms and policies for getting the job done. (p. 175)

It seems that Peter's proleptic ethics is a way of sanctioning the new and of rejecting tradition, rather than being based on any concept of what might be a future in God. In other words, he seems to have reinterpreted divine eschatology in terms of human potentialities that mark a radical departure from the present accepted norms. It amounts to a way of radicalising the concept of human freedom, so that it is orientated not so much towards good in the ultimate sense, as towards 'the long-range good for the human race and for life on our planet as a whole. I recommend beneficence' (p. 178). Yet, because Peters has rejected the classical conception of the good, this teleological orientation is left free-floating, since 'everything is in process'. As applied specifically to genetic technologies, this image of the future is positive in its appraisal of genetic science, for, while recognising that there may be dangers, 'genetic medicine promises a significant measure of potential for relieving crying and pain and mourning for numerous individuals' (p. 178).

THEOLOGICAL TRADITIONS AS BASES FOR ETHICS

The two contrasting approaches to a theological basis for ethics that I have outlined so far could be described as presenting positions of contrast or conciliation. While ethics drawing on dogmatics is more inclined to issue specific rules or deontological principles for ethical consideration of nature, ethics emerging from process thought is more concerned about the future consequences for humanity and for the planet. While the first puts creation in the position of sounding-board for the narrative of salvation history, the second sees creation as the basis in which salvation can be re-described. The former is more inclined to be cautious about recent advances in genetics, while the latter is more inclined to be positive in its affirmation of scientific advances. This does not, of course, rule out the possibility that, even in the first view, some changes in the natural world are permissible, but it is set against particular deontological principles grounded in particular commitments to theological doctrines. Nor does it rule out the possibility that, in the second view, some changes will be resisted; however, in the second case the bright new creation that is inaugurated by Christ's resurrection encourages humanity to enter into genetic science as co-creators with God.

A third possible way of using theology in ethical considerations about genetics is one that draws on certain traditions of Christian teaching and sets these alongside the discoveries of science. James Peterson is a good example of an ethicist taking this stance.[27] For him, 'the classic Christian tradition makes the best sense of a wide range of concerns' (p. 15). What might he mean by this? It seems to be 'the person of Jesus Christ at the universal councils of Nicea and Chalcedon' (p. 16). Nonetheless, like John Polkinghorne, he is happy to adjust the tradition where it suits, rejecting ideas such as the immutability of God.[28] The priority for Peterson is how science is developing and unfolding. He considers genetic science in all its aspects first, before turning to reflect on those areas of Christian tradition that he considers relevant. Ethical evaluation then follows from this alignment. One of his main concerns in drawing on Christian theology seems to be to show that it is compatible with science rather than in conflict with it.[29] He admits that where there is conflict, then both the science and theology have to be reconsidered, though in the history of the debate between science and religion it is usually the scientific perspective on 'the truth' that has prevailed.

For him, exploring particular human attitudes such as humility, respect, community, responsibility and compassion can be illuminated first by genetic science and then compared with theological traditions. He suggests that such an alignment facilitates ethical decisions in genetics. For example, he suggests that humility is inevitable once we ponder more closely on the

---

[27] Peterson, *Genetic Turning Points.*

[28] Polkinghorne, *Belief in God,* pp. 48–75. Polkinghorne poses a sharp contrast between the classic view of God, which he suggests combines atemporality, primary causality, divine impassibility, an inclination towards determinism and an emphasis on divine control, and the modern view of God as showing temporality, top-down causality, divine vulnerability, an inclination towards openness and a recognition of creaturely self-making. It is the latter view that, for him, accords best with scientific and theological thought (p. 74). Yet he is not as committed to process theology as this might imply; in other works he emphasises the importance of Christian creeds as the basis for belief. See Polkinghorne, *Science and Christian Belief.*

[29] This is a trend characteristic of much of the more recent debate in science and religion. See, for example, Peters, *Science and Theology.*

wonder of our genetic makeup. For him, 'humility is not self-deprecation or degradation. It is simple recognition of one's own limitations and the importance of others' (*Turning Points*, p. 44). He goes on to suggest that a similar attitude can be found in Jesus, especially in the narrative of the washing of the disciples' feet. Respect, too, emerges from what we do know about genetics, and this then leads to praise of the God who is also Creator. It is only once we reach the idea of responsibility that some sense of contrast emerges. The fact that people have a genetic tendency to behave in a certain way does not excuse particular behaviours; rather, the 'ultimate standard is God's will recognized through Scripture, tradition, reason and experience such as the direct leading of God's Holy Spirit' (p. 48).

The measure of the distinctive life of a Christian is found in the fruits of the Holy Spirit, and this, for Peterson, shows that our genes do not limit us. When it comes to a discussion of compassion, Peterson omits any discussion of Christian theology altogether; reflection on the brokenness of our genetic makeup through deficiencies of various kinds is enough to engender the attitude that he seeks. His discussion of community, too, includes only a passing reference to God as Trinity, alongside consideration of the communal nature of our genes. It seems, then, that Peterson sits very lightly to the Christian tradition. Where it suits, such as when genetics seems to point in the direction of making immoral behaviour permissible, then Christianity provides a standard. However, we are not told how this standard will serve to influence those outside or even inside the Christian tradition. He claims that 'the distinctive life that can be developed over time for those who belong to Jesus Christ is to stand out as a clear sign that God is at work in the lives of God's people. They could not achieve it on their own' (p. 49). Yet we are not told how this might be the case, except in so far as 'the quality of their lives is to reveal God's presence and intervention'. In what sense God will intervene is left unclear. More to the point, the way in which any such ideal Christian community can influence wider decision-making is unresolved. The main issue as far as Peterson is concerned is that, like Peters, he is anxious to show that 'one is not necessarily limited to the tendencies or even capabilities of one's genes' (p. 49).

Peterson also draws on Irenaeus and other patristic writers to support his idea that creation is in some sense unfinished. For him, God intends creation to be completed, and he suggests that while we can act irresponsibly, part of our nature is to have technologies that lead to change (p. 189). Hence, our mandate as humans is to sustain, restore and improve the world. This gives him particular theological reasons for approaching contested areas in genetics, such as procreation. For, once we understand providence as choosing the genetic start of each human being, Peterson sees no logical reason why this cannot include intentional acts of human beings as well as 'apparently random acts of nature' (p. 190). While he recognises that those who look to the limits of genetic intervention are concerned with human pride, he welcomes the alternative, namely that 'not fulfilling the responsibility to turn genetic intervention to service would reflect a dangerous and destructive attitude of disobedient apathy' (p. 84).

Peterson also draws on the concept of stewardship. However, 'stewardship does not mean that the earth has to be kept exactly as it is found' (p. 87). In fact, genetic intervention becomes an opportunity for such stewardship to be expressed. It is a way of mitigating some of the effects of the original fall into sin. Finding out how to make appropriate changes comes through prayer, acting so as best to express love of God and neighbour. Yet the ethical outcomes of such a view include oddly diverse ideas such as approval of reproductive human cloning, which Peterson prefers to call 'twinning', for reasons of infertility or avoidance of genetic disease, alongside a move towards protecting life in the womb, though he is vague about the point at which such protection should take place (pp. 126–37, 296–305). Indeed, the final criteria that Peterson comes up with for deciding for or against genetic intervention are summarised as first safety; secondly, whether it brings improvement for an individual; thirdly, whether it keeps the future 'open', meaning that it resists any form of genetic determinism; and finally, whether it is the best use of available resources (pp. 304–5). It is clear from this list that the choices for or against intervention are decided on the basis of a secular consequentialist ethic that is then supported by reference to scripture or other Christian traditions, such as that of stewardship.

The notion of stewardship itself is somewhat ambiguous. The ideal of stewardship is a recurrent theme in church statements reflecting on the status of the natural world.[30] It is also evident in Roman Catholic writers such as Benedict Ashley and Kevin O'Rourke, who justify the worth of genetic intervention, so that it is our responsibility to be stewards of the divine creativity that God has given us.[31] The only qualification in this case is that we use such creativity in a prudent way. Northcott has pointed out the difficulty of the use of this term in environmental ethics, for 'the

---

[30] This includes those with evangelical Christian commitments, as well as Roman Catholic documents. See, for example, Berry, *The Care of Creation*; Pope Paul VI, *Humanae Vitae*. It is also noteworthy that some prominent theologians have taken up and used the idea of stewardship as the basis for an environmental ethic; see, for example, Hall, *Imaging God*.

[31] Ashley and O'Rourke, *Health Care Ethics*, p. 327.

fundamental problem with this metaphor is the implication that humans are effectively in control of nature, its managers, or, as Heidegger prefers, its guardians. And yet so much of recent environmental history teaches us that we are not in fact in control of the biosphere.'[32]

Much the same critique could be applied to Peterson's ideal of stewardship. He seems to assume that, while there are some risks that need to be taken into account, nature is to be controlled and manipulated by human ingenuity. In addition, Richard Bauckham has pointed out that the origin of the idea of stewardship arose in seventeenth-century England, and that in this context 'human supremacy over nature was an unquestioned good and technological advance was of unqualified value'.[33] While the notion of stewardship in the context of ecological issues usually includes the idea of the intrinsic value of creation, Peterson seems rather to use the idea in the original sense described by Bauckham, namely meaning human responsibility to use creation for human advancement. Concerning stewardship Bauckham suggests that

It is the old Renaissance dream of humans as gods of the world, its all-wise and all-powerful rulers, exercising divine creativity in remaking the world to their own design, treating nature as the raw material from which to create a world more adapted to its purely human ends. Biotechnology is the proof that this dream is now entering a whole new phase of attempted realization. (p. 106)

Thomas Shannon's approach is, perhaps, rather more promising, as he claims to find ideas and ethical perspectives from the medieval Franciscan theologian, St Bonaventure, and from the medieval Franciscan philosopher John Duns Scotus.[34] He suggests, for example, that the common nature in Duns Scotus' writing has its equivalent in the genome, so that it can be used in order to arrive at generalisations about who we are as human beings. Nonetheless, this is not the most significant aspect of who we are as persons, for 'how this will be done or resolved is the function of neither the common nature nor the genome; it is the function of the individual as he or she acts in freedom' (p. 92). But if all that the idea of the common nature does is to affirm our genome as characteristic of who we are in a general sense, what ethical purpose does this serve? It seems to me that Shannon has not really answered this question; rather, he has simply aligned his traditional theology to the science. He goes on to suggest that over against the idea of common nature Duns Scotus affirms the unique significance of the individual, so this should guard us against any attempt to use the genome as a template for human worth

[32] Northcott, *Christianity and Environmental Ethics*, p. 129.
[33] R. Bauckham, 'Stewardship and Relationship', in Berry (ed.), *The Care of Creation*, p. 101.
[34] Shannon, *Made in Whose Image?*, pp. xiii–xiv.

or significance. However, the question that arises here is: does the concept of individuality and freedom that Shannon promotes necessarily take its precedence from medieval Franciscan theology and philosophy?

His brief consideration of Duns Scotus' ethics is more interesting in that the latter asks us to consider the intention of the agent as well as the circumstances surrounding the action. He also explores the manner in which the act is performed; hence, 'An act is not something external to us; rather, what we do and how we do it shapes and forms us' (p. 128). Duns Scotus also includes the idea of success, which, for Shannon, 'opens the door to a risk–benefit and benefit–burden analysis in terms of calculating the actual success of the act' (p. 128). Furthermore, his idea of circumstance of place, though vague, encourages that the act be set in a broader social context. Unfortunately, he does not then go on to suggest how these ideas might specifically apply to the ethics of genetic engineering. While he seems, like Peterson, to have hinted at the idea of virtue, it is left undeveloped.

AN ALTERNATIVE ETHIC ROOTED IN WISDOM

The focus on human freedom, affirmed directly as a theology of freedom in the case of Peters, or more indirectly through the notion of stewardship in the case of Peterson, betrays a move away from more classic understandings of humanity as being dependent on God. While, as Peters has forcefully argued, an increase in human freedom does not necessarily weaken the power of God, the attitude of seeking after human freedom is one that, I suggest, is conditioned partly by the American cultural dream of liberty. Sarah Coakley argues that resistance to understanding God as one who intervenes in the world, along with an increasingly popular idea that God has withdrawn power in order to allow the world to be itself, combined with the correlate urge for human liberation, has gender connotations. Coakley suggests that such a stance is conditioned by gender, so that the male child's repudiation of the power of the mother and urge for freedom understood as independence are echoed in this stance towards theology.[35] This is not intended to imply that all sons inevitably resist their mother's attention, but rather that the urge to do so is perhaps connected with this style of theologising. Moreover, process theologies necessarily deny the authority of God as understood in the classical traditions of theology. While the concept of freedom is significant in relation to the new genetic

---

[35] S. Coakley, 'Kenosis: Theological Meanings and Gender Connotations', in Polkinghorne (ed.), *The Work of Love*, p. 205.

technologies, without a clear sense of what freedom might mean it easily becomes reduced to freedom of choice and autonomy, as discussed in the previous chapter. Freedom in the classical tradition was not so much freedom of indifference in the face of numerous possibilities set before it, as freedom for excellence, orientated towards the common good, expressed through the virtues and an understanding of the good as envisaged in the Eternal Law.

I suggested in the previous chapter that Christian ethics needs to engage with and draw on insights from current philosophical discussions in virtue ethics. There are, of course, a variety of ways in which Christian ethics has drawn and is drawing on the various traditions of the virtues.[36] In the first chapter I also pointed to some of the virtues that are likely to be most relevant in consideration of issues in genetics, namely the cardinal virtues of prudence, justice, fortitude and temperance. Wisdom acts like an intermediary between these virtues and the theological virtues of faith, hope and charity. But what is the theological context for consideration of these virtues? I suggest that the classic framework for considering God as Creator, as developed in the thought of Thomas Aquinas, situates ethical reflection in a cosmological vision of the world that is thoroughly theocentric, while incorporating and affirming insights from current science and philosophy.[37] Of course, Aquinas' own detailed cosmological concept of the world as a Chain of Being has now proved to be incommensurate with modern scientific cosmology.[38] Yet I suggest that it is not compulsory to accept his particular understanding of cosmology, any more than it is compulsory to accept his negative view of the treatment of animals, while at the same time viewing his work as being that of a brilliant synthesis between the philosophical insights of Aristotle and the theological insights of Augustine. His understanding of wisdom and its relationship both to the world as created and to the practical virtues is also highly suggestive of ways of performing ethics that take into account the particular

---

[36] For an excellent historical and contemporary overview, see J. Porter, 'Virtue Ethics', in Gill (ed.), *The Cambridge Companion to Christian Ethics*, pp. 96–111.

[37] James Gustafson has also described his work as theocentric and claims to be following in the tradition of Thomas Aquinas: Gustafson, *Ethics from a Theocentric Perspective*, I: *Theology and Ethics*; II: *Ethics and Theology*. Nonetheless, Jean Porter suggests that his reappropriation of Aquinas simply represents fragments of the latter's thought: Porter, *The Recovery of Virtue*, p. 15. It is also interesting to note that, unlike Michael Banner, Gustafson affirms the sense of the sublime as being a genuinely religious experience of nature. His stance towards nature is that of humans as participants with nature. See Gustafson, *A Sense of the Divine*, pp. 21–58.

[38] Judith Barad has argued that Aquinas' views are, nonetheless, compatible with evolutionary theory. See Barad, *Aquinas on Animals*.

stance of Christian theology while permitting insights to be drawn from secular science and contemporary philosophy.

How might Aquinas' focus on God as Creator serve to ground a Christian ethic for genetics?[39] In one sense his strong acknowledgment of God as Creator, which is presupposed throughout his work, gives meaning and purpose to creation as such; creation is *good* as it is creatively thought by the Creator.[40] Furthermore, his concept of natural law is not just understood as a philosophical orientation to the Good for humanity, but takes its bearings from the Decalogue, the commandment to love God and our neighbour as ourselves.[41] Yet to read his ethics as that which simply refers to natural law, giving rise through neo-Thomistic interpretations to the detailed prescriptions in casuistry, is to miss the point. Rather, even though contemporary interpreters of natural-law theory have revised such a rigid understanding, his ethical stance needs to be reviewed in terms of the priority he gives to the virtues, and to wisdom in particular. As noted in the previous chapter, practical wisdom or prudence takes precedence in his list of moral virtues.[42] He draws this insight from Aristotle, yet takes this further theologically through his notion of wisdom as that which is both learned and divinely bestowed.

I suggest that an understanding of God as creating through wisdom but out of love puts our understanding of who God is in the foreground of ethical reflection. I would argue that the concept of God as ontologically related to wisdom is commensurate with the thought of Thomas Aquinas, who affirmed that God is divine Wisdom. Affirming God as Creator and as God who is Wisdom helps to shape an ethic that is theocentric and that values all of creation. While this might seem to be more relevant to a discussion of environmental ethics, I believe that our understanding of nature needs to embrace more than human interest if we are to put ethical debates about genetic change, human or otherwise, into proper perspective. Above all, it is important to distinguish clearly between secular notions of *sōphia* that we find in Aristotle and the notion of wisdom found in Aquinas. In a way that is somewhat analogous to his treatment of prudence, Aquinas claims that wisdom can be learned, but it also comes as a gift of the Holy Spirit. Furthermore, human attempts at wisdom that

[39] For a more general discussion of how Aquinas' theology can inform an ethic of nature, see Deane-Drummond, *The Ethics of Nature*.

[40] The Roman Catholic philosopher Josef Pieper was one of the first ethicists to consider the use of virtues in ethics. See his *The Silence of St Thomas*, pp. 56–9.

[41] I am in full agreement with Jean Porter in this respect. See Porter, *Moral Action*, p. 108.

[42] See, for example, Deane-Drummond, *Creation through Wisdom*, pp. 99–101.

simply fix on creaturely loftiness Aquinas names as 'devilish . . . because it copies the pride of the devil, and of all the sons of pride he is king' (*Summa Theologiae* 2a2ae q. 45.1). Yet he also recognised that wisdom can be learned, that is, it is an intellectual virtue that seeks to establish the relationship of everything with everything else.[43]

The gift of wisdom, unlike acquired wisdom, presupposes faith, for 'faith assents to divine truth for itself, the gift of wisdom judges things according to divine truth. Hence the gift of wisdom presupposes faith, since a man judges well what he already knows' (2a2ae q. 45.1). Wisdom for Aquinas is rooted in piety and faith, for 'if a man fears and worships God he shows that he has right judgment about divine things' (2a2ae q. 45.1). It is this rootedness of the gift of wisdom in the life and liturgy of the Christian community that is of special importance. In other words, it is not so much a theology emerging from assent to received doctrines, though it certainly includes this, as a theology grounded in the Christian narrative experience of lived witness and shared story. Hence Christian wisdom is not simply theosophic knowledge leading to intellectual rewards, but a speculative and practical knowledge rooted in an understanding of and participation in salvation history, obliging the believer to perform certain moral actions. The relationship between the gift of wisdom and faith is analogous to the relationship between the virtue of wisdom and the intuitive habit of grasping first principles. While the acquired virtue relies on intellectual judgment, for wisdom is one of the intellectual virtues of speculative reason, the gift of wisdom arises through fellowship with the Holy Spirit. Hence, it raises the intellectual virtue to new heights, though the brief of both includes theological knowledge. Both Aristotle's and Aquinas' views of wisdom coalesce in as much as they give a high place to wisdom among the intellectual virtues, so that Aquinas can claim that 'prudence, or political art, therefore is, in this way, the servant of wisdom, for it leads to wisdom, preparing for her, as the doorkeeper for the king' (1a2ae q. 66.5).

While prudence considers the way of acquiring happiness, wisdom considers the object of happiness, namely the supreme truth. Such perfection cannot be reached in this life, and in this sense even the gift of wisdom points towards the future eschaton; thus 'the act of wisdom is a beginning or anticipation of future happiness'. Aquinas is therefore modest in his assessment of how far humanity can genuinely participate in divine

---

[43] Aristotle's view of wisdom is related to the divine in as much as it can be understood by human reason. But, for Aquinas, 'theological virtue, on the other hand, is concerned with the divine as surpassing human reason': Aquinas, *Summa Theologiae* 1a2ae q. 62.2.

wisdom, for 'wisdom, to which knowledge of God belongs, is beyond man's reach, especially in this life, as though he could grasp it; for this is for God alone ... Yet the modicum which can be had through wisdom is preferable to all other knowledge' (1a2ae q. 66.5). In this sense wisdom, especially as gift, reaches out to the mystical dimension of human experience of God, while being grounded in a search for the truth. Aquinas puts this in another way, thus:

> To know the meaning of being and non-being, of whole and part, and of other consequences to being, which are the terms which constitute indemonstrable principles, is the function of wisdom; since universal being is the proper effect of the highest cause, which is God. Thus wisdom makes use of indemonstrable principles, which are the object of understanding, not only by drawing conclusions from them, as other sciences do, but also by vindicating them against those who deny them. (1a2ae q. 66.5)

It also follows that the virtues flow from grounding in wisdom, including the virtues of prudence, justice, fortitude and temperance (1a2ae q. 59.3).

How might one align oneself to divine things and divine norms? Aquinas hints at the way this is achieved in his suggestion that 'to regulate human life according to divine norms is in fact the work of wisdom, and the first indications of this ought to be reverence for God and subjection to him, with the consequence that in all things whatsoever a person will shape his life in reference to God' (2a2ae q. 19.7). Aquinas develops this idea further in his notion of charity, for charity leads to a sense of sympathy with divine things. In this way he argued that 'wisdom which is the gift does have its cause in the will, namely charity, but essentially it has to do with the intellect, of which the act is to judge aright, as we have said' (2a2ae q. 45.2). In addition, the movement of wisdom is from contemplation to right action, from seeking to understand divine realities to human action according to divine truths, which leads ultimately to happiness even in tasks that might otherwise be burdensome.[44]

Moreover, such an understanding does not ignore a Christological dimension, for the wisdom of God in the biblical tradition is also the cross of Christ.[45] Such a theological insight has a bearing on how far Christian wisdom can be said to be contradictory to human wisdom, and

---

[44] In this way he claims that 'this guidance of human actions by wisdom does not bring bitterness nor toil, rather by wisdom the bitter becomes sweet and the toil a rest': Aquinas, *Summa Theologiae* 2a2ae q. 45.3.

[45] For a discussion of the idea of wisdom as the wisdom of the cross, see Deane-Drummond, *Creation through Wisdom*, chapter 2.

echoes the view of Aquinas outlined above, where he names human conceit, parodying wisdom, as a property of the devil himself. Indeed, it is the particular emphasis in Christian theology on forgiveness, reconciliation and humility that marks it out as distinctive from secular virtue-ethics approaches, which commonly point to human self-advancement. Banner's concern that Christ be given sufficient prominence as a foundation for ethics is thus included, but, by contrast with Barthian dogmatics, I suggest that wisdom lends itself to deeper reflection on the worth of the natural order, of an affirmation of being in the manner suggested above. Furthermore, while in the case of Barthian dogmatics the relationship to creation is somewhat strained, the wisdom ethic flows quite easily and readily from a theology of wisdom.

Consideration of God according to the wisdom motif in many respects counters the view of God according to process theology. God does not emerge from the world or from evolutionary thought, neither do humans have their work baptised through such evolutionary ethics. Rather, wisdom, for Aquinas, refers to ideas in the divine mind that are then reflected in the way creation emerges. Accordingly, divine realities are 'the measure of contingent things', so that 'it belongs to wisdom first to contemplate the divine realities, and this is the vision of the source. Afterwards it directs human action according to the divine reasons. This guidance of human acts by wisdom does not bring bitterness or toil, rather by wisdom the bitter becomes sweet and the toil a rest' (2a2ae q. 45.3).

The goal or *telos* of each creature is valuable, as it moves towards the ultimate good or flourishing. Hence, it is possible to see an eschatological or even consequentialist element in his thought that is often missed. The consequences are not just those set by evolutionary process; rather, they are measured in relation to the ultimate intention of God for all created beings. Thus the final consummation is not necessarily a return to a fixed and static beginning, but an unfolding participation in the life of God. Even the idea of natural law leaves far more room for manoeuvre than many authors have supposed, for Aquinas suggests that natural law can be changed, apart from the first principle, which is to love the good and hate evil (1a2ae q. 94.5).

In contrast with the idea of the Sabbath, which in Banner's interpretation seems to lead to a passive stance towards the natural world, and in contrast with the ideas of stewardship and freedom of indifference, which encourage human mastery over nature, I suggest that the wisdom motif fosters *both* contemplation *and* self-reflexive action. The Sabbath motif is helpful in this context in as much as it can lead to a fostering of charity, and to an eschatological connection between creation and redemption, so that in one sense learning to live from the Sabbath serves to root and ground the development of the virtues.[46] Such a view is implicit in the priority Aquinas gives to contemplation and charity in the development of the gift of wisdom. Knowing that God has created all things in wisdom through love encourages a sense of wonder in the world. Aquinas, approaching the end of his life, declared that all of his work was 'as straw'. He said this because he had a profound mystical experience of God that seemed to him to show the limitations of his theological reflection on God.[47] Yet contemplation can be more than this, for it can also foster reflection and critique of our own past attitudes towards the natural world. Wisdom is self-reflexive in the sense that it is related to prudence, or practical wisdom, which includes elements of taking counsel, judging and acting.[48] However, it is more than this in that wisdom comes by gift of the Holy Spirit.

The picture of wisdom that, I am suggesting, forms the basis for ethical reflection has some resemblance to the idea of transformed judgment discussed by L. Gregory Jones.[49] For him the moral life requires not just formation, but transformation in moral judgment, so that our lives are reorientated towards the Triune God. Moreover, it is a quality of life learned in the context of a particular Christian community, that is, it is set in the context of a particular social and political life. For Jones, the community acquires a *phronēsis*, which for him means a shared ability to think in common under the guidance of the Holy Spirit. While, following Alasdair MacIntyre, I would agree that particular traditions are fostered in particular communities, ethical reflection, especially on issues such as genetics, has a broader significance that means it cannot be restricted to a community's self-deliberation. I would, therefore, wish to find ways of extending the ethical base so that, while the community remains important, it also moves to a global human context and beyond, to an ecological community of life. The move out to a global ethic serves to break down the distinction between the two rival positions of communitarianism and cosmopolitanism in ethics.

---

[46] For a development of the importance of the Sabbath in affirming human connectedness with the earth, and the fostering of virtue, see C. Deane-Drummond, 'Genetic Interventions in Nature: Perspectives from a Christian Ethic of Wisdom', in Edwards and Worthing (eds.), *Biodiversity and Ecology*, pp. 30–44.

[47] Pieper cites Thomas as saying, 'All that I have written seems to me nothing but straw ... compared to what I have seen and what has been revealed to me': Pieper, *The Silence of St Thomas*, p. 46. While this leads to a strong mystical element in his theology, it hardly points to the kind of thoroughgoing existentialism that John Caputo suggests. See Caputo, *Heidegger and Aquinas*.

[48] For further discussion see Deane-Drummond, *Creation through Wisdom*, p. 101.

[49] Jones, *Transformed Judgment*.

Ethical decision-making in genetics is, like that for environmental concern, necessarily complex. With increasing public interest in genetics come broader social and political aspects, as well as theoretical aspects regarding the value of nature.[50] Human technological intervention is fraught with difficulties, as we need to be accountable for the outcomes in nature that are presently unknown and unprecedented. Gustafson suggests that 'we may be able to define limits beyond which our interventions ought not to go, though agreement on these is difficult because persons or groups value different things in relation to themselves or to the natural world'.[51] The theologians writing on ethical issues in genetics have not fully taken this into account. For Gustafson, we are simply left with an unavoidable moral ambiguity. While God orders the natural world, there is no clear end in view. In so far as Gustafson stresses human attitudes, his stance shows some affinity to virtue ethics.[52] However, his strong acknowledgment of human dependence owes more to the liberal theological tradition, especially to Frederich Schleiermacher, rather than to the classic understanding of God that I am proposing here. Yet he does not seem to move us much beyond a sense of ambiguity in moral choice. An ethic of wisdom, by contrast, while still acknowledging a sense that outcomes are not always clearly defined, at least offers some principled frameworks in decision-making. Moreover, it is realistic, in that it recognises the limitations of human reason while at the same time encouraging a positive attitude towards the created world. We are not left simply in a sea of ambiguity, as Gustafson suggests. Rather, prudential wisdom acknowledges that risk is present, but is still able to engender both justice and fortitude in our decision-making. Fortitude comes from knowing that the wisdom we dimly perceive is a reflection of divine wisdom, the end of all things in God.

CONCLUSION

I have indicated so far that much of the current literature on Christian ethics of genetics is, for various reasons, disappointing. While, on the one

---

[50] For discussion of sociological aspects, see, Deane-Drummond and Szerszynski (eds.), *Re-Ordering Nature*.

[51] Gustafson, *A Sense of the Divine*, pp. 68–69.

[52] Jean Porter has suggested that Schleiermacher is one of the forerunners of contemporary Protestant virtue ethicists, and notes that Gustafson follows in his tradition. It is noteworthy, however, that Gustafson has not taken up Schleiermacher's theory of virtue, which is related to the Aristotelian idea of practical wisdom; rather, he has been influenced far more by his overall piety, maintaining that we need to develop a sense of the divine. See Porter, 'Virtue Ethics', p. 105.

hand, it is entirely possible for Banner to engage successfully in public policies about new technological developments, on the other hand the relationship of his reflections to his theological starting point in Barthian ethics is much more difficult to discern. I maintain that in spite of Biggar's qualification we can find hints at natural law in Barth; overall, his theology places the natural order of creation in the background to his main theme of salvation history in Jesus Christ. Creation has no real theological content as such. This might open up the possibility of human manipulation of the world; indeed, Banner does seem to allow for this, with some qualifications.[53] He does not, however, go on to discuss how we can choose between the different alternatives. For example, what happens if a particular manipulation is considered to be intrinsically wrong for some but not for others? The motif of the Sabbath can be imbued with various contents, though for Banner it seems to encourage reflection on the natural world as given. While the Sabbath is undoubtedly included in Barth's corpus, it seems to me to strain his overall theological stance if we use it as a basis for ethical reflection on our relationship with the natural world. The alternative of Hefner and Peters, focusing particularly on human freedom, seems to emerge from their understanding of the importance of evolutionary concepts. God as process neatly fits into their scheme, which affirms humanity's importance as a co-creator with God. Other theological approaches, which claim to draw on Christian tradition in their account of an ethics of genetics, seem to use Christian theology as a way of affirming scientific practice. While we have hints at possibly interesting ideas about virtue, the overall motif of stewardship is dominant. This is not stewardship in the participatory sense of some contemporary ecological theology; rather, it is stewardship understood as the human mandate to reform the world. In its place I have suggested that the ethics of virtue, especially drawing on the wisdom motif, grounds ethical discussion in a theology that is appropriately affirmative of creation and also capable of offering a critique of contemporary practice. The precise way such practice might be critiqued through such a Christian virtue-ethic approach will be explored in the chapters that follow.

---

[53] Banner strongly resists the consequentialist approach to ethics that he finds in public reports on the ethics of genetic intervention. He does, however, suggest that 'some genetic modification may be intrinsically objectionable as manipulative of an animal's good, some not; some may be neutral in relation to an animal's welfare, some may actually result in an improvement, and some may do severe harm'. *Christian Ethics*, p. 219.

CHAPTER 3

Living in the shadow of eugenics

Exploration of eugenics in the twenty-first century inevitably brings with it a memory of the horrors of eugenics at its worst expressed in the racist practices of Nazi Germany. Eugenics in this regime was predominantly negative, the prevention of birth or even the active killing of those considered 'undesirable'. What was at stake was the quality of the 'genetic stock' of the human race. Less well known is the fact that an alternative eugenic also exists, one that has implications for discussions about genetic therapy, namely the encouragement of reproduction of those judged as 'favourable'. Historically, those who supported eugenics in its various formulations came from a wide range of political and cultural backgrounds, with the shaping of eugenic policy reflected in the light of those framings. The seeming biological support for certain views of what might be desirable or not represents a fascinating case study in the way science is perceived or used in order to bolster political ideologies and practice. Exploring the more negative aspects of eugenic policy is not a comfortable exercise. One might say that it is genetics in the absence of Christian ethics, or indeed any ethics. Yet those who supported eugenic trends often did so for what they mistakenly presumed were thoroughly altruistic and noble reasons. Women were prominent in the eugenic movements both in North America and across Europe. This chapter attempts to enlarge on the historical background to eugenics in order to provide insights about its relationship to current practice in genetic screening, therapy and counselling that will be discussed in more detail in subsequent chapters. In itself, eugenics is a fascinating case study in the history of ideas, having used genetic science as its basis, but having outgrown the science to spread into dubious practical policy-making and political control.

WHAT IS EUGENICS?

Among the fascinating issues in the history of eugenics are the way an understanding of its meaning has shifted from its original conceptions and how the application of its principles has varied across different cultures and historical periods. The exclusion of certain individuals from mainstream society, and even the killing of young babies declared 'unfit', has a long history, going back to ancient classical times. Plato, writing in the fifth century BC, suggested in his fifth book of the *Laws* that human breeding and animal breeding were analogous, affirming legal 'purification' of the state. In his *Republic*, rulers hid away imperfect offspring, and also decided who would bear children and how many be born.[1] Yet it was only in the nineteenth century (1865) that Francis Galton, Charles Darwin's cousin, officially coined the term 'eugenics', from the Greek *eugenēs*, meaning 'good in birth'. He saw more than Darwin was prepared (at least initially) to admit, namely the possibility that human beings could now take charge of their own evolution. Galton defines eugenics as

the science of improving stock, which is by no means confined to questions of judicious mating, but which ... takes cognisance of all influences that tend in however remote degree to give the more suitable races or strains of blood a better chance of prevailing over the less suitable than they otherwise would have had.[2]

His later definition is rather more precise, but again stresses the positive eugenic that he had in mind; eugenics is defined as 'the science which deals with all influences which improve the inborn qualities of race; also with those that develop them to the utmost advantage'.[3]

Galton's book *Hereditary Genius* (1869) set out his argument for explaining all human characteristics in genetic terms. In an essay he suggested that even if we made an investment in human reproduction that was just 5% of that in animals, this would lead to a 'galaxy of genius'.[4] The capacity for religious belief and intellectual activity were, according to his views, inherited by natural selection. Hence, humanity is not so much a 'fallen angel' as a 'risen ape', and the development of moral efforts would be pointless, since we are victims of our heredity. His social programme was described by Darwin as 'grand, but Utopian'.[5] Galton, nonetheless, represents a relatively mild form of social genetic policy. Darwin argued against even this version by suggesting that altruism, like other qualities, arose through natural selection. The task of humanity becomes one of 'bearing with' those who are unfortunate, rather of than trying to eradicate those who are afflicted.

---

[1] Cited in Paul, *Controlling Human Heredity*, p. 5.   [2] Galton, *Inquiries into Human Faculty*, 3.24.
[3] Galton, 'Eugenics: Its Definition, Scope and Aims'.
[4] Galton, 'Hereditary Talent and Character', p. 165.   [5] Darwin, *The Descent of Man*, pp. 168–77.

It was only in the post-Darwinian era that eugenics took the form of more robust social policies linked with coercive state intervention. Karl Pearson, for example, believed that if compassion was over-exaggerated it would have negative effects on the long-term health of a population. Instead, racial purification was needed in order to promote long-term changes for the good. In the midst of these harsher definitions of eugenics, there were those who challenged such beliefs. Alfred Russel Wallace, for example, claimed that 'eugenics is simply the meddlesome interference of an arrogant scientific priestcraft'.[6]

Many contemporary definitions of eugenics assume that it is combined with coercive social policies, leading to a split between modern genetic technologies and eugenics, and allowing a clear division between them. Whether such a definition is permissible, given the complex history of eugenics, is open to question.

MOTIVATIONS FOR EUGENICS

As far as Galton was concerned, it was quite simply 'inconsistent to improve the varieties of domestic animals while leaving human heredity to chance'.[7] The idea that we can somehow offset the seemingly random deliverances of our genes is a popular theme today among geneticists, though in this case IVF and pre-implantation genetic diagnosis (PGD) are the scientific tools called upon to help in this exercise. Early geneticists, however, were more or less united in their (mistaken) view that social issues such as poverty, crime, prostitution and so on are direct results of hereditary defects. The worry, particularly potent in Victorian Britain, was that the human genetic 'stock' was rapidly degenerating, with the most prolific individuals being least suited to lead responsible and upright lives. Galton's understanding of eugenics, although largely positive, also approved of negative eugenics, so that each citizen would be required to reproduce according to a 'ranking' of desirable physical and mental qualities. He believed that those who violated these guidelines should be given fines or sent to labour colonies.[8]

Charles Darwin was more hesitant than his cousin to publish his ideas, but he eventually expressed his views on eugenics in his book entitled *The Descent of Man*. He was far less cavalier than Galton about the measures needed in order to follow up his belief in the analogy between human and animal breeding. While Darwin's personality was relatively mild and loath

---

[6] Wallace, Interview fragment (1912) in Smith (ed.), *Alfred Russel Wallace*, p. 177.
[7] Galton, *Hereditary Genius*.   [8] Pearson, *The Life, Letters and Labours of Francis Galton*, p. 420.

to offend, Galton was the opposite. Darwin's encounter with 'savages' in his voyages in the *Beagle* convinced him of the continuity between animals and humans in all manner of traits, including emotions, morals and behaviours. It did not take much imagination to draw some social classes and races closer to the ape than others. Hence, while Darwin accepted that if the 'lower classes' outbred their social superiors this would lead to evolutionary regress, he was reluctant to withdraw aid from the weak. Darwin's theory of hereditary units included the possibility that traits acquired by organisms during their lifetime could be transmitted to the next generation by a process called pangenesis. According to this hypothesis, minute granules or gemmules come from all parts of the system in order to make up the sexual elements. It did not explain why certain characteristics sometimes 'jumped' a generation, or reverted to ancestral traits, or how gemmules could reflect the state(s) of the cells. Francis Galton tested his theory by conducting a blood-transfusion experiment with different varieties of rabbits. He found that no matter which blood was received by a given strain, it made no difference to the offspring, who always resembled their parents.[9] Darwin was, naturally, shocked to the core that his cousin opposed him in this way.[10] He attempted to defend his position by claiming that he had never presumed that transmission of gemmules was through the circulatory system.

Yet Darwin's idea of pangenesis was never really accepted, and similarly the Lamarckian theory of acquired characteristics seemed too weak to explain many apparent anomalies. It took the German scientist August Weismann (1834–1914) to propose an alternative, namely that Darwinian natural selection works by selecting out the weakest individuals, who are limited by their hereditary material.[11] Distinguishing the body cells (*soma*) from the germ cells allowed Weismann to put forward a principle of heredity based on the continuity of the germ plasm.[12] The origin of variations via direct environmental influences on future progeny seemed open to question, and Weisman conducted a number of experiments with mice to show that this was the case.[13]

---

[9] Galton, 'Experiments in Pangenesis'.

[10] Darwin, 'Letters to the Editor'. Galton eventually conceded to his cousin, but not without some protest. See Galton, 'Letters to the Editor'.

[11] Weismann, 'On Heredity' (1883); Poulton et al. (eds.), *Essays upon Heredity*, pp. 67–106.

[12] Weismann, 'The Continuity of the Germ-Plasm as the Foundation of a Theory of Heredity' (1885), in Poulton et al. (eds.), *Essays upon Heredity*, pp. 163–256.

[13] He cut off the tails of the mice, and then found no difference in progeny, even after experiments with six generations of mutilation. See Weissman, 'The Supposed Transmission of Mutilations' (1888), in Poulton et al. (eds.), *Essays upon Heredity*, pp. 431–61.

The motivation for more direct interventionist eugenics aligned with more conservative politics grew stronger after Weismann's discoveries. For, if changing social conditions could not change germ plasm, the only available option would be to curtail the reproduction of those with undesirable qualities. France and Brazil, where Lamarckian ideas were still popular, rejected more coercive measures to achieve eugenic goals, such as enforced sterilisation. Yet occasionally Lamarckians did accept sterilisation in those situations where they believed that degeneration had gone too far. While they, like their American counterparts, wanted to prevent what they perceived as biological degeneration, they thought that changing the social conditions of the poor would automatically lead to an improvement in heritable good qualities, such as physical and mental strength.

In Britain the form of eugenics was related to anxiety about the declining birthrate, which was especially acute among favoured classes. While Americans feared an influx of immigrants, Britons were worried that the poorer classes would become dominant in society. Some even believed that shifts in population would eventually undermine Britain's military prowess. The life of Victorian Britain was dominated by bitter class conflict and social turmoil, with both rampant disease and disorder attributed to social and biological decline summarised in the term 'degeneration'.[14] In the United Kingdom the birthrate declined from 34 per thousand population in 1870 to less than 15 per thousand in 1930, with children per marriage going down from an average of five or six to just over two.[15] The common explanation for this sudden drop is that socio-economic factors were responsible, as were medical advances that meant that more children would survive. Richard Soloway suggests that one of the reasons why eugenics gained popular appeal in the early part of the twentieth century was the decline in birthrate:

Eugenics, as formulated by Galton, was inspired by this mixture of popular social assumption and observation, positivistic confidence in science, and the *Origin of Species*. It was moved in the early twentieth century from the realm of mathematical neo-Darwinian esoteria, which few people could understand, to the public arena by something most people could comprehend and were increasingly concerned about – the declining birthrate. (pp. 353–4).

The linkage between worries about the population issue and eugenics meant that the latter had far wider appeal than is commonly presumed. The postwar boom in fertility laid many of these anxieties to rest, though

---

[14] Paul, *Controlling Human Heredity*, p. 22.   [15] Soloway, *Demography and Degeneration*, p. xviii.

by then there were other reasons why eugenics lost credibility. Some of these factors will be dealt with further below.

In both Britain and the United States, eugenic societies became established, but attracted only just over a thousand members, mostly from the professional classes, including some Protestant clergy. In the USA the Eugenic Record Office (ERO), based at Cold Spring Harbor in New York, proved very important in its public influence. The number of American colleges offering courses in eugenics rose from 44 in 1914 to 376 in 1928. In addition, eugenics also seeped into high-school texts and was presumed to be a good.

A common assumption in much of the early eugenic propaganda was that mental defects were the root cause of many social ills. While Francis Galton popularised the idea that achievement and esteem run in families, those family studies initiated in the United States emphasised the connection between crime, pauperism and heredity. Richard Dugdale, who had been appointed to investigate state jails by the Prison Association of New York, conducted the first such study. He found one family, given the pseudonym Juke, were particularly prolific in their criminal record, being accused of assault, rape, murder, burglary and cruelty to animals.[16] He assumed that the Lamarckian pattern of inheritance follows, so that a 'cure' would be readily available by changing the environment in which the Jukes lived, through a comprehensive re-education programme. At this stage he believed that degenerates were accompanied by high rates of infant mortality and sterility, and so would be self-limiting. By the turn of the twentieth century the assumption tended to be that such families were particularly prolific in reproductive terms.

Subsequent family studies absorbed the results of Weismann's research – that is, they rejected the Lamarckian philosophy underlying the policy suggested by Dugdale. One, more famous, example is that of Henry H. Goddard, who conducted research on a family known by the alias of the Kallikaks (*kalos* means 'beautiful' and *kakos* means 'bad' in Greek).[17] His research followed a family that, as the name he invented for them implies, had a mixed history. Those who were 'feeble-minded' dominated one side of the family, while successful achievers, well integrated into American society, were dominanton the other side. Goddard decided to train eugenic field workers in order to track down family members and diagnose their

---

[16] Dugdale, *'The Jukes'*.   [17] Goddard, *The Kallikak Family*.

physical, mental and moral condition. He employed a former school-teacher called Elisabeth Kite. Like many of his contemporaries, he believed that women were ideal for this kind of work, having the ability to build confidence with those they interviewed, and giving sharp attention to detail. They in turn enthusiastically accepted this role, often on pitifully low salaries, given that other outlets for women's professional employment were in short supply. She found that 143 out of 480 descendants of Martin Kallikak were 'feeble-minded'.

Kite discovered that the genetic line containing the affected offspring were descended from a casual encounter between Martin Kallikak and a 'feeble-minded' girl that he had met at a tavern. The other line came from his marriage. Goddard concluded that 'feeble-mindedness' was hereditary, and a recessive trait; but he also assumed all other social ills were hereditary, including pauperism, criminality, prostitution and drunkenness. He was preoccupied with the inheritance of mental defects, setting up a classification of those with a mental age of one or two as 'idiots', those with a mental age of three to seven as 'imbeciles', and those with a mental age of between eight and twelve as 'morons'.[18] The 'feeble-minded' were incapable of telling right from wrong, hence the connection with criminal and other antisocial activities such as drunkenness and prostitution. He recommended segregation of those who were affected. He recorded a sample of the actual interviews that Elisabeth Kite carried out. They show that she made 'swift, superficial and subjective judgments'; even a single glance was, for her, enough to show whether someone was affected by the condition.[19]

Goddard's book detailing his research, entitled *The Kallikak Family: A Study in the History of Feeblemindedness* (1912), was an immediate success, going into twelve reprints. His story had a moral lesson as well; spreading one's seed too liberally would have dire consequences. This book was among those that helped to promote the idea that such families were parasites on society.

A further outlet of eugenic 'research' came through the testing of US army recruits at the turn of the twentieth century.[20] Nearly half the white draft was classed as 'feeble-minded', a fact that rang alarm bells about levels of national intelligence. While British propaganda tended to point to the lower classes and the urban poor as the source of some of the eugenic ills,

[18] See Paul, *Controlling Human Heredity*, p. 59. The test was so stringent that more than half of those identified as normal by the Stanford-Binet test, which came into use in 1916, would be classified as morons under Goddard's system. See S. Gelb, 'Social Deviancy and the Discovery of the Moron', *Disability, Handicap and Society* 2 (1987), pp. 247–58.
[19] Paul, *Controlling Human Heredity*, p. 54.   [20] Ibid., p. 65.

US propaganda pointed to immigrant policy: in 1840, for example, 40% of children in state mental institutions were of immigrant origin.

The eugenic climate in the USA became particularly obvious through propaganda designed to promote withholding of treatment to babies born with various disabilities. This was achieved through campaigns, such as that of the notorious Dr Haiselden, and the distribution of films, such as the 1922 film *The Black Stork*.[21] Dr Haiselden was eventually expelled from the Chicago Medical Society, not because he had done anything illegal, but because he had publicised the cases. The general consensus at the time was that actions such as these were against good taste and unfit for public discussion. The gradual slippage of eugenic goals, from excluding so-called unfavourable births, into euthanasia (also called mercy killing), which assumes that there are those who are better off dead, is evident in the popular literature of the time. Dr Haiselden was not alone in his belief that 'defective' children should be allowed to die. Some eugenicists, such as British-born Stanley Hall, believed that medical efforts to save life in such circumstances were inappropriate, as they interfered with the 'wholesome' process of natural selection. There was also wide public support for such practices, with a significant minority (4%) even supporting active killing of affected infants.[22] The majority of Roman Catholics stood out against the practices of allowing to die and active killing. Cultural assumptions about defectiveness and degeneracy were also associated with certain races, *The Black Stork* linking black skin colour with defective inheritance, even claiming to have a scientific basis for such presumptions. It is noteworthy that such defectives were still thought to be within the scope of human salvation, rather than being sub-human. The 'soul' of the defective baby was thought to be received by Jesus, implying that there would be, at least, some consolation in heaven. Haiselden viewed the medical advances that allowed premature babies to live, and even the idea that science might cure certain diseases, as a 'vicious fraud, poisoning human germ plasm'.[23] These extreme views would be broadly abhorrent today, except for scholars holding to Peter Singer's position, given the extent of care available for pre-term babies, most of whom are genetically perfectly 'normal'.

Not everyone followed this popular trend; G. K. Chesterton (1874–1936), for example, denounced eugenics as a 'modern craze for scientific official-ism'.[24] Like those of other Roman Catholics at the time, his views were rejected as remnants of a superstitious religion that was out of touch with

[21] Pernick, *The Black Stork*.   [22] Ibid., p. 31.   [23] Ibid., p. 111.
[24] Chesterton, *Eugenics and Other Evils*, p. vi.

contemporary concerns. Yet the fact that prominent American Protestant clergy, such as the Revd W. T. Sumner, Dean of the Episcopal Cathedral of St Peter and St Paul in Chicago, were prepared to embrace eugenics, even refusing marriage to those considered 'unfit', shows the pervasiveness of eugenic ideas.[25]

EUGENIC POLICIES

Although eugenicists were all united in their belief that social issues should guide reproductive decisions (assuming, of course, that there was a link between them), there was hot debate over the practical implementation of these policies. For example, who should be urged to breed? Should it be middle-class college graduates? Who should be discouraged – mental defectives, immigrants, criminals? Who should make the decisions about policy? Should it be the families themselves, or other social organisations, or the state? How should eugenics be expressed in practical policy? Through tax incentives, education, birth-control availability, or sterilization?[26]

The way eugenic policies were formulated depended on particular cultural and political restraints; and (as one might have anticipated), as socio-economic conditions deteriorated, more voices were clamouring for more stringent eugenic policies, such as sterilisation. Denmark passed a law on the coercive use of sterilisation in 1934, and the practice was legalised around this time in many American states. British eugenicists encountered much more resistance to sterilisation laws. However, there were those who offered alternative measures; Julian Huxley, for example, suggested in 1931 that the unemployed should be sent to labour camps and barred from reproducing. Some segregation of those who were mentally ill was allowed under the Mental Health Act of 1913.

Eugenic policies were clearly politically diverse, being held by members of varied political persuasions from the left-wing American geneticist H. J. Muller, who spent some time in Russia trying to implement eugenic policies, through to the more conservative J. B. S. Haldane in Britain. Eugenicists in Britain tried to distinguish the respectable working class from the poorest of the poor, who became the chief objects of eugenic policy. Some eugenicists were members of the left-wing Fabian Society, who managed to hold together a double view of the poor as both 'unfit' and

---

[25] Paul, *Controlling Human Heredity*, p. 10.
[26] The tensions apparent here are noted by Paul, *Controlling Human Heredity*, p. 72.

victims of oppression. Fabians promoted eugenics alongside other socialist policies that offered wider access to health, education and welfare.[27] H. G. Wells was a British author who believed in the 'sterilisation' of failures; George Bernard Shaw believed that 'eugenic religion' would ultimately save the civilised world from collapse. Both authors helped to popularise the idea in the United Kingdom that human reproduction, like animal breeding, could be selective. The idea of sterilisation never took hold, partly because there was a general belief that education would be sufficient to overcome social problems.

In the USA around the turn of the last century, social unrest, strikes and violence followed in the wake of an uneven wealth created by industrialisation. Along with rising crime and prostitution, there were overcrowded prisons and asylums for the insane and feeble-minded. Diane Paul points out that the middle classes, naturally enough, 'called for factory inspection, child labor laws, a shortened workday, community clinics, probation and parole, a federal income tax, workmen's compensation, the direct election of US senators, prohibition. And eugenics.'[28]

Eugenics was seen as a welcome science that allowed greater socio-political control. While segregation of undesirables was favoured in some circles, economically it was very expensive. Castration was the only method of sterilisation until 1899, when a Chicago surgeon, A. J. Ochsner, described the relatively simple procedure called vasectomy. Some, such as Dr Harry Sharp of Indiana State Reformatory, went ahead and sterilised 500 males with no legal warrant from 1899 to 1907. By 1912 there were sterilisation laws in eight states. Yet there were those who were prepared to challenge the state laws on constitutional grounds, and most of the operations were performed on those who were insane. In 1927 a famous case of *Buck v. Bell* upheld the sterilisation statute introduced in Virginia, Justice Oliver Wendell Holmes suggesting that 'it is better for all the world if, instead of waiting to execute degenerate offspring for crime, or to let them starve for their imbecility, society can prevent those who are manifestly unfit from continuing their kind ... Three generations of imbeciles is enough.'[29] Following this ruling, thirty states adopted sterilisation laws, with 60,000 persons legally sterilized. Public opinion was in favour of sterilisation, which was relatively inexpensive if it meant that individuals could be discharged rather than kept segregated in institutions at the

---

[27] See Paul, *Controlling Human Heredity*, pp. 74–6.   [28] Ibid., p. 77.
[29] Cited in ibid., p. 83.

taxpayer's expense. The economic difference explains why some women also were sterilised.

German eugenic programmes commonly drew on American models for support. Like other European and American counterparts, the political support for eugenics in Germany covered a broad spectrum. The German Society for Race Hygiene was founded in 1905 in order to counter the declining fertility of the professional classes. The Jewish geneticists Richard Goldsmidt, Franz Kallmann and Curt Stern were all active eugenicists. Just before the close of the Weimar Republic, a draft law was in place to permit sterilisation, subject to consent. Two months after the Nazis came to power a new Law for the Prevention of Diseased Progeny was in place, permitting compulsory sterilisation. Compulsory sterilisation of a number of individuals followed, including those with congenital feeble-mindedness, schizophrenia, manic depression, severe physical deformity, hereditary epilepsy, Huntington's chorea, hereditary blindness and deafness, and severe alcoholism. Genetic health courts evaluated cases, and, although the law did not specifically mention those who were considered 'asocial', in practice this followed.

Up until 1933 the Scandinavian countries (that is, Denmark, Sweden, Norway, Finland and Iceland) developed their eugenic policies on lines broadly similar to those found in Germany. The justification for sterilisation was spelt out, not in eugenic terms, but in social terms, pointing to the incapability of the individual to raise a family and educate children. Germany applied the law indiscriminately to all those whom they considered racial undesirables, including Gypsies and Jews. Between 320,000 and 400,000 were sterilised in the Nazi era, about 100 times the number in Denmark. Both Germany and Denmark conducted a social register of Gypsies, but, while German policy led them to concentration camps and eventual death in gas chambers, in Denmark the data were used in order to propose integration into the wider community. In 1939 all mental patients in Germany were subject to an extensive euthanasia programme.

It is less well known that Germany practised some positive eugenics towards those especially racially favoured. For example, the Well of Life programme allowed those women who passed a race test, whether married or single, to give birth in maternity homes run by the SS.

The influences of Nazi eugenic policies were not confined to their shores. Marie Stopes, for example, campaigned in Britain for birth-control methods, and also for sterilization of the poor, actively supporting Adolf Hitler. She was appalled by what she perceived as the fertility of the 'unfit'. In the United States, similar fears were directed towards the immigrant population, though there is no evidence that second-generation immigrants are more fertile than average – if anything, the opposite is the case.[30] Madison Grant was among those Americans who perpetuated more extreme racist views against immigrants. He popularised the view that crossing Americans of Nordic stock with immigrants would lead to biological degradation. In Britain, sentiment that saw immigration as posing a 'mongrelising threat', as expressed by post-Second World War personalities such as Enoch Powell, eventually proved an embarrassment to a Conservative government, reflecting the shift away from eugenic policy in the wake of the collapse of the Nazi regime.[31]

Eugenic movements were also scattered in different parts of the world, and their appropriation of genetics was similarly varied, ranging from Latin American through to Russian advocates of eugenics.[32] Eugenics even found a hearing among anarchic groups in Spain, though the forms that eugenics took were as changeable as one might expect of anarchic politics.[33] Like their contemporaries, anarchists wanted to find explanations for good and bad traits in people they encountered, speaking of the 'race of the poor', and condemning the capitalist erosion of equalities and access to health benefits. Eugenics among anarchic groups in Spain also presupposed that science was an objective good, though these groups believed that if it fell into the 'wrong' hands it could be abused.

Latin American appropriation of eugenics did not follow the more extreme policies of sterilisation found in the United States, Scandinavia and Germany.[34] One of the most likely explanations is cultural: the strongly traditional attitudes to family and gender would have revolted against extreme measures such as sterilisation. Eugenic policy was implemented through environmental reforms, though of course this was premised on the fact that Lamarckian theories of inheritance were more widely accepted.

POPULATION GENETICS AND EUGENICS

At the turn of the twentieth century the most commonly held view of eugenics was that it was simply applied genetics. Propaganda from eugenic societies tried to convince the public of its worth, and were generally successful in persuading people to accept the view prevalent among

---

[30] King and Ruggles, 'American Immigration'.   [31] Soloway, *Demography and Degeneration*, p. 352.
[32] Adams, *The Wellborn Science*.   [33] Cleminson, *Anarchism, Science and Sex*.
[34] Stephan, *The Hour of Eugenics*.

geneticists that social issues such as poverty, crime and so on were linked with an unfortunate endowment of 'bad' genes. Galton's version of population genetics assumed that all heredity was continuous in distribution, rather than inherited according to discrete units. He founded what was known as the 'biometric' school, which was later discredited.[35] William Bateson argued, instead, for Mendelism, based on the findings of the scientist and monk Gregor Johann Mendel, whose work had been ignored for some time, but then 'rediscovered' by those searching for an alternative explanation for heredity. Mendel had argued that inheritance in pea plants was through discrete units, and he conducted a series of careful experiments in his monastery garden. His work, although published, was not thought to be relevant to heredity more generally. His relative lack of status suppressed his work.[36]

It took G. H. Hardy to work out what might happen if Mendelian patterns of inheritance worked in a population. In 1908, his research was formulated in a mathematical way, known as the Hardy-Weinberg law, showing that the gene frequency of any given mutant or normal allele does not change under ideal conditions.[37] The equation is as follows. For two alleles, the distribution of a gene in a population would be according to $a^2 + 2ab + b^2 = 1$, where a is the frequency of the dominant allele and b is the frequency of the recessive allele. Hence, if a recessive gene is in 40% of the population, it will yield 16% homozygous recessives and 48% heterozygous carriers. This totally challenged the two main assumptions of eugenicists: first, that 'like always begets like', and second, importantly, that removing those who were affected would automatically reduce the level of the undesirable gene in a given population. While the Hardy-Weinberg law rarely applies in a strict way, because it is based on the assumption of 'ideal' conditions, it does, at least, show that the assumption that removing the recessives from a population would 'purge' it of undesirable genes makes no sense. If, for example, feeble-mindedness was inherited by a single recessive gene, then it would take literally hundreds of years to remove that gene from a population simply by sterilising those affected: too many people were carriers, and no one suggested that carriers should be sterilised; although this would of course be the logical development, it would lead to depopulation. There was the added difficulty of recognising

---

[35] Carlson, *The Unfit*, p. 342.   [36] See ibid., pp. 132–7.
[37] Because Hardy's formula was also suggested by Wilhelm Weinberg virtually simultaneously, it came to be known as the Hardy-Weinberg law.

carriers without suitable tests to find out who were the affected members of a population.

Even if we adopt the simplistic view that defects of all kinds are the result of single recessive character traits, then, it becomes clear that the sterilisation of those who were affected (that is, the recessives) would not remove the genes from the population, as a large proportion of those unaffected would be carriers of the genes. Even when a condition is rare in a population, there are still relatively large numbers of carriers. The carrier numbers are approximately twice the square root of the incidence of a mutant gene. Thus, if 1 in 250,000 babies is born with a particular condition, 1 person in 80 carries that gene. Even if the parents who gave birth to the affected child were sterilised, it would still leave 78 carriers, and the rate of reducing that gene by sterilising methods would be virtually unnoticeable.

The term 'feeble-minded' gradually came to be discredited as the variety of disorders came to light, only some of which were hereditary. Dr John Langdon Down (1828–96) described a condition he called 'mongolism', attributing the characteristic features such as small stature and slanting eyes to an ancestral, less robust form of human evolution originating in Asia. His view reflected his own prejudice against other races. The complex patterns of inheritance made it very difficult for eugenicists to predict the value of enforced sterilization. Some traits were also complicated by being variable in their appearance and/or in their expression, sometimes even skipping a generation. Geneticists describe these effects as having a high or low penetrance or weak or strong expression, depending on background genotype. This made it even more difficult to predict the outcomes of eugenic policies.

Given the increasing knowledge of population genetics and the futility of sterilisation practice on the frequency of gene expression, it is worth considering why so many distinguished geneticists still apparently advocated eugenic policies. For example, the academic journal *Genetics* was founded in 1916, and every member of its editorial board supported eugenics.[38] In interwar Germany, the support for eugenics by geneticists was virtually unchallenged. While some believed in trying to reform eugenic claims, the overall belief that it was beneficial for society remained intact. Eugenicists were united in their enthusiasm for the idea that technocratic solutions could be brought to bear on social problems. While some of them accepted the implications of the growing field of population genetics, they believed that those who were mentally defective

---

[38] Paul, *Controlling Human Heredity*, p. 18.

in any way would not have the ability to be competent parents. In addition, there were some who thought of all defective genes as representing an 'evil' that needed to be eradicated where it was known, even if such policy did not lead to its disappearance in the population.

The results of population genetics did little, it seems, to dampen eugenics policies, though after the 1930s there was a gradual change in attitude towards eugenics. The most likely explanation for the eventual rejection of eugenics is that a combination of social and political shifts rendered it no longer acceptable as a basis for policy. Yet this shift took some time, and scientists were among those who continued to support eugenics. For example, five of the first six presidents of the American Society for Human Genetics, founded in 1948, were also members of the board of directors of the Eugenics Society.[39] By the 1940s the idea of compulsory sterilisation was out of fashion, but many geneticists saw reformed versions of eugenics as a way of highlighting the importance of their work, so that medical genetics was simply good eugenics. While they admitted that race and class had biased eugenics in the past, they insisted that the premise of eugenics, that some genes were 'bad', remained intact. Devastating diseases such as Tay-Sachs, muscular dystrophy and Huntington's chorea were thought of as 'evils' needing to be eradicated.

Some scientists did actively reject eugenics, among them the American geneticist Lionel Penrose, who insisted that an index of a civilised society is whether it can care for those unable to take care of themselves. T. H. Morgan was another prominent American geneticist who spoke out against eugenics, arguing strongly that the genetic and environmental context in which genes are expressed was ignored by simplistic eugenic 'solutions'.

Other scientists adopted an intermediate position. Professor H. J. Muller was highly critical of establishment eugenics; he wanted it to be reformed, believing that economic inequality masks genetic differences. He was also aware that eugenics was frequently based on false assumptions about genetic inheritance according to the false common-sense rule that 'like begets like'. In general he was more in favour of positive eugenics for encouraging reproduction among those with beneficial endowments, rather than supporting a negative programme of removing the undesirables. He was also keen to stress the importance of the environment as a factor in gene expression. In particular, he wanted to stamp out the idea that those in the lower classes are automatically inferior in intelligence,

[39] Ibid., p. 121.

claiming that 'there is no scientific basis for the conclusion that socially lower classes, or technically less advanced races, really have a genetically inferior intellectual equipment, since the differences found between their averages are to be accounted for fully by the known effects of environment'.[40] For him, it was society that was to be blamed for social problems, not individuals for their faulty genes. In 1934 his socialist leanings took him to the USSR, where he laid out plans for a socialist version of eugenics. In a book called *Out of the Night*, published in 1935, he described a programme for artificially inseminating women with sperm from 'superior' men. In this book he made bold predictions about the future possibilities for positive eugenics. He argued that

It is easy to show that in the course of a paltry century or two (paltry considering the advance in question) it would be possible for the majority of the population to become of the innate quality of such men as Lenin, Newton, Leonardo, Pasteur, Beethoven, Omar Khayyam, Pushkin, Sun Yat-Sen, Marx (I purposely mention men of different fields and races), or even to possess their varied faculties combined ... We do not wish to imply that these men owned their greatness entirely to genetic causes, but certainly they must have stood exceptionally high genetically; and if, as now seems certain, we can in the future make the social and material environment favourable for the development of the latent powers of men in general, then, by securing for them the favourable genes at the same time, we should be able to raise virtually all mankind to or beyond levels heretofore attained only by the most remarkably gifted.[41]

His belief that his eugenic policy would lead to a pantheon of genius was totally misguided. His book was warmly received in Britain, but Stalin did not accept his ideas, even executing two of his post-doctoral students in 1936! Eventually Muller was forced to flee. Once back in the United States, he waited until the 1950s before reintroducing his eugenic ideas. In their new form he argued that voluntary means should be used to promote education for the correct 'germinal choice'. He sought to establish a 'Foundation for Germinal Choice', but, once he realised that those who provided financial support for this foundation were strongly capitalist – a political position he clearly disparaged – he withdrew his support. The sperm bank for geniuses, as it came to be called, has been largely ignored despite widespread publicity.

---

[40] H. J. Muller, 'The Dominance of Economics over Eugenics', in *A Decade of Progress in Eugenics*, pp. 138–44 (pp. 141–2).
[41] Muller, *Out of the Night*, p. 113.

PAUL RAMSEY'S 'FABRICATED MAN'

The ethicist Paul Ramsey was convinced that all forms of genetic control were unethical, whether expressed through the extreme negative eugenic policies in the Nazi regime, or through the positive claims of contemporary genetics in the second half of the twentieth century. He was keen to point out the pessimism of writers such as H. J. Muller regarding what he perceived to be the apocalyptic future of the human race, citing work he published in 1959 entitled 'The Guidance of Human Evolution'.[42] Ramsey argued that, from a theological point of view, the deeply pessimistic tone of Muller's writing was simply un-Christian. For Muller, the answer was a positive eugenic intervention through human choice, but one that was informed by genetic futures envisaged by science. Muller predicted that, if nothing was done to intervene, there would be a total collapse in civilised communities. He explains the basis for his positive eugenics by saying that 'it would in the end be far easier and more sensible to manufacture a complete man *de novo*, out of appropriately chosen raw materials, than to try and refashion into human form those pitiful relics which remained'.[43] It seems, then, that although Muller advocated a positive eugenics, it was based on the assumption that negative eugenics was impossible, because the degeneration was much too far gone. His view regarding those with recognisable genetic defects is therefore even more extreme than might have been apparent at first sight.

Paul Ramsey argued that it was extremely difficult for positive eugenics to free itself from culturally bound views of what constituted good qualities, which is one reason why he favoured limited negative eugenics. Ramsey held on to this view, in spite of his knowledge of population genetics, on the basis that to remove any defective individual from a population was, in a small way at least, a 'gain' (p. 56). Yet he went further and suggested that those who were carriers of known genetic disorders should have only half as many children as they might otherwise have had if they had not been so affected (p. 56). He had strong views on couples who decided to take a chance and have a child even though they were both carriers of a recessive defect and so had a one in four chance of having an affected child. He described such couples as showing 'genetic imprudence, with the further notation that imprudence is gravely immoral' (p. 57). He argued for voluntary childlessness, though of course he was writing at a time when pre-implantation genetic diagnosis (PGD) was not a feasible

---

[42] Ramsey, *Fabricated Man*, p. 23.   [43] H. J. Muller, cited in ibid., p. 24.

option. It is ironic, perhaps, that clinical genetics has allowed the kind of negative eugenics Ramsey advocated to be applied in theory, though even with these techniques only those who are bearers of the double recessive gene, rather than the carriers, are eliminated. Ramsey could hardly avoid the charge of advocating eugenics in this instance, and it is clear that he was writing at a stage when the possibility of state control of genetic choice was gradually being replaced by individual familial decisions. We might ask ourselves what such an attitude says about those who are affected by genetic disease. It seems to suggest, in common with other negative eugenic policies, that it would have been better if such people had not been born. Although Ramsey is better known for his critique of positive interventions in genetics – what he termed 'playing God' – it is worth asking if his own strident attitude towards reproductive choices are any less aimed at gaining 'control' over what is clearly a complex pattern of inheritance.

IS CLINICAL GENETICS EUGENICS IN DISGUISE?

Diane Paul highlights how reproductive autonomy, rather than state control of 'germ plasm', has become a dominant feature of contemporary culture. She suggests that 'revelations of Nazi atrocities, the trend towards respect for patient's rights in medicine, and the rise of feminism have converged to make reproductive autonomy a dominant value in our culture' (p. 71).

The shift from state intervention in human genetics to individual choice means that most, if not all, geneticists wish to distance themselves from eugenic language. Eugenics has come to be associated with oppressive regimes; we live under the shadow of a distorted negative eugenics that has left an indelible mark on the human landscape. Most scholars agree that not all evolutionary psychology is racist, nor is an expression of interest in genetic science evidence of Nazi leanings. Such views would defy any reasonable historical appreciation of the history of eugenics. However, some are prepared to ask if the new clinical practices of genetic medicine, such as are found in its screening and selection programmes, are really a form of 'backdoor' eugenics. Dan Stone, for example, suggests that 'there is a sense in which what we are witnessing now is a return of eugenics to mainstream science, and in some ways in an even more insidious form, since it is being presented not as government coercion, but as individual choice'.[44]

---

[44] Stone, *Breeding Superman*, p. 137. Robert Song seems to adopt a similar stance in his suggestion that 'eugenics may not so much have died as adopted a new mask': Song, *Human Genetics*, p. 49. Where is the new eugenics? According to him, this is 'the pre-natal screening suite, the genetic counsellor's

Genetic counselling today has its historical roots in heredity counselling clinics that were supported by the American Eugenics Society. The first clinic in the USA was the Dwight Institute for Human Genetics, founded in 1941 at the University of Minnesota.[45] Charles Dwight even went as far as praising Hitler for his plan to stamp out mental inferiority. Heredity counselling was highly directive in its early years, its practitioners believing that clients needed guidance as well as information. By 1947, Sheldon Reed had coined the term 'genetic counselling', but he argued that counsellors should respect the decisions of those whose lives were affected. One of his reasons for this shift was in itself eugenic: those who came to clinics were almost certainly above the average in terms of ability, so it would be worth preserving their genes in a population. The concept of non-directive counselling was really accepted only following a shift in public attitudes to reproductive choice in the 1960s and 1970s, when concern for the future of a population was replaced by concern for family welfare. In practical terms, genetic testing has overtaken genetic counselling, so that women are more likely to receive information from doctors worried about potential lawsuits than from trained counsellors.[46] It is these subtle pressures on women to make the 'right' choice that has led some to equate contemporary medical practices with eugenics.

Understandably, the association of eugenics and genetics offends many scientists, even though, half a century before, when eugenics seemed to promise so much benefit to the human race, scientists were instrumental in the leadership of eugenic societies. One way to counter this offence is to argue strongly that eugenics is not necessarily an agent of oppression, nor is it always associated with right-wing policies. The historical analysis presented so far underlines this case. Elof Carlson seems to support the use of genetics in negative eugenics in as much as it can reduce the number of sick

---

office, the general practitioner's surgery, the abortion clinic' (p. 50). But is he correct to amalgamate all these practices? In the chapters that follow I will seek to distinguish current screening practices from, for example, genetic counselling practice or abortion. The shadow of eugenics may hang over them all, but, arguably, not to the same degree in each case. I do, however, concur with Amy Laura Hall, of Duke University, when she says that the Revd Joanna Jepson's legal and political struggle against late abortion for an apparently 'trivial' reason, namely cleft lip (from which she herself suffered as a child), is an area of grave concern, especially for Christians, and arguably back-door eugenics. The medical practitioners in this case argued that cleft lip is associated with other 'serious' conditions, but the nature of their seriousness is not clear in the media reporting of this case. In any event, very late abortion amounts to infanticide, which is always unacceptable. I am grateful to Amy Laura for allowing me to read a draft of her article entitled 'Public Bioethics and the Gratuity of Life: Joanna Jepson's Witness against Negative Eugenics' prior to its publication in *Studies in Christian Ethics*.

[45] Paul, *Controlling Human Heredity*, p. 123.

[46] I will discuss genetic testing and counselling in chapters 4 and 5.

babies being born. He is confident that 'each generation will add more conditions that they would prefer to see prevented rather than treated. This will not lead to a super race. It will not lead to a uniformity of personalities, physical appearances, or a new species of humanity' (p. 377). Yet, while he claims that the idea of the 'unfit' is a bad one, this seems to be the very position that he advocates in the application of genetic technologies. Other scientists, however are more concerned to detach eugenics from contemporary genetic practice altogether. One argument for this that might be advanced is that, if contemporary genetic screening were really eugenic in its goals, then carriers would have to be removed from a population as well. Carlson, for example, states that, in the case of recessive genes, 'the use of prenatal diagnosis with elective abortion does not constitute a eugenic procedure because it does not change gene frequency' (p. 370). However, this is a weak argument, since it is clear that, even at the height of the eugenic dream, virtually no one made such extreme policy recommendations, even when it was known that carriers were responsible for the maintenance of genetic defects in a given population. Because it was quite simply socially unacceptable and impracticable even to try to remove the carriers in the population, eugenicists needed to conveniently play down this aspect in order to win public support.

In addition, the cases in which the modern genetic techniques *can* remove genes are those of dominant disorders, where there are no 'carriers' as such, but only those either affected or unaffected by the trait. Huntington's chorea is one such condition. In these cases there is every possibility that the gene will be removed from the population in one generation if selective abortion is used. A similar scenario exists for X-linked disorders, where the recessive hemizygous gene would be removed in one generation by screening, or over a two-century period if it were just left with no interference. Carlson believes that categorising any screening programme as eugenic is wrong, since such programmes simply speed up what would happen anyway for dominant and hemizygous genes, and is ineffective in removing those genes that are recessive. He seems to be against positive eugenics of all kinds through genetic science, believing that we do not yet have the knowledge to undertake such experiments, and we cannot be sure about the outcome of such actions (p. 377). Yet it is ironic, perhaps, that the very processes that he affirms can be used to make the kinds of changes that he is anxious to resist. At the same time, he believes that fears that genetic engineering might be eugenic fail to capture the relatively small scale of genetic engineering compared with the total pool of available genes; in this way it would be the same as 'trying to construct a towering cathedral using one-centimeter bricks and a pair of tweezers to align them' (p. 392).[47] I suggest that what has persisted in both the eugenics of the last century and more recent contemporary medical practice, including reformulated versions of eugenics advocated by Carlson, is the view that there are those in the population whom society would be better off without. Hence, while in most cases genetic screening would not be 'eugenic' in the sense of being an effective means of removing genes from a population, it is eugenic in as much as it assumes that there are undesirables in our midst.

Of course, the counter to this position is that clinical genetics, in any case, is not intended to be a directive against those who are affected by the condition, but more a resource of information in order that informed choices may be made. Yet it is clear that the fact that such acts are acts of private citizens, rather than a result of coercive government policies, does not make them benign.[48] The history of eugenics has shown its chameleon quality, originating as it does in ideas such as 'degeneracy'. It therefore seems unlikely that hopes to improve the hereditable qualities of the human race will disappear altogether; rather, they are likely to emerge in a new form, shaped according to the dominant values of the time; that is, according to the mantra of individualism, economic rationalisation and reproductive choice. The chapter that follows takes up the more contemporary political agenda of genetic choice through screening and testing, and it is worth considering such an agenda in the light of historical issues presented in this chapter.

---

[47] For a discussion of different patterns of inheritance, see Carlson, *The Unfit*, pp. 369–77.
[48] Paul, *Controlling Human Heredity*, p. 35.

CHAPTER 4

Genetic testing and screening

One of the growing applications of new genetic knowledge is seen in the development of policies that foster both genetic testing and screening. Both are linked with a perception of improved health and healthcare, personalised prediction of risk, more precision in diagnosis, and more precise targeting of drug therapy and prevention according to individual genetic profiles. The benefits seem, at first sight, obvious, and integral to the aims of the medical profession. Genetic profiling can, of course, also be used to track criminal activity or to determine paternity, though the main concern of this chapter will be the issues associated with health and medical ethics. More general issues arise, such as the 'geneticisation' of knowledge about humanity.

The UK Government White Paper on genetics, entitled *Our Inheritance, Our Future: Realising the Potential of Genetics in the NHS*, launched in June 2003, represents a remarkable endorsement of the application of genetics to healthcare services, with the promise of a £50 million investment over three years.[1] In addition to more specialised services in genetics, UK Government policy is to integrate genetics-based approaches into mainstream healthcare, so genetics is set to be a key characteristic of healthcare policy for all patients, not just those with defined genetic disorders. Ethical concerns, where they arise, seem to be based on fears about misuse of an individual's genetic information for commercial or other gain, while exempting its use for police or medical purposes. Such an approach relies on the professional ethical policies that already exist, with public consultation amounting to receipt of information followed by comment rather than providing any serious challenge to the implementation or goal of given policy decisions.

This chapter will focus particularly on the genetic science behind genetic testing and screening, but will also offer a critical analysis of the

---

[1] Department of Health, *Our Inheritance, Our Future.*

secular ethical and policy debates. UK policy will act as a case study, and will serve to inform ethical discussion in the light of practical changes that are taking place, though the ethical and social issues raised will also apply to contexts outside Britain. I will deal with the more general ethical issues surrounding the nature of genetic risk in the next chapter, on genetic counselling, for communicating a clear and realistic sense of what that risk might mean is integral to counselling practice. Chapter 6, on gene therapy, will also build up an argument for an alternative approach to ethical decision-making in socio-political contexts, drawing on the virtues, as outlined in the first two chapters, as an approach that is fruitful to consider even in the arena of institutional ethics, which this present chapter seeks to address.

FINDING THE WAY THROUGH SOME DEFINITIONS

At the outset, it is important to distinguish the various forms of genetic knowledge, as there is a tendency for the boundaries between them to become blurred. The ethical issues associated with each aspect are distinct, though related. *Genetic testing* is confined to individuals. While it can be performed on those who show symptoms of a disease, it can also be performed on those who show no symptoms. People in the latter category might be carriers of a defective gene and *asymptomatic*, or they might be likely to develop a disease at some time in the future, either later in childhood or, as in Huntington's chorea, as an adult, and so are *presymptomatic*. Genetic testing can also, in its broadest definition, cover the testing of the genes of body cells (somatic testing), as opposed to the material inherited through the germ line. Somatic testing applies to genetic disorders such as many cancers, though of course, there are also heritable genes that make an individual more likely to contract different forms of the disease. One could argue that most diseases involve some alteration to the genetic constituents of cells; bacteria and viruses invade the 'host' cells and take over the genetic machinery for their own ends. Genetic testing in the narrower definition, as applied to the germ line, has more ethical connotations, since its characterisation will impact on the children of the individual concerned. The genetic testing of inheritable characteristics is not necessarily just DNA analysis; it might also include analysis of gene products, or proteins, that are known to be characteristic of the condition. Peter Harper has suggested a helpful working definition of genetic testing:

Genetic testing is the analysis of a specific gene, its product or function, or other DNA and chromosome analysis, to detect or exclude an alteration likely to be associated with a genetic disorder.[2]

Sometimes biochemical variations found in population studies are related to a particular disease susceptibility trait. For example, A-polipo-protein E, used as a population marker, is also correlated with susceptibility to Alzheimer's disease.[3] Genetic testing that is diagnostic of a particular disease is uncontroversial; it simply helps to identify the genetic contribution to a disease pattern. However, genetic testing that is pre-symptomatic is performed in cases where the probability of developing a disease is almost inevitable. Predictive testing, on the other hand, gives a probability only, with numerous other environmental and genetic background factors contributing to the likelihood or not of the onset of the disease.

Those who might be carriers of faulty genes may want to undergo a genetic test in order to help their reproductive decisions. One difficulty is that even in these cases the individuals may be treated like 'patients', although they are completely healthy themselves. Genetic testing normally involves an initial consultation, followed by laboratory testing, followed by further support. The initial preparation and follow-up support are the remit of genetic counsellors, though it is fair to say that, in the United Kingdom at least, the need and availability of laboratory tests far exceed the numbers of trained genetic counsellors. Thus, many of those tested will not necessarily have the benefit of access to genetic counselling services.

The commercialisation of genetic tests, such as that for the breast cancer BRCA1 gene by the American-based company Myriad, is unfortunate, since those who are on the receiving end of the results of such tests do not have access to the kind of counselling required. There has been a case reported of a woman opting to have a double mastectomy on hearing that she had inherited the gene for breast cancer.[4] Such actions are inappropriate in view of the outcomes of genetic tests, which usually predict susceptibility rather than guaranteeing a particular outcome. In addition, there is always the possibility that mistakes may occur in laboratory test results because of human error.

---

[2] P. S. Harper, 'What Do We Mean By Genetic Testing?', in Harper and Clarke (eds.), *Genetics, Society and Clinical Practice*, pp. 7–14 (p. 8).

[3] Ibid., p. 9.

[4] See S. A. M. McLean, 'The Genetic Testing of Children: Some Legal and Ethical Concerns', in Clarke (ed.), *The Genetic Testing of Children*, pp. 17–26 (p. 19). The fact that this is also a recommended 'therapy' for disease carriers shows the bizarre nature of healthcare in this respect. I will come back to this discussion in more detail below.

Genetic screening refers to genetic testing carried out on a whole population, or sub-population, rather than being performed in individuals or their families. For example, a Swedish screening programme identified all infants affected by alpha-1 antitrypsin deficiency, because such children were far more susceptible to lung disease. Subsequent research found that their fathers smoked even more heavily after the results were known, so it was clearly ineffective as a disease prevention programme, and was eventually dropped.[5] Screening of babies for phenyketouria deficiency is now performed on a routine basis in the United Kingdom, and has largely prevented the onset of this disease, since the condition can be treated with dietary supplementation.

GENETIC DISEASES: A MEDICAL VIEWPOINT

In order to understand the enormous growth in interest in genetic manipulation and treatment, which serves to shape both the way policy is emerging on both testing and screening and the motivation behind such changes, we need to consider, at least very briefly, the genetic basis for some patterns of inheritance and disease. Such 'genetic facts' are also useful in the context of current genetic counselling practice, since, although counsellors are not necessarily medically qualified, they will have a good understanding of patterns of disease inheritance and their underlying genetic causes.

Genetically determined diseases may result from (a) chromosome abnormalities, (b) single-gene defects, (c) polygenic defects, or (d) somatic gene defects, as in cancer.

Chromosome abnormalities are found in about 1% of all newborn babies and in 50% of miscarriages, and, since 50% of conceptions lead to miscarriage (most unrecognised), it follows that a quarter of all conceptions fail because of some chromosomal abnormality.[6] When a chromosome is present three times, this is known as *trisomy*. Down syndrome is the most widely recognised and is trisomy of chromosome 21. This disorder is more likely in offspring of older mothers. The general medical term for abnormalities in chromosome numbers is *aneuploidy*.

There are about 4,000 known single-gene disorders, which may be inherited according to traits that are autosomal dominant, autosomal recessive, or X-linked through the chromosomes that determine sex.

[5] A. J. Clarke, 'The Genetic Testing of Children', in Harper and Clarke (eds.), *Genetics, Society and Clinical Practice*, pp. 15–29 (p. 23).
[6] Connor and Ferguson Smith, *Essential Medical Genetics*, p. 3.

Autosomal dominant diseases mean that the heterozygous individual is always affected by the disease. In this case, if the individual married someone who did not carry the disease, there would be a 50% chance of their children being affected. Huntington's chorea is of this type. This picture is refined somewhat by the fact that this pattern assumes 100% *penetrance* and 100% *expressivity*. 'Penetrance' refers to the numbers of individuals in a population who are heterozygous and who show symptoms of the disease. Autosomal recessive traits, on the other hand, show symptoms of a disease only if the individual has two defective alleles, so there is a large number of heterozygous carriers who show no symptoms. Some of these are very common, such as the allele leading to enhanced susceptibility to familial hypercholesterolemia, found in one in 500 of the population (1:500). The occurrence of defective genes leading to familial breast cancer is 1:300, as is the occurrence of those leading to familial colon cancer. Cystic fibrosis is found in a ratio of 1:2000 in the white population, sickle-cell anaemia in 1:400 of the black American population, and Tay-Sachs disease in 1:25 in European Jews. X-linked diseases, on the other hand, are carried on the X chromosome and will show only in male children who have received the chromosome carrying the faulty gene.

All single-gene disorders may vary in expressivity; that is to say, the extent and degree of the symptoms that appear vary from one individual to the next, and depend on both the *genetic background* in which the gene is placed and the *environmental factors* that the individual has encountered. Some dominant inherited diseases increase in severity from one generation to the next, through a process known as *anticipation*. The molecular basis for this is known in some cases. For example, the disease known as myotonic dystrophy leads to a muscle-wasting disease that becomes far worse in each generation. The untranslated 3-region of the gene normally contains between 5 and 35 copies of the guanine-cytosine-thymine triplet (GCT), but in affected individuals it rises to over 50, increasing to 1000+ in subsequent generations. This is known as *expansion of triplet repeats*, and is also characteristic of fragile X syndrome and several other adult-onset neurodegenerative diseases, including Huntington's, where the age of onset is inversely related to the number of triplet repeats. Polygenic diseases are those that follow from a combination of different defective alleles, and they may also be multifactorial, which means that factors such as environment and lifestyle play a part in disease susceptibility. Diabetes, coronery artery disease, schizophrenia and congenital heart disease are all of this type.

The great variety in patterns of inheritance and severity of diseases, even when faulty genes are present, strongly cautions against the formulation of any policy that smoothes over the differences likely to be encountered. Medical practitioners themselves might easily be tempted to offer a technological or even surgical fix where none can be reasonably offered. At the end of a medical textbook in genetics the authors made the following comment:

A major challenge to tomorrow's physicians will be to balance the tremendous advances in technology that allows more accurate diagnosis and more effective treatment with the need to maintain a warm, empathetic and ethical approach to patients and their families, struggling with difficult issues of illness or threat of illness. Physicians of the coming years would be thus well advised to heed the Russian proverb, 'let your brains be loving and your heart be wise'. We owe to ourselves, our patients, both present and future, nothing less.[7]

It is understandable, given the complexity of the issues in different genetic contexts, that the authors adopt a case-study approach to ethics. However, there are other social and cultural factors that need to be considered in developing an ethical approach to genetics. If, on the one hand, the case study is a good reminder of the need to be aware of individual contexts, on the other hand there is a danger that technological solutions may be offered where such a solution is ethically impermissible. An implicit awareness of this possibility is hinted at in the quotation above, but leaving medical students with such vague directives and such simple encouragement towards empathy will do little to encourage a careful ethical response.

ETHICAL ISSUES IN GENETIC TESTING

Testing children

Genetic testing of children who show disease symptoms is ethically non-controversial, and is part of medical diagnosis. Families who discover that their children are *likely* to have the genes for a genetic disease, appearing either later in childhood or in adulthood, will often want their children to be tested to see if they have the faulty genes. Genetic counsellors are trained to be non-directive, but this practice assumes that the families of those involved are capable of making an 'informed choice'. The language of choice also dominates prenatal testing, as we shall see below. However, there are considerable social pressures on parents of children likely to be

---

[7] Ibid., p. 339.

affected. Parents are faced with a dilemma. If a child is identified as having the faulty gene, then he or she is likely to be stigmatised by family and friends, or even treated differently by their parents compared with their siblings. In addition, parents may not feel that there is sufficient social support available if they discover that they have an affected child.[8] This is especially the case when the condition they will encounter is incurable, so that there are real possibilities that both the child and parents will feel that the knowledge is too devastating. In addition, genetic testing has an impact on the whole family, not just on the individual, for it will raise the likelihood that other family members are also carriers of a genetic disease. Legally, medical intervention, including genetic testing, must be carried out in the 'best interests' of the child.[9] If this is not done – that is, if a procedure is carried out without a legally valid consent – this amounts to an assault. The parents may argue that the knowledge will help the child to adjust, but it is more likely that other factors are involved, such as the need to know in order to relieve anxiety and for the sake of the extended family. There is, broadly speaking, support for parental consent in cases where children are tested for disorders that appear in childhood, but not normally in cases of late-onset disorders. Sheila McLean argues that the rationale for testing for earlier-onset conditions, namely helping a child to adjust, would also apply to late-onset conditions, so the reasoning is faulty (p. 23). She argues in favour of *even more* restrictions on parental consent for testing, rather than fewer. The problem with her position is that it would seem to deny to the *parents*, who will be the ones bearing the burden of care when the disease appears in childhood, knowledge that would be useful to them. Moreover, there are clear benefits to the child in having a test for some diseases. For example, familial adenomatous polyposis coli (FAP) predisposes those who are affected to bowel cancer.[10] Children likely to be affected start colonoscopy screening from between ten and twelve years old. A genetic test shows who needs to be screened, hence sparing those who do not carry the gene both the anxiety and the unpleasantness of the process. Testing for Duchenne or Becker muscular dystrophy is also permitted on the basis that it helps to prevent anxiety in parents, who might otherwise misinterpret symptoms such as fatigue. It is clearly of benefit to those children who do not have the genetic fault to have the test, since it will relieve both their anxiety and that of the parents. In addition,

[8] A. Clarke, Introduction, in Clarke (ed.), *The Genetic Testing of Children*, pp. 1–16, esp. p. 5.
[9] McLean, 'The Genetic Testing of Children', p. 22.
[10] Clarke, 'The Genetic Testing of Children', p. 17.

parental anxiety is likely to be relieved in the case of a possibly affected child once the condition is confirmed, such knowledge being preferable to living in uncertainty.

There are other features that distinguish between testing children for childhood diseases and testing them for late-onset disorders. Those likely to suffer late-onset disorders may be subject to discrimination from employers or insurance companies if the knowledge became available, and this fact strengthens the case against allowing such tests on children unless there are particular reasons why the information might be important, such as in other medical treatments. The UK Government White Paper on genetics, published in 2003, agreed to a moratorium on the disclosure of genetic information for insurance purposes. The child, if subject to parental decision-making, is denied the freedom of choice that adults have in relation to genetic tests. Most adults who are at risk of developing Huntington's chorea, for example, prefer not to have the genetic test. This factor would not apply for childhood diseases. In addition, those who have a disease that will appear later in adult life may be treated differently by parents and family, leading to psychological damage. Of course, the situation is more complicated if adolescents who are no longer under the official guardianship of their parents (e.g. those over eighteen) seek to have the test.[11] At the time of writing there is a moratorium on insurance companies and employers gaining access to genetic knowledge held by the National Health Service.[12] Rather than tightening litigation at this stage, so that all testing of children is more regulated, I suggest that greater access to counselling is called for, and also a greater sharing of information on the ethical issues at stake, rather than simply informing parents of the medical 'facts'. In addition, we need to create a culture in which those with disabilities of any sort, whether their origin is genetic or otherwise, are welcomed as part of the human community. Such a culture would help to alleviate the fear of some of the commoner genetic diseases, though the real tragedy and horror of untreatable conditions, such as Huntington's chorea, are no less real in this context.

A case that falls between testing for late-onset disorders and for childhood diseases is the testing of children for carrier status for recessive diseases. Children may strongly wish to be tested in these circumstances.

---

[11] J. Binedell, 'Adolescent Requests for Predictive Genetic Testing', in Clarke (ed.), *The Genetic Testing of Children*, pp. 123–32.

[12] This applies to adults as well as to children. For more details, see the Government White Paper, *Our Inheritance, Our Future.*

This is often the situation in families where one of the siblings has the disease. Mucopolysaccharide (MPS) and related disorders, for example, affect lysosomal storage and lead to mental retardation and death early in childhood. In this situation, consultation with the child who is likely to be a carrier is important, for carrier status affects his or her subsequent reproductive decisions. Even quite young children can be involved in making the decision whether to be tested or not. However, there are increasing calls for testing on children under sixteen years old to be tightened up, even though, from the point of view of likely carriers, it is often of psychological benefit to know whether they have this condition before they embark on relationships, even if the probability of their having an affected child themselves may be very small.[13] More general psychological research has yielded inconclusive results on the psychological impact (on either children or families) of predictive testing for different genetic conditions, whether for carrier status or for susceptibility to genetic disease.[14] The inability of some parents or children fully to understand the implications of carrier status suggests that tests are being carried out without adequate counselling support.

Prenatal and pre-implantation genetic diagnosis

Prenatal diagnosis (PND) has been available for some time, and is also informed through population-screening programmes that detect the likely occurrence of a particular genetic disease, as discussed below. Prenatal diagnosis takes place through invasive procedures such as amniocentesis, chorionic villus sampling (CVS) and cordocentesis, which are offered to pregnant women considered to be at risk of bearing a child with a genetic disease. Techniques such as these rely on the fact that some foetal tissue appears in the amniotic fluid surrounding the growing baby. The difficulty associated with these techniques is that only relatively rarely can treatment of a condition be offered *in utero*; normally, the only possible 'therapy' is termination of the pregnancy. For amniocentesis, the genetic test takes place relatively late in the pregnancy, at sixteen weeks' gestation. CVS, while it can be performed earlier, carries a relatively high risk of complications, such as spontaneous abortion and thus the unnecessary death of

---

[13] C. Lavery, 'On the Receiving End of Genetic Medicine', in Clarke (ed.), *The Genetic Testing of Children*, pp. 47–50.

[14] S. Michie and T. M. Marteau, 'Predictive Testing in Children: The Need for Psychological Research', in Clarke (ed.), *The Genetic Testing of Children*, pp. 169–81.

healthy foetuses. It is ironic that viability of pre-term babies comes very close to this gestation; while some medical practitioners are happily destroying the life of one pre-term baby, others are fighting to save the life of another.

In some situations, for example where the foetus is known to be suffering from a fatal condition such as anencephaly (where there is no brain at all), it may be very difficult for the mother to know what course of action to take. She may not wish the dying process to take longer than necessary; certainly, the assumption of medical practitioners would be that this is the most logical course of action to follow. Simply asserting pro-life or pro-choice positions makes no sense in these situations, for a woman who has received such news is likely to feel so distressed that she will follow whatever medical practitioners recommend. In addition, if the foetus is aborted at this stage, the mother is not offered any statutory support by employers, and so has less opportunity to grieve and to deal with the likely guilt implicated in such a choice. There are other conditions, however, where a relatively long life is possible, the most obvious example being Down syndrome. Mothers are routinely expected to take up the offer of a prenatal test, as if this were the most responsible and reasonable option available. The needs of the foetus, which is so close to viability, are not really considered, for the procedure remains a legal one. Down-syndrome children are generally happier, on average, than most other children. Having Down syndrome is therefore not the terrible affliction that it is often assumed to be. Individuals with Down syndrome will often live much longer now than previously, possibly well into their fifties, thanks to medical intervention that helps to delay death arising from associated congenital defects of the heart and so on. Of course, parents are then burdened with the respon-sibility to care for these children well into their old age, and may well not outlive their children. This adds to the anxiety about what might happen to the adult children when the parents are no longer alive, given the limited mental capacity of those with the condition. However, parents would no longer be subject to such intense pressure and anxiety if better social support existed for those with disabiliites. The routine testing and screen-ing *against* Down syndrome builds up a sense of societal rejection of care for those afflicted.

In these circumstances, mothers are under immense pressure to abort affected foetuses. Indeed, amniocentesis is not normally offered where the mother insists that if an affected child were found, she would choose not to have a termination. To assume that this is a genuine 'choice' on her part is to ignore the social pressure on and stigmatisation of all those with learning difficulties. How much is this really a choice, and to what extent would the mother be forced, bizarrely, into feeling irresponsible if she did bring such a child into the world? This is one reason why the routine testing and screening for Down syndrome amounts to a form of eugenics, for those with the condition are considered to be 'unacceptable' members of society, as in the earlier eugenic programmes, which focused on mental incapacity. But if screening and PND for conditions such as these become integral to our society, what kind of message is given to those who do have these conditions already? Those involved in the medical profession are apt to point out that they would treat those who have a genetic disease in exactly the same way as any other patient.

Preimplantation genetic diagnosis (PGD) offers couples the opportunity to select those very early embryos that do not carry disease, before they are implanted in the womb. The ethical rights and wrongs of PGD overlap with those of *in vitro* fertilisation (IVF), for it depends on prior IVF fertility treatment. If IVF is unacceptable, then so, of course, is PGD. IVF has been castigated by opponents as being detached from sexual relationships, and for allowing embryos that are not implanted to die even though they allegedly have the 'potential' to become human persons. The 'wastefulness' in IVF treatments, and the rare mixing up of samples (so that the eggs are given a different donor sperm) show some of the unethical aspects of this practice. Yet this practice can hardly be put in the same category, ethically, as the termination of twenty-week-old foetuses. While I believe that all human life is to be respected, therefore, access to IVF is not as irresponsible as pro-life activists would have us believe. Quite simply, there is an important ethical distinction to be made between abortion and IVF fertility treatments. On the other hand, IVF should not be offered for relatively trivial reasons, such as to ensure a child of a preferred sex.

IVF when combined with PGD offers the opportunity to select out those foetuses likely to carry serious diseases. In the United Kingdom, six centres are currently licensed to carry out PGD; it was first offered in 1990 at Hammersmith NHS Hospital in London. One or two cells from each of the newly fertilised eggs are tested for specific genetic defects. Removal of these cells at a very early stage appears to have no effect on the subsequent development of the embryo. The Genetics Commission Advisory Group (GenCAG) recommends that commissioners of NHS services should accept a limited place for PGD as part of the national health scheme available to those who are most in need.[15] The Human Fertilisation and

---

[15] GenCAG, *PGD – Guiding Principles for Commissioners.*

Embryology Authority (HFEA) has licensed the use of PGD for a range of serious conditions, including Fragile X, muscular dystrophy and Huntington's chorea. PGD can also be used for aneuploidy screening, although, for reasons similar to those expressed above, in relation to PND, it would be a matter of ethical concern if this method were to be used routinely to screen for Down syndrome in all those who were attempting IVP over the age of thirty-six. On the other hand, in the relatively limited circumstances where the risk of incidence is similar to that for which the screening of monogenic diseases is licensed, aneuploidy screening may be appropriate. The HFEA has approved the use of PGD for a serious genetic disease, combined with tissue-typing, in order both to prevent a child being born with a genetic disease, and to treat an affected sibling. The use of PGD to generate stem cells to treat a sibling affected by genetic disease, where the disease has arisen spontaneously, is ethically more complex, since it entails the use of IVF where there are no fertility problems, and the use of PGD for a related sibling rather than specifically for the benefit of the resulting child. Both uses of PGD inevitably involve more treatment cycles for the mother of the affected child, and also 'wastage' of otherwise healthy embryos.[16] While trends to enlarge the use of PGD need to be watched very carefully, the objection that any resulting child will feel 'used', rather than wanted for his or her own sake, is not sustainable in practice. If PGD were to be used for an increasing range of genetic conditions, for example through DNA chip technology, this would come up against a practical as well as an ethical limitation, for the screening method would almost inevitably mean that no embryos free of multiple conditions would be available for transfer. There is therefore little practical possibility that PGD could lead to a fully 'designed' baby, or, more accurately, to one that has slipped through all the negative screening. It is worth noting, however, that, where the test is available, the science of PGD allows carriers of autosomal recessive genetic diseases to be recognised. This raises the possibility that selection against those who are carriers of a disease may become available through PGD, even though these carriers do not, except in rare circumstances, show symptoms of that disease. Arguments in favour of such selection would emphasise the increased reproductive choice of the resulting child. Selection against symptom-free carriers of disease in order to eliminate a gene from a population moves PGD beyond even the eugenic proposals of the last century. It ignores the important point that,

---

[16] These issues will be dealt with again in chapter 8.

in many cases, recessive genes can confer some advantages on those who are carriers, as, for example, with sickle-cell anaemia.

ETHICAL DIMENSIONS IN GENETIC SCREENING

Genetic screening for known or suspected genetic disorders

For many medical professionals, screening is acceptable if it meets the following criteria:[17]
1. The disorder screened for is clearly defined.
2. It is present in appreciable frequency.
3. Early diagnosis is advantageous.
4. There are few false positives, thus it is specific.
5. There are few false negatives, thus it is sensitive.
6. The benefits outweigh the costs.

Screening can be of two types: the routine prenatal screening of pregnant mothers, and the screening of particular groups or populations known to have a high risk of being either carriers of a disease or susceptible to a disease. Of course, testing highlights the social importance of such a disease; marking it as worth screening raises the level of anxiety in a group about the likelihood of being affected.

Prenatal screening of pregnant mothers is commonly through blood-serum tests at between sixteen and eighteen weeks' gestation. These check for changes in maternal alphafetoprotein (AFP) levels. AFP levels are raised when a woman is pregnant with a foetus that has neural-tube defects. However, the specificity of this test is weak, since there is a strong overlap between the upper limit of AFP in normal pregnancies and those with affected foetuses. AFP levels are also reduced in those with Down syndrome, but human chorionic gonadotrophin (hCG) levels are elevated. The Government White Paper previously cited recommends prenatal screening of all expectant mothers for Down syndrome, with counselling provided by midwives.[18] In this case it might be asked whether the sensitivity of the screening tests is sufficient, though those who are identified at 'high risk' are then offered the opportunity to have amniocentesis.

Policy-makers who decide whether or not to undertake population screening, or to increase the availability of genetic tests more generally, usually use criteria such as access, accuracy, quality of care and cost-effectiveness as

---

[17] Connor and Ferguson Smith, *Essential Medical Genetics*, p. 204.
[18] *Our Inheritance, Our Future.*

markers in deciding whether or not to introduce particular screening programmes. Genetic diseases that are polygenic, or that are affected by environmental factors, or that are expensive to monitor are likely to be low on the list of priorities. One of the reasons the British Government has approved serum screening for Down syndrome for all pregnant mothers in the United Kingdom is likely to be its relatively low economic cost. However, the social effects and ethical implications of such screening were accounted for only by a policy of maternal 'informed choice'. Follow-up tests through amniocentesis is the only accurate and specific screening method for Down syndrome; a low specificity initial screening test is offered in the understanding that a more specific test is also available. In this particular case the results following amniocentesis and karyotyping of the cells are highly specific, and have become more rapid and accurate with the development of new cytological techniques.[19] Molecular cytogenetics has developed the use of fluorescent DNA probes that then hybridise with specific regions of the chromosome(s), a process known as fluorescent *in situ* hybridisation (FISH). This technique has speeded up the process of identification of trisomy and/ or gender of the foetus in order to test for likelihood of chromosomal disorders or sex-linked diseases.[20] The specificity and sensitivity of detection of these conditions are good in these cases, but there is always the possibility of human error, for example through inaccurate sample labelling.

Those who come forward for testing normally assume that the results are 100% accurate. Any decisions that they make to go ahead or not with the 'treatment' are therefore based on a total trust of scientific procedures.[21] The level of specificity also varies depending on the particular condition being screened, and while there is a general agreement that specificity and sensitivity must be high, the accuracy of such techniques is often described in statistical terms that are very difficult for untrained members of the public to understand and appreciate fully in terms of their likely implications. While this can and should be alleviated through effective genetic counselling, the increase in the number and availability of genetic tests is such that counselling cannot keep up with the increase in demand. For screening programmes, the extent of counselling support given is unlikely to be at the same level as that for familial genetic diseases because of the relatively high cost.

---

[19] Karyotyping summarises the genetic information about a particular individual, including chromosome number and any identified genetic defects.

[20] For colour images of FISH see, for example, Bonthron et al., *Clinical Genetics*, pp. 34–6; also Kingston, *ABC of Clinical Genetics*, p. 16.

[21] Most common errors are technical failures and interpretation errors. See Dequeker and Cassiman, 'Genetic Testing and Quality Control'.

Once a pregnant woman has accepted the initial invitation to have her serum screened, she is on the slippery slope to medical intervention, which is very hard to resist. She may well assume at this stage that, because the blood test is non-invasive and therefore cannot affect her foetus, there is little reason *not* to have a test. In addition, her levels of anxiety are likely to rise considerably when the results of the blood test show a positive in the direction of either neural-tube defects or Down syndrome. Midwives do not have the time or training to give sufficient counselling regarding the likely future implications of accepting serum tests, which are often labelled as 'routine checks' in much the same manner as ultrasound scanning. The latter has been popularised as a way of seeing a picture of one's baby and thus of promoting bonding, but in reality it represents a national screening programme offered to all pregnant mothers in the United Kingdom in order to detect abnormalities of the foetus. The most likely 'treatment' offered following the discovery of a condition is termination. Midwives are reluctant to speak about ultrasound in these terms; hence mothers are encouraged to undergo a battery of tests without always being aware of their implications. The idea that there are ethical safeguards through 'informed choice' becomes somewhat ludicrous in these circumstances.

Population-screening is also possible for those who are likely to have haemoglobin disorders such as thalassaemias and sickle-cell anaemia. A simple blood test will confirm carrier status, thus enabling couples to decide whether or not to have the prenatal genetic test once a pregnancy is confirmed. Children with beta thalassaemia major die between two and seven years of age, unless treated with regular blood transfusions, though there are drawbacks to this method because of iron overload. The number of live births judges the effectiveness of genetic screening, so the number of terminations is considered to be the measure of the effectiveness of genetic services.[22] A similar approach applies to Down-syndrome screening reported in standard medical textbooks, where live births of those affected are considered a 'negative' result as far as the screening programme is concerned.[23] Therefore, in spite of the rhetoric of parental choice, it

---

[22] OECD, *Genetic Testing*, p. 26.
[23] See Connor and Ferguson Smith, *Essential Medical Genetics*, pp. 204–9. The OECD report was rather more aware of the variable termination rate after PND of Down syndrome across Europe, ranging from 67% to 95%, and they were conscious of the fact that culture, religion and provision of services differ, with the need for screening programmes to be developed in parallel with the development of social and medical services for the disabled. Yet this seemed to be a passing comment in the document; the full impact of what this might mean in policy terms was not addressed. OECD, *Genetic Testing*, pp. 24–5.

becomes clear that underlying the availability of genetic services and screening is the hope that those who do discover that they have an affected foetus will decide to terminate the pregnancy.

Those who have breast-cancer carrier status for the genes BRCA1 and BRCA2 are at an increased risk of contracting the disease, but it does not predict when in a person's lifetime the disease will appear. Once again, it is possible to screen those populations that are at greater risk. Ashkenazi Jews, for example, have a greater risk of contracting breast cancer than the population at large.[24] Screening can lead to a decision to treat the patient with chemical preventative medicines, or to perform prophylactic surgery. According to this model, women need to be prepared to undergo surgery in order for screening to be 'cost-effective', increasing life expectancy by an average of a little over four years if ovaries are removed as well, or by an average of two years if tamoxifen is administered.

This crude calculation of life expectancy seems to force ethical concern about cancer-screening into an economic model, in much the same way as Down syndrome prenatal serum screening. Women who are found to be carriers of the genes will face an unwelcome choice, being either under pressure to have both breasts and ovaries removed, or subject to unpleasant chemotherapy, even prior to symptoms appearing. It represents a desperate attempt by clinical geneticists to be seen to be doing something positive for their patients when, in practice, no treatment is available. Four extra years, or an increase in life expectancy of about 10%, represents a crude measure of 'success' that can hardly be regarded as such. For example, BRCA1 carriers have a 48% chance of developing breast cancer by the time they are fifty and a 64% chance by the time they are seventy; the figures are slightly elevated if BRCA2 is also present.[25] Thus there are 52% of carriers who are *not* affected before they are fifty and 36% who are *not* affected by the time they are seventy. It is hard for those receiving the information to be positive, given that the results are reported in probabilistic terms of whether or not the person will contract the disease. In the proportion of cases that do not go on to develop disease, surgery or chemotherapy is completely unnecessary, but it is done for the sake of those who will be affected. The psychological effects on the patients and their families under-going traumatic surgery need to be taken more fully into account. It is not enough to regard this as a 'quality of life issue' that is relevant only for younger people, labelled as 'patients', who are carriers of a disease but not

---

[24] OECD, *Genetic Testing*, pp. 34–5. [25] Ibid., p. 36.

showing symptoms of it.[26] Carriers of genes such as BRCA1 have an increased likelihood of contracting the disease, but this is not the same as, for example, Huntington's chorea, where carriers almost inevitably show the symptoms of the disease later on in their lives. Thus the relatively low *penetrance* of cancer-carrying genes, along with the variable *expressivity* because of environmental factors, make such drastic treatment of carriers completely inappropriate.

Population genetic profiling: the UK Biobank

Another phase in screening that will become increasingly widespread is the matching of genetic profiles to disease susceptibility or drug sensitivity. The creation of human genetic databases raises a number of important ethical and social considerations about access to genetic information. The UK Biobank project, initially termed the UK Population Biomedical Collection, was approved in 2002 and represents the joint initiative of the Wellcome Trust, the Medical Research Council and the Department of Health.[27] An initial sum of £45 million has been earmarked for the project. It can be viewed as one of the aftermaths of the success of the Human Genome Project. Dr John Newton, the Chief Executive Officer of the UK Biobank, is enthusiastic about its potential, announcing at an event organised by the Parliamentary and Scientific Committee that

> The last few years of the last century saw biomedical science transformed by the Human Genome Project. The new genetics provides a stunning opportunity to move ahead in our understanding of variability in human health. But the genome itself is not the answer. If these extraordinary insights are not to be relegated to a contemporary museum exhibit, we need to be able to develop practical intelligence. The UK Biobank is part of the continuing national effort to achieve just that.[28]

The specificity of the research follows three years of debate, including issues such as the role of general practitioners, the age range used, types of information to be gathered and the diseases to be investigated. The research for this study will look at the relationship between lifestyle, environment, genetics and health for a sample of the population of 500,000 volunteers

---

[26] This labelling of carriers as 'patients' simply reinforces the mistaken notion that those who carry a disease gene are 'ill', further reinforcing the myth that carriers of defective genes should not be permitted equivalent access to insurance and employment.

[27] Public Health Genetics Unit, 'Brief UK Policy Update'. Other large-scale population studies are planned for Iceland, Singapore, Estonia and Tonga.

[28] Press release, 'New CEO Announces His Vision for UK Biobank at Parliamentary Event'.

gleaned through participating general medical health-service practices. The 'volunteers', picked at random by their GPs, would be aged between forty-five and sixty-nine, and their health followed over ten to fifteen years. It is hoped that the research will help uncover the relative contribution of genes and environment in the development of important diseases such as Alzheimer's, diabetes, cancer and heart disease. The genetic bases for such diseases are complex, and involve normal gene variants, or poly-morphisms, which increase or decrease the likelihood that a disease will appear. Individually, such genes have low penetrance, but when together the risk is increased. The study will see how far different genetic combin-ations fare in relation to particular environments and lifestyle options.

Yet the study itself is not ultimately for the benefit of those taking part, as Newton suggests in the same speech:

Studies using the UK Biobank resource will identify associations between discrete environmental, lifestyle and genetic factors and important interactions between these factors. This will allow the risk of disease to be predicted in populations. Predicting risk in individuals is not the aim of the study. Knowing difference in risk in populations can provide direct evidence for the scope of prevention.

Those individuals who take part in the study are therefore unlikely to benefit directly during its implementation, but will provide, instead, a legacy for future generations. This raises ethical issues that will be discussed in more detail below.

The study will also facilitate measurement of the difference in response to different treatments, depending on the person's genetic profile, hence eventually allowing, following analysis of the results, a more individual 'designer' drug-therapy regime depending on the person's genetic make-up. The study also aims to allow more accurate predictive tests for those of a given genetic profile, and thus raise the specificity and selectivity of the currently available predictive tests, which rarely take into account either environmental factors or lifestyle issues. The University of Manchester was named in May 2003 as the UK Biobank co-ordinating centre, or 'hub', overseeing a number of regional centres or 'spokes' for the project.

The sponsors of the project claim to be committed to an ethically sound approach to the collection, storage and use of samples, as well as to extensive public consultation. Focus groups broadly divide into 'public groups', 'nurses groups', and 'GP groups'. In February 2003 an Interim Advisory Group on Ethics was set up in order to provide information about a suitable ethical framework. Later, in April 2003, the Association of the British Pharmaceutical Industry co-hosted, with the funders, a consultation meeting with senior research managers about the use of the information arising out of the UK Biobank.[29] The policy of the UK Biobank is to allow pharmaceutical companies access to the information, but it will be kept anonymous in order to protect confidentiality. Of course, in order to track the disease history back to a particular patient over the timescale envisaged, the data cannot be fully anonymous, and so will be encrypted.

Like other genetic tests, the UK Biobank tests will be conducted through the 'informed consent' of participants, though it is clear that the way the information is presented on the website actively seeks to promote the project. Yet the idea of informed consent makes this national project differ from other similar national studies in Iceland, Estonia, Singapore and Tonga, which are both more broadly based (that is, more than a subset of the population is measured) and compulsory.[30] In this sense the UK Biobank project has rather more safeguards compared with similar projects internationally. In addition, insurance companies or employers cannot use the Biobank data, and the Human Genetics Commission (HGC) rejects the idea that it can be used for forensic purposes.[31] This seems to depart somewhat from the Biobank website, where the possibility of access by the police is recommended where there is a court order requiring such information.[32]

The ethical guidelines proposed for the UK Biobank involve initial approval by the Ethics Committee and ongoing audit by an independent committee. Key areas are under review, according to the principles of informed consent, confidentiality, and risk/benefit assessment. In the third category the risk to the volunteers in the study is thought to be minimal in a direct sense, though the pilot study also monitors study methods. The genetic profiles of individuals who take part in the study will not be disclosed to them; the only information they receive will concern more immediate physical symptoms such as high blood pressure or dysrhythmias. Individuals will, nonetheless, have a legal right to obtain the information about themselves if required, though the impression given by the protocol statement is that individuals who are worried about

[29] UK Biobank, 'Ethics and Consultation'.
[30] Public Health Genetics Unit, 'Brief UK Policy Update'. The national genetic profile screening programmes in Estonia and Canada do not include the effects of environmental factors or lifestyle in the study, but, more crudely, attempt to relate genetic profiles with susceptibility to disease. See 'Protocol for the UK Biobank: A Study of Genes, Environment and Health', February 2002, p. 13.
[31] Public Health Genetics Unit, 'Brief UK Policy Update'.
[32] UK Biobank, 'Frequently Asked Questions'.

particular disease susceptibility would be expected to go through the more usual process of individual genetic counselling and advice.[33] The protocol also believes that the involvement of the pharmaceutical and biotechnology industries in the project is 'essential to maximise delivery of the health benefits'. In addition, while the protocol states that potential participants will be kept informed of the likely involvement of commercial bodies, it is not clear if consent to use the data could be withdrawn at a later date if an individual felt uncomfortable about the participation of additional pharmaceutical companies in the project once it had started.

The HGC undertook a public consultation, entitled *Whose Hands on Your Genes?*, on the storage, protection and use of genetic information. They found public support for the use of genetic information in medical goals, such as in improving medical care and in disease prevention, but aversion to its use for commercial purposes.[34] Given the intertwining nature of these two processes, it is very difficult to know what kind of development would meet public approval. The House of Lords Select Committee on Science and Technology initially challenged the adequacy of the oversight of the use of genetic information by the UK Biobank. The committee recommended setting up a Medical Data Panel (MDP), which would approve and oversee projects that involved the use of human medical and genetic information.[35] The government rejected this recommendation on the basis that the Patient Information Advisory Group (PIAG) would cover the roles suggested by the MDP.

The more specialised committee overseeing the ethical implications of the Biobank, known as the Interim Advisory Group (IAG), was chaired by Dr William Lowrance, a consultant in health policy and ethics, whose research interest is the protection of health information in research. The IAG undertook to develop an Ethics and Governance Framework (EGF) for the UK Biobank, reporting to the UK Biobank Joint Project Board (JPB), which links directly to the three core funders of the project.[36] The IAG also took into account the results of the public consultations to date in drawing up the framework. However, it seems that the general terms of

---

[33] 'Protocol for the UK Biobank', p. 32, states that 'individuals concerned about their risk of particular conditions will be encouraged to consult their general practitioner or other health professional'.

[34] Human Genetics Commission, *Public Attitudes to Human Genetic Information*. One noticeable feature about this report is the varied responses across ages, with very different attitudes in younger age groups than in older. Older people supported the use of genetic information by insurance companies.

[35] Report by the House of Lords Select Committee on Science and Technology, March 2001.

[36] UK Biobank, '*What's new?*', <http://www.biobank.ac.uk/whatsnew.htm>, accessed 27 August 2003.

reference for the IAG were to increase public confidence in the Biobank, rather than to offer substantive challenges to its practice. Thus their first term of reference is to 'advise the funders on best ethical practice, which will provide a sound basis for fostering public trust and confidence in the project. This should take due account of the practical constraints of implementing the scientific protocol in a cost-effective and timely way.'[37] It is clear from this statement that the IAG was limited by the funders' desire for public confidence in the project and for cost-effectiveness. In addition, the role of the IAG is to determine how best the Biobank can be 'governed' by an oversight body that serves to ensure compliance with best practice according to quality assurance measures. Yet, given the first proviso of the ethical objectives, namely to foster public confidence and to work within cost-effective implementation of the scientific protocol, it is hard to envisage the governance body as having any authority other than the implementation of existing practice. In addition, only a selection of discussions taking place between IAG and the funders were open to public scrutiny, and the authority to disclose seems to be in the hands of the funders of the project: 'The funders may disclose the advice received by the IAG as they think fit, except that such advice will not be attributed to individual members.'[38] In addition, the funders have a right to ask a member of the group to resign should they consider that member to have a 'conflict of interest'. The IAG was short-lived, being dissolved by the funders after July 2003. In addition, the oversight body, in discussion with the hub company based in Manchester, is allowed to adjust the EGF. Moreover, the group responsible for the final drafting of the EGF was not, as one might anticipate, the IAG, but the JPB, linked directly with the three funders. It is clear that such adjustments to the EGF by the JPB and the oversight body may not necessarily be in line with the ethical principles set out by the IAG, once again weakening its terms of reference. It also flies in the face of the Human Genetics Commission, which has strongly recommended that 'the governance of genetic research databases and DNA collections should allow for oversight by an independent body – whether it is an ethics committee or another body – which is separate from the owners and users of the database (5.45)'.[39]

[37] UK Biobank, *What's New?*, The UK Biobank Interim Advisory Group (Ethics and Governance), 11 March 2003, p. 2.
[38] Ibid.
[39] HGC, *Inside Information*, p. 9. The Government White Paper on genetics (2003) has committed itself to introduce new legislation on DNA theft, so that it will be an offence to test individuals'

The summary of the IAG report of its second meeting, in April 2003, showed that they were concerned that not all future uses of the resource could be predicted; participants would need to be aware of this at the start. However, I suggest that this is a very vague statement of intent. It is clear that even geneticists themselves cannot fully predict the potential usefulness of information collected in this way, so preparing participants for such events, quite apart from keeping them informed of current possibilities, is a very difficult and problematic area. The interests of the participants were much more to the fore in the IAG interim report, compared with the final scientific protocol, which seemed cavalier in its approach to access of information. The IAG was also aware that information gained for commercial purposes might not necessarily be in the public interest, so there needed to be safeguards in this respect.

The HGC ethical guidelines recommend, in particular, ethical concepts such as *genetic solidarity* and *altruism* in the disclosure of genetic information (p. 7). This is on the basis of a common inheritance of genetic material in the human population, so that 'We all share the same basic human genome, although there are individual variations which distinguish us from other people. Most of our genetic characteristics will be present in others. This sharing of our genetic constitution not only gives rise to opportunities to help others, but it also highlights our common interest in the fruits of medically based genetic research' (p. 16).

This would be particularly relevant to the UK Biobank project, since the benefit accrued to the individuals themselves would be minimal, especially as the designers of the project assume that mortality or contraction of disease in particular circumstances will be an indicator of high-risk factors. Any hypothesis linking particular lifestyles and genetic profiles would not be disclosed to the participants, nor would they have access to their genetic information without considerable difficulty, since a sudden change in their lifestyle would upset the consistency of data recovered. Hence one might argue that, assuming that the participants are fully aware of the purpose of the study, it is a Biobank of those who are also predisposed to show solidarity to others. Whether such a tendency comes from a combination of nature and nurture or religious commitment is not the point; the issue is that the Biobank is a further subset of those who are prepared to offer their biological makeup for the service of others. Now, if the results of that research were to be used for the purpose of

DNA without their consent except for medical or police purposes. There is already a moratorium in place on the 'unacceptable use of genetic tests by insurers', though what this means in practice is still somewhat vague at present.

making substantial commercial profits, there would be a considerable breakdown in trust on the part of participants. The difficulty is that while the UK Biobank has worthy aims that are for the benefit of the community as a whole, it is inextricably linked with commercialisation of tailor-made treatments through the pharmaceutical industry. Offences designed to protect the individual from abuse of genetic information apply only for 'non-medical' purposes, thereby shielding the pharmaceutical companies involved in medical practice. In addition, while the information for the Biobank is anonymous as presented to the pharmaceutical industry, the ability to trace individual cases back is an essential component of the project if it is going to be successful. The results may show that an individual has a particular tendency to a disease through a mutant gene, but the individual is not told about this information unless he or she makes a special case for access, as mentioned above. How far relatives of those who are afflicted once mortality or disease occurs would be prepared to accept the lack of disclosure remains to be seen. Genetics is a familial affair, but the proposed Biobank project does not seem, so far, to have taken this into account.

The HGC also recommends the ethical mandate of *respect for persons* for disclosure of genetic information, which means in practical terms that

(a) Through the principle of *privacy*, no one would be forced to disclose genetic information.
(b) Obtaining genetic information requires the *consent* of the individuals concerned.
(c) Personal genetic information should be *confidential* and should not be disclosed to others without consent.
(d) Through the principle of *non-discrimination*, no one should be unfairly discriminated against on the basis of genetic characteristics (p. 7).

So far the Biobank is following the guidelines suggested above, except that personal genetic information will be passed on indirectly through the accumulative process of building up a databank. Its justification is that it will be of 'medical benefit'. As discussed earlier, this is a grey area, for, while the data are encrypted, it cannot be totally anonymous or tracking of health and disease over time would be impossible. Although it would be illegal to hack into the computer systems in order to obtain genetic information, one could envisage a scenario where an unscrupulous individual decides to decode the identity of participants in the Biobank and pass them on to insurance companies or a research organisation. The HGC did not think there was sufficient legal protection against this kind of abuse (p. 9).

Like the IAG, the HGC was also wary of allowing the police access to genetic research databases, including the Biobank. However, they add a clause to their recommendations allowing an exception to this ruling, namely: 'In some cases a person may wish to disclose confidential information if he or she feels that is necessary for reasons of public safety. We believe that in exceptional cases it should be permissible to reveal personal genetic information in order to avert substantial harm to others' (p. 19). Hence the police could, in some circumstances, gain access to the information. There is a clear difference between the use of genetic information by the police in order to identify particular criminals, and access of genetic profiles by the police more generally. The release of genetic information to the police needs to be tightly regulated; if it is not, it will give the impression that the police service was becoming an authoritarian regime, which would generate public hostility and suspicion.

CONCLUSIONS

So far, this chapter has aimed to set out the feasibility of genetic testing and screening of human individuals, in the context both of familial diseases and of population studies. Although testing for particular diseases as a diagnostic tool is uncontroversial, particular ethical issues arise where testing occurs either before a baby is born (prenatal or pre-implantation testing), or before symptoms of late-onset diseases develop, or for carriers, where genetic testing will affect their reproductive decisions. The assumption in many medical texts seems to be that genetic testing is performed in order to facilitate the decision to terminate a pregnancy, thereby preventing a disease by drastic culling of affected foetuses. While 'informed choice' is the rhetoric that is used, other social and discriminatory factors that militate against those with genetic disabilities serve to foster a culture of rejection of all but the 'normal', as defined by genetic profiles. Genetic screening of much larger population groups is becoming increasingly established. The UK Government has enthusiastically endorsed the growth of genetic testing and profiling. One of the largest research efforts to date is the UK Biobank, set up to analyse the genetic profile of middle-aged subgroups of the population over a decade or more. The influence of lifestyle and environment will be taken into account. In these circumstances fears about abuse of genetic information are protected against by the ethical principle of respect for others, which means, in practice, a right to privacy, consent, confidentiality, and non-discrimination. Such protection at the individual level is balanced by the view that such results will promote the common good, leading to notions such as solidarity and altruism. Such worthy goals are possible only if there is tight regulation of the information; and, while the benefits may accrue to the wider community, it is worth considering the relative gains that are to be had by different sections of that community. The genetic conditions to be researched will largely be determined by commercial factors in the development of targeted drug therapies. Like many other medical advances, the public-interest gloss may well cover up less worthy aims. Therefore, as well as the ethical mandate for altruism and solidarity, it seems to me that total transparency and open governance are required for such large-scale projects, where the potential for abuse is enormous. We should not need to be reminded that we are living in the shadow of eugenics, where what began as a relatively worthy and innocuous goal (namely the enhancement of our genetic 'stock', which was, of course, impossible anyway) was soon turned to less worthy and even deplorable aims. While genetic testing and screening are most akin to negative eugenics (that is, the means of removal of less favoured genotypes), genetic therapy offers a different tactic, one that aims both to treat disease and to enhance human evolution along certain lines. Genetic counselling aims to offer information to individuals and families about the possibilities for genetic intervention. The next chapter deals more specifically with the approaches taken by genetic counsellors. One of the difficulties, of course, is that public genetic services may well 'escape' the filter of counselling. In what sense is counselling both embedded in medical science, but also anxious to detach itself from 'public-health' concerns? This question, among others, will be the subject of what follows.

CHAPTER 5

Genetic counselling

Genetic testing and screening necessarily mean that some individuals will be found to be vulnerable to genetic disease, either immediately or in the longer term. Genetic counselling differs from other medical practices, such as consultation, in that it is designed to give those families with particular burdens about genetic disease the time and space to reflect on both the nature of their condition and the likely consequences of it, either for themselves or for their children. This chapter will consider the ethics of current practice, and situate this discussion in the context of broader social questions about the nature of genetic risk. Genetic counselling presupposes that the information given about one's genetic makeup needs to be handled with discretion; counsellors are the new priests, giving access to services such as pre-implantation genetic diagnosis (PGD) or other available 'treatment' options. I will suggest that counselling cannot be separated from the medical sub-culture in which it has grown and evolved, and that trying to suggest otherwise is disingenuous. I argue for a greater need for a culture that strives to welcome those with disabilities into the human community and to support families who are likely to be affected, instead of rendering those with genetic disease as 'unfit'. Such a shift requires a rethinking of prudence at an institutional and political level as well as at an individual and familial level. In addition, prudence needs to be combined with justice, but justice in its broadest sense, rather than simple access to counselling services and resources.

WHAT IS GENETIC COUNSELLING?

Genetic counselling, at a bare minimum, seeks to give families who are affected by genetic disorders the opportunity to gain information about a particular condition. Unlike much other medical information, genetic tests give rise to probability statistics that are difficult for the average person to interpret. Genetic counselling helps clients to cope with the gap between diagnostic knowledge of a disease and the possibility of treatment, leading to psychosocial and ethical problems either prior to or following a test result. Genetic counselling can also help clients understand the likely course that the disease will take, and steps that could be taken either to alleviate symptoms or to manage the problems associated with the disease where this is possible. Counselling will also help individuals understand how the disease is inherited, and what effects this may have on reproductive decisions that have been taken already, if the client is pregnant, or will be taken in the future. As discussed in the previous chapter, the extent of penetrance and expressivity often varies considerably. Sometimes the counsellor will have to break the news that very little is known about a particular genetic condition. The number of instances of genetic diseases that can be identified, but not treated, is likely to increase as knowledge about human genetics expands. Both of the latter scenarios may be unwelcome news to those seeking help. Very often the genetic counsellor will have gained prior knowledge of the family history from a genetics nurse who has conducted interviews with those members of the client's family who are on the 'family tree' of those who are affected by the disease. While genetic counselling has information-giving at its core, one of its intentions is to facilitate the client's sharing of anxieties and doubts occasioned by genetic knowledge, so it serves to provide emotional support as well as simple impartation of facts, much of which is subject to considerable uncertainty because of the probabilistic nature of genetic disease.

Angus Clarke argues strongly that genetic counselling should be monitored according to a broad category of quality of service, rather than according to specific outcomes such as influence on clients' reproductive plans or behaviour. 'For clinicians to know that their work would be evaluated in this frankly eugenic manner would impose intolerable burdens on them.'[1] The ethical presuppositions are that the counsellor is 'detached' from the client in the sense of being non-directive, while at the same time being prepared to show empathy for those affected or likely to be affected by genetic disease. By facilitating the clients' free choice, counsellors believe that they have a role to play in an ethically sound use of genetic knowledge. Nonetheless, while this may be a goal, the extent to which counsellors do achieve non-directive statements may vary between cultures, and across medical professionals. Obstetricians, for example, are more likely to be directive compared with genetic counsellors, who, in

---

[1] A. Clarke, 'Outcomes and Process in Genetic Counselling', in Harper and Clarke (eds.), *Genetics, Society and Clinical Practice*, pp. 165–78 (p. 168).

turn, are more likely to be directive compared with non-medical support staff. German genetic counsellors are more likely to recommend continuation of a pregnancy, whereas Portuguese are more likely to recommend termination.[2] Some tricky ethical situations may arise as a result of genetic counselling. How should a counsellor respond, for example, to a family's request for confidentiality, which is the hallmark of all counselling, when other family members are likely to be put at considerable risk by non-disclosure? These professional judgments will be situated within a general assessment of the harm done by non-disclosure needs to be set against the likely harm of full disclosure against a family's wish. Peter Harper argues that genetic information should be given out only rarely in this situation, and certainly never to third parties, such as insurers or employers, who may have an indirect vested interest in the information.[3]

One of the stronger desires of those involved in genetic counselling is to focus on the *family*-related nature of their task, and to detach themselves from the practice of population-screening and testing, associated, as it is, with campaigns for public health. While screening programmes themselves may operate somewhere between the two paradigmatic extremes of 'genetic cleansing' and 'informed choice', any shift towards a genetic-cleansing model for genetic counselling would be unethical and unwelcome as far as the majority of practitioners are concerned.[4] Clarke sets up an opposing list of those who are screening under the auspices of a 'cleansing' model, compared with those who are 'choosers'.

Given this, it is understandable that genetic counsellors would want to distance themselves from 'cleansing' screening models that minimise their input in an overall programme and have strong resemblances to eugenic programmes of the last century. However, as population-screening becomes more widespread, it is going to become increasingly difficult for counsellors to detach themselves from screening practice; that is, they are

---

[2] A. Clarke, 'The Process of Genetic Counselling: Beyond Non-Directiveness', in Harper and Clarke (eds.), *Genetics, Society and Clinical Practice*, pp. 179–200 (pp. 183–4). Robert Song has pointed to the hollowness of so-called informed consent by 'genetic professionals and the health service as a whole', believing that many women facing difficult choices about continuation of pregnancy show simple 'acquiescence' to pressure. While I would agree that this applies in many prenatal screening programmes (which I will discuss later in this chapter), genetic counsellors attempt, at least, to be rather more impartial than he implies. Information supplied by midwives in the UK in 2005 raises the possibility that some women will not want the tests, in a way that was not apparent even five years earlier. Song, *Human Genetics*, pp. 53–4.

[3] P. S. Harper, 'Genetic Testing and Insurance', in Harper and Clarke (eds.), *Genetics, Society and Clinical Practice*, pp. 49–59.

[4] See, for example, A. Clarke, 'Prenatal Genetic Screening: Paradigms and Perspectives', in Harper and Clarke (eds.), *Genetics, Society and Clinical Practice*, pp. 119–40.

Table 5.1. *Counselling in two opposing paradigms for screening programmes*[a]

	Choosers	Cleansers
Goal	Provision of information	Reduction in birth incidence
Economics	Costs permitting	Cost effective
Consent	Fully informed	Assent or opt out
Pre-test counselling	Unlimited and integral	Minimal
Post-test counselling	Unlimited and integral	Minimal
Client satisfaction	Studied systematically	Irrelevant
Social evaluation	Careful search	Nil
Focus of audit	Informed autonomous choice	Selective abortion

[a] Adapted from Clarke, 'Prenatal Genetic Screening', p. 126.

likely to be called upon to give individuals information if they have been detected as being 'at risk' through prior screening. Moreover, in the public mind, at least, genetic services fall under the same category – be it screening, counselling or prenatal diagnosis and so on. The various philosophies behind the practice of each are likely to be lost on the average individual, who is made aware of genetic 'risks' through screening rather than through familial history of a particular genetic disease. Clarke argues that genetic screening of the cleansing type gives little place for genetic counselling, but one might ask whether any screening programme has the capacity to promote 'choice' in the way he implies from the twin paradigms. In other words, the rhetoric of 'choosers' may be far more acceptable in screening, but where it has the net effect of giving the impression that there are 'unfit' members of the human race that we would be better off without, it ultimately fails in its task, for the choice is facile, rather than real.

COUNSELLING IN A RISK SOCIETY

The language of clinical genetics is the language of probability, rather than of certainty. It is a way of trying to manage and control the concept of 'high risk' or 'low risk' by evaluating the future in terms of likely outcomes. Risk thinking has replaced the broader uncertainty and incalculable 'chance' or lottery, so that

risk thinking tames chance, fate and uncertainty by a paradoxical move. By recognising the impossibility of certainty about the future, it simultaneously makes this lack of certainty quantifiable in terms of probability. And once one has quantified the probability of a future event's occurring, decisions can be made and justified about what to do in the present, informed by what seems to be secure, if probabilistic, knowledge about the future.[5]

Ulrich Beck has argued, more generally, that we now live in an unpredictable and even hazardous 'risk society', one that has replaced the overall paradigm of scientific progress and confidence about the future.[6] Gene technology, in this scenario, does not so much reduce risk as heighten its possibilities for disaster, so that

Gene technology pits humankind into an almost godlike position, in which it is able to create new materials and living creatures and revolutionise the biological and cultural foundations of the family. This generalisation of the principle of design and constructability, which now encompasses even the subject whom it was once supposed to serve, exponentiates the risks and politicises the places, conditions, and means of their origin and interpretation. (p. 200)

In other words, the possibility of redesign of humans through genetic technologies actually *increases*, rather than reduces, the overall sense of anxiety about the future. He is particularly critical of the 'creeping' nature of techno-economic sub-politics, which has informed medical practice, but which has, remarkably, escaped public discussion, becoming aware of itself only after the event. He therefore goes on to suggest that medical, including genetic, progress becomes institutionalised; further, it is 'the institutionalised revolution of the lay public's social living conditions without its consent' (p. 206). It amounts to a 'noiseless social and cultural revolution'. Yet because it is not yet in the official political sphere, decisions are imposed in a way that would be totally unacceptable in a democratic society. One could even view the British Government White Paper on genetics (2003) as following in the wake of medical change, rather than serving to shape its development.

Beck has sounded some alarm bells that may be quietened only by public rejection of medical technologies that the White Paper seeks to endorse. It is hardly surprising, in such a context, that he suggests that

the practice of having public political discussions only after research and investment decisions have been made needs to be broken up. The demand is that the consequences and organisational freedom of action of microelectronics or genetic technology belong in parliament before the fundamental decisions on their application have been taken. The consequences of such a development can easily

---

[5] N. Rose, 'At Risk of Madness', in Baker and Simon (eds.), *Embracing Risk*, pp. 209–37 (p. 214).

[6] Beck, *Risk Society*, pp. 51–2. Beck has been criticised for not taking into account the risk of being poor, but in this context genetic risk would add to this risk, rather than replace an existing sense of confidence.

be forecast: bureaucratic obstacles to plant automatic and scientific research. This is, however, only one variant of this model of the future. (p. 229)

Alternatives include intermediate forms of social control, which avoid the centralisation of government, but still create compulsory jurisdiction. The Human Embryology and Fertilisation Authority (HFEA) seems to fall into this category, mediating between research scientists, government policy and law, and public interests. It is able, then, to perform a critical role in helping to avoid the kind of tendencies implicit in Beck's critique. Yet, in the past at least, one of the main sounding-boards for its decisions has been what is already within the legal sphere, rather than the creation of new restrictions outside the law.[7] This has begun to change with the realisation that the authority can also make a contribution towards the processes required in order to tighten up current legislation where it is seen to be 'leaky' (as in, for example, controversy about what constitutes an embryo). Although the HFEA has been criticised by some medical practitioners for its bureaucratic cumbersomeness, it is clear that without some form of intermediary govern- ance the possibility of public input into decision-making in genetics would be bypassed, left at the mercy of political representation through parliamen- tary processes that it is habitually able to escape.

Genetic counsellors have to work in the social and political context in which sensitive decisions about human genetics have escaped the normal democratic processes and become embedded or even enshrined in government policy. This, combined with the uneasy sense that humanity is attempting to recon- struct itself, means that the rhetoric that counsellors use in the quiet of their consulting rooms, of 'free choice' and 'autonomy', begins to sound a little shallow. The generalised sense of 'risk' becomes translated into a practical fear of the unfit that might even, unawares, affect the attitudes of genetic counsel- lors towards clients. Clients may well seek more genetic counselling as the status of genetic knowledge continues to accelerate in contemporary society.

In these situations it is worth asking why the public might come to trust the genetic counsellor at all. In many cases individuals are ambivalent about trusting experts in complex decision-making about human genetics. Would a decision to trust a genetic counsellor be a simple trust in expert knowledge, or a leftover willingness to trust those considered knowledge- able because of the clients' sense of lack of control over their lives?[8] Or is the trust a deliberate choice on their part, a selective trusting after carefully

---

[7] Deech, 'The Ethics of Embryo Selection'.
[8] This would be what Anthony Giddens describes as a premodern confidence in scientific truth as such. See Giddens, *Modernity and Self-Identity*.

weighing up the evidence?[9] The second alternative seems unlikely because of the lack of choice; the only option presented to the client who has anxieties about genetic disease is referral to the expert clinical geneticists. Yet we might see this desire to win trust in small measure once the counselling has started, for the counsellor may seek to dispel the anxieties about his or her role in the process. The quite adamant separation of public-health genetics and clinical-counselling genetics is a case in point. A third possibility, offered by Brian Wynne in relation to public behaviour towards those with expert knowledge, is that the trust is disingenuous, that underlying the trusting behaviour there is a deeply suspicious mindset, unaccompanied by feelings of trust.[10] The fact that most of those who see genetic counsellors do not subsequently show any difference in reproductive decisions might suggest that this kind of trust is operative; that is, the view of the clinical geneticist, only thinly disguised under the rhetoric of choice, is accepted at one level only.[11] Yet there is a fourth alternative, namely that the 'trust' in the genetic counsellor could even be said to be exhibiting a 'performative dimension', that is, one where trust is so designed as to elicit trustworthy behaviour by the one trusted. Bronislaw Szerszynski has suggested that this 'performative' behaviour accounts for apparently anomalous actions on the part of the lay public towards those whom they believe are not necessarily candidates for such trust. One example is in the case of a resident who approached an operator of a local chemical plant for information about safety procedures in the case of an accidental leak.[12] This last suggestion is the most challenging and interesting as far as the ethics of genetic counselling is concerned, for it is seeking to provoke trustworthy behaviour on the part of those who are approached for help. Given the sensitivity and personal nature of human genetic knowledge, such performances might have played a part in preventing genetic counselling from becoming totally absorbed by the public-health culture in which they are embedded, and might be one of the reasons genetic counsellors take a stance against such policies.

---

[9] This is Giddens' preferred model for 'late modernity', the sense that active trust has to be 'won' by those who are to be trusted.

[10] B. Wynne, 'Interpreting Public Concerns About GMOs – Questions of Meaning', in Deane-Drummond and Szerszynski (eds.), *Re-Ordering Nature*, pp. 221–50.

[11] Alan Clarke has suggested that there is no evidence to suggest that either reproductive behaviour or decisions are affected by counselling, and to make this a marker of the success of the counselling process would itself be 'eugenic' and, by implication, unacceptable. See Clarke, 'Outcomes and Process in Genetic Counselling', in Harper and Clarke (eds.), *Genetics, Society and Clinical Practice*, pp. 165–78.

[12] Szerszynski, 'Risk and Trust: The Performative Dimension'.

COUNSELLING AND PRE-IMPLANTATION
GENETIC DIAGNOSIS

Although the scientific technique of PGD and its implementation in current policy-making in the United Kingdom was mentioned briefly in the last chapter, it is worth coming back to this practice in the light of genetic counselling, because PGD seems to fit somewhat uneasily and even precariously between individual familial genetics and the overall genetic screening and testing project with its public-health goals and aims. Those who demand access to this 'treatment' include couples already seeking fertility treatment through IVF, those with a known risk of a genetic disease, and those who want a specific child, such as one of a desired gender. Current UK regulation rules out the use of PGD for gender selection, unless used for a sex-linked genetic disorder.

Even at the start of IVF treatment, some foresaw a time when it would be possible to use the technique to select out unwanted embryos; technology bred more technology, based on the premise that genes 'caused' disease in a deterministic way. The construction of the process is that IVF/PGD is relatively neutral; the 'benefits' focused on the outcome – a 'healthy' baby, judged by the absence of a specific disease – rather than on the means to obtain this end, namely, the increased destruction of embryos and the intervention in women's reproductive biology. One might even argue that the anti-abortion lobby has served to foster the idea that PGD constitutes preferable, or even desirable, progress over prenatal diagnosis (PND), since in the latter case there is late analysis of the genetic disorder followed by termination of the pregnancy.[13] By contrast, PGD seems to be detached from women's bodies; the reproductive processes become one step removed and therefore subject to control from the 'outside', without the same degree of protection as is afforded to embryos that are implanted. In PGD it is the doctor who decides which embryo will be allowed to live and which will be prevented from living, based on assessment of genetic tests. It is noteworthy that prior to the Human Embryology and Fertilisation Act of 1990 there was no legal protection at all of human embryos created outside the womb.[14]

Deborah Steinberg offers a feminist critique and suggests that the language of PGD is one that focuses specifically on the technical process and the embryo, taking insufficient account of the role of women. Because

---

[13] Steinberg, *Bodies in Glass*, pp. 106–12.
[14] Brahams, 'Ethics and Law of the Diagnosis of Human Genetic Disease', in Edwards (ed.), *Preconception and Preimplantation Genetic Diagnosis*, pp. 315–28 (p. 317).

the success rate for PGD is less than that for IVF, women are subjected to many more difficult treatments. She suggests that seemingly taking women out of the process echoes a more deeply encultured anxiety about women's sexuality and reproduction, the site of pollution and danger in ancient religious ritual.[15] I suggest that the removal of women from PGD talk is not deliberate in the way she suggests, but a necessary outcome of the techno-logisation of human biology in general. Yet she is correct, it seems to me, to suggest that one of the latent anxieties among those with religious senti-ments is that it does interfere with processes that have traditionally been under divine providence alone. It therefore goes to the deepest aspects of human experience. While those who object to the technology may be drawing on deeply held cultural views about the place of reproduction in human society, then, it is unlikely that those who perform the acts are doing so because they want to control or even suppress women's sexuality in the way she implies. Genetic counsellors who fail to give sufficient information about the likely trauma for women in the process of PGD are not performing their duties. The difficulty that Steinberg envisages would arise if the language of PGD research that tends to ignore women's experience were translated into counselling practice, so that women become objects of a technological process of which they were only dimly aware at the start of the 'treatment'.

At the moment, PGD is restricted to 'serious' conditions. The licensing of those conditions approved by the HFEA for PGD is likely to increase as more disease genes are discovered in the absence of possible cures. But in this context we need to ask two separate questions. The first is: what is serious or not serious? Søren Holm warns against what he calls 'severity creep', whereby more and more conditions will be labelled as serious over time.[16] Some American deaf couples have sought to use PGD to select positively for deaf children, who could be part of the deaf community. Are they allowed to bring only the 'best possible' *hearing* child into the world, judged by medical science? Or are they permitted to bring the 'best possible' *deaf* child into the world, according to their own judgment? In addition, those who are given the responsibility for genetic counselling would need to make clear to couples the extent of the possible penetrance and expressivity of a particular condition. A more common sentiment is

[15] She draws on Mary Douglas's work, *Purity and Danger*, for this assessment: Steinberg, *Bodies in Glass*, p. 106.
[16] S. Holm, 'Ethical Issues in Pre-Implantation Genetic Diagnosis', in Harris and Holm (eds.), *The Future of Human Reproduction*, pp. 176–90 (p. 185).

that 'the investment of a genetic disease with the spectre of an inevitably terrible life and early death fuels the sense that genetic screening is not only necessary but the only possible response'.[17] Action is slanted in favour of rejecting those who, in probabilistic terms only, have a high chance of developing a disease with varying degrees of severity. In this context it is worth asking if a genuine choice is being presented, or whether the choice is thrust upon patients and forced upon professionals by the increasing availability of genetic services. In these situations the pregnancy becomes 'tentative' until all tests have been carried out. Of course, PGD removes the possibility of tentative pregnancies, though the success rate is about as low as in IVF, so it is doubtful if this is a valid argument in its favour. The 'good' of the increase in reproductive choices is one that is assumed, but it is not necessarily a good, for it disguises other social changes that go unnoticed.

COUNSELLING AND DISABILITY

How would those who suffer from a particular condition feel if they knew that programmes were in place to selectively screen out those in their situation? Those who support PND and PGD will argue that the techniques are not there as a means of discriminating against those with the disability; rather, the 'good' is in preventing the suffering of the individuals who would otherwise be born with the disease, and the suffering of their families. More liberal ethicists will argue that removing a foetus, judged as non-personal, does not judge those who are suffering from the condition. However, there are two issues at stake here. The first is that, under current law, those mothers who are pregnant with a disabled child can abort right up to the expected birth date; no viability time limit is set on her 'right' to terminate. Such a policy is clearly eugenic, for it seeks to remove those considered 'unfit' from society. In this context, speaking of PND as if it were not a slur on those with disabilities sounds very hollow. Secondly, if our moral obligations are to persons only, then why not do anything we want with PGD? Why not screen out one or other of the sexes? For one might argue that in certain cultures, at least, a family without a son would suffer social stigma and discrimination.

Again, why not try to enhance other characteristics, such as intelligence?[18] While this is unlikely to be possible at present, since intelligence is mutifactorial, polygenic, and likely to owe as much to environment as to genetics, what if certain genes *were* found that partially contributed to higher

---

[17] Steinberg, *Bodies in Glass*, p. 118.   [18] I will return to this aspect in chapter 6.

intelligence? This does not seem beyond the realm of possibility, especially in view of the high social and cultural value given to intelligence. In these scenarios, how would those with learning difficulties of all kinds respond? Given that PGD has been allowed for aneuploidy, effectively allowing selection against those with conditions such as Down syndrome, what if the mother undergoing PND decided to continue with a pregnancy in these circumstances? Would she be considered irresponsible, given the techniques available, both to her family and to the wider social community?

This desire for children regardless of the condition of the foetus may apply not only to PND. Informal conversations with consultants suggests that in some cases of PGD, where all embryos are found to be affected by the condition(s) that is/are being screened, parents have requested that the affected embryo(s) be put back in the mother's womb. So far, clinicians have resisted this request, as it goes against the original purpose of PGD, namely to select *against* certain conditions. It is, nonetheless, an interesting twist to the way informed consent has come up against its limits. It also shows that the suspicion that PGD *inevitably* leads to negative attitudes by parents towards those with disabilities is oversimplified, though more research would be needed in order to test the prevalence of such views. Of course, if the conditions being screened were not life-threatening, then one might argue that it is an improper use of the technology in the first place. The outcome in this case demonstrates the imprudence of using PGD unless absolutely necessary, that is, for life-threatening conditions. Where such couples are also infertile, would IVF be refused on the basis of the risk of disease? In Italy, where the law stipulates that all IVF embryos must be transferred, regardless of quality or risk to the mother, clinicians are put in a difficult position. For example, an egg fertilised by two sperm is known to be unviable, but according to the law has to be put back into the mother's womb. In the case of IVF where there is simply a risk of disease, the lack of certainty is more likely to allow clinicians to go ahead without breaking the Hippocratic Oath to do no harm.

Alan Clarke has pointed to the significance of these issues in terms of counselling practice. He believes that

It is also most unlikely that the possibility of *actively welcoming* a child with Down syndrome is very often presented in antenatal clinics as a real ('reasonable') option, and if a woman makes that decision then personal values attributed to some unusual cultural or religious factors are likely to be invoked to account for her decision.[19]

---

[19] Clarke, 'The Process of Genetic Counselling', p. 186.

If, on the other hand, the woman decides to go ahead with a termination, the probable anguish, guilt and depression that follow are not raised as an issue worth discussion. Genetic counsellors are also far less likely to confront a woman who has opted for termination with positive messages about the variability of a particular disease and the quality of life of those with learning difficulties and other genetic disorders, many of whom go on to have highly productive and fulfilled lives. If a woman expresses her wish to continue with the pregnancy, a counsellor is far more likely to point out the possible severity of the condition and its impact on the family. In these scenarios, choice is offered in the context of a socially coercive structure that rejects those who are biologically 'unfit'.

Has disability become the new taboo in place of death and sexuality and race?[20] In such a social context, the idea of non-directive counselling becomes virtually impossible in practice. It is also worth asking why other measures are not used to improve the health of future babies, rather than adopting a policy that focuses so sharply on genetic disease and screening. In this scenario, 'society and health professionals jointly decide to devote resources to prenatal genetic screening when alternative approaches to improving outcomes for mothers and infants are neglected, even though social and nutritional approaches to improving outcomes in high risk pregnancies may be available and could be simpler and cheaper'.[21]

What about the views of those who are disabled themselves? Tom Shakespeare, who is a research officer at Policy, Ethics and Life Sciences Research Institute in Newcastle, suggests the following:

Reducing suffering and preventing impairment are goals that most people would support. But in our focus on genes and diseases, we should not ignore people and relationships. Disability is a fact of life. The human population is different in all sorts of ways; we should preserve diversity and recognise the moral value of every individual. Non-disabled people fear impairment. Disability is regarded as a medical tragedy, which should be avoided at all costs. Yet disabled people can enjoy a good quality of life, in a society which promotes more independent living and civil rights. Disabled people's voices need to be heard in genetics debates, including the voices of people with learning difficulties.[22]

We also need to account for the fact that since only 1% of the 12% of the population who are disabled are so because of congenital abnormalities, the prospect of 'genetic cleansing' of disability is a myth. Not only are screening programmes ineffective in removing a disease gene, as discussed in the

---

[20] Ibid., p. 188.   [21] Ibid., p. 187.
[22] T. Shakespeare, Foreword to Ward (ed.), *Considered Choices?*, p. 4.

previously, but the majority of those who suffer disability do so because of environmental factors, lifestyle or ageing. One disabled participant in a workshop on genetics commented:

People with learning difficulties are different to other people. We get picked on – others make fun of us. People shout at us in the street sometimes. Black people with learning difficulties get picked on even more. People with learning difficulties should be treated fairly and not discriminated against. Scientists should find the gene that makes people pick on those who are different. Then our lives would be better.[23]

This person also felt strongly that any mother who is pregnant with a baby with learning difficulties should not terminate her pregnancy:

I think babies with learning difficulties or disabled are good, very, very, good. They should be born, not aborted. There should be tests for women who are pregnant to see how the baby is. If it has Down's syndrome, the parents need someone to talk to. They need to find out what people with Down's syndrome can do. You should think of a baby as a baby first, not just that it has Down's syndrome. (p. 39)

The fear of bearing a child with a learning difficulty seems to be one of the main reasons why those over thirty-five years old accept the amniocentesis offered as part of a screening programme.[24] Their perception of risk as 'high' may be unrelated to the actual probability based on maternal age; some older mothers even felt a sense of guilt at putting their baby at risk by conceiving in the first place. The way the doctors frame a particular risk of having an affected child will also influence the perception of risk on the part of the mother. A woman in her late thirties, for example, might think of herself as at high risk if compared with younger women, or at low risk if compared with older women. An older woman who rejects a test can even be made to feel irresponsible for deciding against testing, depending on how the risk equation is framed. In addition, the age at which amniocentesis is automatically offered seems to have been set on the basis of the relative capacity of laboratories to cope with testing. Conveniently, it coincided with the apparent risk of spontaneous miscarriage during amniocentesis. In other words, doctors were steering women into invasive tests on the basis of the level of resource funding for genetic screening and testing.[25] Now that there are enhanced funds for screening for Down syndrome,

---

[23] Anonymous participant in J. Howarth and J. Rodgers, 'Difference and Choice: A Workshop for People with Learning Difficulties', in Ward (ed.), *Considered Choices?*, pp. 27–50 (p. 39).

[24] This is based on information from case-study work reported in Heyman and Henrikson, *Risk, Age and Pregnancy*, pp. 115–44.

[25] Ibid., p. 211.

following the Government White Paper on genetics, the conditions set for high risk may well shift again.[26] The possibility of legal action by women above a certain age who are not offered tests means that doctors are more likely to be concerned that tests are positively offered, and are recorded as having been done, than to engage in any form of genetic counselling. What is interesting, however, is that those who accepted amniocentesis did not view conditions such as Down syndrome as an inherent disaster, but rather 'calibrated its adversity in terms of their own ability to cope and the degree of support they would receive from their family. Hence, their judgments were socially contextualised, while doctors were primarily concerned with reducing the population of children with a medically defined condition'.[27]

One father of two children, both with severe learning difficulties, has commented on the difficulties of bringing up his children:

On the other hand they are happy and they bring happiness to others, including us, their parents, and this is work that really matters. So this is not some kind of dewy-eyed sentimentality for living with them, and making good their disabilities is very hard work. What is more, all sorts of things, for example, a conventional social life or the kind of level of professional work that would bring career advancement, do not and cannot happen. But I would not be without Jo or Matthew to save my life. They strip away pretence and ambitions. They force me to face up to my own faults and limitations ... Who is to judge the value of another's life? Who has the right to say that a life is not worth living, that it should be squashed out? We exist for another and, as a result, none of us has the freedom simply to do as we wish; we delude ourselves if we think otherwise. Rather, we have the duty to care for each other. That is the society I wish to be part of.[28]

In addition, the prospect that genetic screening and testing might be of economic benefit, as it would be cheaper than looking after those with learning difficulties, was, for him, quite simply 'disgusting'. He challenged the idea that 'choice' should be given the status of an 'ultimate virtue', along with material gain and success, regardless of the means of attaining that success.

Overall, then, any apparent good achieved through screening and testing of pregnant mothers seems set, in its present form at least, to widen even more the gap between those who are disabled and those who are not. It seems extremely unlikely that testing and screening will be offered for the

---

[26] See the Government White Paper on genetics, *Our Inheritance, Our Future*. Other aspects of this White Paper were discussed in the previous chapter.

[27] Heyman and Henrickson, *Risk, Age and Pregnancy*, p. 125.

[28] S. Picton and J. Picton, 'What It Means for Us. Two Parents' Perspectives', in Ward (ed.), *Considered Choices?*, p. 49.

sole purpose of preparing parents for having an affected child, yet this is the task of counselling at its best: to offer parents the opportunity to see disabilities in ways that are positive, rather than in ways that serve to reinforce cultural and social prejudices.

AFFIRMING A SUFFERING PRESENCE

It almost goes without saying that one task of the Christian community is to act in such a way as to provide a place of welcome for those who are affected by disabilities, including those who have genetic diseases. Instead of viewing such persons as the 'unfit' members of the human community, we need to relearn what Stanley Hauerwas has described as the 'suffering presence' of those who are part of the community in which we are placed.[29] Although he was writing at a time before the rapid explosion in genetic testing, he recognised the cultural shift with its emphasis on individualised choice and apparent freedom, so that 'the birth of a child is no longer a gift of God, but an event for which we can be held accountable' (p. 11).

Although he was writing at a time when babies born with serious difficulties were often allowed to die, rather than being terminated in pregnancy, he suggests that viewing their suffering as a justification for such inaction (letting die) misses the point, for 'we all, healthy and non healthy, normal or abnormal, are destined for a life of suffering' (p. 172). Viewing suffering simply as 'unbearable' is probably a projection of how we would feel in their situation, but we often do not know, for we cannot know, to what extent individuals may suffer from their disability. Therefore,

> We do not know how much pain they will undergo, but we nonetheless act to justify our lack of care in the name of our humane concern about their destiny. We do so even knowing that our greatest nobility as humans often derives from the individual's struggle to make positive use of his or her limitations. (p. 172)

More often than not, the feeling that suffering is unbearable for another is a result of our own inability to cope with another person's open suffering, so we resent both those who suffer without apology, and the loneliness that it opens up by our denial of our neediness of others. He suggests, importantly, that once we learn not to fear those with learning difficulties, they

[29] Hauerwas, *Suffering Presence.*

also learn not to fear their own neediness. He rejects the idea that we should use the notion of 'God's will' to justify avoidable suffering and injustice. Rather, turning the notion of avoidance on its head, he suggests that

Quite simply, the challenge of learning to know, to be with, and care for the retarded is nothing less than learning to know, be with, and love God. God's face is the face of the retarded; God's body is the body of the retarded; God's being is that of the retarded. For the God we Christians must learn to worship is not a god of self-sufficient power, a god whose self-possession needs no one; rather ours is a God who needs a people, who needs a son. Absoluteness of being or power is not a work of the God we have come to know through the cross of Christ. (p. 178)

It would be unrealistic to expect the secular practice of genetic counselling to express the possible beneficial effects on parents for those who have an affected child. Hauerwas's approach is directed unashamedly at the Christian community, the church, as a way of expressing its particular vocation in the world. How might this apply to secular practice? I suggest that even secular counsellors need to try to help parents overcome negative feelings of rejection towards children who have already been born with genetic defects, rather than simply offering 'solutions' of avoidance through PND and termination. The idea that women *need* such screening processes came into vogue after the practice was devised, so to some extent it is putting women into a situation where they feel obliged to have healthy children.[30] We therefore need to ask ourselves: 'Is the story claiming that the pregnancy has malfunctioned (by not spontaneously aborting), resulting in a baby with malformations, any "truer" than the story suggesting that society has malfunctioned because it cannot accommodate the disabled in its midst?'[31]

In such situations, where PGD is available, parents may come to the conclusion that their actions are ethically more acceptable than aborting an affected foetus. Yet it is in these circumstances that the positive option of accepting the gift of care for a life that is disadvantaged needs also to come into view.

---

[30] A. Lippman, 'Prenatal Genetic Screening: Constructing Needs and Reinforcing Inequalities', in Clarke, *Genetic Counselling*, pp. 142–86 (pp. 148–9).

[31] Ibid., p. 160. Robert Song offers a similar commentary on disability. I would endorse his suggestion that Christians must be far more aware of the social pressures that reject those who are disabled, and must become far more proactive in welcoming those who are disabled. Song, *Human Genetics*, pp. 23–5, 51–8, 70–2.

BEYOND THE PRECAUTIONARY PRINCIPLE

Learning how to manage and communicate the risks that are presented through genetic science is one of the tasks inherent in genetic counselling. François Ewald has commented on the emergence of the precautionary principle in the context of scientific uncertainty and the possibility of serious and irreversible damage.[32] Although the particular social conditions in which the precautionary principle came to be used reflected anxiety about environmental change, much the same could be said about the new reproductive and genetic technologies. In seeking to minimise 'risk' through more and more intervention, the possibility of serious damage comes into view. A precautionary principle would serve to challenge the basic assumptions inherent in a given programme, which presupposes inevitable progress and benefits. Thus, 'precaution appears when scientific expertise comes up against its own limitations and forces the politician to make sovereign decisions, alone and without recourse to others' (p. 295). Risk measurement, when taking due account of precaution, will allow for the possibility of irreversible accidents in exerting human power over nature. Although this is more likely to be evident in non-human genetically modified organisms, the spectre of irreversibly altering the course of human genetics carries with it the same kinds of risk. While genetic therapy is at present permitted on only somatic cells, genetic counsellors may find themselves in a situation where they are called upon to advise when and if, as seems likely, the legal structures are loosened to take account of increased demand. PGD followed in the wake of IVF, and inherited genetic modification is the next logical step. There are prominent ethicists, John Harris among them, who argue strongly that if it is possible to manipulate our hereditary material 'safely', then there is no reason not to do it. He sees no ethical objection to allowing such a development to take place.[33] The point of mentioning this here is that the nature of genetics is such that it cannot be contained in the way he envisages; in any scientific discovery there is always an element of uncertainty about the outcomes.

The unique situation about human genetic technologies is that they create new kinds of dependencies rather than equalities, and new forms of power over others. The precautionary principle would allow for the fact

---

[32] F. Ewald, 'The Return of Descartes' Malicious Demon: An Outline of a Philosophy of Precaution', in Baker and Simon, *Embracing Risk*, pp. 273–301 (p. 292).

[33] J. Harris, 'Rights and Reproductive Choices', in Harris and Holm (eds.), *The Future of Human Reproduction*, pp. 1–37, esp. pp. 31–3. I will come back to a discussion of genetic enhancement in the next chapter.

that these inequalities exist and would try to confront them. The idea that justice is exercised in genetic services is a myth; even allowing for the fact that it may be available to all, justice is not simply about availability of genetic services but about the much broader question of whether it will ensure the greatest good for the greatest number, that is, social justice. Hauerwas rejects IVF on the grounds that it is an unjust use of economic resources, while holding to the view that IVF research should be allowed to continue (p. 155). The current widening access to IVF through the National Health Service in the United Kingdom, along with expansion of genetic services in general, suggests that the public-health lobby to promote genetic services has won through. How far this represents a form of social injustice by siphoning off scarce resources that could be used for other medical conditions is open to discussion. If it does not, one might envisage that a driving motivation for the new technologies is an economic goal rather than an altruistic one. The precautionary principle should, in theory, allow for this form of self-criticism of practice to take place.

In addition, the precautionary principle is not simply a matter of spreading risks throughout the population, but of preventing harm in the first place. Today the only acceptable kind of war is one that is virtually zero-risk to combatants, a very different cultural scenario compared with the two World Wars of the last century. In much the same way, we might ask ourselves whether the attempts to manage the unmanageable will eventually lead to a greater intolerance of risky procedures in assisted reproduction.

Is there more that might be said about the future of genetic counselling, other than advocating a greater awareness of the precautionary principle? Scientists tend to look at particular case histories and then devise an ethical approach based on the particular circumstances of that case. Joseph Fletcher similarly believed in situation ethics, but, once he applied this to human genetics, it seems that any sense of restraint or precaution was muted, though he admitted that the fact that we *could* do something did not mean that we *should* do it. He invited us to choose between situation ethics and arguing from principles, suggesting that a pragmatic approach is the most reasonable one. He suggested that most medical ethics was based on the kind of argument that reasoned according to good consequences or outcomes. Yet, given his approach, it is surprising, in the context of the real possibility of human cloning, to see the outcome of this kind of approach. According to him, 'if the greatest good of the greatest number (i.e., the social good) were served by it, it would be justifiable not only to specialise the capacities of people by cloning or by constructive genetic engineering, but also to bioengineer or bio-design parahumans or "modified men" – as chimeras (part animal) or cyborg-androids (part prosthetes)'.[34]

Such views seem extreme and unwarranted, but are the consequence of a complete lack of any principles about the worth of human nature as such. The opposite alternative, presented by Paul Ramsey, namely a rejection of all forms of assisted reproduction, including IVF and artificial insemination by donor (AID) as against Christian values of the family, might seem extreme in the more conservative direction. Ramsey is well known for his belief that we must learn to be human before we can 'play God'.[35] Ramsey, it seems, believes that we simply do not have the wisdom to tamper with the genetic future of the human race. Although he was writing at a time when geneticists were particularly despairing about the present genetic state of the human race and the likely demise of the latter, pitching forth their utopian dreams in such a context, his remarks are at the opposite end of the spectrum compared with Joseph Fletcher's positive affirmation of combining humanity and technology. Ramsey's reaction against such utopianism is understandable, but not necessarily always helpful. Yet there are elements of his account that are still relevant. One aspect is the attempt to render human personhood as that which can be manufactured, the language of DNA effectively squeezing out other forms of discourse about what it means to be human.[36]

Ramsey also wants to make sure that the person is not squeezed into a non-person or simply an interesting member of the species, thereby losing his or her human dignity, sacredness and rights. One of the tasks of the genetic counsellor would be to make sure that the person remains one who does not simply become a non-person, a tendency Ramsey has picked up in the medical profession as a whole. Because of the time allowed for each person in genetic counselling sessions, this is unlikely to happen, though clearly counsellors need to be kept on their guard for trends in counselling practice. IVF, and any genetic engineering for positive or negative eugenic reasons, are, for him, immoral and refuse to recognise the right of the child to be.[37] Ramsey also objects to IVF and other artificial procedures on the

---

[34] Fletcher, *Humanhood*, p. 85. See also Fletcher, *The Ethics of Genetic Control*.

[35] Ramsey, *Fabricated Man*.

[36] A rather more up-to-date and sophisticated form of this argument has been offered by Bronislaw Szerszynski: B. Szerszynski, 'That Deep Surface: The Human Genome Project and the Death of the Human', in Deane-Drummond (ed.), *Brave New World?*, pp. 145–63.

[37] Ramsey, *Fabricated Man*, pp. 76–113. His main reason for rejecting IVF seems to be that it dispenses with 'mishaps', those embryos discarded as not worth implantation. Yet not only is it unlikely that such 'mishaps' would be viable, but deliberately to place damaged embryos into a womb would be considered irresponsible on the part of the medical practitioner. He also objects on the basis of the

basis that it undermines parenthood and family life. His argument here is a biblical one, that one should not split apart the union of love and procreation that is implicit in the prologue to John's Gospel.[38] Yet the categorical denial of the worth of parenthood achieved through IVF is neither self-evident nor borne out in the light of experience. Although similar arguments have been used against cloning, cloning involves the more extreme example of asexual reproduction, by contrast with IVF, which involves sexual reproduction, albeit outside its more usual context. Those who do achieve pregnancies following IVF often show a much greater degree of commitment to their children than those who bear children through 'natural' or in some cases 'accidental' sexual acts. Ramsey's argument does not ring true to practical experience, even though he is correct to raise the issue of family life in the context of genetic technologies. Genetic counsellors should help those faced with difficult decisions about whether to go ahead and try to have a child, in spite of the risks, through the means and options open to them. I suggest that the cultural trends inherent in technologies such as IVF, PND and PGD are of greater ethical concern than simply isolating IVF and naming it in terms of inadequate parenting.

An alternative approach, which is supported by Hauerwas, though not explicitly applied in the context of genetic technology, is one that draws on virtue ethics. I suggest that the precautionary principle is a secularised version of the tradition of prudence.[39] Given that this is the case, developing a prudential understanding along more Christian lines would seem to offer a mediating approach towards secular ethics. The precautionary principle allows for self-criticism of policy and practice in a way that fails dismally when a case-study approach is used, for attendance to individual cases necessarily narrows the attention of the observer on to the details and specifics of particular problems and dilemmas. I am not suggesting that we should never consider problematic cases, but setting policy simply on the basis of case analysis will not do, for we end up with a ragbag approach that fails to take into account the wider concerns of society and the need to work for the common good.

---

unknown risks of the procedure, though such risks are thought to be minimal today in the light of the experience of delivering healthy IVF children. Ramsey is worried because the child is not in a position to give consent, though presumably if PGD was used to prevent an unwanted disability, this is unlikely to be refused, as choice in this context is meaningless, as the affected child would not have existed.

[38] Ramsey, *Fabricated Man*, pp. 32–45; see also Ramsey, 'A Christian Approach to the Question of Sexual Relations Outside Marriage'; 'Shall We Reproduce? I. The Medical Ethics of In Vitro Fertilization'; 'Shall We Reproduce? II. Rejoinders and Future Forecast'.

[39] See Deane-Drummond, *The Ethics of Nature*.

Prudence, when viewed in a Christian way, becomes the means of deciding what it is to express a particular virtue, be it charity, justice, temperance or fortitude. It is one of the reasons why it is the first of the four cardinal virtues. Prudence, then, expands the notion of the precautionary principle by allowing precaution to be just one of the virtues associated with it. The others are memory of the past, insight into the present, shrewdness about the future, reason, understanding, and openness to being taught.[40] Memory of the past would, of course, include a deep awareness of the way the 'unfit' have been abused through genetic means in our recent history. Genetic counsellors have a greater sense than many other medical practitioners of the dangers and difficulties of treating those who are different as unfit members of the human community. Genetic counsellors also need to have insight about the present, that is, a clear sense not just of the genetic 'discoveries' being made in the name of science, but also of their social and cultural consequences. Shrewdness about the future is rather different from simply acting out of precaution, for it implies an ability to act which precaution does not; it implies realism about human motivations and tendencies to sin, as well as ability to achieve goals. Reason and understanding go together; they express the ability to synthesise information as well as simply to acquire knowledge. Doctors faced with the task of managing pregnancies may well resort to information-giving that lacks understanding and empathy in the particular situation facing an individual. Ironically, perhaps, even though genetic screening and testing are thoroughly individual in many respects and are presented as 'free choice', the communication by medical practitioners with those who are undergoing such tests can seem impersonal and even dehumanising. Openness to being taught would also include openness to learning from those with genetic disorders, as well as openness to acquiring knowledge through the latest research journals and projects. A Christian would argue that those who have learning disabilities have much to teach those who do not, so the tendency to render them as worthless members of a community or, worse, as not deserving to exist, needs to be challenged and confronted. Such attitudes and prejudices are hard to break; even the smallest degree of self-examination will show degrees of prejudice towards those who are different from us. However, prudential living requires us to take responsibility for such inner transformation of self, so that we learn to move beyond the barriers that have enclosed our lives through the absorption of unchallenged cultural prejudices.

[40] See Deane-Drummond, *Creation through Wisdom*, p. 100.

Ewald criticises the notion of prudence as leaving no room for the victim. He suggests that, according to this model, those who do not exercise it have no excuse; they have simply failed to express virtue.[41] However, this reading of prudence is faulty, for a number of reasons. First of all, prudence is closely allied to justice, which would include the principle of equal dignity and rights of all human beings. Secondly, I argue that there needs to be a greater sense of responsibility for one's own actions. In a risk society it is easy simply to follow the path of least resistance and to accept what seems to be the least risky course of action to take. But this is making a judgment on a narrow interpretation of risk and benefit, seen in a pseudo-scientific context, detached from wider social issues. Prudence, instead, encourages a sense of stillness, a silent contemplation that facilitates decision-making, rather than an impulsive reaction to perceived threat. Genetic counsellors not only need to display prudence in their decisions about what to tell or not to tell their clients; they also need to encourage this virtue in others. Thirdly, the precautionary principle does not actually tell us what to do; it is an element of prudence, which Ewald ignores, so it leaves us without any basis for activity as such. He tries to get round this by suggesting that it must remain 'reasonable', but what is reasonable action in the light of precaution? Surely this, too, is a form of prudence. Finally, from a Christian perspective the notion of prudence needs to include both fortitude, which is a sense of willingness to suffer for the sake of the good, and charity, the ability to love beyond what we might be capable of through our natural instincts.

The discussion would be incomplete without some reference to the virtue of wisdom in the context of genetic counselling. As the techniques for different methods of genetic testing and analysis become more widely known and recognised, those who find themselves in the profession of genetic counselling can usefully call upon wisdom as a motif for their activities. Wisdom in this secular sense means viewing things from a holistic perspective, not just taking in one narrow issue or factor, but trying to see the whole picture that looks beyond the immediate problem in hand. Such a virtue may be difficult, given the pressing and often anxious demeanour of those who approach genetic counsellors for help. However, without wisdom, genetic counselling will become simply information-giving that is detached from its social context. Rather than facilitate choice, it is more likely simply to bolster the establishment position in which genetic counsellors are located, namely the sub-politics of the

---

[41] Ewald, 'The Return of Descartes' Malicious Demon', p. 275.

medical profession. Wisdom in practice is, of course, another name for prudence, and in this context it is worth mentioning that prudential reasoning is not just confined to the individual or family, but that it reaches out to political and institutional organisations as well. It is one reason why PGD is an issue for both government and genetic counsellors; I suggest that it is virtually impossible to screen off the tasks of genetic counsellors as if they have nothing to do with broader genetic policies, however distasteful some of this may be to the practitioners themselves. In this context, one task of genetic counsellors may be the critical one of mediating between the wider medical professionals and those with particular genetic diseases, and of providing ways of introducing more ethical approaches to institutional policy-making.

Those in the Christian community will also seek deeper forms of wisdom that come as the gift of the Holy Spirit, rather than those that are learned as such through education or family life. One might even see the lives of those families that have a disabled child as lives that are specially blessed with the possibility of receiving the grace of wisdom. Yet it is in that suffering face that the face of God begins to show through, as Hauerwas suggested, and, in this, wisdom grows. What of those situations where a genetic disease has devastated a family, leading to situations of mistrust or even more extreme forms of depression and domestic violence? In these circumstances, claiming to find God in the suffering may seem somewhat shallow and unrealistic. However, Christianity cannot deny the ultimate faithfulness of God in spite of sin and devastation. In such situations, the virtue of wisdom is clearly insufficient, even if we see in it the dim reality of the wisdom of the cross.[42] It is here that the virtue of charity comes into its own, for no family or individual is an island; and the task of the Christian community is one of solidarity, not just in the sense of sharing our genetics, but also in the sense of sharing love and compassion towards those who find it impossible to love. Hence, the destructiveness of individual suffering needs to be set in the context of the wider social response of the community as a whole. In a cultural and social context that accepts those with disabilities, the possibilities for the isolation and devastation of relationships that I have just described are far less likely. The Christian community needs to be one that serves to create such an ethos of acceptance, so the task of wisdom would be to find ways to facilitate such change at all levels, individual, familial, community and political.

---

[42] Deane-Drummond, *Creation through Wisdom.*

CHAPTER 6

Gene therapies

The concern of this chapter is to interrogate those genetic practices that either directly or indirectly draw on genetic knowledge in order to change human functioning. It is important to elaborate, at the outset, what is known scientifically about the possibilities on offer arising out of genetic knowledge, as well as the implications of this knowledge. Our current state of knowledge about how genes work, for example, will give some indication of the prospects for both somatic gene therapy and inherited genetic modifications (IGM) of all kinds. Other areas that are relevant for ethical debate include those fields that draw specifically on genetic knowledge in order to design novel treatments for disease, as in, for example, stem-cell 'therapy'. In parallel with genetic screening, the ethical issues arising out of this burgeoning genetic knowledge include not only immediate cases to hand, but also wider social issues connected with the impact of medicine on societal and political functions, such as those concerned with autonomy, justice and community. I will argue for the relevance of situating prudential decision-making with the cardinal virtues of justice and temperance in order to discern the way forward in contested areas of ethical debate arising out of these relatively new technologies.

SCIENTIFIC ISSUES IN GENETIC INTERVENTION

Because genetic science is so complex, this section can do no more than highlight those areas that are relevant for an adequate understanding of the possibilities inherent in genetic modification in humans. The multi-million-dollar Human Genome Project, which sequenced the human genome in draft form, was completed at the dawn of this century.[1] Although this was heralded as a scientific breakthrough, there is an enormous gap between gaining an understanding of the sequence, relating this

---

[1] For further discussion of the science and ethics, see Deane-Drummond, (ed.), *Brave New World?*

to genetic function and malfunction in genetic disease, and translating this knowledge into clinically effective therapy. It is important to note that the genetic 'blueprint' is not sufficient to tell us both why humans are humans, and why some individuals suffer disease and others do not. Scientists, especially when they are communicating with each other, are quite prepared to admit that a veil of ignorance hangs over genetic knowledge. They are increasingly aware that the regulation of the human genome is much more significant than previously thought. In other words, saying that humans share 98% of their genes of chimpanzees, or that we share the bulk of our genes with mice, or even that we share 50% of our genes with daffodils, might imply that genetically we are related to plants, close to mice and even closer to primates. However, the same gene can code for very different phenotypes (in other words, physical characteristics). Why is this the case? The most likely explanation is that, while there are some clear differences in genes, there are also much wider differences in the regulation of expression of such genes.[2] If the regulation of the gene improves the number of offspring, then long-term changes arise out of such regulatory differences, including the possibility of new species. Evolutionary biologists have tended to speak about genetic variation in terms of genes, rather than acknowledge the significance of non-coding DNA that is now coming to light as a result of research in molecular genetics. Of course, scientists are not implying that such changes in regulation come about simply because of environmental factors, for, if this were so, it would lead to Lamarckian versions of evolution, where permanent genetic change is induced by environmental influences on individuals. While there may well be some such influences, these changes are not normally inherited, and the majority of regulatory processes are themselves coded for genetically, perhaps involving the so-called 'junk' DNA in between the 'genes' known to code for various functional proteins.

Some of the regulatory genes, such as transcription factors, will be identifiable as protein products, but others are likely to be much shorter stretches of DNA. Buried in the DNA sequence, therefore, is a highly complex 'regulatory code' that is of equal importance to the 'genetic code' specifying particular gene products. At present, simply by examining the sequence of DNA, researchers cannot predict the way regulation will work. Research in this field has really developed only since 2002. Regulatory DNA is also known as 'modules', and these are near or next to a gene. Those that stimulate DNA expression of a gene are called *enhancers*, while

---

[2] For an excellent article on this topic see Pennisi, 'Searching for the Genome's Second Code'.

those that suppress DNA expression are called *silencers*. Enhancers, thought to be small stretches of DNA about 500 base pairs long, have binding sites that, by virtue of their ordering and pattern, are able to influence which genes are 'switched on' and for how long. There may be as many as 100,000 enhancers and silencers in humans, but only 100 or so have been identified to date. Developmental biologist Cooduvalli Shashikant, of Pennsylvania University, has shown that changes in enhancer affect the vertebrae configurations in a range of different species, from zebrafish and pufferfish to mice. The importance to gene therapy of this fundamental research is that changes in gene regulation are likely to be important, not just in differences in gene expression between species, but also in disease function.

Another area of continued discussion is the genetic difference between primates and humans.[3] Popular books on genetics and ethics regularly make the claim that, since humans share 98% of the genetic code of chimpanzees, this means that there is practically no genetic difference between humans and primates. However, anyone who cares to make even a casual observation of the great apes will recognise that, while there are lines of continuity, there are also important physical, mental and social differences. While part of this difference is likely to be attributed to complex differences in gene regulation, which are only just beginning to be understood, the crude percentage measurements camouflage some important distinctions within genes. For example, close analysis of shared genes has shown that the gene called 'forkhead box P2 transcription factor', which is required for proper speech development, has undergone major changes in human evolution. Other human genes that showed greater than average divergence from a common ancestor were those coding for olfactory and hearing functions. The researchers were also surprised to find that many of the genes that they identified as undergoing rapid evolutionary change in humans were also responsible for disease. This may provide one way of helping to identify the genetic basis for disease.

Given this complexity, it is, perhaps surprising that scientists have achieved any deliberate changes in the human genome. By distinguishing between somatic gene therapy, which affects the body cells of a given patient, and germline genetic therapy, which affect gametes, scientists were able to win public support for somatic therapy in humans. They also distinguished, in both somatic and germline contexts, between 'therapy', used to treat disease, and 'enhancement', a term used to imply an

---

[3] A rough draft of the primate genome was published in December 2003. For discussion see Pennisi, 'Genome Comparisons Hold Clues to Human Evolution'.

improvement in 'natural' capacities. Many authors prefer to speak of inheritable genetic modification (IGM), rather than of germline therapy, since the former widens the discussion to include those changes that may or may not be beneficial for humans and successive generations.

One of the most common techniques for somatic gene therapy is the use of viral agents (vectors) in order to move the required DNA into the nucleus of cells. Of course, such viruses need to be disarmed of their normal disease function, and modified so that they carry the appropriate DNA. Retroviruses work when the amount of DNA to be transferred is relatively small, and when the target cells are actively dividing.[4] Genes that are normally responsible for the regulation of expression of the genes cannot normally be included, because of the limitations of size of transferable elements. Adenoviruses are alternative viral vectors, and have been used in cystic-fibrosis and cancer trials. These agents can carry larger amounts of DNA and are not restricted to dividing cells. However, the genes in the virus that normally code for suppression of immune response in the host cells are deleted to make room for the new DNA, which means that repeated doses have to be given, as the virus is subject to immune response from those receiving treatment.[5] Given that the newly introduced DNA rarely, if ever, combines with the host DNA at a given site on the chromosomes, it is surprising, perhaps, that somatic gene therapy is clinically effective at all. Therefore, the DNA expression is rarely regulated, and the dosage required becomes a matter for clinical trials, in much the same way as the clinical testing of pharmaceutical products.

So far, the diseases that have evoked clinical trials using somatic gene therapy include severe combined immunodeficiency (SCID)-X1 disease, using retroviruses; haemophilia B, using AAV virus vectors; and ornithine transcarbamylase deficiency and cystic fibrosis, using adenoviruses.

---

[4] For discussion of scientific methods, see B. Pathak, 'Scientific Methodologies to Facilitate Inheritable Genetic Modifications in Humans', in Chapman and Frankel (eds.), *Designing Our Descendants*, pp. 55–67.

[5] Adenoassociated viruses (AAV) have also been used, and so modified that they do not integrate into the genome at a specific site. Another technique uses liposomes, small lipid vesicles that act like carrier vehicles for either drugs or new genetic material. The vesicles may be modified so that they are less likely to be attacked by the immune system. Some cancer patients have received DNA using liposomes in order to delay progress of the disease. Liposomes might also be useful in order to carry artificial chromosomes that are still under development as a means for gene therapy. Artificial chromosomes have the advantage of being able to be carried to the next generation of somatic cells through mitosis, that is, the normal process of cell division. This technique has not yet proved to be clinically viable, partly because the centromere (or middle section of a chromosome) cannot, as yet, be duplicated in an artificial chromosome. For discussion, see Willard, 'Artificial Chromosomes Coming to Life'.

By 2002 there were over 500 gene-therapy protocols approved for evaluation in clinical trials, and by 2004 there were closer to 700.[6] Yet it is
important to note that many somatic gene-therapy trials are not specifically
geared to the treatment of genetically inherited diseases, but are targeted at
more general diseases, such as cancer. Patients may have a genetic propensity for a disease in a way that is not always identified prior to treatment. In
order to be effective in, for example, treatment of cancer, researchers need
to gain information on the specificity of target sites, the toxicity of gene
therapy and the possibility of novel vectors. Often gene therapy is tried in
combination with other conventional drug-therapy methods. The effectiveness of the genetic methods for the treatment of all diseases has been
somewhat patchy, and scientists are trying to design new ways to tackle the
problem. The treatment of cystic fibrosis is a case in point, in that, in spite
of initial great optimism about the effectiveness of somatic gene therapy, its
performance has been disappointing clinically. Scientists have endeavoured
to find other means for making treatments more effective. For example, it
might be possible to target gene expression at the mRNA level, rather than
at the DNA level, thus introducing short sections of DNA coding for an
RNA decoy that is then incorporated into the final mRNA required for
normal function.[7]

Rather more serious are those occasions where the somatic therapy itself
has produced negative or lethal side-effects. The most famous example was
the case of Jesse Gilsinger, who died in September 1999 following a somatic
therapy trial on ornithine transcarbamylase deficiency. Jesse was a healthy
eighteen-year-old volunteer, who, prior to the trial, suffered relatively mild
symptoms from the disease. His death occurred in phase 1 of the trial,
which was designed to test dosage levels. The lethal effects came from an
overreaction of his immune system to the adenoviruses used as vectors in
the trial, thus serving as a cautionary tale for other somatic therapy trials
using this method of delivery. While, subsequently, scientists found that
Jesse had a faulty immune system that may have led to the unusual
reaction, insufficient ethical stringency was ultimately responsible for his
death.[8] Although precautionary blood tests will help to prevent more
deaths from faulty immune functioning, the scientists concerned seem to
accept that unexpected risks are part and parcel of somatic gene therapy.

---

[6] Hunt and Vorburger, 'Hurdles and Hopes for Cancer Treatment'.
[7] Crystal, 'Fooling Mother Nature'.
[8] For Bostanci, 'Blood Test Flags Agent in Death of Penn Subject'. The FDA's reaction was to halt all
     gene-therapy trials conducted by the University of Pennsylvania; Marshall, 'FDA Halts All Gene
     Therapy Trials at Penn'.

In October and December 2002 the Necker Hospital in Paris admitted that two boys in a SCID trial had developed leukaemia because the retrovirus had inserted near an oncogene, LMO2. The likelihood of such an adverse reaction happening again is very difficult to discern accurately. Even more recently, in June 2004, a haemophilia trial involving use of the AAV vector carrying the gene for factor IX was halted because seven patients developed signs of mild toxicity.[9]

Given this uncertainty in relation to the safety of somatic gene-therapy trials, it is hardly surprising that few scientists are sanguine about the possibility of deliberate IGM. James Watson, the pioneer in the structure of DNA, is perhaps a notable exception, and is remarkably cavalier about the possible benefits and uses of IGM. For example, he suggests that we should 'never postpone experiments that have clearly defined future bene-fits for fear of dangers that can't be quantified', including any aspects of enhancement that might improve the characteristics of human beings for the better, such as the elevation of human intelligence.[10] This gives a somewhat distorted impression of the actual expectations of most scientists working in the field, who are generally rather less likely to succumb to scientism. There is also a genuine anxiety that some techniques, which are used to undertake somatic gene therapy, could also affect inheritable genetic material. The US Recombinant DNA Advisory Panel halted clin-ical trials of haemophilia B because there was some concern that the procedure might alter the inherited genetic material of the patients in the trial.[11] This risk was also evident in suggestions made as early as 1999 for *in utero* genetic transformations, where there was a perceived risk of genetic transformation of the precursor tissues for gonads.[12] The rationale for *in utero* treatment is that many genetic disorders give rise to irreversible damage before birth. Pre-implantation genetic diagnosis (PGD) is avail-able for only a restricted number of genetic diseases, and not all parents will want to pursue this route. So far, *in utero* treatment has succeeded in animals, but has not yet been tried in humans. There is also ongoing research to improve the specificity for action of inserted DNA, but, while this has been achieved in human cell cultures,[13] it has not, thus far, been

[9] Kaiser, 'Side Effects Sideline Hemophilia Trial'.
[10] Watson, *Passion for DNA*, pp. 228–9. For further commentary, see C. Deane-Drummond, 'How Might a Virtue Ethic Frame Debates in Human Genetics?', in Deane-Drummond (ed.), *Brave New World?*, pp. 225–52.
[11] Marshall, 'Panel Reviews Risk of Germ Line Changes'.
[12] Zanjani and Anderson, 'Prospects for In Utero Human Gene Therapy'.
[13] Such results were published *in vitro* some years ago; see, for example, Guo et al., 'Group II Introns'.

successfully used in clinical applications. Other apparently novel techniques for correcting DNA defects were initially reported in 1996 to be a
million times more potent than standard methods, but the results have not
been repeated.[14]

What might be the most likely means of achieving IGM in the future?
Given the complexity of the genome, there is the ongoing worry that the
newly introduced DNA could have undesirable and unforeseen consequences. The alteration of even one of the 3 billion nucleotides in the
human genome can have severe or even life-threatening outcomes.[15]
Nonetheless, forms of genetic modification are being developed that do
not so much introduce new DNA permanently in the cells as 'repair' the
function of an existing mutant gene. In this method the regulation of gene
function would remain intact, so there is no need to introduce more DNA
in order to code for regulatory aspects. Scientists have developed short
strands of DNA containing both a duplex binding domain (DBD) and a
normal repair domain (RD), which together make up triplex forming
bifunctional oligonucleotides (TFBOs). These TFBOs can bind to the
existing double strand of DNA at specific sites, alongside a mutant gene.
In a fraction of the cells, the RD invades the existing duplex of the DNA
while it is replicating, so that the resulting DNA is normal rather than
mutant. The procedure is only about 1% efficient.[16] Other techniques
under development involve a combination of RNA and DNA, again
with the same result in view, namely the repair of existing DNA. The
risk of unwanted changes using these methods is thought to be relatively
small, since the cells degrade the oligonucleotides, and they do not induce
an adverse immune response.[17]

The most likely candidates for initial alteration using IGM are spermatogonia cells, that is, the cells responsible for producing male sperm.

---

[14] Taubes, 'The Strange Case of Chimeraplasty'.

[15] K. W. Culver, 'Gene Repair, Genomics and Human Germ Line Modification', in Chapman and
Frankel (eds.), *Designing Our Descendants*, pp. 77–92.

[16] Another, similar technique involves the use of single-stranded DNA in the mutant region, known as
small fragment homologous replacement (SFHR), which leads to the same end result, that is, repair
of the existing DNA.

[17] It should be noted that even oligonucleotides can induce changes in RNA expression. As part of any
safety protocol, RNA from treated tissues would need to be measured, as well as changes in proteins.
The most efficient way of marking such changes would be to use RNA chips and protein chips,
which would be used to detect subtle changes in RNA and protein expression in human tissue. RNA
chips, for example, work by exposing fluorescent-tagged RNA molecules derived from patients to
chips containing millions of DNA single-stranded molecules on glass or silica wavers. Protein chips
would work in much the same way, except that antibodies would be used on the chips instead of
DNA. The antibodies, like DNA, serve as binding sites.

Kenneth Culver believes that such studies could provide a model system for other IGM changes.[18] In this scenario the germinal stem cells could be modified and then injected back into the man. It is unclear how effective such a transformation would be, so it is worth bearing in mind that many scientists believe that targeting embryonic stem cells or cloned cells would be the easiest way of approaching most other cases for IGM. The embryonic stem cells would need to be viable for implantation, and for this the most likely technology that would be used is a cloning procedure, that is, the transfer of a somatic nucleus into an enucleated egg.

It is worth asking at this juncture what are the realistic scientific possibilities for IGM in clinical practice in the immediate future.[19] The availability of PGD in the minds of some, at least, alleviates the pressing need to pursue IGM, since the mutant gene is selected against prior to implantation. Many clinical practitioners are therefore pessimistic about the practical applicability of IGM, because there are alternative, safer methods that 'screen out' genetic disease. But other scientists are more positive about the need for IGM from a clinical point of view, while recognizing that if somatic gene therapy became efficient enough, it might alleviate the pressure for IGM.[20] Some couples may object to PGD, but are willing to consider modification of sperm, since such a process would not involve the destruction of embryos. Ironically, perhaps, such a 'model' system could then be used to develop strategies for IGM for other 'enhancement' purposes. Possible candidates include the introduction of tumor suppresser genes, suppressor genes for rheumatoid arthritis, and γ-IFN, which protects against infections. Extra copies of these genes would be a preventative rather than a 'therapeutic' strategy, in advance of the appearance of the disease. Such a procedure would sit uneasily at the borderline between enhancement and therapy, since it takes the form of preventative medicine and protection against disease, rather than of therapeutic treatment to alleviate an existing condition. Presumably, candidates targeted for such a treatment would be those with a pre-existing genetic disposition for the disease in question.

Prior to such expansive changes in genetic intervention, a more likely clinical application of the new genetic knowledge is the development of targeted drug therapy, based on the genetic profile of particular candidates.

---

[18] Culver, 'Gene Repair, Genomics', pp. 87–9.

[19] For a review, see R. M. Blaese, 'Germ Line Modification in Clinical Medicine', in Chapman and Frankel (eds.), *Designing Our Descendants*, pp. 68–76.

[20] C. H. Evans, 'Germ Line Gene Therapy', in Chapman and Frankel (eds.), *Designing Our Descendants*, pp. 93–101.

The potential medical benefits of detailed knowledge of a patient's genetic profile are one motivation behind the genetic database collection discussed in chapter 4. Gefitinib, or Iressa, is a drug that inhibits the tyrosine kinase activity of the epidermal growth factor (EGF) receptor activated during tumour growth in lung cancer.[21] Patients who respond to the drug have mutations in the EGF receptor, though, so far, a diagnostic test for this mutation has yet to be developed. Herceptin, developed by Genentech, allieviates an aggressive form of breast cancer by blocking a growth-related protein receptor called HER-2/*neu*.[22] Only those patients who carry the HER-2 gene can be treated with Herceptin. The diagnostic test is aimed at the molecular detection of the protein receptor, rather than at the gene itself. Unsurprisingly, the same company sells both the diagnostic kit and the drug associated with the treatment of sensitive patients. This form of treatment relies on molecular knowledge of the disease in terms of genetics and expression.[23]

ETHICAL ISSUES IN GENETIC THERAPY

The aim of this section is to explore more fully the ethical debates both arising more directly out of the scientific analysis of genetic therapy, while also being conscious of wider social issues in which such analysis is embedded.

Somatic-gene therapy

Some religious writers have concluded that no specific ethical issues are associated with somatic-gene therapy; it is simply another means of treating a patient, using gene probes rather than drugs.[24] However, while this is

---

[21] Editorial, 'Toward Tailored Cancer Therapy', *Science* 304 (4 June 2004) 1409i.

[22] Service, 'Recruiting Genes, Proteins, for a Revolution in Diagnostics'.

[23] Most of the proteins expressed in complex diseases, such as cancer, have an unknown genetic base. In these cancers one developing technique is trying to identify the very complex patterns of protein expression in particular cases without full knowledge of the functions of individual proteins. It leads to what some have termed 'clinical proteomics'. DNA chips have reached a more advanced stage and have been used in a number of clinical trials where the genetic defect is known to cause a particular disease. Most of the studies have targeted forms of breast cancer or mutiple myeloma. Louis Staudt's research on lymphatic cancer and a specialised gene chip suggested that the genetic profile of patients could be used to predict which ones were the most likely to recover. However, in spite of the promising research, commercial pressures may mean that many of these diagnostic approaches do not go far beyond the research stage.

[24] See, for example, early discussion by A. Dyson, 'Genetic Engineering in Theology and Theological Ethics', in Dyson and Harris (eds.), *Ethics and Biotechnology*, pp. 259–71.

true to some extent – in that there are no obvious reasons in principle why somatic-gene therapy as such is any less ethical than other medical treatments – I suggest that such blanket approval can too often foreclose the need for a careful ethical approach to the technology, and for the lessons that can be learnt from its use in other genetic applications. New technologies both carry a higher risk and are more likely to be highly lucrative if they prove successful. Arguments for enhancement of characteristics using somatic methods have also met with opposition from the start, not least because of the likely exaggeration in respective benefits on a global scale, exacerbating the differences between the northern and southern hemispheres. In addition, it is enhancing technology that is likely to be the most lucrative in terms of sales and market opportunities.[25] While the ethical issues associated with somatic therapy for specific diseases may not be particularly controversial, it is important to stress the need for adequate ethical review, especially where the techniques used for somatic therapy become possible models for IGM.

The case of Jesse Gilsinger, who died as a result of a gene-therapy trial (discussed above), is a good example of the controversy surrounding an application that raised a number of significant ethical concerns. In the first place, the director of the Institute for Human Gene Therapy, James Wilson, had a financial stake in a company that Wilson founded in order to develop the technology. The likely personal financial gains raised important issues about the overlap between scientific and financial portfolios.[26] The FDA investigated the institute and found that it fell foul of both clinical protocol and regulatory requirements. Adverse effects had been found in monkey trials, and the patients were not given sufficient information about the potential risks. Jesse Gilsinger's father sued the research team and settled out of court for an undisclosed amount. Jesse's death served to tighten up regulation on somatic gene therapy in all adenovirus trials. Additional US legislation was introduced in order to increase the supervisory aspects of human gene-therapy trials, responding directly to these ethical concerns.[27]

In October and December 2002, however, more problems arose with the X-SCID trial in France, where two young boys being treated for the disease developed leukemia. In this case there had been prior studies with

[25] S. Holm, 'Genetic Engineering and the North–South Divide', in Dyson and Harris (eds.), *Ethics and Biotechnology*, pp. 47–63.
[26] Marshall, 'Gene Therapy's Web of Corporate Connections'.
[27] For discussion, see Spink and Geddes, 'Gene Therapy Progress and Prospects'.

monkeys, suggesting the potential mutagenic effects of retroviruses and their cancer-causing potential. It is not clear how much risk might be posed in other retroviral studies, which is one reason why trials have stopped in some countries (such as France and Italy), while in the United Kingdom the trials are reviewed on an individual-patient basis depending on a number of factors, such as the seriousness of the disease; in the United States, the temporary moratorium on clinical trials was lifted after a year.

The Gilsinger trial raised procedural issues to do with a lack of attention to the enabling of adequate informed consent. Of course, it may be difficult in practice to achieve properly informed consent because of the difficulty in explaining the detailed science behind genetic trials.[28] But should we effectively give up on this aspect by admitting that 'what patients really consent to is placing their faith (and life) in the hands of the physician/scientist'?[29] Søren Holm argues convincingly that consent for medical intervention that is achieved because patients are vulnerable, in that they are dying anyway, is ethically acceptable, as the patient is coerced by *nature*, not by the researcher.[30] Consent also has to be informed; that is, minimally, the participant is to be given clear information about (a) the objective of the research, (b) the role of the research subject and (c) the risks and inconvenience involved. Jesse Gilsinger's case was significant, as he was in the first phase of the trial, which was in effect to test out any toxic effects of the treatment on humans. He was not suffering from a life-threatening disease, and some have queried whether it would have been more appropriate to conduct this phase of the trial on those sufferers (mostly babies) who were at high risk of death prior to treatment. However, in these cases it might have been difficult to test efficacy, and there were worries that parents of such babies might feel coerced. Yet, if Holm's criteria on coercion were applied in this case, then coercion would be one induced by nature, not by the researchers involved; though of course the parents would be giving the consent. The motives of the researchers were also mixed in this case, since they were clearly in a position to make considerable financial gains once the method was released on the market for patenting and sale. Jesse offered to help out of a sense of wanting to bring forward research into a disease that afflicted so many others more severely than him. He could be said to be a 'martyr' for such a cause, though it is very

---

[28] See, for example, discussion in P. R. Lowenstein, 'Gene Therapy for Neurological Disorders: New Therapies or Human Experimentation?', in Burley and Harris (eds.), *A Companion to Genethics*, pp. 18–32.

[29] Lowenstein, 'Gene Therapy for Neurological Disorders', p. 26.

[30] S. Holm, 'The Role of Informed Consent in Genetic Experimentation', in Burley and Harris (eds.), *A Companion to Genethics*, pp. 82–91 (p. 85).

doubtful that he would have offered to help in this way if he had been properly informed about the fatal risk associated with the early phase of the trials.

These outcomes have led some authors to suggest that there is an inherent risk in all somatic gene-therapy trials that will be impossible to predict with any certainty.[31] In both the cases in the United States and France, however, there was a failure to take into account published research in monkeys that indicated that it would be inappropriate to continue with the trials. The deeper question, therefore, is *why* such research was brushed aside, and the most likely explanation is that there was too much haste in clinical application because of the lucrative gains predictable from patents on the process.[32] Some scientists are inclined to suggest that somatic gene therapy is bound to involve some risks, which may occasionally be fatal, just like any form of drug treatment. The fact that adverse drug reactions are the sixth leading cause of death in the United States, however, does not amount to an adequate ethical argument in support of slackening ethical responsibility with respect to somatic gene therapy. Any death, especially if it could have been foreseen, amounts to an unacceptable diminishment of humanity. It is, therefore, somewhat disturbing to note that gene-therapy trials often compress phase 1 and phase 2, which combine dosage effects and efficacy, and then miss out phase 3 trials, which are larger-scale trials aimed at detecting rare side-effects. In effect, gene-therapy trials move straight into phase 4, so that 'as soon as some evidence of efficacy is produced, the therapy often enters routine clinical use immediately'.[33] By calling such treatment 'therapy', rather than an 'experimental trial', those patients who are subject to such treatment are not given the same kind of protection as true research subjects. Religious commentators on somatic gene therapy, who tend to endorse such practices without adequate scrutiny, have not, apparently, noticed such difficulties.

The use of somatic therapy *in utero*, although not yet attempted, is also under discussion and regulatory guidelines were drawn up for its use in 1998 (UK) and 1999 (USA). One of the main ethical concerns is related to the possible impact on the inheritable genetic material of the foetus. There is also the ethical issue of not being able to obtain informed consent – though this presumably would also be the case for other drug treatments used *in utero*. As a minimum standard, there is a need to strike a balance between the risks to the mother and the risks to the foetus. Although the

[31] Spink and Geddes, 'Gene Therapy Progress and Prospects'.
[32] For a wider discussion of gene patenting, see the next chapter.
[33] Holm, 'The Role of Informed Consent', p. 87.

conclusion reached by the regulatory authorities in both the United States and the United Kingdom was a moratorium on the use of *in utero* treatment, some scientists would like to see the discussion reopened in the light of ongoing preclinical research. Of course, with the advent of PGD and PND, there is a lowered incentive to develop such methods. However, from an ethical point of view, as long as there could be adequate monitoring of outcomes in terms of likely effects on the germline and other risks, *in utero* treatment would be worth considering, since it avoids the ethical difficulties associated with PGD and PND. Therefore, to view such methods as the *status quo*, not in need of alternatives, is, in my opinion at least, a diminishment of ethical reasoning.

There has also been the suggestion that *in utero* somatic gene treatment that inadvertently led to IGM should simply be accepted; after all, drug treatments also unintentionally affect the germline.[34] However, in those cases it is an *adult*, rather than a foetus, who is treated with potentially mutagenic agents, and the adult has the possibility of the removal of their gonad stem cells or ovaries for later reimplantation after treatment, as well as the possibility of informed consent. In other words, the cases are not equivalent. Of course, one might argue that, from the patient's perspective (in this case that of the foetus), it would be better to have a life, with the possibility that deleterious genes in subsequent generations would indirectly result from *in utero* gene-therapy treatment, than to have no life at all; but this would in no way alleviate the need for careful scrutiny of unintended IGM, so that such genes were genuinely unintended, rather than simply thought of as an inevitable unfortunate side-effect. The most liberal approach might even lead to *in utero* experiments becoming 'test cases' for IGM. This would be an unhelpful strategy to adopt, since, while it might draw something good out of an unfortunate accident, to have this in place as a policy decision would lead to a cavalier attitude to the possibility of IGM that would be extremely ill advised. To suggest that unintentional IGM should be accepted in the light of naturally incurred spontaneous mutations and the instability of the genome[35] is again somewhat presumptuous about the risks associated with those changes caused by human intervention.

---

[34] For a discussion, see Blaese, 'Germ Line Modifications in Clinical Medicine', pp. 73–4.

[35] While it is true that the background of spontaneous mutations needs to be known in order to assess the true level of unintended IGM, this does not reduce the need to be vigilant about human induced changes. Blaese, 'Germ Line Modifications', pp. 74–6.

Inherited genetic modifications

The ethical discussion of IGM has tended to polarize around the acceptability, or not, of therapeutic treatments (those designed for the treatment of disease) and those treatments known as enhancements, which elevate desired characteristics of an individual in terms of specific functioning. IGM is currently banned in most jurisdictions, largely because of fears over the safety aspects in the light of available scientific techniques. This has not stopped many ethicists, including religious ethicists, speculating for some time on the ethical implications of IGM technology.[36] Almost without exception, the ethical evaluation among both scientists and bioethicists alike is that the current state of knowledge renders IGM unacceptable at present, because of the clear risks associated with an insufficient understanding of the processes involved, and lack of adequate and safe means to introduce new genetic material into the inherited material. An exception is the case of mitochondrial disease, in which case faulty eggs could be given a fresh 'boost' by treatment from a donor's cytoplasm. Of course, another ethical issue appears in this case, namely that the resulting egg would have genetic material from two maternal sources, a human chimera. More general discussions have been aired in religious ethical circles for some time, so much so that Robin Gill, in commenting on Audrey Chapman's book on the ethics of genetic science, remarks that 'there are as yet only so many points to be made about the merits or otherwise of novel, but circumscribed, areas such as genetic engineering or reproductive cloning'.[37] Yet, since 1999 the field of somatic genetic therapy has exploded, the possibilities of IGM have come closer, and the ethical debates continue. Much of the religious discussion entails a debate between the ethical acceptability of 'therapy' over against 'enhancement', with more liberal positions endorsing both, more conservative views rejecting both, and intermediate positions arguing for therapy but not enhancement.[38]

It seems to me that we should not give up on ethical engagement with the issues, which inevitably raise important questions over and above

---

[36] See discussions in, for example, Dyson and Harris, *Ethics and Biotechnology*; Peterson, *Genetic Turning Points*; Cole-Turner, *The New Genesis*; Deane-Drummond, *Biology and Theology Today*; Song, *Human Genetics*; Shannon, *Made in Whose Image?*; Harris, *Clones, Genes and Immortality*; Shannon and Walter (eds.), *The New Genetic Medicine*; Peters, *Playing God?*; Smith and Cohen, *A Christian Response to the New Genetics*; Vardy, *Being Human*; Bryant and Searle, *Life in Our Hands*; Hui, *At the Beginning of Life*; Chapman and Frankel, *Designing Our Descendants*; Coors, *The Matrix*.

[37] Gill, 'Review: Unprecedented Choices'.

[38] See discussion in C. B. Cohen and L. Walters, 'Gene Transfer for Therapy or Enhancement', in Smith and Cohen (eds.), *A Christian Response to the New Genetics*, pp. 53–74.

simply how to engage with novel techniques. In the first place, we might challenge whether the distinction between enhancement and therapy is particularly helpful. From a scientific perspective it is clear that some 'treatments', such as those to support an immune system, would be 'enhancements', but would protect against the onset of a disease. Secondly, the distinction implies that there are 'normal', or 'desirable' features of human life that, when missing, invite therapy. But who is to say what this normalcy entails?[39] Hence it is unclear whether the distinction will provide a sufficient guiding line for moral decision-making, apart from giving a crude indication of what is not acceptable at one end of the enhancement spectrum. An alternative ethical approach would be to use prudential reasoning in order to arrive at a decision in each case, rather than a simple labeling according to 'enhancement', or 'therapy', which tends to bias automatically in favour of the second. The latter is particularly in evidence in the discourse on stem cells, which I will discuss in more detail below. Some new techniques may be more acceptable than others, and we need to find a way to decide which ones are permissible, other than simply extrapolating from what has gone before. The case of Jesse Gilsinger is a good example; until this time (1999), many ethicists had a permissive attitude to somatic gene therapy, failing to take into account both the risks it posed, and the temptation to overlook these risks in the interests of commercial success. Those scientists who were actively engaged in the Jesse Gilsinger case have reacted similarly: there was too much haste, so that there is an admission that 'some clinical applications have simply outstripped scientific understanding of the disease model or the properties of the vectors, representing an army too far ahead of the supply lines'.[40]

There is also a range of positions that could be taken with regard to IGM, assuming that the risks could be avoided. The most liberal thinkers believe that IGM needs to be integrated into other aspects of medical care, but see no reason in principle to resist the technology, including so-called enhancement, that introduces desirable characteristics into the human genome.[41] Underlying such views is a liberal politics that believes that an overriding good is the individual choice of the agent. As long as consent is

---

[39] This issue was discussed by a number of authors in Deane-Drummond, *Brave New World?*

[40] Friedmann, 'Principles for Human Gene Therapy Studies'. His suggestion that some deaths must be expected in clinical trials, as for any new advances, was not only insensitive, given the recent death of Gilsinger, but also dubious as an ethical policy, as it could lead to complacency about fatalities and to paying insufficient attention to safety and other precautions.

[41] John Harris is a staunch advocate of this position; see, for example, his *Clones, Genes and Immortality.*

gained, therefore, IGM should be permitted. Of course, this avoids to some extent the possibility that consent might be gained by future generations. The reply John Harris often makes, namely that such generations have similarly been 'subject' to the social conditions imposed by prior generations, ignores the likely irreversible nature of IGM. Further, to suggest simply that these changes could be removed later also ignores the fact that those on the receiving end are themselves limited by such choices, in that IGM changes the options that are available to them in a more drastic way than environmental changes, which could, in theory, be altered in someone's lifespan. In addition, under a philosophy that has been called 'post-humanity', or even, 'transhumanity', there are serious academics who are arguing that human capacities should be pushed ahead on all fronts, regardless of the past, without restraint, in ignorance of social impacts, and simply in the hope of perceived enjoyments and higher human capacities in the future.[42] Such a philosophy fits neatly into the technophile aspects of youth culture, and so is likely to convince many of those who subscribe to what we might call the computer generation; the borderline between artefact and human becomes one that is automatically welcomed, rather than resisted.

Given this shift towards an interest in all things artificial in the service of perceived gains, it is hardly surprising that there has been a backlash against these technologies by some philosophers. While Francis Fukuyama has been criticised for his lack of attention to scientific detail, especially in the cases of genetic engineering that he discusses, his book, *Our Posthuman Future*, sounded particular alarm bells about the possibilities for negative effects on human identity raised by human genetic engineering. More recently, Bill McGibben has joined the fray, arguing that the ability to say no, to say *enough* when it comes to the new technologies, is what distinguishes us from the animals.[43] Mere lust for more and higher capacities clouds our human capacity for compassion for those without such capacities, and renders us blind to human suffering. Jürgen Habermas, in his book *The Future of Human Nature*, is similarly sceptical of much of the modern biotechnology project, believing that only very limited cases of IGM would be warranted, perhaps those associated with severe and life threatening disease. All these writers view genetic engineering as just one example of the relationship

---

[42] Space does not permit a detailed discussion of this movement. It is worth noting that philosophers in such established universities as Oxford are promoting this position; Nick Bostrom, for example, is one of the most active proponents of transhumanity. See Bostrom, 'Human Genetic Enhancement'.
[43] McGibben, *Enough*.

between humanity and technology, though in this case the argument made is that the interventionist technology threatens to change who we are as persons as well.

How valid is this criticism? Is there a middle way between the somewhat facile acceptance of technology by those in the more extreme liberal camp, and its rejection by the critics of post/transhumanity? It is clear that many scientists, at least, cannot identify with the cultural movement of trans-humanity that seemingly draws on its activities in order to support its claims. For many clinicians, the desire for genetic engineering comes simply in response to a medical challenge, rather than from a more sinister desire to change human nature. Of course, it might be possible to argue that rendering what is acceptably normal in genetic terms as the base line for gene therapy effectively damps down the differences between human beings, and uses a medical model for what is normal and, by implication, acceptable. The chances that IGM will become so widespread as to lead to such population effects is, however, far-fetched, especially as there has been no hint, so far, that those having carrier status would be genetically modified. But, while these population effects are unlikely, we need to ask more closely what such technologies serve in terms of particular human interests. Who gains most by such technologies? Is it the sufferers themselves, or the multinational companies armed with patent rights? If such techniques became an aspect of a public healthcare system, who would have access to the technology, and what other areas of medical provision might be affected?

These questions represent utilitarian arguments about gene technology, that is, those predicated on the outcomes of particular decisions. As well as the social risks mentioned above, it is important to bear in mind that it is very unlikely that all possible risks will be fully known and understood before the technology is approved. Somatic gene therapy is a case in point. In addition, some technologies may be more readily acceptable in principle than others. For example, even if one has some hesitation about perma-nently changing inherited genetic material, it seems to me that there are fewer inherent objections to *repair* mechanisms, which aim to correct DNA so that the mutant reverts to wild type, compared with those techniques that add additional DNA to the existing genome. There may be other novel ways round the problem, such as use of artificial chromo-somes that would be unrecognized by the immune system – but this again raises issues about permanent changes to genetic makeup.[44]

---

[44] Artificial human chromosomes in a hybrid with mouse centromeres have passed from one gener-ation to the next in experiments on mice. See Willard, 'Artificial Chromosomes Coming to Life'.

Theologians are divided about the acceptability or otherwise of IGM, while most are more inclined resist enhancement techniques. Paul Ramsey, for example, famously declared that we should not learn to 'play God' before we have learnt how to behave responsibly as humans.[45] His comments, made at the dawn of genetic engineering, when optimism about the possibility for genetic change was at its highest, need to be seen in this context. Others, nonetheless, have questioned the wisdom of tampering with the genome through IGM, reflecting, perhaps, a sense that our genetic makeup serves to set our biological limits of being. Ted Peters argues that much of the religious resistance to changing the genetic makeup of humans reflects an unwarranted philosophy of genetic determinism.[46] Yet is this a fair criticism? Certainly, anyone who believes that our genetic code completely determines human behaviour has failed to understand the complexity and subtlety of genetic knowledge. In fact, it is this subtlety that should give us pause for thought, for one might doubt whether it would ever be possible to remove all the contingencies associated with changes, expect perhaps in a few isolated cases where there are known single-point mutations leading to serious disease. I suggest, therefore, that the science should give us pause for thought, and a means to resist the somewhat wild speculations of transhuman philosophers.

Another area worth considering in this context is the methods and means to arrive at the desired ends. While we may debate which genetic changes might be acceptable or not, the *means* to achieve such ends also needs to be taken into account. If those means draw on cloning technology, where embryos are routinely destroyed, new ethical concerns are raised relating to the perceived status of the human embryo. Similar ethical debates rage over the use of stem cells to treat human disease, where these are derived from embryos left over from *in vitro* treatments, derived *de novo* from embryos created for the explicit purpose, or cloned using enucleated eggs and somatic nuclear transfer. The fact that this has become an important political and public issue became very clear in the run-up to the US elections in the autumn of 2004, when John Kerry used his stance on stem cells to try and win over public support for his campaign.[47]

In the latter context it is worth noting with some care the way the language used in discussions about the science can serve to influence the ethical conclusions reached. For example, stem cells had their roots in the nineteenth-century science of teratology, which was concerned with the

---

[45] Ramsey, *Fabricated Man.*   [46] Peters, *Playing God*, pp. 1–26.

[47] Malakoff, 'The Calculus of Making Stem Cells a Campaign Issue'.

science of malformations in the embryo, or 'monstrosities'.[48] Embryonic stem cells were linked with the monstrous properties of teratomas, teratocarcinomas and parthenogenetic growths. Teratomas are a mix of undifferentiated stem cells and varieties of differentiated tissue that are disorganized in structure and have no co-ordinated function. Teratocarcinomas can, like embryonic stem cells, become established cell (EC) lines and show unregulated growth. Embryonic stem (ES) cells are, in many respects, analogous to cancer, and tumors are often derived from the failure of resident stem cells to differentiate. It is worth noting how ES cells would have been perceived a century earlier, namely as a 'monstrous growth', that is a growth without limits; but a century later they become not so much pathological as sources of healing and regeneration. It would, therefore, have been impossible for the early scientists to view such cells as having therapeutic potential. Perhaps the close connection between EC and ES cell lines should give us more pause to reflect on the pathogenic potential in ES cells. The lack of attention to the risks associated with ES cell treatment reflects the enthusiasm of many scientists to develop the technology. It is also thought that ES cells derived from cloned embryos, which are advantageous in that they are less likely to lead to an immune reaction, may also increase the risk of cancer. In addition, as mentioned above, transformation of ES cells combined with cloning is the most likely route to be recommended in order to achieve IGM. Such a route would, it seems to me, be unethical as a means to achieve the goal of IGM. While a case might be made for the use of stem cells from spare IVF early embryos, which would have been destroyed anyway, to treat someone suffering from a lethal disease, the use of cloning technology to achieve such cells, either for the treatment of disease or for IGM, would be unacceptable, since it would destroy potential human life either for an existing life or for another life that has not yet come into being. Such a projected life would not have an ethical claim on the other life that is deliberately created and destroyed, even if, arguably, one might press the case for balancing the claim of a life that is dying with early embryonic life originally intended for reproduction that would otherwise be destroyed.[49]

---

[48] Cooper, 'Regenerative Medicine: Stem Cells and the Science of Monstrosity'.

[49] Note that even in the latter scenario it would be preferable to opt for the more conservative position, since there is no reason, *per se*, why embryonic stem cells, which are therapeutically more potent than adult stem cells, could not come from spare IVF embryos, assuming that a tissue match is possible. Scientists are right to claim that it is technically easier to use 'cloning' to achieve this end, but the ethical difficulties outweigh such technical advantages. See also Deane-Drummond, *The Ethics of Nature*, pp. 124–9.

Are there any specific ethical issues associated with targeted drug treatment? This technology is likely to mushroom in the future, and deserves rather more attention than it has previously been given. The heated speculation on IGM may have clouded due attention to the pharmacogenetics that is evolving very rapidly in Western societies. It is also likely to become embedded in mass screening programmes and database collection, which raise their own ethical issues, as discussed in chapter 4. This technology might seem to be the answer to clinicians' prayers for targeted treatment for individualised patient care. However, it is worth pausing to consider what impact universal applications of these methods might have on patients themselves. In effect, we would *all* become patients, all with a 'disease liability' profile that could be targeted by certain arrays of drugs. No wonder the monitoring of the relationship between human genomics and disease is becoming a government-sponsored project in the United Kingdom, for it seemingly opens the possibility of tailored treatment that would cut costs at the clinical level and ensure that only those likely to benefit would receive the expensive drugs to hand. However, such amassed knowledge raises issues about confidentiality; employers and insurers would have a keen interest in gaining access to such information for their own assessment of risk. Who would really want to know of all the diseases that are likely to affect them in the future? Would it raise the levels of anxiety in the human population to such an extent that there would be an increase in use of neuropharmacological drugs?

REDISCOVERING THE VIRTUES OF PRUDENCE, JUSTICE AND TEMPERANCE

So far, the ethical arguments for genetic intervention in human beings have broadly divided into spheres. Much of the secular debate concerns whether it is right or wrong because of the positive or negative consequences, either immediately, because of the perceived benefits or risks to the patient, or related to longer-term social goods or ills. The latter would include discussions about social justice. There is little resistance to somatic gene therapy in principle, other than among those currently guiding clinical practice. Marilyn Coors's approach is, perhaps, an exception, in that she attempts to devise a grid or matrix that takes into account varied ethical insights arising out of principles, consequences and virtues, so that every possible development in IGM is screened according to whether it meets the following criteria: benefit, justice, responsibility, valuation of difference, integrity, discourse, and wisdom.[50] While this proposal is interesting, it is not entirely clear how we might decide what amounts to demonstrating such characteristics; in other words, it would be difficult to arrive at a neutral position for any of these criteria. Her notion of wisdom includes 'ultimate ramifications', but it is important to ask what this might mean, in concrete terms. I suggest that the specific virtue of prudence, combined with justice and temperance, is helpful in this context, because of the temptations towards greed, a narrowing of ethical discussion to immediate impacts rather than giving wider consideration to social justice, and too-hasty action stemming from the highly competitive nature of biotechnological applications. Prudence, with its threefold activity of deliberation, judgment and action, includes the possibility of slow and careful deliberation where new technologies are introduced for the first time. While there will always be some unknown risks, it seems to me that there was a lack of prudence in the cases discussed above that have had serious side-effects. Rushing ahead with clinical trials without taking sufficient account of the available research on primates is a case in point. The figure of Folly in the biblical wisdom literature is one who acts in haste, without adequate preparation.[51]

Prudence also includes the possibility, not only of individual prudence, relevant for those developing the technologies, but also of familial and political prudence. It is relevant to consider familial prudence where genetic technologies are situated at the borderline of reproductive and regenerative biology. Stem-cell therapy, for example, might be perceived from a scientific point of view as a kind of somatic gene therapy; the tissue to be treated is likely to be defective genetically because of the disease it harbors, and the stem cells make up for this loss, providing a source of fresh, healthy cells, without any complications such as arise from the viral carriers of DNA used in somatic gene therapy. In those cases where the patient has a genetically inherited disease, the stem cells will need to be genetically modified prior to injection into the diseased tissue. If stem cells are derived from adult tissues, this poses few ethical questions other than the safety of the techniques used and the possible side-effects of the treatment. Yet stem cells, where they are derived from either embryonic or cloned embryonic sources, are also implicitly life-giving in another sense; that is, they have a potential to become a human being, rather than just to serve as a regenerative tissue source for another human

---

[50] Coors, *The Matrix*, pp. 127–46.
[51] See discussion in Deane-Drummond, 'Come to the Banquet'.

being. The ethical question is related to the prevention of the flourishing of human life, rather than to causing direct harm to the embryo as 'personal'.[52] Those attracted to utilitarian arguments will generally play down the means used to achieve a good end, and focus on the beneficence achieved in alleviating the suffering of the patients using this form of therapy.[53] Those attracted to deontological arguments will be more concerned about the principle of using human embryos or embryonic tissue, treating the potential life of this human being as the vulnerable 'neighbourly' life that has need of ethical protection.[54] From the point of view of prudence, when considered in a familial sense, it is also vital to consider the relationship between parties. For stem-cell therapy using somatic nuclear transfer from 'body' cells of the patient – in other words, therapeutic cloning – the source of new stem cells depends on the destruction of an early blastocyst. Of course, if there could be a way, scientifically, of telling the difference between partly reprogrammed cells that could produce ES cells, and those which are known to be potent in creating an embryo, this would avoid the ethical concerns of even the most conservative ethicists. In other

---

[52] Most conservative positions equate the beginning of personhood with the moment of conception of an embryo. David Jones, for example, in his book *The Soul of the Embryo* (published as the present volume went to press), puts forward a case that the 'soul' of the embryo is embedded from the moment of conception, and such a high status is the dominant view in Christian history. His views are likely to find acceptance among those who are already committed to a conservative position on the status of the human embryo. While his book provides a valuable resource on historical debates, other Roman Catholic historians, such as Jean Porter, take a very different stance towards contemporary issues. See Porter, 'Individuality, Personal Identity'. His position also seems to endorse a form of genetic determinism, in which personhood or ensoulment is quite literally determined by our genetic makeup. This downplays the importance of the environment, and of implantation in particular, as essential for human formation; equating the start of development with conception misses the point here. Hence I would argue that a gradualist view can still give some status to the human embryo, even if it is not as high as the most absolute position would wish. A gradualist view does not, in other words, automatically lead to the most liberal policy on the use of stem cells and cloning in the way Jones seems to imply. The ethical harm in destroying early embryos, for a more conservative gradualist, which I find the most convincing position to adopt, would be indirect; that is, the possible prevention of human life from growing and developing, rather than the literal destruction of a person. Further, we are not required to draw the line where Aquinas suggested, namely when he considered the possibility that rationality might be present some forty days following conception. While the most conservative stance arguing for protection from the moment of conception is the easiest in terms of where to draw the line for more stringent protection, and also gives, perhaps, a greater sense of security for those who believe, this position seems to me to resist the possibility of prudential discernment in this area, for it forecloses discussion in much the same way as an absolute liberal stance. A gradualist can give value to the early embryo, but not to the same degree as later in development.

[53] See, for example, T. Peters and G. Bennett, 'A Plea for Beneficence: Reframing the Embryo Debate', in Waters and Cole-Turner (eds.), *God and the Embryo*, pp. 111–30.

[54] See B. Waters, 'Does the Human Embryo Have a Moral Status?', in Waters and Cole-Turner (eds.), *God and the Embryo*, pp. 67–76.

words, if scientists could partly reprogramme a somatic cell so that it was able to produce more effective stem cells (i.e., it became pluripotent), while still having no inherent potential to produce a human being (i.e. without becoming totipotent), perhaps by relocating these cells in an artificial medium rather than in an egg, then these cells could be treated more like the tissue from which the cells were derived, rather than as an early embryo. So far, because human cloning is banned under the law, it is impossible to say whether pluripotency is also implicitly linked with totipotency. Unfortunately, scientists are unable to make this distinction, so the ethical dilemma remains. Some authors regard the need for a suitable environ-ment for viability – that is, an intact blastocyst and uterus – as ethically significant,[55] but this does not avoid the ethical dilemma associated with the prior destruction of potential human life that this technique entails. In addition, isolating egg elements in order to generate stem cells would not, as Harris seems to suppose, avoid the ethical difficulties, since such stem cells could still have totipotency if placed in a suitable environment.[56] His suggestion that the use of enucleated animal eggs avoids the problem ignores the ethical difficulties associated with the creation of chimeras. While I would resist giving such an early embryo the full status of person-hood (and in this context I believe that speaking in terms of 'neighbour' is not particularly helpful), there is room to argue that what these cells might become also needs to be taken into account in ethical decision-making. In this sense the embryonic stem cells become connected in an oblique way to *familial* relations, rather than simply being a tissue transplant from a healthier part of the body. Would families agree to such treatment if it were presented to them in this way? Does informed consent load the response by referring to stem cells as regenerative sources, ignoring their historical connection with teratocarcinomas? Virtue ethics also is careful about intentions, and of course this factor needs to be taken into account; the intention is to work for the healing of the patient, which is a good aim. Yet Aquinas is keen to point out that even if the aim is good, if the means used to achieve this aim are suspect, this leads to what we might call *sham prudence.*[57] However, prudence will try to balance the intention of the

[55] Towns and Jones, 'Stem Cells, Embryos and the Environment'. For further discussion see Song, *Human Genetics.*

[56] Harris, 'The Ethical Use of Human Embryonic Stem Cells', p. 162.

[57] This is one of the forms of sham prudence; see Aquinas, *Summa Theologiae,* 2a2ae q. 55.8. For a discussion of the different facets of distorted prudence, see Deane-Drummond, *The Ethics of Nature,* pp. 12–13.

actors, the means used to achieve the ends, and the overall effects and impacts in arriving at a right judgment.

It is in those cases that are less clear-cut that the greatest ethical difficulties arise, and the possibility of mistakes in ethical judgment need to be acknowledged, so that it is never too late to review a policy or guidelines. This has particular relevance at the political policy-making and regulatory level, which needs to adjust in the light of new evidence and prospects. In the United Kingdom in the summer of 2004, the Human Fertilisation and Embryology Authority (HFEA) granted researchers in Newcastle licences to use stem cells generated by cloning technology in order to conduct research on therapeutic treatment for those who are suffering from diabetes. The research will involve genetically modifying the stem cells prior to treatment. The decision is in itself controversial, for the reasons indicated above; and I suggest that this policy needs to be open to review in the future in the light of further ethical, public and scientific discussion. Regulatory bodies in the United States have been criticised as simply means through which scientific developments gain public approval, without the need for a tight legal system, rather than anything more stringent in terms of appraisal. In other words, regulation is seen as something of a sham process through which scientists can achieve their goals, while hiding under the cloak of a regulatory body. It is particularly important that the HFEA does not come to be seen in this light, or adopt liberal policies that simply follow scientific developments without careful consideration of ethical issues from a range of perspectives, as well as genuine public appraisal. It is always tempting in a culture that gives approval to 'evidence-based' styles of medicine that the loudest voices will come from those sections of society that offer hard scientific facts. Nonetheless, the fact that the HFEA set up a citizens' jury of young people in order to listen to their views on 'designer babies' is a hopeful sign in this context.[58]

Much of the anxiety about the impact of IGM concerns not just immediate effects, but also the unknown impact on future generations. Consideration of the impact on future generations is an important ethical quandary, since it sits at the border of consequentialist and deontological theories about ethics. Secular ethical theories do not seem to be able to deal adequately with ethical questions about future generations. Of course, the most liberal will reject the idea that an impact on future generations has any ethical significance, arguing that we should not really concern ourselves

---

[58] Citizens' Jury on Designer Babies, sponsored by the Wellcome Trust and held in Cardiff in September 2004. The summary report, *The Verdict*, is available from the HFEA.

where there is no definite harm envisaged. The most extreme view is that only actions that entail the risk of extinction of the species are morally questionable.[59] While I would argue that there is far more to human identity than genetic essentialism, genetic changes stand to set the *biological boundaries* within which human flourishing takes place. There is, therefore, a moral imperative to consider such issues very carefully, rather than brushing them aside as irrelevant to contemporary concerns.

Rachel Muers has discussed the question of responsibility towards future generations in a helpful article in connection with environmental problems.[60] Some of this discussion is relevant to particular questions about genetic technologies for future generations. Discussion of the responsibility to future generations in a modern context is related to our ability to change the conditions in which humans exist by our impacts on the external environment. However, I suggest that this question is deepened still further by the possibility of changing not just our external conditions, but our genetic makeup, which evolves in relation to such conditions. For this reason an analysis of human responsibility needs to take account of *both* genes *and* environment. Does IGM represent a radical break with the past, a moving into a new human future that is unprecedented, in such a way that those future persons will barely recognise themselves in their historical antecedents? Or is it a continuum with respect to human history, as humanity has always pressed and will continuously press towards a goal of progress? Is it a destabilisation of what it means to be human or not? While we may not expect 'the possibility of a catastrophic breakdown of the conditions of social existence', in the manner projected for environmental collapse, the possibility of an alienation from self if IGM is taken continuously towards its scientific limits needs to be set alongside the more positive view that each generation has its own capacity to exercise freedom and capacities and to pass these on to future generations.

We sense intuitively that we have responsibilities towards future generations, but this clashes with the difficulty of giving any such future persons rights or other contractual means of having a relationship with those existing in the present. It is one area where rights language comes up against its own limits, reciprocity is impossible, and we reach an 'incoherence of talking about merely "possible" persons as objects of ethical concern'.[61] Of course, in reproductive biology 'possible persons' as embryos have become objects of moral concern, but the two situations are different,

---

[59] S. Holm follows Hans Jonas in this respect. See Holm, 'The Role of Informed Consent', pp. 88–9.
[60] Muers, 'Pushing the Limit'.   [61] Ibid., p. 41.

for, short of freezing such embryos for another generation, discussion about future generations represents persons who have not yet even begun to come into existence. Does a communitarian philosophy fare any better? Muers argues that it does not, for a community is itself bounded by particular limitations, including its propensity to break down and its inability to secure indefinite continuity (pp. 41–2). She is also correct to challenge the notion that belief in eternal life *necessarily* means that humanity will be unconcerned about the impact on future generations; one might equally argue that timeless value and shared meanings actually make consideration about future generations more relevant for ethical concern. Yet, while the language of intergenerational responsibility may indeed open up questions about the ultimate and penultimate, which Muers takes from Bonhoeffer's ethics, it would be a mistake to imply that this gap is the only place where theological ethics can gain a voice. In other words, while theological reflection can find an opening where philosophical ethics reaches a limit, this should not imply, as Muers seems to suggest, that theology is most useful only in such contexts. To adopt this understanding might suggest a theological ethic of the gaps, filling in where secular reasoning breaks down.

How might intergenerational responsibility fare from the perspective of a theological approach to the virtues? I suggest that this connects with the philosophical intuition that future generations matter, set amid the virtue of wisdom, which is the intellectual virtue that connects everything with everything else, including humans and God in relationship. There is a sense in which wisdom has an eschatological dimension, for we can ask: is this the future of creation that God intends for humanity and the earth, or not?[62] Does the future, envisaged in God, lend itself to this development, and how do we know what this future entails? The practical element of prudence that is worth considering in this context is *foresight*, the ability to anticipate what the future might bring about.[63] Prudence directs decisions in such a way so as to maximise, through foresight, what would honour God and work for the good of humanity and the natural environment. While prudence cannot predict, in advance, what might happen to future generations, by concentrating on circumspection in the light of the future possibilities, it has the capacity to take the needs of those future generations into account. The following considerations are relevant in this context.

---

[62] For a discussion of the relationship between creation and eschatology in the context of wisdom, see Deane-Drummond, *Creation through Wisdom*.

[63] Deane-Drummond, *The Ethics of Nature*, pp. 14–15.

Would it be honouring to God to enhance human capacities for future generations so that they move beyond what is currently possible today? If so, which human capacities might be changed? How would a coming generation judge the action of present actors on their behalf, and what might they wish for? In other words, is it possible to imagine ourselves into the future to such an extent that we have at least some empathy and compassion for those who follow in our footsteps? Or would such enhancements make it more difficult for humanity in the future to accept human limitations and finitude, an illicit grasping towards immortality? Or, given the limited availability of such treatments, would such enhancements create a new social sub-class of persons who consider themselves superior to those who have not had such enhancements? What are the resource implications, in terms of cost both to human society at large and to the natural environment? Or will parents be subjected to such strong pressure to deliver such enhancements to their children that they believe that they ultimately have no choice?[64] If limits are imposed, who decides what these limits are, and can they be revised? Who is responsible for watching over the stretching of these limits, which has become characteristic of allied fields such as genetic screening in reproductive medicine? These and other related questions make up the ingredient of foresight in prudential decision-making.

Since prudence is closely linked with justice, a prudential approach to justice serves to set the mean of this virtue, so that it becomes orientated towards the common good. Thus, through foresight, those elements of action that might lead to situations of injustice would be resisted. Justice as virtue is that which judges by external rules and boundaries, and in this sense differs from prudence, which is more about an internal disposition towards correct decision-making, taking into account a number of different factors. Does it make sense to talk about justice towards future generations? If justice is measured merely in terms of human rights, it certainly becomes philosophically difficult to sustain coherence. However, justice as virtue means that, through empathy, the present generation can try to envisage what intuition demands, namely, that those unknown people in the future deserve to inherit those conditions appropriate for a rich human life. While it is easier, perhaps, to envisage what this might mean in terms of environmental resources, the availability of human resources and the richness available in human being and becoming also

---

[64] A. Newson, 'Is There a Cost in the Choice of Genetic Enhancement?', in Almond and Palmer (eds.), *Ethical Issues in the New Genetics*, pp. 23–38.

needs to be taken into account. Attempts to reduce biodiversity in the human population makes sense only where it is recognised definitively that the human species would be better off without that variation. Sickle-cell anaemia is a good example, where the mutant gene led to protection against malarial infection. Fortunately, given the way genetic disease has evolved, any prospect for complete removal of a gene is somewhat remote.

Temperance as virtue also makes sense in those cases where it is clear that IGM arises out of motives that are not so much about providing good for the human community as about an incessant drive for progress or for profit. Temperance, or knowing what can satisfy our basic needs, does not imply lack of joy in life or of enthusiasm or fascination for scientific discovery. It does, however, set such discoveries in the context of human life as a whole, creating a balance in attitude so that the real motivations of those involved in a given activity are uncovered. What may be entirely appropriate as an academic exercise in understanding genetics may not be appropriately applied to clinical medicine. Temperance reinforces the tendency of prudence to apply caution, and to set limits to given developments. A philosophy that avoids discussion of temperance, or is disdainful towards it – such as the transhuman philosophy – runs the risk of overreach, of making claims for humanity that are appropriate for only a minority of the population as a whole.

How realistic might this turn to the virtues be in the context of the secular debates and current controversies on human genetic interventions? Underlying this position is another theological precedent, namely that virtues evolve in the context of a reformed understanding of human freedom.[65] Where human freedom is judged to be freedom of choice, initiating an ethic that depends simply on parental or patient consent, then autonomy trumps the other virtues for which I have been arguing in this and earlier chapters. However, while the possibility of human sin cannot be ignored, it seems to me that a convincing approach to bioethics is one that recognises the importance of being human. Such a view seeks to challenge those who equate humanity with human autonomy to the isolation of other goods; they are revealed as those who are holding on to an impoverished position that has arisen in the context of modernity and Enlightenment philosophy. In addition, while the theological virtues of

---

[65] I have discussed the importance of human freedom in the context of modifications to inherited genetic material in other work. See, for example, C. Deane-Drummond, 'Freedom, Conscience and Virtue: Theological Perspectives on the Ethics of Inherited Genetic Modification', in Cole-Turner (ed.), *Design and Destiny*.

faith, hope and charity will inform those in the Christian community, parallel virtues of compassion and trust are also inherent in secular philosophical debates about responsibilities towards others in the human community. So the approach being argued for here finds common ground with those secular theorists who argue on the basis of virtue ethics, but also situates such virtue within a theological view of the place of humanity on earth. Freedom for excellence, that is, freedom that is orientated towards the common good, facilitates the development of the virtues; it is the air in which the virtues can breathe. While an overriding virtue in this respect is charity, prudence helps orientate the believer towards correct decision-making under charity, and towards the common good. Where there is a clash between a secular understanding of what this might mean and a Christian understanding, the virtues that are relevant are not only humility (the readiness to admit both the strength and the limitations of one's knowledge) but also fortitude (the readiness to challenge and confront where the developments go against what prudential reasoning has discerned as the common good). Such fortitude has the ability to resist where it becomes obvious that the motivations for action are evil, though the ability to discern good and evil is a task of prudence. It is those cases that are ambiguous in ethical terms that are most difficult to discern. It is in these cases that slow deliberation is required, for, over time, the process of weighing arguments on both sides becomes clearer and more transparent. As well as charity, prudence presupposes faith – that is, a commitment to see good ends as ends under God, and the means to achieve such ends as means under God. Arguments alone will never entirely convince, which is one reason why a theological interpretation of the virtues makes sense, for it situates virtues in the richer context of theological virtues arising in the human community.

CONCLUSIONS

I have argued in this chapter that insights into the present state of genetic knowledge give some important indicators of the prospects and possibilities for human genetic interventions. In particular, unravelling the complexity of the regulation of gene expression qualifies any concept that knowledge of the sequence of human genes is sufficient for understanding the complexities of the human genome. The hidden code becomes another Holy Grail that geneticists are actively pursuing, though, even when this is discovered, further complexities and unresolved difficulties will remain. There is a sense, in other words, in which geneticists seem more prepared to admit than, perhaps, was the case even a decade ago that there are severe limitations in our knowledge of human genetics. New examples of this trend occur all the time; for example, the thirty or so genes on chromosome 21, once thought to be important in expressing the characteristics associated with Down syndrome, are not thought to be sufficient to cause characteristic symptoms, thus making therapeutic treatments based on the modification of these genes or their products less likely.[66] Even the partial success of attempts at somatic gene therapy is surprising, given the level of complexity involved in gene regulation. More careful and detailed comparative analysis between humans and primates shows that humans have diverged in key areas in terms of the molecular evolution of certain genes, so any popular understanding of genetics that suggests that humans are virtually equivalent to apes in genetic terms needs to be challenged. While a discussion of the genetic or other sociobiological or cultural basis for human behaviours was outside the scope of this chapter, deliberate reflection on what is permissible or not in terms of genetic intervention is undoubtedly a characteristic of humanity alone.

In a discussion of the gradual development of somatic gene therapy, I drew attention to the use of viral vectors in transmitting new portions of DNA into cells. The safety of somatic gene therapy is qualified both by the specificity of vectors to target particular cell types and insertion points on the genome, and by the immune reaction of the patient to these invading agents. Clinical trials on humans also relied on prior animal and primate experimentation, but in some cases these results seem to have been overlooked. The web of corporate connections in this case was predicated on the possibility of extremely lucrative patent rights for such treatments. In the case of Jesse Gilsinger, the code of ethical practice that is recognised as being minimally required in terms of giving of sufficient information for the person in the trial to make an informed consent was blatantly brushed to one side. While this oversight may not have been deliberate, succumbing to the temptation to take short-cuts in order to speed up the process, and sales, of the therapeutic protocol shows a degree of folly that amounts to more than simply distorted prudence. Nonetheless, the general response of the global community to this crisis has been to tighten up regulatory control. While some scientists may resist this, overall it seems to me to be in the public interest, and to represent a good example of political prudence.

---

[66] Gould, 'Key Genes May Not Create Down Syndrome'.

The ethical issues raised by pharmacogenetics are more complicated in that they relate to patient rights over personal information and over the political pressure to release such information to insurance companies and employers keen to have the knowledge. In addition, the pressures that pharmacogenetics will bring to bear on patients' own sense of psychological well-being need to be taken into account. Will we all become patients now, given that we will all have the propensity to contract diseases, to greater and lesser extents? Will I really want to know which diseases I, or my children, will be likely to suffer in my lifetime or theirs? If DNA chips become more readily available in clinical practice, which diseases will be targeted, and how might this affect the allocation of healthcare resources? Would those who are unlikely to respond to a given treatment be abandoned as lost causes? The virtue of political prudence is needed in order to help shape this developing science and to challenge the market-led approach that seems to be dominating the evolution of new drugs. If this is to have a realistic chance of happening, the Government will need to develop strategies for fostering the development of targeted drugs that are going to be of most benefit for the common good, rather than simply being developed in response to the global market economy.

In utero genetic modifications sit uneasily at the boundary between somatic therapy and intentional IGM, as they raise the possibility of unintentional IGM. While any virtue ethics will argue that *intentions* are important, the shift towards IGM is recognisably a highly significant move to make. The situation is somewhat ambiguous ethically, as one could argue that it represents a positive move towards the *treatment* of genetic disorders, rather than simply offering termination as the only alternative to continuation with the pregnancy. Yet, on balance, a prudential judgment would, it seems to me, hold the moratorium on this process for sufficient time to allow the safety aspects to be addressed, including the likelihood of transfer to precursors of inherited genetic material. Of course, one could argue that gaining a life with instruction not to reproduce would be better than no life at all, but such a restriction would amount to an unacceptable infringement of civil liberties. Scientists would also need to be wary of the possible negative impact that germline modifications may have on the public mind; whether such modifications are intended or not would seem less important than the fact that they had been achieved. Any suggestion that *in utero* experiments could in some way use foetuses as guinea pigs for the subsequent development of IGM seems to me to be unethical, and to fail to respect what is due to the foetus, even though in law a foetus does not have 'rights' as such.

The scientific development of IGM would need to proceed very cautiously and, in my opinion, be limited to severe genetic diseases where these can be corrected safely using 'repair' methods that do not introduce new elements into the genome. In addition, while some of the safety aspects would be alleviated if embryonic stem cells were to be used – cells derived from cloned embryos, or even developed into spermatogonia cells or egg cells[67] – serious ethical questions still surround this technology. Testa and Harris argue that stem-cell technology would allow infertile couples to reproduce, using cloning technology to produce the embryonic stem cells that are then used to create gametes. However, this would be to use an unacceptable means, namely the destruction of human life through cloning, towards a good end, that is, a cure for infertility. The resulting gametes could also be genetically modified, hence providing another route towards IGM. While it might be argued that, in the case of therapeutic cloning for disease, the ethical claim is for one potential life against one that is dying, in this case the procedure is even more problematic, since it involves the destruction of life for a life that has not yet come into existence. Harris argues that conservative attitudes to stem-cell therapy are ill founded, as couples regularly accept the near inevitability of the natural 'destruction' of embryos in the course of trying to have a baby in natural conception.[68] For him, the positive good of having a baby accepts the early destruction of embryos. By extension, he argues that it is more rational to accept that the positive good of saving a life in therapeutic treatments makes such destruction acceptable. In much the same way, he could argue for the positive good of treating infertility.

Infertility is an agonising and traumatic condition that afflicts many millions of couples throughout the world. Yet, while the intention of IVF is to generate as many healthy embryos as possible, the intention of this cloning method for the creation of 'artificial' gametes, which may or may not have been modified at the stem-cell stage, would be the deliberate destruction of early embryos for the sake of gamete production. In other words, there is an important distinction between the good envisaged in human reproduction, and the goods envisaged in embryonic stem-cell technologies. If there were a way, scientifically, of retrieving all those embryos conceived using IVF that are known to be unviable, this might

[67] For discussion of the ethics of gamete production from stem cells see Testa and Harris, 'Ethical Aspects of ES Cell-Derived Gametes'.

[68] J. Harris, 'The Ethical Use of Human Embryonic Stem Cells in Research and Therapy', in Burley and Harris, *A Companion to Genethics*, pp. 158–74.

make the technique of stem-cell generation more acceptable. What Harris has in mind in the discussion of 'artificial' gamete production, however, is the use of cloning technology to generate stem cells, which are then induced to form gametes. Production of 'artificial' gametes through cloning technology attempts to overcome some of the ethical problems associated with human cloning in that sexual fertilisation is necessarily prior to the final generation of the embryo that is to be implanted. But what if this method failed? The use of cloning to generate gametes would encourage the movement towards complete reproductive cloning of the individual if cloning failed to deliver gametes in the manner anticipated. Human cloning is made particularly problematic by its reliance on asexual reproduction, with its associated identity problems for the child thus produced.

There are also other possible techniques on the horizon, relating to cloning technology, that could be used in the future either for fertility treatment or for the treatment of serious diseases. One is to use enucleated animal eggs to produce oocytes containing animal mitochondrial DNA with the diploid human DNA from a somatic source. The technique has been possible for some time, since American researchers combined an enucleated cow egg with a salivary cell nucleus. It is argued this technique should have wider application, as there is a current shortage of human eggs for research. The human DNA seems to dominate the resulting cell lines, but traces of animal mitochondrial DNA are still present. So far, this technology has not been used in the treatment of human disease. Given the correct chemical treatment, human eggs can also divide spontaneously as if they had been fertilised. The term used for this, parthenogenesis, is strictly speaking something of a misnomer, as the egg requires chemical activation, and the procedure therefore differs from the cases occasionally found to happen spontaneously, none of which are viable. Both the human–animal hybrid and the parthenotes could be induced to produce stem cells; in other words, they could be used as a source for treatment of disease or to model research. At first sight, both of these techniques look like ingenious solutions to very practical medical problems, namely the shortage of an adequate supply of eggs or stem cells for the treatment of disease. Also, given the similarity between animal and human DNA, would the eventual introduction of very small amounts of animal DNA into human cells be an issue of concern?

Why, then, would I hesitate to endorse such techniques? In the first instance, I think we need to draw a distinction between modelling a disease for research purposes and its use in the actual treatment of disease. The approval by the HFEA in February 2004 of the use of therapeutic cloning for modelling motor neuron disease relates to its use as a model system in developing new drug therapies.[69] But one might ask, in this case, how far it was really necessary to use specifically embryonic stem cells as model systems, even if it could be argued that this is much more efficient in the actual treatment of diseased patients. The nature of the disease also has to be life-threatening. This partly relates to the perceived status of the early life that is under consideration. While I would reject the concept that such life forms have the status of personhood, such life is still human life, and needs to be treated as having value. Neither the animal–human hybrid nor the parthenotes is viable in the strict sense of having the potential to become viable embryos (that is, they would probably fail to implant). Yet the life that they embody is still human life, and we simply do not know how far such life could develop, as, thankfully, the experiment has not been undertaken. The fourteen-day limit for the creation and use of embryos still holds, but there is increasing pressure to raise this limit. This illustrates once more that 'therapeutic' cloning opens the way to other, related technologies that are even more ethically ambiguous. At the very least, for policy-making, there needs to be a moratorium on the use of such technologies in medical practice until time for adequate political discussion and public debate has elapsed. Another new technology being developed, namely inducing an adult stem cell to dedifferentiate so that it can become pluripotent, strikes me as just another way of manipulating cells so that they behave like early embryos. Of course, if there were a way of separating the pluripotency so achieved from embryonic potential, that would amount to a breakthrough in the research, as cells that were simply pluripotent would not carry the same ethical ambiguities.

What if *adult* stem cells could be induced to form 'artificial' gametes and thence be used for fertility treatment? I have already mentioned the use of embryonic stem cells in this respect, discussed by Harris. The answer to this partly depends on the answer to the preceding question, namely how far pluripotency can be distinguished from embryonic potential. A further technique for the creation of artificial gametes involves an initial somatic nuclear transfer into an enucleated egg, followed by the reduction from a diploid set of chromosomes to a haploid set, a process that normally happens to egg cells undergoing their first cell division. The egg cell that results would have to be fertilised in the normal way, and at first sight this seems more acceptable than the other techniques so far discussed. If it were

---

[69] Ian Wilmut, the 'father' of cloning, was given a licence for this research. See the report by M. Henderson, 'Cloning Gets Green Light to Find Cure for Nerve Disease', *The Times*, 9 February 2005, p. 22.

used with enucleated eggs from a donor, which seems likely, then the ethical difficulty relates to the combination of mitochondrial DNA from one maternal source with the somatic nuclear source. Of all the processes suggested to create artificial gametes discussed so far, this one seems to me to be the most acceptable from an ethical point of view. It is, of course, a form of inherited genetic modification, as in this case there would be a combination of mitochondrial DNA from one egg with nuclear DNA from another egg. Considerable care would need to be given to the welfare of any resulting child, in much the same manner as the current regulatory process set up for donor eggs. In addition, it would be more acceptable to use eggs that are already surplus to requirements in existing IVF treatment, as in the current 'egg-share' schemes available, rather than to take more potentially exploitative measures involving payments, which could take advantage of economically vulnerable women.[70]

Another approach to infertility that is currently under discussion is the IGM of spermatogonia, using gene-transfer techniques. Once the technique was developed it could, perhaps, be applied to other inheritable genetic conditions involving male sperm, where the couples concerned were unwilling to use PGD. Although this seems like an attractive ethical possibility at first sight, since it does not involve the destruction of embryos, one needs to consider the long-term implications. The technique provides for the means of development of IGM methods that could be used for other applications that would be less defensible, such as the one outlined above, combining cloning and gamete formation. It would, for example, be difficult to hold the line between therapy for treatment of a disease and enhancement. This is one reason why I have argued for restriction of the therapy to serious, life-threatening diseases, using systems of repair rather than the introduction of new genetic material.

Finally, I have argued throughout for a recovery of the virtues of prudence, justice and temperance, in the light of both current philosophical discussion and the shift towards liberal politics of the market in setting the agenda for the ethics of genetic interventions. Even liberal writers greet the possibility that a man could become the source of eggs using cloning technology with a certain amount of caution, though they note that a homosexual couple would still need a surrogate woman to harbour such an embryo. Yet the overall positive

---

[70] Although payment for donated eggs is, at the time of writing, vanishingly small, this is likely to change following public consultation conducted by the HFEA in 2004–5. The European Tissue Directive, which prohibits monetary payments for human tissue, will act as a brake on excessive payouts; the payments should reflect considerable levels of 'inconvenience' for donors, rather than be seen as a monetary reward for the 'selling' of eggs.

appraisal of such a move by Testa and Harris demonstrates that the only ethical consideration seems to be that of safety.[71] Those who might resist such notions on philosophical or theological grounds are dismissed as following unwarranted versions of natural-law theory, where the natural is pronounced good. While the authors compare this technology with the early days of IVF, as is common among more liberal proponents of new genetic technologies, the possibility that seems to be ignored is the historical location of stem cells in the science of 'monstrosities', and its derivation from the latent potential of that science. It seems very unlikely that such difficulties could ever be overcome, and scientific researchers would be advised to search for other means to overcome infertility, rather than promoting bizarrely novel techniques in the interests of a false sense of political correctness. Of course, once the experiments have proved successful in animals, then discussions about legitimacy or otherwise in the human sphere become more relevant. Yet we need to ask serious questions about the reasons why such experiments are even being considered. Is this a good example of *curiositas* run amok, a lack of temperance, and indeed lack of prudence? Such drastic changes in reproductive treatment need to be resisted using the virtue of fortitude, for such a change would, it seems to me, be counter to the common good, both in principle and in terms of use of resources.

This discussion illustrates how cautious we need to be when it comes to initiating changes that will affect not just the present generation but the following generations. I have argued that, while the secular ethical approach to future generations reaches a limit, in that it has no real way of dealing with the issues, an ethic that draws on the theological ground of the cardinal virtues in the speculative virtue of wisdom enables such considerations to come into view. Wisdom is also relevant in that it helps to resituate theology in an overall discourse about human genetics, without alienating those who are committed to secular philosophy, since wisdom is also a good that can be understood in scientific terms as that human characteristic which recognises complex elements in any debate. Of course, the questions of what wisdom is, and how it might be expressed in terms of science and theology, are outside the scope of this chapter. Suffice it is to say that, once it becomes grounded in practical wisdom, prudence gives some guidance about how to act, while recognising the possibility of mistakes and the need for revision and further reflection. In the following chapter I will take up in more detail the vexed issue of gene patenting, mentioned in passing here, and the ethical debates about the validity of such a means of protecting clinical applications of gene technology.

---

[71] Testa and Harris, 'Ethical Aspects of ES Cell-Derived Gametes', p. 1719.

CHAPTER 7

Gene patenting

Patenting of genes, whether of non-human or human origin, raises strong reactions both within and outside the Christian community. There are some who argue vehemently that nothing living or of biological origin should be subject to patent law. Others argue, equally passionately, that without patent protection the funding for expensive research and development would be impossible. There are philosophical and religious reasons why many oppose patenting of life forms. These include, for example, the contention that knowledge and 'life' can never be treated as 'property'. Religious opposition can either focus on the idea of going beyond acceptable limits, similar in tone to objections to gene therapy, or raise broader concerns about the common good and about justice issues in terms of access to those goods. The resistance to outright, absolute objections to DNA patenting has shifted the discussion to more specific questions about the consequences of DNA patenting and its scope.[1] For the purposes of this chapter I will outline more precisely what patenting law entails and contrast the position in the United States with that in the European Union when dealing with biological materials. Case studies, especially controversies surrounding the patenting of stem cells, help to illustrate the limitations of the legal frameworks developed in Europe and the United States. I will also seek to address the question of how far the churches have sought to influence developments, and, in the light of wider issues covered under the TRIPS (Trade Related Intellectual Property) Agreement, consider the suggestion of the Human Genome Organisation (HUGO) about benefit-sharing. Discussion thus far has concentrated on deontological and consequentialist ethical arguments.[2] While it is important

[1] David Resnik discusses the arguments for and against DNA patenting in his book *Owning the Genome*. While he makes brief reference to religious arguments, his discussion is more focused on legal, philosophical and scientific issues.
[2] Resnik's comprehensive philosophical survey allows for deontological and consequentialist approaches, but does not mention virtue ethics. This is, perhaps, surprising, as he does try to develop a more synthetic approach using the precautionary principle. Resnik, *Owning the Genome*, pp. 10, 110–12, 125–6, 196–7.

to consider such arguments, I suggest that it is equally important to include in the discussion some consideration from a virtue-ethics perspective. Above all, I will argue that as a human community we need to take greater responsibility for fostering the common good by considering the virtues of prudence, justice, fortitude and temperance as those virtues orientated specifically towards its development.

WHAT IS PATENTING?

Henry VI first granted a UK patent to John of Utynam in 1449 for his method of making stained glass. John had to teach others his trade in return, making his method public; a more common reaction by manufacturers then was to keep their methods secret. Patents gradually became part of the commercial life of the nation. In the United States the first patent law to be introduced in 1793 covered 'any new or useful art, machine, manufacture, or composition of matter, or any new or useful improvement thereof'.[3] Congress replaced 'art' with 'process' in 1952. At the turn of the last century ornamental-plant lobbyists campaigned to include plants within patent law, so that in 1930 a US Plant Patent Act established the right to patent new cultivated varieties, but held back from permitting patenting of 'wild' varieties in the field. At this stage the Act limited protection to those plants that could reproduce asexually. Human intervention was, of course, required in order to gain a patent licence. There was a general consensus that anything 'natural' could not be patented. By 1970 the US Plant Variety Protection Act had been extended to allow intellectual property rights (IPR) for sexually reproducing plants (in other words, seed-bearing varieties), though such rights were not, strictly speaking, patents, as they were less extensive and, significantly, allowed farmers to save protected seed for their own use or for sale on other farms.[4]

Patenting is the reward given to groups or individuals for a specific invention, rather than for a 'discovery'. This invention must be *novel* (that is, it is not obvious to others) and also *useful* (that is, it has some application that is of economic value). The issue of a patent takes the form of a 'negative right', in that third parties who make use of this inventiveness are required to pay a fee covered by patent law. The fee is justified on the basis that the time and money spent on research and development require a payback, over and above the marketing of the final product. Note that if a

---

[3] Kelves, *A History of Patenting Life*, p. 1.
[4] R. S. Eisenberg, 'Patenting Organisms', in Reich (ed.), *Encyclopedia of Bioethics*, pp. 1911–14.

patent is not granted, the research is not prevented from going ahead; it merely means that others can use the methods published without penalty. Scientific discoveries are not subject to patenting because scientific advance grows from pre-existing knowledge, which should be accessible to all for further research, without penalty. Such knowledge is very broad in its applicability, so if it were subject to a patent it would, in effect, grant a reward to a single group and curtail further research. In theory, patent law was designed to facilitate socio-economic functioning at a national and global level by providing incentives to develop innovative and useful research that would benefit the whole community. The 'secrets' become 'shared' through patent protection. This is balanced by the need to reward individuals for their creative contribution to the process, though increasingly, and perhaps ironically, the reward is given not so much to individuals as to multinational companies. Companies have their own means of rewarding employees who are responsible for achieving patentable commodities.

In a famous case, Ananda Chakrabarty filed a US patent for a modified bacterium (*Pseudomonas*) that was genetically modified in order to degrade components of crude oil. His application in 1976 was initially rejected on the basis that nothing 'natural' could be the subject of a patent. He worked for General Electric, a company that was accustomed to dealing with processes as 'inventions'; other, biologically based companies, would have more readily assumed that patenting of such an application would be refused as not meeting the criteria. The US Supreme Court, in 1980, made a landmark decision by a narrow 5:4 majority, ruling that in *Diamond v. Chakrabarty* the GM bacterium could be protected by a patent. The court held that 'his discovery is not nature's handiwork, but his own', and is 'the result of human ingenuity and research'.[5] This was a watershed, as it allowed an increase in filing for patents of living things, including newly developed plant varieties, the protection of which had previously been more restricted. The patents were, in some cases, far too broad. For example, they covered all genetically engineered seeds and plants of a particular species.[6] By 1987 provision was made to extend patentability to non-human living multicellular organisms, which included animals. By 1988 a mouse, genetically engineered so that it developed cancer, known as the Harvard oncomouse, had been patented.

[5] Cited in M. Sagoff, paper for American Association for the Advancement of Science Dialogue Group on Genetic Patenting, 1996, p. 13. For discussion see Chapman, *Unprecedented Choices*, p. 132.
[6] Hettinger, 'Patenting Life'.

PATENTING IN THE USA AND EUROPE

The 1976 European Ruling on Patents contains a clause, 53(a), that prohibits patents that are contrary to public order or morality. Another clause, 53(b), prohibits patents on plant or animal varieties, or anything produced by a 'natural process', except microbiological products. As one might expect, the creators of the Harvard oncomouse were initially refused a licence to patent, and the development was subject to fierce opposition by groups filing objections based on the morality clause. However, by 1991 a patent was granted. This time, the morality clause was used to support the case, on the grounds that the creation of the oncomouse would serve the interests of cancer patients.[7] The US Congress, in rejecting the idea that morality could ever be a factor, held that patent policy was necessarily amoral, shaped by economic considerations alone; at the same time it claimed that other regulatory areas of government should deal with the issues of the legitimacy or otherwise of particular actions. William Cornish and David Llewelyn argue that, on the contrary, 'it seems disingenuous to view the patent system as some morally neutral form of state aid in recognition of the cleverness of the inventors'.[8] In other words, the granting authority cannot disclaim their responsibility for inventions that are protected by patent law, hiding behind the negative character of patent right. If this aspect is given too much emphasis, it merely assumes that patenting is morally neutral, which is clearly not the case. While, for example, it seems to me that it is correct to point out (as Donald Bruce does) that lack of patenting will simply allow others to use the invention, and so in one sense enable the process, such enabling is unlikely in practice, since patent royalties are a means both of providing needed income and of preventing further competition without penalties, at least for the duration of the patent.[9] In 1997 Jeremy Rifkin tested the USA system further by filing a patent with a biologist for a human–animal chimera, but this was rejected on the grounds that it was 'injurious to the well being, good policy, or good morals of society'.[10] Of course, US patent lawyers criticised this decision, as it seemed to go against the stated policy that patenting could not include morality in its brief.

---

[7] Eisenberg believes that permission was inconsistent with current law of the time that prohibited animal-variety patents; in this case the permission was apparently justified, as it covered the broader category of rodents. Eisenberg, *Patenting Organisms*, p. 1912.

[8] Cornish and Llewelyn, *Intellectual Property*, p. 833.

[9] D. Bruce, 'Whose Genes are They? Genetics, Patenting and the Churches', in Deane-Drummond (ed.), *Brave New World?*, pp. 257–73, esp. pp. 259–60.

[10] Kelves, *A History of Patenting Life*, p. 80.

SOME CASE STUDIES

The following case studies illustrate the difference in practice between the patents that can be granted under US law and those that can be granted under European law. The European Patent Convention (1973) distinguishes between claims for a product patent and claims for a process patent. It also sets out to prevent very broad claims that go beyond product description. Patents relating to embryonic stem cells have been applied for and obtained since as early as 1987 in USA, and by October 2001 over 500 patents had been applied for or granted. The European Union Biotechnology Directive, published in 1998, allows for the patentability of biological material. In this case it seems to liberalise the Patent Law of 1976, which rejected the patentability of plant or animal varieties. While the directive rejects the view that discoveries of that which can be found in nature can be patented, including those relating to the human body, body parts or gene sequences, it does allow the *processes* used in, for example, the isolation of DNA fragments to be patented, as long as the DNA sequence has some identified function (art. 3.1). In 1992 the EU ruled against patenting the products of conception, but the status of embryonic stem cells was ambiguous, because they were *derived from* conception. It also allowed for the patentability of isolated human elements, such as stem-cell lines.[11] The Group of Advisors on the Ethical Implications of Biotechnology to the European Commission (GAEIB) argued that patenting would be permissible only in those cases where genuinely new possibilities could emerge from the patent.[12] The European Parliament was also concerned that patent applications in Europe did not violate the principle of non-patentability of humans, or their genes or cells in their natural environment. However, the clause about the 'natural environment' can easily be sidestepped in existing law, as the processes used to isolate stem cells for research or other cell lines inevitably entail that such lines are not in their 'natural' context. It is worth considering these patent applications in a little more detail.[13] 'Products', in the case of stem cells, for example, would refer to stem cells, stem-cell lines or differentiated stem-cell lines.

[11] I argued in chapter 1 for the inclusion of stem-cell debates in discussions about the ethics of genetics.
[12] Van Overwalle, *Study on the Patenting of Inventions*, p. 54.
[13] These details were correct as far as I was aware at the time of writing, but may have altered since then. The most important point to note here is the initial resistance by the European Office, compared with the US Patent Office. For discussion, see Overwalle, *Study on the Patenting of Inventions Related to Human Stem Cell Research.*

'Processes' refers to those methods used for isolation, cultivation, cloning or treatment of cells.

The first type of example where human embryonic stem cells are patented arises *indirectly* through research using other primate species. A patent applied for protection of the methods of growing primate embryonic stem-cell lines as a model for human tissue lines.[14] The United States granted patent protection in this case, but protection was not granted in Europe. A second type of application arises when a patent is issued for animal stem cells, but there is no specific claim that the technique will be confined to non-humans. A third type of application that has been successful in the United States, but not in Europe, directly involves human embryonic stem cells; for example, where human embryonic stem cells have been treated so that they become blood stem cells.[15]

In August 2001 the very liberal approach to patenting stem-cell research in the United States came under attack indirectly by President George W. Bush's restriction on federal funding of stem-cell research. He specified that public funds could be used only if the following criteria were met:

1. That cells were derived from existing stem-cell lines.
2. That use came with informed consent of the donors concerned.
3. That stem cells from embryos were taken only from embryos 'left over' from fertility treatment, and that embryos should not be created *de novo* for this purpose.
4. That donors were not given financial incentives, but only reasonable cover for expenses.

In addition, he specified that no federal funds could be provided for

1. Creating new stem-cell lines from embryos, whether those embryos resulted from IVF treatment or not.
2. Creating embryos for research.
3. Cloning of human embryos for any purpose.

This restrictive move met with much resistance in the United States, among biotechnologists and scientists alike, accustomed as they were to a much more liberal policy on patenting. This trend towards a tighter control on human stem-cell lines seems at first sight to cohere with a more specific statement against patenting of the human genome that had been issued on 14 March 2000 as a joint statement by President Bill

---

[14] In this case the patentees argued that, since the method works for Rhesus monkey cell lines and marmoset cell lines, from Old World and New World species, then it would almost inevitably work for human embryonic stem-cell lines as well.
[15] This is known as haematopoietic differentiation.

Clinton and Prime Minister Tony Blair the previous year.[16] However, the resemblance is superficial. In the first case, President Bush was influenced by deontological considerations about the status of the human embryo, and therefore wanted both to 'gain' from the research that was possible using stem cells, and to avoid being seen as directly culpable for acts that destroy embryos, so that 'this allows us to explore the promise and potential of stem cell research, without crossing a fundamental moral line by providing taxpayer funding that would sanction or encourage further destruction of human embryos that have at least the potential for life'.[17] It did not, of course, prevent or sanction applications for patents for research using stem cells from newly destroyed embryos, or even the creation of embryos for research by privately funded companies. However, the statement did recognise the importance of moral issues in funding research, even though the President's stance on the use of existing cell lines is itself open to some question from an ethical point of view.[18] In the second case, the Joint Statement against human genome patenting, the ethical basis in this case is more consequential. Blair and Clinton were not alone in that many in the scientific community also called for a revision of patent law so that it could not be used to control more fundamental research. On 23 March 2000, nine days after the Joint Statement was issued, the Royal Society of Science and the National Academy of Sciences issued a statement urging that the human genome should be freely available to all those who wish to benefit from it. However, the US Patent Office seems to have ignored such requests, since patenting of human DNA is still possible in principle.

David Resnik has challenged the notion that patenting DNA restricts scientific research by examining correlations between the granting of patent permission and research activity.[19] His conclusions are based on

---

[16] 'To realize the full promise of this research, raw fundamental data on the human genome, including the human DNA sequence and its variations, should be made freely available to scientists everywhere ... We applaud the decision by scientists working on the Human Genome Project to release raw fundamental information about the human DNA sequence and its variants rapidly into the public domain, and we commend other scientists around the world to adopt this policy.' The White House, 'Joint Statement by President Clinton and Prime Minister Tony Blair of the UK', 14 March 2000.

[17] The White House, press release: 'Remarks by the President on Stem Cell Research', 9 August 2001.

[18] Conservatives would be unhappy with the complicity in the crime arising from making 'use' of embryo cell lines, while liberals would argue that his stance fails to recognise the risks associated with existing cell lines. For example, mouse feeder cells were used at one stage, which could run the risk of viral transmission. In addition, liberals would argue that potential for research is far too restricted if all the conditions specified are met.

[19] Resnik, *Owning the Genome*, pp. 136–40.

a science citation index approach that simply extracted those articles that featured the words 'gene', 'genome', 'DNA', 'genomics' and 'genetics' in their titles. The explosion of DNA patents appeared to have no impact on such citations. However, what this research failed to demonstrate was the *direction* of research activity, and the identity of those conducting the research at an international level. While DNA patents will clearly not prevent research in genomics, it is more likely to move it in some directions rather than others, and to be restricted to those research groups that can afford the payments required. Resnik's analysis was simply too crude to lead to any firm conclusions about the impact of DNA patenting on genomics research. Furthermore, the argument that basic DNA research should serve to resource a common pool undermines the argument that the only alterative to patenting DNA is secrecy. Of course, Resnik believes that patenting does not pose a threat to openness of access to information either, but such openness includes a financial cost, and it is this aspect that many find objectionable.

Resnik also argues that if DNA were not patented, then other 'downstream' products would be patented, such as proteins or RNA (pp. 142–4). However, this is exactly the point made by HUGO, namely that the restrictions under patent law should be more specific, rather than based on DNA, which could potentially be useful for multiple purposes.[20] In addition, a discovery is very often the result of years of painstaking research that has built on the knowledge gained by others, and will often be made virtually simultaneously in different laboratories. It would be inappropriate to reward those who were the first to achieve the final step required for the development of all subsequent applications. Rather, a patent that focuses on a specific application of a more theoretical process provides an incentive to look for those applications, though they are often, but not always, less prestigious in the scientific community than 'basic' research.[21]

The 1998 EU directive rejects the possibility of patenting for cloning of human beings, or for modifying the human germline, or for the use of human embryos for industrial or commercial purposes. However, it is worth asking whether therapeutic cloning can be patentable under European law. Van Overwalle suggests that recital 41 hints that only reproductive cloning is strictly banned, for it defines cloning as any process

---

[20] Rossiter, *HUGO Statement on the Patenting of DNA Sequences*, January 1995.

[21] This is changing now that the research assessment exercise in the United Kingdom is giving credit to university departments that are successful in patenting the 'inventions', leading to the double reward of (a) further research funding and (b) recognition and status in the scientific community.

'designed to create a human being with the same nuclear genetic information as another living or diseased human being'.[22] There is no definition of
what human being might be, except that it is 'from the embryonic state'.
This question is taken up further in the European Commission *Opinion on
Ethical Aspects of Patenting Inventions Involving Human Stem Cells*, published in May 2002. The dilemma discussed in this opinion relates to both
the need for patents to foster research and the restriction in access to
healthcare resulting from expensive patents. The ethical issues, according
to the opinion, relate both to the prohibition of profit from the human
body and to the principle of free and informed consent by the donor. In
balancing the difficulties associated with access with the demands by
biotechnology companies, the opinion recommends that simple isolation
of embryonic stem cells is not sufficient to warrant patent, which may be
granted only if some modification has taken place, either *in vivo* or through
genetic engineering for specific therapeutic uses. Of course, the issue of
'consent' in this case applies to the mother or parents of the 'spare' IVF
embryos, or to the gamete donors, or to the mothers of aborted foetuses, as
the likely sources of embryos. They did not approve patenting of stem-cell
lines derived from cloning created through cell nuclear transfer, because
the process of cloning is the same as that used for reproductive cloning.
However, they were prepared to leave the matter open for further public
discussion. This, in itself, demonstrates that European law is not clear-cut
in its legislation on cloning, which opens the way for further liberalisation,
subject only to the public-order clause. In view of the way this has been
interpreted in the past to favour, for example, patenting of the oncomouse,
it seems unlikely that this clause will provide restrictions on therapeutic
cloning where benefits to sick humans are consequential.

THE CHURCHES' RESPONSE TO THE 1998 EU DIRECTIVE

The bioethical working group of the European Ecumenical Commission
for Church and Society (EECCS) and its successor, the Church and Society
Commission of the Conference of European Churches (CEC), provide
helpful insights into the particular religious issues thrown up by the EU
directive and into attempts by the church to influence European policy.[23]

---

[22] Cited in Van Overwalle, *Study on the Patenting of Inventions*, p. 58.
[23] Donald Bruce writes from particular experience of involvement with both these groups, as discussed
in Bruce, 'Whose Genes Are They?', pp. 262–73. The EECCS working group originally comprised
mostly representatives of Protestant churches, though the CEC included Orthodox and members
from Eastern Europe.

The European directive of 1998 was eventually accepted after some bitter controversy and opposition, leading to a rejection of an original proposal for a directive in 1995 by the European Parliament. The bioethics working groups opposed the original draft, which they believed, failed to take into account in an adequate way the ethical and social issues involved in patenting. The proposal assumed that genes could be patented, arguing that isolated human genes could be classified as inventions. To claim that the copying of DNA makes the material significantly different from that in nature seemed disingenuous.[24] Although the EU directive allowed for an ethical clause so that something could be excluded from patenting, it did not require that the process itself be stopped. The bioethics group argued that this made no sense; what was needed was another ethical body to evaluate those patents that had been approved, and presumably to have a regulatory role in permitting the research to take place at all. The European Commission rejected this proposal as one that would 'disturb' the patenting process, regarding the churches' response as 'emotional evaluation'. This, of course, was not only incorrect but a great disappointment to those engaged in this discussion. It is unfortunate in some ways that, while secular philosophical arguments were used in addition to religious ones, the use of religious language gave the commissioners a convenient excuse – namely that religious belief in itself should not be allowed to interfere with the patenting process.

Because theological arguments that rely on insistence that such action is against 'God's will' are not valid in the lawcourts, it is more appropriate to seek arguments that will be convincing from a pragmatic point of view, even if more theological arguments might be appropriate in discussion within the Christian community as such. This is, of course, the disadvantage of forms of ethics that include theological language: that those who do not adhere to the same beliefs can dismiss it as unreasonable. However, important secular reasons were embedded in the churches' response, and these the commissioners conveniently ignored. Other voices were equally doubtful about the wisdom of EU policy. The biotechnological lobbyists also used the bioethics group as a means to support their case, claiming that it was against helping those suffering from debilitating diseases because it wanted to block patents. This is, of course, far from the truth, and the use of emotionally loaded stories to support their case is a good example of lack

---

[24] Of course, those who support the policy would agree with Resnik that isolating and purifying DNA *does* change the DNA in significant ways, in that it is not identical to that in the 'natural' state, and new sequences may be added. However, it seems to me that such changes are relatively insignificant compared with retention of the identity of the original gene sequence. Resnik, *Owning the Genome*, p. 89.

of integrity and honesty in the discussion. The European Parliament made some strong amendments to the original proposed directive, but these were then ignored by the Commission, leading to a final text that was, according to Bruce, 'almost as flawed as the original'.[25] Many members of the European Parliament who witnessed this process sensed that this was a real failure of proper democratic process. It is witness to the almost inexorable rise of the power of biotechnology and of the promise of its commercial gains to seduce those involved. In this case it is not so much a case of genetics slipping into public policy without going through the normal democratic processes, in the manner that Ulrich Beck has observed, but of the actual democratic rejection of aspects of the technology, followed by the failure of democracy itself to contain the process.[26] There have, nonetheless, been attempts to correct this failure. The Dutch Parliament has tried unsuccessfully to challenge the legality of the directive, and the French National Ethics Committee has argued that patenting of human genes should be illegal.[27]

THEOLOGICAL ARGUMENTS FOR AND AGAINST GENE PATENTING

What were the underlying religious reasons why the bioethics group objected to gene patenting? Most of the discussion here centres on the subject of human dignity. This can take the form of putting emphasis on the special relationship between God and humanity, humanity being made in the image of God, *imago Dei*.[28] However, such an approach can be challenged by other theologians – notably those in the USA, such as Ted Peters, who argue that patenting of life, including human DNA, is morally acceptable from a Christian point of view because it rewards creativity, itself a characteristic of human image-bearing.[29] Audrey Chapman observes that 'the affirmation of humanity as the image of God does not in and of itself provide a clear grounding for opposing patenting of altered human tissue or DNA fragments'.[30] She also suggests that, since human beings share their DNA with other creatures (having up to 98% in common with other primates), such an affirmation cannot be used as a claim for human distinctiveness. While it is true that human evolution is suggestive of a

---

[25] Bruce, 'Whose Genes Are They?', p. 265.   [26] See Beck, *Risk Society.*
[27] Bruce, 'Whose Genes are They?', p. 266.
[28] See, for example, Land and Mitchell, 'Patenting Life: No'.
[29] Peters, 'Patenting Life: Yes', and Peters, *Playing God?*, p. 139.
[30] Chapman, *Unprecedented Choices*, p. 149.

common link with animals, to claim that the commonality itself is enough
to question its distinctiveness is, it seems to me, a false move. The subtle
differences between human DNA and primate DNA are, after all, sufficient
to code for a huge plethora of different proteins and processes. However,
localising human dignity in DNA is misguided in as much as it seems to
imply that 'human nature' is resident in the genes. Rather, the dynamic
interplay between genes and environment serves to facilitate the emergence
of the human person. Yet it also seems to me important to stress that,
though human DNA does not carry the same ethical weight as 'personhood', this does not mean that it lacks value, or that it lacks distinctively
human value through its ability to set biological limits within which human
beings emerge. European law excludes the products of human conception
from patenting, which suggests that different levels of patentability are
needed, depending on the particular links with human personhood. The
secular arguments against patenting of DNA fragments seem to me to be
more convincing than specifically religious claims related to image-bearing.
However, this does not rule out the possibility that there will be additional
theological reasons for resisting patenting where human integrity seems to
be at stake, as, for example, in the patenting of human beings, or of human
body parts or products of conception.

Another theological challenge takes the form of attributing ownership of
life to God; patenting represents the usurping of such ownership.[31] This
view, of course, presumes that life can be 'owned' and made the object of
property. The analogy with God's ownership is not very helpful, therefore,
in challenging the root of another objection, namely that living creatures
cannot be the object of ownership in the first place. It is also inconsistent
with other theological positions that lay more emphasis on life as gift, since,
if life were given, God would no longer be the rightful owner.
Furthermore, it could be said that patenting is not so much the giving
ownership as a negative right protecting the interests of those who have
'invented' something. Finally, the kind of ownership that God exercises in
relation to creation is not based on property rights, but rather 'God's
ownership of things is best understood as God's reserving the right to
define their purpose, value and relationship to other creatures. God owns
the land, not to exclude creatures from it, but to give it for their right use
and set the limits of proper use and care.'[32] To try to suggest that God's

---

[31] See, for example, Land and Mitchell, 'Patenting Life: No', pp. 20–2.
[32] R. Cole-Turner, 'Theological Perspectives on the Status of DNA: A Contribution to the Debate
Over Genetic Patenting', in Chapman (ed.), *Perspectives on Gene Patenting*, p. 152.

rightful ownership challenges patenting, therefore, seems wide of the mark, for God's ownership is not in the same category.

A further theological challenge is that the sacredness or sanctity of life, and aspects associated with but not identical to this perspective, such as the concept of life as a gift from God, are further warrants against gene patenting. These views are usually associated with the more general notion that we are wrong to 'play God'; that is, we have usurped God's intentions for life as gift and as sacred by treating it in this way. While the human body might be given respect, why should a sense of the sacred, or, in secular terms, human dignity, necessarily include fragments of DNA or tissue lines?[33] In addition, since the logical conclusion of an absolute view of sacredness of life is that all genetic engineering should be opposed, rejecting patenting is a false move, as it simply prevents the originators from gaining profit from their 'invention', rather than stalling the research as such.[34] Some objections to patenting may, therefore, be viewed as indirect objections to the technology, rather than to patenting as such. Patenting might be thought of as a way of controlling research without going down the route of an outright ban.[35] Ronald Cole-Turner's reply to any objections that use the language of the sacred is that genes are not sacred; since God, who alone has the status of divinity, is the Creator, they cannot be refused a patent on this premise.[36] Yet does the fact that God creates genes necessarily mean that they are *not* sacred? If 'sacred' means 'divine', this objection holds. If 'sacred' means acquiring special dignity in view of a *relationship* to God the Creator, however, this objection is not tenable. Cole-Turner's other suggestion, that this effectively counters religious objections to patenting, applies only to the former category of discussion. He seems to go further in suggesting that there should be no objection to biological patents as long as individuals and corporations exercise their intellectual property rights in a way that is consistent with God's purposes. This implies that all forms of patenting of biological material are, in principle, acceptable theologically. This seems to be a consequentialist approach that explores purpose narrowly in terms of goods achieved. It is by no means clear that the overall purpose to which intellectual property rights are assigned is necessarily directed to the common good, even though the patent application, considered narrowly, may name a given good, such as a form of therapy or treatment.

[33] Chapman, *Unprecedented Choices*, p. 150.   [34] Ibid., p. 147.
[35] Eisenberg, 'Patenting Organisms', p. 1912.   [36] Cole-Turner, 'Religion and Gene Patenting'.

While to declare genes as 'sacred', or even linked ontologically with image-bearing, seems to me to be a false move because it tends towards an elevated view of human genetics in a reductionist way, a more convincing theological objection comes from reflecting more deeply on the nature of the *relationship* between humanity and God, rather than from fixing on particular deontological characteristics, such as image-bearing, whether of DNA or other life forms. Esther Reed argues that the relationship between God and humanity can be perceived as gift, gift viewed liturgically in relationship with Christ; and therefore to subject human beings or their parts to trade offends against the invitation to participate in Christ's life, which leads to a true sense of human integrity.[37] She suggests further that, just as in the biblical account the temple is named by Christ as an inappropriate place for trade, so is the human body (and, by implication, parts) also. This is a more convincing approach than the language of *imago Dei* or the language of the sacred, where these are detached from relational aspects, since Reed's position would in theory permit genetic engineering, for it is the notion of trade itself that seems to be the object of offence. What does the language of integrity suggest about the permissibility of genetic engineering? Genetic engineering that is directed towards human integrity (for example, through the removal of a diseased gene) could be seen as having a redemptive capacity that would be in line with a liturgical approach.[38] In addition, Reed suggests, convincingly, that we need to opt for a 'capacity' approach that takes into account the particular character-istics of a species in deciding whether that species can be the subject of patent protection. Thus, while a bacterium could be patented, a modified higher animal or primate could not.[39] Of course, this approach has its limitations, in that it would seem to promote the idea that plant varieties can be patented as a matter of course. Certainly this would make sense on these criteria alone. By using the language of integrity, Reed is hinting, though not stating explicitly, that such participation implies an extension to all parts of the human body and its fragments, in a somewhat analogous way to Land and Mitchell's extension of image-bearing to all parts of the human body, as they are still identifiably human.[40] It is not clear, however, why it is necessarily offensive to trade in DNA fragments even though it is clearly inappropriate to trade in human bodies and their parts. While the

---

[37] Reed, 'Thinking Liturgically', pp. 282–3.
[38] Reed does not consider this aspect, but it is suggestive of such a move. See chapter 6 above.
[39] This discussion relates to animal rights more generally, which I have discussed elsewhere; see C. Deane-Drummond, *The Ethics of Nature*, pp. 60–5.
[40] Land and Mitchell, 'Brave New Biopatents', p. 21.

boundary between humanity and animals makes it clear that human beings in themselves cannot be subject to trade, but some animals can, why is it so offensive from a theological point of view to trade in fragments derived from human beings?

Part of the objection here seems to be related to the sense that patenting leads to the commodification of life.[41] In the narrow sense, commodification means regarding the object merely as something to be bought or sold in the marketplace, and patenting highlights the objectification of parts of human beings in a way that seems to treat them as things rather than subjects. Why does the commodification of a part or a fraction of the human body necessarily lead to humanity's losing its subjective status, becoming an 'it' rather than an 'I'? There seem to be two trends here that those who object to patenting on religious grounds find offensive. The first is the slippery-slope argument: that once human fragments are bought and sold, it is a short step to treating human beings in this way. The second relates to the ethos that patenting promotes, namely that living things can be reduced to commodities that can then be bought and sold.[42] Such objections might be answered by claiming that patenting does not necessarily mean that the subject of such a patent is treated as property, or commodified, any more than life insurance automatically renders such a person's life as having *only* a market value. There are clearly difficulties in defining whether something can be classified as 'natural' or 'artificial', in which case the question arises: how do we decide whether this is a product of human ingenuity or not? Resnik contends that no clear criteria exist; rather, 'we must appeal to normative concerns, such as our goals, purposes and values in drawing this distinction'.[43] In other words, in those areas where it is ambiguous, we must make a decision to call something a human invention, based on the purposes intended.

However, there are also social and political implications of this commodification process that have far-reaching consequences.[44] These and other, related, social-justice issues also come into play in consideration of patenting, and, as I will show below, have an important bearing on Christian theological responses to gene patenting. It is these social-justice issues that seem to have been marginalised in the American theological discussion, which has tended to focus on the somewhat rarefied theoretical point about

[41] See Chapman, *Unprecedented Choices*, pp. 151–2.
[42] Hanson, 'Religious Voices in Biotechnology'.   [43] Resnik, *Owning the Genome*, p. 86.
[44] For discussion, see J. Clague, 'Genetic Knowledge as a Commodity: The Human Genome Project, Markets and Consumers', in Junker-Kenny and Cahill (eds.), *The Ethics of Genetic Engineering*, pp. 3–12.

the extent to which patenting offends against the *imago Dei*. While such debate has its place, any objections so raised can be challenged by equal and opposite theological reasons to support patenting, leading to a stalemate.

ETHICAL DEBATES IN GENE PATENTING

Philosophical issues

The defence of intellectual property rights rests on three justificatory schema.[45] The first is instrumental; that is, individuals have a rightful share in the benefits of their invention. The second justification is self-developmental; namely, individuals can develop freely without interference from others.[46] Yet it is also important to point out that patents are normally issued to companies rather than to individuals, which weakens any sense of individual ownership or development. The third justification is economic; namely, that patenting brings benefits to wider society by allowing transfer of property in a market system, leading to an overall increase in efficiency and productivity.

A core area for philosophical debate is whether knowledge itself is an appropriate area to be covered by patent law, in that it assumes that knowledge is a commodity that can be bought and sold. John O'Neill, for example, suggests that the market provides the wrong kind of test for knowledge, skewing research in a direction that favours multinationals and away from projects that are likely to be of public benefit.[47] Intellectual property rights disregard the way scientific knowledge has accumulated over generations of scientific work, recognising only the active, innovative aspect of that knowledge as having economic ramifications. It rewards only those who have come to this step first, even though competing groups may be very close to hitting upon the same 'invention'.

The newness of the knowledge is also open to some challenge, especially given the way patent law is currently set up to allow for patenting of DNA fragments. The Human Genome Organisation (HUGO) strongly resists patenting for DNA sequences, arguing that the kind of work required to generate expressed sequence tags (ESTs) is routine rather than innovative,[48] for it draws on techniques that had been developed since the mid-1980s.

---

[45] For discussion see May, *A Global Political Economy of Intellectual Property Rights*, pp. 92–4.
[46] Marx suggested that individuals lacked a stake in their labour under capitalism, and in this sense patenting, as originally devised, might seem to work in the opposite direction.
[47] O'Neill, 'Property in Science and the Market'.
[48] *HUGO Statement on the Patenting of DNA Sequences*, January 1995.

HUGO therefore maintains that, although the overall Human Genome Project was large in scale, the simple generation of ESTs lacked innovation in terms of its science.[49] If patenting were confined to ESTs, the more difficult steps would go unrewarded while being subject to indirect patent controls. It argues that

it would be ironic and unfortunate if the patent system were to reward the routine while discouraging the innovative. Yet that could be the result of offering broad patents to those who undertake massive but routine sequencing efforts – whether for ESTs or for full genes – while granting more limited rights or no rights to those who make the far more difficult and significant discoveries of underlying bio- logical functions.[50]

HUGO's views against the patenting of ESTs were reiterated in a further statement, issued in 2000.[51] It clarifies its position that single nucleotide polymorphisms (SNPs), like cDNA or ESTs, or whole genomes of patho- genic organisms, should be viewed as 'pre-competitive information'. Thus, while patent law is intended to enhance innovation and development, HUGO suggested that, in some respects at least, it could serve to work in the opposite direction, by restricting knowledge that should be open to all. It therefore argues, convincingly in my view, that the process of generating such DNA fragments does not deserve to be patented, as it is not sufficiently novel, and actually blocks the really novel research that follows the basic research effort.

The biotechnological industry has given a mixed response to such doubts expressed by scientists regarding the worth of gene patenting. The company Merck Sharp & Dohme has argued that genetic sequences should be placed in the public domain, while SmithKline Beecham disagrees.[52] Some have argued that the restriction in knowledge that can be anticipated by so many patent payment requirements amounts to a 'tragedy of an anticommons'.[53] In other words, such restrictions are counter to creativity, favouring those who have captured patents on the initial processes.

---

[49] It did, however, suggest that obtaining a full-length DNA sequence was much more challenging, involving a detailed piecing together of the maps, followed eventually by the use of these maps to obtain proteins that could eventually lead to diagnostically useful results in terms of identifying biological functions.

[50] *HUGO Statement on the Patenting of DNA Sequences,* January 1995.

[51] Such claims are known in patent jargon as 'reach-through' claims, as they go beyond an acceptable boundary in limiting research. *HUGO IP Statement on Patenting of DNA Sequences in Particular Response to the European Biotechnology Directive.*

[52] Cited in Chapman, *Unprecedented Choices,* p. 135.

[53] Heller and Eisenberg, 'Can Patents Deter Innovation?'

Audrey Chapman has identified four areas of concern expressed in the secular debates on patenting.[54] The first, related to whether life or non-life can be patented, is separate from discussions about whether knowledge is patentable, but both debates question the legitimacy of awarding patents in areas that would not normally be commodified, as discussed above. The second idea, that basic knowledge of human DNA (such as that to be found in ESTs) is a common inheritance of humanity and should not be patented comes through clearly in HUGO statements and also in the joint statement by Tony Blair and Bill Clinton, even though HUGO, at least on the surface, seems more concerned about the impact of such restriction on scientific research. The UN General Assembly made a Universal Declaration on the Human Genome and Human Rights that reinforced this position, namely, that the human gene could not be the subject of property since it underlies the unity of all members of the human family. However, the specific clause (art. 4) that referred to DNA of the human genome 'in its natural state' led to some ambiguity over interpretation, for, arguably, the EU 1998 directive also bans patenting of DNA 'in its natural state', but allows for patenting of DNA sequences. The UN also lacks legal muscle, and was largely ignored by biotechnology companies. Of course, the 'common heritage' idea could be understood in two ways: as a common right of access to the *benefits*, or as common heritage of groups to preserve DNA as a *resource*. If the former position is taken, then, even if DNA is a common heritage, as long as global and intergenerational distributive justice prevails, DNA could still be patented.[55] It is naïve to presume that, if common resources were to be commercialised, genuine distributive justice would be possible in practice. There are also complex debates surrounding the possibility of intergenerational justice that seem to reach a limit in terms of secular approaches to the discussion.[56]

The third contested area is the link between human dignity and integrity; this link is also raised as a possible reason for objecting to human gene patenting in secular terms. It is a secular equivalent of theological arguments discussed earlier in this book. Those who express concern are aware of the history of eugenics and conscious of the need to protect the human person against eugenic alterations. Chapman argues that the 1998 EU directive has responded to this by banning patenting on cloning human

---

[54] Chapman, *Unprecedented Choices*, pp. 137–45.
[55] P. Ossario, 'Common Heritage Arguments and the Patenting of DNA', in Chapman (ed.), *Perspectives on Gene Patenting*.
[56] Muers, 'Pushing the Limit'.

beings, germline genetic identity, and commercialisation of embryos.[57] However, it seems to me that the legislation is not as watertight as Chapman implies, since it would be possible to patent embryonic stem cells under current legislation (as discussed above), and the cloning directive seems to leave open the opportunity to patent stem cells produced through therapeutic cloning.

The fourth area, namely social-justice issues, will be outlined below. Here it is worth noting that campaign groups have identified inappropriate use of genes from indigenous groups; that is, the genetic material has been used although the proper procedures for obtaining informed consent have not been adhered to. The Human Genome Diversity Project, which attempts to collate samples from ethnic groups before intermarriage has taken place, has been heavily criticised both for this reason and for the fact that it infringes on the beliefs and values of the groups concerned. These patents confer benefits on the researchers, but do not reward the donors. Such patenting therefore represents a human-rights issue of some importance.[58]

Justice issues

Those who support gene patenting argue that it is a matter of individual and corporate justice that those who are inventive should have a market share in the profits arising out of this invention, leading to social goods in terms of transfer of knowledge. However, the outcomes are not always as anticipated, but lead to effects that are less beneficial than were predicted, and to unfair advantages accruing to those in receipt of patents. The purported economic benefits of patenting assume liberal values, namely that a free-market economy is necessarily the best means of transferring goods. However, one could equally argue that, far from encouraging transfer of knowledge, the present system of patenting effectively leads to enclosures of natural resources that were once open to a wider number of people. In those cases where traditional knowledge is gleaned and then patented under the patent law of richer states, this leads to a double form of enclosure, both of the raw materials themselves and of traditional knowledge.[59]

---

[57] Chapman, *Unprecedented Choices*, p. 143.

[58] Benjamin, 'Indigenous Peoples Barred from DNA Sampling Conference', pp. 5, 18.

[59] May, *A Global Political Economy*, pp. 101–2. The patenting of products isolated from the neem tree, used in India for generations for traditional medicinal purposes, is a good example of such double enclosure. Numerous other plant varieties native to developing countries have been 'pirated' for their products, including genetic variability, and have been developed commercially under patents in developed nations. See Shiva, *Biopiracy*.

Given the context of gene patenting of crops for food and medical resources, it is hardly surprising that many of those in the poorer communities in the world are deeply suspicious of human gene patenting. The issue in this case is not so much about procedural justice (that is, to what extent the patenting system can reward those who are truly inventive, a point raised by many scientists) as about distributive justice, since human gene patenting is unfairly skewed towards benefiting a narrow sector of the human community. This is a point that has not gone unnoticed by the ethics committee of HUGO, which claims that

At present there is a great inequality between the rich and the poor nations in the direction and priorities of research and in the distribution and access to the benefits thereof. When there is a vast difference in power between those carrying out the research and the participants, and when there is a possibility of substantial profit, considerations of justice support the desirability of distributing some profits to respond to health care needs.[60]

However, concerns about just distribution of benefit are not confined to the poorer nations, but also impinge more specifically on differential access to benefits in the richer nations, especially those that rely on private systems of healthcare, such as insurance.[61]

Consideration of global-justice concerns includes consideration of the Trade Related Aspects of Intellectual Property Rights (TRIPS) agreement, set in place in 1996 and signed by 140 nations. Statements by UNESCO, WHO and HUGO are influential, but, unlike TRIPS, have no legally binding authority. The TRIPS agreement establishes minimum standards on a range of intellectual property rights, including patents, supplementing the established agreements set in place through the Paris, Berne, Rome and Washington Conventions. The TRIPS agreement emerged as a result of fears, mostly among Westerners, about piracy; but it was not welcomed by the developing nations: 'industrialised countries forced developing countries to initiate negotiation of an agreement on TRIPS with the clear objective of universalising the standards of IPRs protection that the former had incorporated in their legislation, once they had attained a high level of technological and industrial capability'.[62] As far as the developing nations were concerned, the TRIPS agreement seemed to enshrine a policy of 'technological protectionism', consolidating a further division between the Northern nations that generate the technology, and the poorer

---

[60] HUGO Ethics Committee, *Statement on Benefit Sharing.*
[61] See below, chapter 8.   [62] Correa, *Intellectual Property Rights,* p. 3.

Southern nations that make up the market for the resulting products and services. The TRIPS agreement amounts to a blatant failure of procedural justice, whereby not all parties had an equal share in drawing up the legislative rules. Carlos Correa believes that the United States aggressively sought to set in place international rules that would help to re-establish its competitive position in the economy, a position that had started to decline through competition from overseas.[63] The US pharmaceutical industry was one of the main lobbyists pressing for an expansion in patent protection.[64]

Prior to 1999, the TRIPS agreement contained an article that allowed for the non-patentability of substances existing in nature or animals or plants. Just as in Europe, however, this clause could be interpreted in such a way as to allow for patents on isolated fragments, such as DNA. Under TRIPS it is possible for countries to opt out of patenting natural materials; for example, Brazilian patent law excludes genome, germ plasm of any natural living being and natural biological processes, and Argentinian patent law excludes any kind of living material or substance existing in nature.[65] However, Correa notes that the developing countries do not have the capacity for proper examination of patent applications, a situation that may allow patents to be set up in a way that virtually guarantees monopoly status over given products. This opens the opportunity both for *procedural injustice* and for *distributive injustice* in relation to genetic goods. Correa suggests that TRIPS may work against those cases of bioprospecting, where patents are applied for on natural goods growing in the wild.[66] Christopher May, on the other hand, suggests that under the terms of the agreement even natural products can be appropriated and removed from the public realm.[67] The TRIPS agreement still allows biotechnological, including genetic, resources to be patented; and once they are patented in one

---

[63] Correa, *Intellectual Property Rights*, p. 5.

[64] Because the use of generic drugs by India and other developing nations relied on no patent protection, the introduction of TRIPS has led to an increase in their price and consequent health risks. In Argentina it has been estimated that there has been a 45.5% reduction in consumption of medicines, because of the 270% increase in price, leading to an increase in revenue of $370 million by the producers of the drugs, based in the Western world. While article 30 includes the right to grant compulsory licenses in the situations of health emergency, Correa suggests that this does not go far enough: Correa, *Intellectual Property Rights*, p. 217. In 2001 the World Trade Organisation clarified the situation by the publication of the Doha Declaration on the TRIPS Agreement and Public Health, which allowed some provision for overriding TRIPS for reasons of public health or in an emergency. Yet the threat of litigation means that developing nations may not have sufficient wherewithal to execute compulsory licences in order to counter the overall trend towards a failure to meet basic health needs. WTO, *Declaration on the TRIPS Agreement and Public Health*.

[65] Correa, *Intellectual Property Rights*, p. 54.

[66] Ibid., p. 56.   [67] May, *A Global Political Economy*, p. 103.

jurisdiction it becomes difficult to deny patents elsewhere. As May suggests, 'this removal, patenting and return-as-product process is regarded by many in the developing states as theft of their natural resources'.[68] Part of the difficulty here is that patent protection is given to individuals or companies, not to social groups who have developed, for example, traditional medicines and agriculture, so it is unlikely that indigenous seeds or products will be able to be protected using this legislation.

The TRIPS agreement, like the 1998 EU directive, contains a clause that allows consideration of whether a use is against the *ordre public* or morality. But *ordre public* can be interpreted in a narrow way in terms of public order. It also excludes patentability of diagnostic, surgical or therapeutic methods. However, it remains to be seen to what extent this clause could be used to block patentability of, for example, therapeutic cloning, or other gene-therapy methods that are likely to be very expensive. Given the fact that TRIPS has been used to patent indigenous seeds and products, it seems likely that ways will be found around these clauses. In addition, this clause seems to fail to implement what might broadly be termed *contributive justice*, that is, an obligation on all to contribute to the public good. The idea of contributive justice is equivalent to Aquinas' notion of general or legal justice, and is the virtue whereby the good citizen is directed towards the common good.[69] The distinction between general justice and constitutive justice or justice between individuals is brought out clearly in the following way:

The common good is the end or purpose of individual persons living in the community as the good of the whole is that of each part. Yet the good of one individual person is not the end or purpose of another. That is why general or legal justice, which is ordered to the common good, is more capable than particular justice, which is ordered to the good of another individual person, of extending to inner feelings affecting a man in himself. (2a2ae q. 58.9)

The Roman Catholic bishops prefer to name this general justice contributive justice, as it puts particular emphasis on the individual's contribution to the common good.[70] While, in Aquinas' original notion of contributive justice, those acting justly were individuals, that same notion can usefully be applied to multinational companies; and Clague has argued convincingly that far greater attention needs to be paid to contributive

---

[68] See n. 59 above for the example of the neem tree: May, *A Global Political Economy*, p. 103.
[69] Aquinas, *Summa Theologiae*, 2a2ae qq. 58.5, 58.6.
[70] National Conference of Catholic Bishops, 'Economic Justice for All', cited in Hollenbach, *The Common Good and Christian Ethics*, p. 195.

justice by those multinationals that are gaining disproportionate benefits from biotechnology.[71] Much the same could be applied to those companies that exploit genetic resources for their own benefit. While those engaged in patent law claim that issues of morality are outside their brief, the fostering of division between richer and poorer nations could, in its long-term effects, actually be seen as working to disrupt community among the nations, leading to a breakdown in *ordre public*. The case-by-case approach characteristic of patent law misses the global trends implicated in such legislation.

Another area of discussion in relation specifically to issues in genetics has been that of *compensatory justice*. This includes discussion of how far those who have donated their tissue or DNA for research that is then patented should have a share in the benefits arising from that research. Two good examples include the University of California at Los Angeles patent of a leukaemia cell line isolated from the spleen of a patient, John Moore, who refused to sign a consent form. Moore sued the University, but eventually the California Supreme High Court ruled that he could not have owner-ship rights over cells after they had been taken from his body.[72] The case clearly shows that ethical issues were not taken into consideration in the final ruling, which went against the interests of the individual, who was refused a share in the benefits. The United States National Institute for Health (NIH) received a patent for cell lines taken from blood samples from a member of the Hagahai tribe in Papua New Guinea and from the Solomon Islands, both communities known in some cases to carry resis-tance to leukaemia. This was clearly a prospecting move, for the resistance had yet to be identified. The resulting controversy eventually led NIH to back down over their claims under the patents.[73]

BROADENING THE THEOLOGICAL AGENDA: BENEFIT-SHARING AND THE PUBLIC GOOD

The foregoing secular ethical discussion highlights the narrowness of the theological agenda in its consideration of issues such as to what extent DNA represents the image of God in humanity. Relatively few authors have considered the broad social and political issues associated with

---

[71] I am grateful to Julie Clague for allowing me to read her chapter while it was still in press: Clague, 'Patently Unjust? Biotechnology, Commercialisation and the Common Good', in Deneulin et al. (eds.), *Capabilities and Justice*.
[72] Hettinger, 'Patenting Life', p. 271.   [73] See Chapman, *Unprecedented Choices*, p. 134.

patenting.[74] Julie Clague has been particularly concerned about the way commercial investment in biotechnology impedes health goods, especially for the poorer nations. She argues that 'the public good offers a discourse that can be utilised across the worlds of public policy, economics and medicine to express and delineate the humanitarian benefits of biotechnology and the social responsibility of the international community'.[75] In particular, the notion of the public good becomes more than simply a rhetorical device; rather, it is a viable policy initiative once it is understood through the concept of global public goods and benefit-sharing. Clague also notes that one of the most influential strands of moral discourse uses the language of rights, though she resists naming rights as an integral aspect of the public good, for she believes that the global public-good discourse takes us further than the language of rights. UNESCO has also argued that genetic data should benefit all in the context of a human-rights approach.[76] In deliberative discussion about patenting DNA, it needs to be borne in mind that rights language is also common to libertarian arguments for intellectual property rights. The debate then becomes cast in terms of conflict of rights, which can undermine any possibility of further deliberation and compromise.[77] It is therefore my contention that the language of the public good is more helpful in discussions about the legitimacy of DNA patenting than is rights language.[78] The challenge, of course, remains: namely, how such language of the public good can be translated into concrete policy-making, rather than simply informing a public rhetoric. The notion of global public good is an attempt to translate the Christian notion of the common good into public policy.

While the broad idea of health as a global public good is one facet of what the public good might mean, HUGO also identifies genetic databases as global public goods. HUGO defines global public goods as 'those whose scope extends worldwide, are enjoyable by all with no groups excluded and, when consumed by one individual, are not depleted for others'.[79] In order to characterise the form this public good should take in practice in terms of policy-making, especially policy relating to genetic goods, it is worth

---

[74] One notable exception is Clague, 'Patently Unjust?'   [75] Clague, 'Patently Unjust?'

[76] See, for example, UNESCO, *Universal Declaration on the Human Genome*, arts. 12, 18, 19; UNESCO, *International Declaration on Human Genetic Data*, art. 198.

[77] See also Resnik, *Owning the Genome*, p. 65.

[78] I am not here implying that human rights are unimportant, but rather saying that, in discussions about patenting the genome, the *emphasis* must be on alternative strategies in order to arrive at workable solutions. There are, of course, exceptions, such as attempts to patent DNA from indigenous populations.

[79] HUGO Ethics Committee, *Statement on Human Genomic Databases*, December 2002.

considering in rather more detail HUGO's ethics-committee proposal on benefit-sharing. It arises because private expenditures for genetic research exceed those of governments. The committee also argues that benefit-sharing needs to be much wider than that covered by compensatory justice afforded, for example, to those participating directly in the research or gaining therapeutic benefit by such participation. It recognises that international laws on biodiversity in plants have established the principle of benefit-sharing. I suggest, however, that the degree to which this principle has influenced policy-making is doubtful, since there is a distinct lack of benefit-sharing of non-human genetic resources. While the committee recognises that immediate health benefits determined by community needs should be provided, even in the absence of profits, such a goal would be difficult to achieve, given the TRIPS agreement currently in place, which allows for provision only in emergency situations such as a pandemic. The committee also suggests that, in the cases where a small group harbours an unusual gene that benefits another with a particular disorder, then justice may require that the original group be recognised. HUGO suggests that benefits should be shared among the group as a whole, regardless of participation in the research. It also suggests that profit-making ventures, which would include patenting, should include a donation to the healthcare infrastructure or to humanitarian efforts in the communities studied. HUGO sets this at a modest 1%–3% of their annual net profit. This amount seems to me to be mere tokenism, but it would at least be a move in the right direction. It is also worth noting that others have used the rhetoric of 'benefit-sharing', but have come to very different conclusions about what needs to be done. David Resnik, for example, supports the principle of benefit-sharing, but also suggests that there is no need to make substantive changes to patenting law currently prevailing in the United States.[80] However, it seems to me that, in addition to having a general notion of the good and the sharing of benefits, we also need to know both what these goods might mean more specifically, and how such general justice might find expression. For this the virtue of prudence is essential.

THE CARDINAL VIRTUES AND THE COMMON GOOD

In discussion over the public good, one critical issue remains, and that is the extent to which this concept coheres with the Christian notion of the

---

[80] Resnik, *Owning the Genome*, pp. 11, 81.

common good and the means through which such goals can be fostered.[81] The common good links more specifically with teleology associated with the virtues. I will argue in this section that, while the public good is certainly a goal to be achieved, the language of human rights also needs to be supplemented by the language of virtue if the goals of the public good are likely to be achieved. This is for a number of reasons. In the first place, rights language will only impinge on the consciences of those who have already perceived the need for greater distribution of resources and benefit-sharing. Where consciences remained dulled, it is more likely that rights language will be seen conveniently as political issues that are outside the consideration of secular biotechnological organisation, in much the same way that religious issues were dismissed out of hand as being irrelevant to particular aspects of patent law discussed in the European Union. In the second place, rights language will appeal to those who are affected negatively by patent inventions, but equally the language of rights could be used in a counter-attack in order to appeal to a particular right or freedom to carry out research. I am not suggesting that rights language is irrelevant; rather, I am saying I am not convinced that it is the best means of implementing the direction towards the public good that is so vitally needed.

The four cardinal virtues of prudence, justice, temperance and fortitude are also relevant in this context. A file for a patent might seem prudent to a particular biotechnology company, where prudence is seen in terms of decision-making orientated towards the good. However, the motivation behind such application needs to be carefully scrutinised to determine which particular goods it is likely to promote. The good portrayed is often phrased in such a way as to highlight prospective medical benefits for those suffering from debilitating diseases, while the underlying good is simply for the originators of the 'invention'. Of course, beneficence needs to include concern for suffering, but the purported benefit of relief of suffering is not always an inevitable result of the research undertaken and the patent application applied for. In other words, the outcomes of the patent application are not always self-evident, but rather are projections in order to win public support. The motivation for patenting is not always genuine; the real underlying motivation may be, for example, to block someone else's research, to take an unfair share of the market, or to gain power and control over resources that are more properly seen as an aspect of the common heritage of humanity. Many of the proposals for

---

[81] See, for example, Hollenbach, *Christian Ethics and the Common Good.*

embryonic stem-cell research seem to be in this category, where claims for medical cures are exaggerated and the risks ignored in the bid to win both public support and patent rights. The EU 1998 directive on patenting seemed to place economic goals at its heart, and, while it granted the admissibility of a morality clause, in practice it has sought to become more closely aligned to the more liberal patent policy operative in the United States. The case studies suggest that the morality clause may for a time delay provision of a patent in the European Union, but eventually the economic pressures of a capitalist market economy will force the granting of such patents.

In such a scenario it becomes difficult to know how to find ways into changing a system that has succeeded in making the powerful more power-ful than ever before. I suggest that benefit-sharing needs to include, not just the economic and material products of a particular invention in terms of distribution, but also a sharing in *power* so that those who are most disadvantaged overall have a say in the way policy might be shaped and new research conducted. This goes beyond the notion of human rights as such, since it encourages inclusion at an early stage, even *before* the human rights and justice issues become evident. HUGO suggests that 3% be given by those making profits to support health infrastructure. But this still leaves the system intact, with the majority of research directed towards the health needs of a narrow minority. In 1998, for example, the twenty-nine coun-tries that comprised the Organisation for Economic Co-operation and Development (OECD), spent $520 billion on research and development, leading to 91% of patents and representing more than the total economic output of thirty of the poorer nations.[82] Instead, a greater responsibility for global health needs is required so that those multinational companies that make excessive profits from genomic research begin to take more active steps in research that will be beneficial to the poorer members of the human community. Just as there has been a progressive 'greening' of businesses under public pressure for social responsibility, so there needs to be a greater degree of *social accountability* in research, rather than simply orientating research to suit market opportunities.

Of course, while prudence, in the classic tradition, would have fostered decision-making that makes for public goods, the virtue that is most clearly aligned with prudence in this case is charity, or disinterested love of neighbour. Such charity would include not just donation of monetary resources, which can seem condescending to those on the receiving end,

[82] UNDP, *Human Development Report 2001*, p. 109.

but a far greater share in decision-making and policy-setting in accordance with the needs of the community in question. It would make sense for multinationals to liaise with those charitable agencies who have had some practical experience of working alongside communities in this regard, and drawing on shared knowledge about their particular needs and aspirations. There has been some attempt to do this in the sharing of genetic goods of crop plants, such as the development of Vitamin A rice. Unfortunately, the researchers failed to take into account local knowledge, such as the existence of naturally occurring varieties that exceed the vitamin production of the genetically modified rice plant.[83]

I have already discussed the issue of justice, but as far as the virtues are concerned, justice includes both the manner of patent applications and also the way benefits are shared in a community. Clearly, even though justice is measurable according to certain rules, it is important that *justice as virtue* is practised in relation to patenting in order to try to prevent the legal battles and acrimonious struggles that lead to so much strife and misunderstanding. In the first place, justice as procedural requires that those who seek patents do not do so in such a way as to make claims that are unjustified; for example, claiming for novelty, as in SNP sequencing, when such procedures are routine. Of course, admitting that one's research is routine rather than an invention requires also the virtue of humility, a virtue that is vital to the growth of science, relying as it does on the insights of so many others as it takes small steps towards discovering knowledge. Humility is also required in the sense that there needs to be an admission that one's application has been wrong in the past, and a willingness to change in the future. Justice as procedural also requires a measure of inclusion in decision-making of those likely to be affected by particular decisions.

Patent law is not really the right instrument to enforce specific bans on particular processes, so the suggestion of parallel regulatory bodies of the type suggested by the churches' bioethics committee seems to be a sensible one. There are already regulatory bodies in some jurisdictions, determining the legitimacy of certain controversial areas in genetics, such as the UK Human Fertilisation and Embryology Authority (HFEA). Although this group has its critics, it is infinitely preferable to have some sort of regulatory body in place than to have no regulation at all. It would seem entirely sensible to have parallel regulatory international bodies that work in conjunction with TRIPS, and regulatory European bodies that work in conjunction with the European Patent Office (EPO). Such regulatory

---

[83] Shiva, 'Life on a Threatened Planet'.

bodies would oversee the regulation put in place through both TRIPS and EPO to ensure that the public good was achieved in a fair and reasonable way and that justice was done in cases likely to arouse controversy or dispute.

There is also a need for fortitude – that is, the willingness to suffer for the sake of the good. This third cardinal virtue is important in as much as any proposal to change the existing system is almost bound to meet with considerable opposition. This is likely to be the case for those who are within the biotechnological community as well as for those outside it. Not all biotechnological companies have dismissed, for example, the need to desist from patenting fragments of the human genome. While their motivation may, in some cases, be related to a perceived market opportunity in terms of building up public support, all efforts to try to redeem a system that has worked so much to the disadvantage of poor and powerless groups in the community need to be welcomed.

Temperance is, above all, the virtue that urges restraint from taking more than is necessary for one's own health and well-being. In other words, it would challenge the greedy acquisition of resources for individual benefit that seems to have been encouraged indirectly by the way patent law has developed in the Western world.[84] Temperance is also a virtue that has particular relevance when considering the patenting of non-human resources. While there should be some reward for inventiveness, a greater degree of discernment or prudential decision-making should be used in order

1. to distinguish adequately between genuine health needs and cosmetic wants that are merely a luxury
2. to determine what is appropriate as the patent royalty in each case, in order to prevent excessive rewards
3. to distinguish between a good that is common to all of humanity, such as genetic databases or cDNA, and genuine inventiveness that can be rewarded
4. to encourage a willingness, through temperance, to share in any goods gained
5. to encourage a willingness, through temperance, to forfeit the right to patents in those countries that lack the means to sustain basic healthcare provision.

The fifth provision is important, for otherwise, under point 4, the gains obtained from, for example, developing nations through patent payments

---

[84] I am including multinational companies when I speak of individual benefit here.

are simply taken with one hand and then given back with the other, producing no net gain by these nations. A similar situation existed in the past where there was a campaign to cancel the debts of poorer nations, in an attempt to re-establish a level playing field for those who suffer gross disadvantage.

CONCLUSIONS

This chapter has addressed the knotty issue of patenting genes, focusing attention on human genetics and associated questions. I have argued that the patenting of biological processes is bringing to light a number of complex ethical issues that need to be considered through international debates. It is clear that the United States has the most liberal policy on patenting, allowing for the patenting of any living being as long as human intervention has been involved. European law, while including a morality clause, seems so far to have failed to restrain the increasing grip by private companies on biotechnological goods through patenting. Theological discussion on patenting has tended to focus on the morality or otherwise of patenting life, and, while some theologians argue that because life is a gift it cannot be patented, others suggest that the gift of creativity is itself God-given and so deserves to be rewarded. The religious offence caused by patenting of human beings, human cell lines or human DNA is more convincingly addressed through considerations about humanity as being in relationship with God, and the disjunction of this relationship that seems to be served by commodification. However, I have argued that over and above these considerations, the social-justice agenda is one that needs to be much more carefully analysed by Christian ethicists. Patenting of DNA fragments should be banned, not so much because of religious concerns, but because it serves to erode a common heritage of humanity that is a resource to be shared and to provide benefit for all. This makes sense not only in terms of science, but also in terms of the way patent law has been set up, namely to protect inventions that have useful applications. By 'reaching through' to areas that are broadly encompassed in a patent and preventing others from conducting the research, in spite of exclusion clauses on experimental use, such broad-scale patenting serves to shut down research rather than to enhance its progress.

I have also argued that gene patenting needs to be criticised where it seems to work against the public good, as is the case of the international TRIPS agreement as it currently stands. I have suggested that, while human rights have their place in implementing basic justice requirements, in order to challenge the system there must be other ways of reforming the current practice as it stands. One way is through additional regulatory bodies that have the power to ban research in some areas. Another way is through encouraging those in influential positions to develop virtues of prudence, justice, temperance and fortitude. Other virtues, including charity and humility, are also important. This topic clearly goes beyond the scope of a single chapter. I have tried, at least, to offer a preliminary analysis of the kind of direction in which the discussion might go, though the field is evolving all the time with new global regulations and new possibilities for patent applications. In the chapter that follows I will explore more specific questions about women and genetic technologies, especially those involving the new reproductive technologies. This discussion also raises important social and political issues that need to be borne in mind when considering ethics and genetics.

CHAPTER 8

Women and genetic technologies

While women may, like men, be involved in the practice of genetic science, advances in genetics have a differential impact on women. The extent to which women have been excluded from genetic science, alongside other sciences, is not the central concern of this chapter. Rather, its purpose is to tease out feminist ethical debates about new reproductive technologies in relation to their coherence or otherwise with the tradition of practical wisdom, justice and natural law that I have elaborated elsewhere. Feminist standpoints on bioethics are far more diverse than is commonly assumed, ranging across the political spectrum. There are, nonetheless, some overall trends in their approach that are worth noting. These are, broadly: (a) an emphasis on an ideal of care, rather than that which stresses rationality; (b) a stress on interpersonal relationships rather than autonomy; and (c) communitarian responsibility rather than individual rights. This picture is clouded somewhat by some feminists who seek to stress justice for women in the context of new reproductive technologies, and others who are equally comfortable with the language of rights for women and other disadvantaged groups, including embryos. In all cases, nonetheless, the intention is similar, namely to uncover those social and philosophical assumptions that have served to reinforce patriarchal and sexist elements in society, and the extent to which these pervade new reproductive technologies that are now on offer. It is important to consider new reproductive technologies, as they are intricately bound up with genetic screening and the possibilities for IGM. I intend to highlight the main areas for debate and to offer critical commentary on the discussion thus far. I will also develop my own argument for an ethical approach that is sensitive to feminist concerns, using the threads that run through this book, namely virtue ethics drawing predominately on prudence and justice, as well as natural-law theory, traditionally used to promote more conservative positions.

FROM ACCEPTANCE TO RESISTANCE?

Anthony Dyson discusses the changing attitudes to the new genetic technologies among feminists.[1] He suggests that, outside feminist discourse, ethical approaches to the new genetics have often been unaware of the value systems embedded in technology, and of the politics surrounding the discussions. While the enlarging control of the technology through medical practice is reassuring to some ethicists, feminists tend to react in the opposite way, viewing such practices as a further intrusion on women's lives and choices. Of course, early feminist writers such as Simone de Beauvoir, writing in the 1950s and 1970s, before the successful birth of the first 'test tube baby', welcomed the opportunities that the new reproductive technologies might bring for women, since they believed that it could free women from the 'tyranny' of reproductive biology.[2] De Beauvoir believed that reproduction might be achieved through artificial wombs, a possibility that is very unlikely to be realised.

Feminist writing from the 1980s was much more likely to be highly critical of the possibilities inherent in the new reproductive technologies. Hilary Rose and Jalna Hanmer were among a number of feminists who asked how far such technologies would add to the oppression of women rather than liberate them from it.[3] Others, such as Deborah Steinberg, joined in the debates, asking important questions about precisely which women were helped by the new reproductive technologies, and challenging further the failure to question the positivistic assumptions behind such technology.[4] Such issues continue to dominate the debates, as I will elaborate further below. Yet the shift towards challenging the new reproductive technologies among feminists is not quite as linear as Dyson implies. The underlying focus on women's right to choose, the need to care for women who face real distress because of problems with fertility, the challenge of caring for a seriously ill child – all these factors combine with social analysis of a more political nature about the desirability or otherwise of the new genetic technologies.[5] There are also considerable debates on

---

[1] Dyson, *Ethics and the New Reproductive Technologies.*   [2] De Beauvoir, *The Second Sex.*

[3] H. Rose, 'Victorian Values in a Test Tube: the Politics of Reproductive Science and Technology', in Stanworth (ed.), *Reproductive Technologies*, pp. 15ff.; J. Hanmer and P. Allen, 'Reproductive Engineering: The Final Solution?', in Birke and West (eds.), *Alice through the Microscope.*

[4] D. Steinberg, 'The Depersonalisation of Women through the Administration of "In Vitro Fertilisation"', in McNeil et al. (eds.), *The New Reproductive Technologies.* See also Steinberg, *Bodies in Glass.*

[5] For an informative discussion see, for example, Helga Kuhlmann, 'Crisis Pregnancies in the Age of Human Genetic Diagnosis: Women's Right to Self-determined Pregnancy and the Right of the Other', in Junker-Kenny (ed.), *Designing Life?*, pp. 93–111.

how far genetic intervention is desirable or permissible from a feminist point of view. The complexity of the discussion, including its alignment with religious considerations, means that the jury is still out as far as feminists are concerned, on genetic interventions. Nonetheless, it is still reasonable to suggest that, although feminists have raised some of the most critical voices on the underlying social and political issues, it is an area that needs to be of concern to *all people*, not just those with feminist commitments.

AN ETHIC OF CARE?

The development of an ethic of care is a response to the depersonalisation of much of biomedicine, with its stress on rational choice and autonomy of the patient. Margrit Shildrick speaks of the way the healthcare professions have 'pathologised' individuals, making them 'objects of the clinical gaze', and thus have 'silenced the voice of the patient'.[6] A care-based ethic attempts to correct this trend, and has particular resonance with the nursing profession, gaining popularity especially through the work of Carol Gilligan, Nel Noddings and Sara Ruddick.[7] Carol Gilligan based her study on analysis of the way women confronted with an unwanted pregnancy make decisions, and provided a corrective to an exclusive emphasis on justice, impartiality and individual rights, which, she believed, had dominated the discourse in medical ethics. Gilligan argued that, while justice figures more strongly in decisions made by men, an ethic that revolves around notions of care and interconnected relationships is much more common among women. It is important to stress that Gilligan found differences in *tendencies* between men and women from her field work; some men do make decisions in a way that is more responsive to caring needs, but less frequently than women. Such men are more likely to be drawn to work in the so-called 'caring' professions. Nel Noddings, on the other hand, focuses more specifically on the (genetic) maternal instincts of women in their care for their newborn babies, believing that the particularity of such interests excludes issues of justice. Noddings has been criticised by other feminist writers for attempting to remove equality considerations.[8] Ruddick similarly has used mothering as a basis for ethics, but prefers to portray this in gendered language; that is, she suggests that

---

[6] Shildrick, *Leaky Bodies and Boundaries*, p. 76.
[7] Gilligan, *In a Different Voice*; Noddings, *Caring*; Ruddick, *Maternal Thinking*.
[8] See, for example, Mahowald, *Genes, Women, Equality*, p. 152.

'maternal thinking' can be a capacity of men as well as of women. Because she links her ideas with a commitment to pacifism, her thinking includes a social and political component, rather than relating caring to essentialist notions about women as such.

An ethic of care has been developed in a more specifically theological way by authors such as Diana Cates, who has argued consistently for putting feeling back into professional medicine, so that we learn to develop compassion for others unlike ourselves. While it is related to the concept of beneficence, she seeks to go further than this in developing the notion of friendship, and also rooting her discussion theologically through Thomistic themes of friendship with God.[9] Cates suggests that such friendship is not just about mutual regard for those like ourselves, but about wishing and doing good for the other in order to enable the other's flourishing. Charity allows such love to flow out to others, even when they are strangers or hostile towards us, so that such benevolence represents a 'tendency to recognise other humans as being like us in their humanness and to experience towards them a weak, but dependable, sense of affection and good will' (p. 126). Cates reinforces her argument by pointing to the friendship with God in which this good will rests; hence there is a theological basis for her ideas about care:

Friendship with God pursued in friendship with others gives the believer the unforgettable impression that all human beings have a share in the divine life, that all human beings by virtue of our participation in the same life are embedded in each other's lives, that the genuine good of each of us includes inescapably the good of every other, and that finally we will flourish, or wither, together. (p. 130)

Cates has also applied her ethic of caring to biomedical ethics, though disappointingly her edited collection did not include the specific issue of the new reproductive technologies.[10]

I suggest that an ethic of care that puts due emphasis on particular relationships could usefully be applied to areas of genetic practice such as genetic counselling and counselling prior to fertility treatment. Women who come for fertility treatment, for example, are vulnerable in as much as their desire for children has been frustrated. In these circumstances they tend not to hear when told of those aspects of treatment that are negative. Because of the relatively low statistical success of giving birth to a healthy baby (up to about 25%, though the success rate is about a third of this for

---

[9] Cates, *Choosing to Feel*, pp. 119–26.
[10] Cates and Lauritzen (eds.), *Medicine and the Ethics of Care*.

women over forty years old[11]), most women who undergo 'treatment' will be disappointed; so even calling IVF a 'treatment' is a misnomer, as it implies rather more probability of positive outcomes.[12] An ethic of care would both support women in their vulnerability and help them to face up to the practical implications of their choice whether or not to go ahead with one of the new reproductive technologies, depending on which one is medically accessible. There must be sufficient support if the couple decide not to go ahead with the procedure; the common assumption is that their choice will be acceptance once they know about the procedures. These might be, for example, IVF for infertility, or the use of IVF with pre-implantation genetic diagnosis (PGD) where there is a known risk of genetic disease. The processes involved in IVF, for example, involve risks associated with the drug regimes used for stimulating egg collection, such as ovarian hyperstimulation; risks associated with the surgical procedures used for collecting eggs; adverse effects of Clomid, a drug used in the absence of IVF; the enhanced risk of ectopic pregnancy or ovarian cysts; the increase in likelihood of an earlier onset of menopause; and an increase in the likelihood of some forms of cancer.[13] There is also the humiliation and depersonalisation associated with the medical treatment itself, though I doubt whether this is necessarily deliberately misogynist.[14] Other impor-tant factors include the psychological risks associated with the ups and downs of 'treatment' cycles – the intense hope, followed by disappoint-ment with each attempt; the strain in relationships, especially if there is disagreement about the extent to which intervention should be pursued; the effects on family life if other children are involved; and the disruption to work where, as is increasingly likely, the woman is in paid employment. An ethic of care can help to alleviate some of these negative effects by showing appropriate empathy and making sure that relationships are sustained, regardless of the decision made. Above all, an ethic of care needs to respect the dignity of the persons involved and ensure that choices are made with the good of the family at the forefront of any decision-making. Rosemarie Tong suggests that much of maternal desire comes from social conditioning, so that 'to the degree that a woman is convinced that being a genetic and gestational mother is the *sine qua non* for her

---

[11] Success rates are improving with time, and some clinics report up to 40% clinical pregnancies for women under thirty-five years old. Live births are 10% lower than this because of spontaneous miscarriage.

[12] Chadwick (ed.), *Ethics, Reproduction and Genetic Control*, pp. xv–xvii.

[13] For discussion of these and other risks see Tong, *Feminist Approaches to Bioethics*.

[14] For a discussion see Cahill, *Sex, Gender and Christian Ethics*, p. 245.

success as a human being, she will "want" to use virtually any reproduction-aiding technology to achieve her maternal aim'.[15] An ethic of care, in other words, seeks to uncover motivation that presents childbearing as the only way in which women can affirm their humanity or express their role in a committed relationship, but also respects the dignity of an individual and her ability to make choices for herself.

An ethic of care is also appropriate in those situations where a mother may be faced with a termination of a pregnancy because of the genetic condition of her foetus. In such circumstances a great deal of sensitivity is called for and is well channelled by an ethic of care. For example, the practical needs of the family must be considered, and a caring attitude must be fostered towards the mother who has to make agonising choices about what to do in such circumstances. An ethic of care makes less judgment about the rights and wrongs of a given action, but tries to put charity for the mother first, while also allowing for the possibility that the child, if the pregnancy goes ahead, will be born into a loving environment. How one thinks about the status of the human embryo will influence whether or not an abortion is acceptable, in which case care-giving would include care shown to the foetus in the womb as well, though most feminists do not take this position.[16] Even the most conservative position might allow for the abortion of a foetus affected by a terminal condition, where there is little hope for a live birth. Yet an ethic of care would also seek to maintain the interests of those who suffer from disabilities and mental retardation, given the range of conditions that can be classified as allowable for legal abortion. Presenting a positive picture of the kind of life that is possible for someone with a given genetic condition can help to alleviate the more extreme fears associated with having a disabled child. An ethic of care would not, for example, reject those with disabilities, but welcome them as members of the human family.

An ethic of care has also been developed through caring for those who suffer from all kinds of disabilities, so it has the advantage of not prejudging the choice of a mother faced with the possibility of abortion, while recognising that families may not feel equipped to take up this demanding role. Mary Mahowald is right to be critical of those feminists who have declined to support mothers who care for their disabled children on the

---

[15] Tong, *Feminist Approaches to Bioethics*, p. 182.

[16] Some exceptions include those who are more inclined towards traditional Roman Catholic interpretations about the status of the embryo, such as Liz Hepburn, who argues that counselling needs to raise ethical debates about the moral status of the foetus; see, for example, her 'Genetic Counselling: Parental Autonomy or Acceptance of Limits?', in Junker-Kenny and Cahill (eds.), *The Ethics of Genetic Engineering*, pp. 35–42.

grounds that such care-giving reinforces female stereotypes of subservience.[17] She argues that such misplaced mother-blaming ignores the experience of mothers who are vulnerable, in that they are more likely to suffer from the ill health, guilt and anger associated with care-giving. The extent of the physiological and psychological toll on these mothers is also related to their perception of the severity of their child's symptoms, the reality of the symptoms, and their own relationship with the father. Caregiving can be satisfying for men as well as women, but only relatively few men feel able to take up this challenge. The social assumption is that women will be the primary care-giver in such circumstances.

There are, nonetheless, a number of problems associated with an ethic of care, as other feminists have pointed out. Susan Sherwin, for example, is particularly critical of an ethic of care, believing that it simply reinforces the subordination of women.[18] In its emphasis on affective relationships and communities, social relationships and politics can be ignored, including, for example, the wider issues associated with equality in the new reproductive technologies. An ethic of caring can also reinforce stereotypes about women as caring in a way that can, in some cases, be exploitative for women. It seems to me that this is especially problematic where caring is linked specifically to biology rather than to gender, as, for example, in Nodding's version of care ethics, for this tends to reinforce the concept of essentialist differences between men and women. In this respect it serves to reinforce assumptions about women related to their biological function, which is one of the main reasons for feminist rejection of reproductive stereotyping relating to the role of women in society.

There is current academic discussion on how far altruism, common to non-human social communities, has parallels with Christian and humanitarian traditions of charity.[19] This discussion has not been taken into account in feminist discussions about an ethic of care. Such sociobiological research demonstrates that altruistic love, especially that relating to care for our own kind, is linked with deep-rooted biological urges that we share with other social animals. Of course, the social processes involved in complex animal behaviour, including aspects of altruism, can also be discussed in terms of their own development of forms of 'culture', rather than simply assuming that this behaviour arises out of biological 'instinct' that has, for example, genetic origins. The intention to foster love for 'outsiders' and enemies, in particular, does not seem to have any parallel

---

[17] Mahowald, *Genes, Women, Equality*, pp. 154–5.   [18] Sherwin, *No Longer Patient*.
[19] See Post et al. (eds.), *Altruism and Altruistic Love*.

outside the human community, which is one reason why *agapē* seems to reach beyond the boundaries of altruism.[20] Feminist discussion of an ethic of care has not incorporated this debate into its analysis, but it would be helpful to do so, since it would clarify those elements of caring that arise from biologically rooted desires, those that arise from cultural elements that are shared with social animals, and those elements that are distinctive to a particular religious tradition. The self-reflectivity that is possible in such analysis is peculiar to the human community.

In general, feminists have strongly rejected drawing on sociobiological analysis because of a broad tendency among more prominent sociobiologists to reinforce misogynist practice as simply arising out of biological drives. There is also a strong difference in emphasis; while sociobiologists want to put more emphasis on biology as the source of sexual difference, feminists are more inclined to view such differences, in the human community at least, as arising as much out of social construction as out of biology. John Dupré, for example, highlights the way sociobiologists, writing at the beginning of the emergence of the field, served to shock by deliberately sexist remarks, such as that by E. O. Wilson, who claimed: 'It pays males to be aggressive, hasty, fickle and undiscriminating. In theory it is more profitable for females to be coy, to hold back until they can identify males with the best genes ... Humans obey this biological principle faithfully.'[21] Such crude versions of sociobiology, which clearly need to be rejected, are only one possible interpretation, and are not supported by empirical evidence. Dupré suggests that there is no sign that this trend has abated within some more popularist versions of sociobiology; if anything, sociobiologists, especially those seeking popular appeal, have become even less qualified and more confident in their statements regarding the relationships between men and women. In these cases, men are defined through their ability to inseminate women, regardless of the consequences, thus removing them completely from the possibility of any version of a care ethic, or any ethic whatsoever for that matter.[22] It can also lead to crude popularist versions of biological determinism, where genetics becomes the source of all social ills, including tendencies towards sexual abuse and violence. It is understandable that feminists have distanced themselves from such crude and ill-founded analysis.

Given this, it is not really surprising that feminists have failed to consider other aspects of sociobiology that are rather more informative and suitably

[20] See Grantén, *Patterns of Care*.   [21] Wilson, *On Human Nature*, p. 125.
[22] Dupré, *Human Nature*, p. 48.

qualified, at least in some instances: for example, discussions around altruism. It is also apparent that those books that do examine in more detail aspects of altruism in relation to religious faith fail to discuss adequately the philosophical issues that are implicit in sociobiology, including the critique by feminists.[23] On the other hand, an ethic of care that aims to be inclusive – that is, to encourage both men and women to be more conscious of the need for charity both within and beyond the immediate biological needs of the family unit – is to be welcomed as an important ingredient in medical ethics. Care also needs to inform ethical issues around genetics, especially aspects related to making choices about genetic intervention, and fostering care for those who suffer from disabilities arising from genetic conditions.

AN ETHIC OF JUSTICE?

A question that now needs to be asked is whether an ethic that puts due emphasis on equality and justice is more appropriate than an ethic of care, given the gendered nature of genetic disease and its relatively greater impact on women than on men. There are twin sources of gendered differences in genetics, which can be analysed empirically. The first source is related to biological differences; for example, defective genes can be mitochondrial or sex-linked in origin. These gendered differences are unchangeable in that men have Y chromosomes, while women do not.[24] The second source refers to changeable differences in the impact of genetics on women, related to psychosocial attitudes and practices. One example is the differential burden on women in terms of responsibility to care for children affected by genetic conditions. More support should be given to principal care-givers, and men should be encouraged to take a more active part in their children's care, instead of assuming that the burden should fall on the mother of the child.[25] Employers also need to be flexible enough to adjust working schedules in order to facilitate the desire of care-givers to pursue goals beyond immediate care-giving. Another example is that the proliferation of genetic testing has its negative social consequences, felt more severely in those parts of the world where medical treatment is dependent on private health insurance.[26] In these cases, some people will not be able to afford medical insurance if they test

---

[23] See Post et al. (eds.), *Altruism and Altruistic Love.*
[24] This discussion must be qualified by consideration of those genetic defects of the sex chromosomes that lead to failure to develop a normal male or female form and physiology.
[25] Mahowald, *Genes, Women, Equality*, pp. 74–5.   [26] Ibid., pp. 298–9.

positive for certain genetic conditions. This is likely to affect indirectly the health of those who test positive for genetic conditions, and, given that women are less likely to be able to afford expensive healthcare, it is more likely to have a differential impact on women.

In advocating the importance of a reinstatement of justice, it is important to know what is meant by this term. The libertarian version of justice simply refers to equal rights of individuals – in the case of genetic testing, prenatal testing and treatment, to have access to these services and to be charged according to market forces, as long as the individuals are informed about the risks involved. John Rawls's social-contractarian theory attempted to move beyond this simple model and to include alleviation of social and economic inequalities. Susan Okin extends his ideas by pointing to the patriarchal structures of families, which Rawls ignores.[27] Yet one can ask whether an extension of Rawlsian rights theory is sufficient, for it still uses the dualistic language that underwrites superiority of mind over body.[28] Libertarianism also mistakenly assumes that voluntary practice will be sufficient to reduce the inequalities that arise out of different genetic endowments. Libertarians, for example, would reject government interference in principle as an infringement of liberty, even if they were intended to reduce inequalities arising out of genetic conditions. Mahowald argues convincingly that 'at best, a libertarian feminism is a partial feminism because, by limiting its advocacy to procedural freedom, it advocates only for those women who are substantively free already'.[29] Liberal feminism can also be problematic where it deals only with women and does not extend to other non-dominant groups. There are, further, difficulties with communitarian versions of feminism, since in theory a community could support an anti-feminist stance. Where individuals are members of different communities, how does the demand of one group outweigh that of another? Mahowald seems to be on the right track in arguing for a socialist version of feminism, for it challenges inequalities regardless of race, class, gender, ability, sexuality and genetic endowment. She also argues that individual differences can be accommodated within this model, though she prefers the label 'egalitarian', since 'socialist' can sometimes be viewed with suspicion by liberals concerned about individual rights and liberties.

Mahowald raises the possibility of distributive justice in genetics: for example, the relative allocation of resources to genetic research and testing in such a way that other social needs are not considered. Is the Human

[27] Okin, *Justice, Gender and the Family.*   [28] Jagger, *Feminist Politics and Human Nature.*
[29] Mahowald, *Genes, Women, Equality*, p. 80.

Genome Project (HGP) a prime example of this kind of over-distribution of goods in terms of financial cost?[30] Criticism also came from scientists themselves, who believed that the companies likely to benefit from the research should have provided the funds. I suggest that there would, none-theless, have been a drawback to this method, since it could have led to patenting of the human genome (which was attempted by Craig Ventor), and it would not have allowed subsequent sharing of the knowledge for the benefit of basic scientific research (see chapter 7 above). Political interests were clearly at stake in facilitating the HGP, which represents only the tip of the iceberg in terms of understanding human genetics. Care needs to be taken in the release of personal genetic information, so that it is enforced only in those cases where it impinges on the treatment of others likely to be affected, as in some cases of familial genetic diseases (see chapter 5 above). Difficulties are also associated with enforced counselling where this is neither desired or helpful, though I suggest that its opposite, the lack of availability of effective counselling, is much more likely to be a problem. The use of enforced genetic tests, such as the UK Government screening programme for all pregnant mothers for Down syndrome, is another good example of overdistribution of genetic testing and screening (see chapter 4 above). There are other disturbing examples of practice; for example, the use of ultrasound in India and China seems to have promoted the selective abortion of female foetuses. There is some evidence that chorionic villus sampling, which puts the foetus at risk, is routinely used among the wealthy educated sectors in Latin America, regardless of the actual possibility of genetic disease. Such practices amount to an excessive use of genetic technology, which fails to consider the real purpose for such intervention, namely the welfare of both the mother and the baby.

Poor mothers in some rich countries such as the United States do not have access to genetic tests, as they are not available through a national health service. In the very poorest communities of the world the 0.5% risk of having a Down-syndrome baby would be considered insignificant by comparison with the fact that the women who do become pregnant face a 1%–2% chance of mortality, and 10% of all babies die before their first birthday.[31] There are also some discrepancies in the UK national system, since certain forms of testing are available only to those prepared to pay a fee.

---

[30] For further discussion see Deane-Drummond (ed.), *Brave New World?* It is also pertinent in this context that Mahowald was herself partly funded by the Human Genome Project.

[31] Penchaszadeh, 'Reproductive Health and Genetic Testing in the Third World'; V. B. Penchaszadeh, 'Implementing Genetic Services in Developing Countries', in Kuliev et al. (eds.), *Provision of Genetic Services: An International Perspective*, pp. 17–26.

This leads, in turn, to a disproportionate level of disability among the poor, who are often more likely to have affected children because of non-genetic-related influences, such as poor diet, drug abuse, teenage pregnancies and so on. There is also less access to infertility treatment among the poorer communities, leading to enhanced psychological suffering.

The gap between detection of a disease and the treatment for it means that for many women the only options for 'treatment', upon the discovery that their child suffers from a genetic illness, are either termination or to continue with the pregnancy. Of the world's population of women, 40% can, in theory, have access to abortion.[32] Second-trimester abortions can be performed where genetic disability is detected, or where the mother's health is seriously at risk, or where there are reasons why a young girl has concealed her pregnancy (for example, if she has been the victim of incest). The higher cost of abortions in the later stages, and the relatively smaller number of doctors willing to take up this procedure in the second tri-mester, mean that access is frequently denied to women. This leads to a disproportionate burden on poorer women, who are often ill equipped to deal with the burdens of a child with serious health problems. Mahawald defends the legal rights of all women to have access to abortion, although she recognises that, morally, there are debates about the status of the foetus. Mahowald also believes that, where there is conflict between the rights of the foetus and the mother's right to freedom of choice to terminate the pregnancy, then the mother's claim should take priority. I agree that there should be consistency in legal practice, so that poor women are not discriminated against simply because of their poverty, in a way that tends to exacerbate the difference between classes and lead to a much higher proportion of disability among the poor.

Yet the tragic nature of all abortions should not be forgotten. In those cases where late abortions are allowed, especially of foetuses suffering from a genetic condition, abortions are virtually equivalent to euthanasia, or even infanticide. Some of the reasons for permitting abortions at a late stage are far less justifiable than others, especially where the life expectancy and quality of life of the foetus are expected to be reasonably good, as in the case of Down syndrome, for example. In the United Kingdom a battle has been fought over the legality of a late termination of a pregnancy due to 'cleft palate', though of course, this condition is also associated with more serious genetic defects. If abortion is undertaken for apparently 'trivial' reasons, it cannot be justified, and the legislation needs to be challenged

---

[32] Mahowald, *Genes, Women, Equality*, p. 96.

and tightened up to reflect this. In addition, much more social support should be given to those mothers who decide to continue with their pregnancies whatever the diagnosis, so that the social stigma and economic burdens associated with having an affected child are minimised. Women must certainly not be made to feel irresponsible if they decide to refuse the tests offered to them, or if, having had the tests, they refuse to terminate a pregnancy. Ironically, perhaps, the differential access to abortion for rich and poor is likely to reinforce the social rejection of those with disabilities arising from genetic and social pressures, so that the poor are doubly marginalised, on account of both their economic disadvantage and their perceived lack of health.

In the discussion about genetic interventions through somatic or germ-line therapy, Mahowald believes that equality of access is the only criterion for approval or otherwise of both therapy to treat disease and enhancement to add particular characteristics (pp. 228–9). In other words, she believes that there are no reasons in principle why any number of changes cannot be allowed. While I suggest that equal access is important, it is unlikely to be achievable in the foreseeable future for IGM, because of the cost. It is also surprising, perhaps, that Mahowald does not consider the possible disadvantages associated with blanket approval; for example, who will make decisions about what is acceptable or not in terms of enhancement? This is a good example of the way distributive justice can become detached from notions of political prudence, so that the good outcome and the means to that outcome are not kept under review. Decisions are most likely to be taken by an elite, and, while Mahowald argues that women should be given a privileged status in defining use of IGM, it is unlikely to be the case in practice, given the other prevalent inequalities associated with genetic knowledge.[33]

TOWARDS AUTOKOENOMY

Is it possible to steer midway between an ethics of care and the position that puts more emphasis on relationships of power in disputes over bioethics?[34] There is a huge diversity among feminist positions, especially in their approach to ontology, epistemology, politics and ethics. More 'synthetic' approaches include that known as autokoenomy, where the *autonomous* self is affirmed, but in such a way as to take account of a *community with others*. Given the pressure towards autonomy as the

---

[33] For further discussion see above, chapter 7.   [34] Tong, *Feminist Approaches to Bioethics*, pp. 93–6.

prevailing principle in medical bioethics, this concept seems to serve as a challenge to bring such decisions into the context of community life, rather than assuming that individual choice is all that is required. Rosemarie Tong argues for forms of epistemology that recognise that all knowledge is, to some extent, situated in a particular historical context, and to this degree is partial and localised. She affirms the notion of practical dialogue, which is as much about learning to listen to the other points of view as about making one's own position clear. She recognises limitations to this approach; for example, if this process violates cultural conventions about self-disclosure, then it is not practicable; or if participants lack the necessary language skills, again it is unfeasible. Other conditions, such as a history of abuse or mental illness, may make communication difficult or impossible. In spite of these limitations, she argues that practical dialogue as expressive of autokoenomy is the most desirable option in establishing communities where effective decision-making can take place.

How viable and relevant is the notion of autokoenomy and practical dialogue? Difficult areas that are relevant to women's issues in this context include questions around egg or embryo donation. The practice of making this dependent on known donors has been challenged because of the pressure placed on women to help their infertile relatives. It is now much more likely to be anonymous and to entail some commercial reward, although in the United Kingdom these rewards are limited so as to discourage economic motivation for donation. The law in the UK has changed, so that from April 2005 donors who live in the UK are required to identify themselves to any child born from their gametes or embryos, if that child, on reaching the age of eighteen, desires this information. The legislation in this case has some parallels with laws around adoption, though, of course, for artificial insemination by donor (AID) the gametes or embryos are deliberately donated before the pregnancy is achieved. Nonetheless, given the shortage of the supply of eggs, sperm and embryos in fertility clinics in the UK, it is increasingly likely that fertility clinics will be pressing for more funding in order to advertise more widely abroad, where legislation is less tight, for donors to come forward, or to help underwrite the procedures in such practice, or even in some cases to facilitate the exchange of these genetic goods with other clinics that face a limited supply. In these scenarios there is a real possibility that the embryos or gametes could be seen as commodities that can be bought and sold. There is also a very real temptation to exploit women in poorer communities of the world, where the unequal trade exchange offers them sufficient incentive to sell their eggs or embryos to richer Western nations so that Western infertility clinics have sufficient gametes or embryos. It is extremely doubtful whether such women have been given the opportunity for any practical dialogue; rather, their need relates to the intensity of poverty and economic restriction.

Genetic counselling more generally would benefit from a tempering of autonomy so that it can take on board more of the needs of the community. One way suggested so far is through an ethic of care, but the ideal of autokoenomy implies the exploration of wider values and preferences in relation to social needs. While a paternalistic model is commonly rejected by counsellors, a second model is simply 'information-giving'. Counsellors may move towards what might be called an interpretive model, where the counsellor helps the client to articulate his or her own position and to recognise his or her values. However, Tong argues for something more proactive on the part of the counsellor, known as a deliberative model, which allows a genuine discussion to take place between the counselled and the counsellor. A deliberative approach permits an honest expression and discussion of the wider ethical and social issues implicated in each decision, rather than simply leaving it up to the 'client' to make the choice based on a bald knowledge of the science of the genetic disease concerned. I suggest that the danger with this approach is that, where women are vulnerable, they may not be able to engage in adequate argument or discussion, and so may defer to the counsellor rather than having confidence to express their own views in relation to other positions. It seems to me that the counsellor needs to be able to be flexible about the kind of model of counselling that is appropriate in each case. Clearly, raising wider issues about the ethical debates is helpful, over and above simply giving factual information about the scientific facts of the disease, but only as long as it is done in a sensitive way.[35] If counsellors do use deliberative methods, they need to be confident that their ability to articulate their position does not threaten the client in any way. Rosemarie Tong raises the possibility that those who refuse gene therapy, if it becomes routine, might be considered irresponsible, or might even be penalised, just as those who knowingly take drugs that harm their foetus may be prosecuted.[36] Such a move needs to be resisted strongly, especially where the only 'therapy' is termination of pregnancy. Tong is also more sensitive than Mahowald on the question of what defines genetic disease, and resists the idea of enhancement,

---

[35] Antony Dyson also argues that the trust implied in the giving of consent, and the autonomy implied in non-directional counselling, should not be separated from a commitment to help search for what ought to be done, that is, ethical issues. See Dyson, *Ethics and the New Reproductive Technologies*, p. 23.

[36] Tong, *Feminist Approaches to Bioethics*, p. 239.

regardless of how far it is readily accessible, for she recognises that many ideas about perfection (including, for example, beauty) are heavily conditioned by social and cultural norms.

The balance between the right of the individual to choose and the needs of the community is also expressed in attitudes to abortion, raised in our earlier discussion of the model of justice. Laura Purdy is one of the few feminist authors who argue that it is not in the embryo's interests to exist at all if it harbours a genetic disease such as Huntington's disease; thus it is 'immoral' to bring such children into the world.[37] Of course, other feminists have rightly criticised Purdy heavily, as they believe she has succumbed to a model of perfectability as being the only desirable way of being human.[38] Mahowald, as discussed above, accepts selective abortion as desirable as long as it does not discriminate against poor women. Adrienne Asch is more sanguine about the possible negative social consequences of genetic knowledge – if it is not perceived as random, communal commitments to those who are suffering from the disease will probably be reduced.[39] If genetic testing is perceived as an individual choice, social issues and responsibilities are weakened. She also argues that once parents have control over the characteristics of their children, they could become less accepting of their children's flaws, for the control is in fact illusory, since it is about selecting out certain genetic diseases. It is here that counselling needs to be seen as a way of breaking down illusions of perfectibility associated with genetic knowledge. Asch resists the idea that women should abort foetuses with genetic diseases that are not immediately fatal, such as Down syndrome, spina bifida, cystic fibrosis or muscular dystrophy, since all such sufferers can have meaningful lives. The difficulty, of course, is that abortions for such reasons are legally permissible in most countries, so women need much more social and moral support if they are to be convinced that they will be able to cope with the level of care that is required to look after an affected child. One should, however, note a highly objectionable trend observed by Michelle Stanworth, namely that in the mid-1980s three-quarters of all obstetricians in Britain indicated that, following prenatal tests on women, they had insisted on the abortion of foetuses affected by disabilities or health problems.[40]

---

[37] L. M. Purdy, 'Genetic Diseases: Can Having Children be Immoral?', in Arras and Rhoden (eds.), *Ethical Issues in Modern Medicine*, pp. 311–17.

[38] See Tong, *Feminist Approaches to Bioethics*, pp. 233–5.

[39] A. Asch and G. Geller, 'Feminism, Bioethics and Genetics', in Wolf (ed.), *Feminism and Bioethics: Beyond Reproduction*, pp. 318–50.

[40] M. Stanworth, 'Reproductive Technologies and the Deconstruction of Motherhood', in Stanworth (ed.), *Reproductive Technologies*, pp. 10–35 (p. 31).

FEMINIST THEOLOGY AND ETHICS

I will begin to interweave religious questions in this section by highlighting the theological arguments that have been used in support of the availability of genetic technologies for women. I will next consider how far feminist theologians working within more traditional theological approaches have sought to enlarge the discussion in terms of the common good. I will also ask how far an ethic that draws on natural law and on consideration of the virtues might contribute to feminist debates about the new reproductive technologies.

Theological arguments in favour of more choice

Barbara Nichols presents an argument in favour of prenatal testing for women from a theological perspective.[41] Like many others, she believes that the burden of care for children affected by genetic disease falls primarily on women, and that the assumption that women must be sacrificial in relation to childcare, which pervades traditional Roman Catholic approaches to motherhood, is misogynist and reflects the desire of men to control the sexuality and reproductive capacities of women. In this scenario, women are not viewed as moral agents, capable of making their own decisions and bearing responsibility for these decisions. Drawing on the work of Rosemary Radford Ruether, Nichols argues that women have been portrayed in a way that makes them feel responsible for the sin of humanity; they were the ones who took the forbidden fruit, and God is viewed as the one who then punishes the human race, and women in particular, for this act of disobedience. She argues that if the technology is rejected, the child must be accepted no matter what, but this portrays God as one who punishes women when it is not their fault. The Virgin Mary as the model of perfect obedience reinforces this lack of choice; a child is simply accepted without any real agency on the part of women. Mary as obedient and submissive mother is pitched against Eve, whose choice led to the expulsion of humanity from the Garden, and whose choice reflected a failure to observe limits. Nichols believes that such an interpretation of the Genesis text encourages women to see themselves as submissive, unable to make moral decisions. She suggests that

---

[41] B. Nichols, 'Genetic Testing: The Tree of the Knowledge of Good and Evil', in Ackermann and Storm (eds.), *Liberating Faith Practices*, pp. 153–74.

women have not been encouraged to exercise control over their reproductive capabilities, even while these reproductive capabilities have been used to define their social role. Nor have women been encouraged to protest or question an understanding of God as the one who punishes those who express moral agency, and who does so through the experience birth. (p. 167)

She argues strongly that a woman should not be blamed for a child's suffering a particular genetic condition, so that diseases such as breast cancer, early onset of Alzheimer's or mental deterioration should not be viewed as punishments from God. She believes that 'we do not need a fickle, obscure God who keeps us continually wanting to be punished for not having interpreted his wishes appropriately. Such a theology has more in common with the dynamics of domestic abuse' (p. 168).

Of course, her discussion revolves around the extent to which the Genesis text has been used as an occasion for suppressing women's capacity for decision-making. She cites Walter Brueggeman as suggesting that the Genesis story moves from trust and obedience to crime and punishment, so that choice is seen as a rebellious act rather than as an act of responsibility. She wishes instead to see the choice made by Eve as an act that allowed a more mature relationship with God, a moving into freedom. In response to her analysis, it is worth making a number of issues clear. In the first place, any interpretation of the Genesis story that encourages a view that suffering is always consequential on sin is a mistake, and goes against other biblical texts, such as Job, that challenge such presumption. Secondly, the tree of knowledge of good and evil is not related to the idea of forbidden knowledge as such, for in the earliest version of the story it was simply the tree in the middle of the garden.[42] It is therefore a mistake to interpret this story in such a way that seeking after knowledge is somehow forbidden by God, or that choices in and of themselves are not permitted. After all, implicit in human image-bearing are decisions and choices by both men and women in the naming of the animals and care for the earth. Rather, the choice that is rejected is one that knowingly goes against the covenantal relationship with God; yet even this choice is ambiguous, in that it does allow for some good outcomes in spite of such a decision. The difficulties with Nichols' analysis are, first, that she believes that the text supports a patriarchal and misogynist approach to women, which is not necessarily the case; and secondly, she does not consider the ambiguities for women that surround the new reproductive technologies. How free, for example, are the choices of women in this regard? She ignores the value of the foetus and the impact

---

[42] Westermann, *Genesis 1–11*, p. 222.

of such choices on other marginalised communities. She draws on the book of Job in order to reinforce her view that suffering is not the result of sin. However, she fails to consider the suffering of those who are labelled by genetic screening as having a life not worth living. Of course, we need to resist stereotypical views of women as passive recipients of an agenda set up and endorsed by men. But at the same time, there needs to be a far greater sensitivity to wider social and political issues, and to the consequences of such choices. Looking to novel interpretations of the Genesis text cannot take us very far; rather, we need to understand more fully what freedom means in the context of new genetic technologies, and have a correct appreciation of what it means to act morally under the auspices of a fully informed conscience.[43]

Nichols' conclusion that the new genetic technologies are both 'burden and blessing' raises the possibility that mistakes might be made, but she does not address the question of their nature. Of course, we need to avoid a scenario that she resists, where God simply creates the rules and humanity obeys. She is also correct to point out that women need much more support in their decision-making, but this can apply to either decision; she tends to assume that the decision will be made in favour of abortion rather than its opposite. Nichols fails to consider the tragedy that is implicated in any decision to terminate a foetus. Rather more helpful, then, is Helga Kuhlmann's analysis, which questions the almost hysterical fear of having a malformed child, a fear she believes is fostered through the notion of medical risk.[44] She is careful to distinguish between abortion of a handicapped child as forced by state intervention in the Nazi era, and that which is currently available. In addition, she believes that the pain and guilt associated with any termination, however it has come about, needs to be addressed by liturgical expressions that deal with the loss of and sorrow for the life that is killed. This would, of course, be most relevant in relation to pregnancies in the later stages, but earlier terminations still represent loss of potential life, regardless of one's views about the status of the embryo.[45]

---

[43] For more detailed discussion of the relationship between freedom, conscience and virtue, see C. Deane-Drummond, 'Freedom, Conscience and Virtue: Theological Perspectives on the Ethics of Inherited Genetic Modification', in Cole-Turner (ed.), *Design and Destiny*.

[44] Kuhlmann, 'Crisis Pregnancies', pp. 98–101.

[45] Maureen Junker-Kenny argues that the embryo should be given the status of personhood from the moment of conception, because of its potential for human life. I am less convinced by this argument, but at the same time I recognise that any decision to terminate, even for fatal conditions, always carries with it an element of the tragic that needs to be addressed by a sensitive and caring theological response. See M. Junker-Kenny, 'Embryos in Vitro, Personhood and Rights', in Junker-Kenny (ed.), *Designing Life?*, pp. 130–58.

There are important areas to discuss in relation to whether controlling life is itself desirable from a theological point of view. Maureen Junker-Kenny, for example, argues that the battle against natural chance immediately instrumentalises the one who is the recipient of the technology, robbing the person so conceived of his or her freedom, for it is 'designed in her specifically by another human will. Instead of being regarded as a threat to be minimised, natural chance needs to be acknowledged as the guardian of freedom' (p. 150). But this assessment assumes that the process of genetic intervention removes all elements of chance, which it clearly does not. At least in its acceptable form, it can be used to detect those conditions that are likely to be lethal for the child or to lead to severe suffering. Moreover, this assessment also implies that we are determined solely by genetics, that it is possible to 'design' our children, which is clearly not the case. Environmental factors play a highly significant role in human development. I agree with Junker-Kenny that we need to keep a close watch on the mentality of control that is implicit in the new reproductive technologies, to recognise all children as gifts, rather than as human products, and to be very wary of crossing any line that seems to suggest otherwise. I suggest that an intermediate approach between Nichols' affirmation and Junker-Kenny's rejection of the reproductive technologies is more in keeping with the tradition of prudence, as I will elaborate further below.

Theological arguments in favour of familial relationships

Lisa Cahill takes a rather different approach to Roman Catholic attitudes to the new reproductive technologies and is more liberal than Junker-Kenny.[46] She situates her discussion in the context of debates about sexuality and the family. She argues that ethical discussions about donor relationships, including, for example gamete and embryo donation, do not consider child welfare and family relationships adequately, but focus instead on consent and issues around autonomy. While the desire for a genetically related child is, she believes, legitimate, it is now possible to have a separation of genetic (through egg and sperm or embryo donation), gestational (through surrogate arrangements) and nurturing mothers. She

---

[46] Cahill, *Sex, Gender and Christian Ethics*, pp. 217–54. See also Shannon and Cahill, *Religion and Artificial Reproduction*, pp. 37–62, 105–38. Cahill is correct to identify the illogical position adopted by this instruction, namely that contraception, masturbation, adultery and rape are all categorised as similarly 'intrinsically evil' (p. 113). Cahill criticises the assumption that sex, love and the possibility of procreation are necessarily integral to every conjugal act, rather than needing to be considered in terms of the totality of the relationship.

raises an important question, namely: how far will such biological asymmetries affect family ecology? She recognises that while the Warnock report (1984) affirms 'family values' and attempts to look at a range of possible positions, it does not give a clear rationale for its liberal position. The USA Office of Technology Assessment (OTA) Report on Infertility (1988) makes little attempt to disguise its advocacy of reproductive choice as having primary value. Cahill is critical of the Vatican instruction on the new reproductive technologies, *Donum Vitae*, which, she argues, is mistaken in its assumption that simply affirming human dignity will work to curtail the spread of reproductive technologies. The official Roman Catholic position insists on a clear link between sexuality, marriage and parenthood, which the new reproductive technologies, including, for example, IVF, PGD, AID and artificial insemination by husband (AIH) all violate. While the OTA stresses freedom of choice, privacy, pragmatism and tolerance alongside the rights of would-be parents, the Vatican document stresses the duty of the couple to preserve the nature of marriage and the family, which they view as ineluctably linked to the procreative partnership of one man and one woman. Human rights are not so much the right to choose as the right of every human being to enjoy physical integrity in relation to his or her parents. Cahill characterises the OTA report as 'aggressively liberal', while the Vatican document puts more emphasis on duties than on rights. It also draws on the natural-law tradition to insist on its own conservative view regarding the new reproductive technologies.

Of course, there is a dilemma here, for natural law as such concerns that which all reasonable men and women can believe, but the Vatican interpretation of its meaning does not approach social consensus. Cahill is prepared to ask challenging questions about the official Vatican view: for example, do couples undergoing IVF necessarily experience this means of reproduction as a violation of married love? She also believes that the use of donors, including AID and egg donation, is morally far 'more dubious', since it involves a third party in the married relationship, who is detached from the social and psychological relationship with the child. As we have already noted, since 2005, in the United Kingdom at least, donors are required by law to identify themselves to any child resulting from their gametes (or embryos) who, on reaching the age of eighteen, wishes to trace his or her biological identity. Cahill argues that the media have contributed to a view of parenthood as essential for adulthood and social appeal, which has encouraged a sense of desperation among those who seek fertility treatment. Certainly, the view that becoming a gestational mother is necessary for a woman's identity needs to be resisted.

Cahill is not alone in pointing to the ambiguities involved for women seeking fertility treatment, as I have discussed in more detail above. I am, however, less convinced than she seems to be that donor relationships inevitably damage family life. I do agree that it adds another ethical dimension over and above that which arises out of what she terms 'homologous' relationships, namely the use of the gametes of both partners through IVF and presumably PGD as well. It seems to me that where a woman has become a gestational mother, the bonding that can arise is likely to be much stronger than that resulting from adoptive arrangements. Of course, there is an issue around the legitimacy of using gamete donation for such purposes, given the possibility of adoption.

Cahill argues that adoption is a viable way of channelling parental aspirations, and of course this possibility should be encouraged as one of the options for would-be parents. However, it also needs to be borne in mind that the number of babies available for adoption, certainly in the United Kingdom, is becoming severely restricted, and many of those babies who are available suffer from severe disabilities. Many children who are offered for adoption are older and have suffered physical or emotional abuse. While some couples will have the emotional and physical resources to deal with these problems, should those who, for whatever reason, cannot have a child of their own feel compelled to do so? I suggest that clear limits need to be set; for example, the use of egg donation for mothers well past child-bearing age is unacceptable, as is its use for 'family balancing' reasons.[47] However, as long as this is carefully considered in the context of the couple and their relationship, and of the welfare of the child, it need not be ruled out of court in the way that Cahill suggests.

Would children born in this way have reason to regret their birth, if they knew they were wanted? Of course, if they were 'purchased' by payments of money so that they could be described as having been 'bought', serious issues could be raised about receiving such children as gifts. But parents who describe the way that they have acquired adopted children from overseas sometimes use the language of purchase, so adoption *per se* does not inevitably prevent incorrect attitudes of commodification towards children. The ethical issues associated with gamete donation include both the broader political issues surrounding the likelihood of the exploitation of women for their eggs or embryos, and clear considerations about the welfare of the child and the effects on family relationships. I suggest

---

[47] Current law in the UK prohibits the use of IVF for gender selection (except for the avoidance of sex-linked diseases), so this would automatically rule out donor arrangements used for this purpose.

that in many cases it is more likely that a child born in this way would have a greater sense of self-worth than children who were born and then abandoned by their mothers, and subsequently adopted. At the same time I would be very wary of simply promoting women's choice in the manner suggested by Nichols, for reasons already noted.

Theological arguments in favour of feminist natural-law theory

What might be an alternative approach to these issues, given the complexity of the debates, the difficulty in ensuring the need to listen to women's voices, to be wary of seemingly promoting their choice, when other political and social forces are at work, and the drive towards perfectibility and its associated rejection of the marginalised and those with disabilities? Deborah Steinberg argues that religious elements are present in the idealisation of new genetic technologies, for it represents the deliberate suppression of women's sexuality and an erasure of consideration of women as such.[48] While it is important to resist the sexist elements in religious tradition, I am less convinced that sexist religious ideals are echoed in the new reproductive technologies. My suggestion is that it is possible to recover a version of natural-law theory, combined with a virtue ethic that draws on the notion of prudence or practical wisdom, in a way that can facilitate mediation around the difficult debates concerning the new reproductive technologies. Cristina Traina has similarly argued that natural law does not need to be abandoned by feminists in their search for ethical frameworks.[49] She comments on the natural-law tradition as expressed in documents such as *Donum Vitae* and finds it wanting (pp. 323–31). She suggests that the document fails to show any sign of having consulted with either women or families, and that it abstracts family relationships from wider social institutions and supporting relationships. The conjugal relationship is elevated even above the persons it represents, in such a way that an obvious conclusion would be the rejection of adoption. Traina asks some important questions of *Donum Vitae* about its assumptions regarding what makes for stable relationships, and the presumption that technological intervention in reproduction is necessarily evil. Traina argues, in my view correctly, that a feminist view needs to consider what is really behind women's desire for children, including the way unexplored social pressures serve to shape human choices. These pressures provide the raw material for human inclinations and prudential judgments. It is not enough, for example, to assume that a woman 'desperate' for

---

[48] Steinberg, *Bodies in Glass*, p. 106.   [49] Traina, *Feminist Ethics and Natural Law.*

a child is expressing the 'natural' desire for procreation in the way that pro-choice and natural-law traditionalists assume. Rather, institutions can serve to force impossible choices between the shame of infertility and the dehumanising procedures associated with the new reproductive methods. She suggests that there are other low-technical means for treating infertility that should be promoted, including better nutrition, reducing exposure to toxins and treating sexually transmitted diseases, all of which can lead to considerable increases in fertility.[50] Importantly, she argues that, while natural desires are important, they should not become absolute, so that 'the "natural" person has a telos, but "natural" desires have no inevitability or ends or even independent existence that exert moral authority over the wisdom and the freedom of the person whom they inhabit'.[51]

It is worth noting that the natural-law tradition is less dogmatic than is often supposed in traditionalist interpretations. Aquinas allowed for considerable variety in interpretation, especially when it came down to applications in particular contexts.[52] A feminist interpretation is more sensitive to historical context, including a discussion of the meaning of terms such as 'natural', in as much as these terms are socially and culturally constructed as well as having some basis in biology. Traina does not really deal sufficiently with the meaning of the common good in such contexts, while she does acknowledge the need to think beyond narrow categories to wider social and political issues.

Theological arguments in favour of a recovery of practical wisdom and virtue

What would an expression of virtues of practical wisdom look like in the feminist context? In the first place, wisdom is rooted in the virtue of charity, and cannot be considered apart from charity. In this sense it would affirm the move towards an ethic of care, but, like the other virtues, charity is both learned and given as gift of the Holy Spirit. It is therefore a virtue that can be shared in the human community at large, but one that needs to be fostered particularly in the Christian community, as expressive of the love of God for creation, and with a Thomistic view of charity as a 'certain kind of friendship with God'.[53] An ethic of care is inclusive, in that

---

[50] She draws here on Sherwin's discussion; see Sherwin, *No Longer Patient*, p. 135.
[51] Traina, *Feminist Ethics*, p. 334.
[52] For further discussion, see Vacek, 'Catholic Natural Law and Reproductive Ethics'.
[53] For further discussion see chapter 9 below, and also Deane-Drummond, *Creation through Wisdom*, pp. 106–7.

it reaches out to those women who struggle to know what to do amid the plethora of genetic choices now available to them, but also considers wider issues about what is the most caring approach, given the existence of those with disabilities in our midst, and the requirement to offer care to those who are less able than ourselves or who suffer from genetic disease. Yet charity is not the only element involved in wisdom, even though it forms its ground. For wisdom expressed as prudence is also linked with justice as virtue, and with temperance and fortitude.

How does justice as virtue compare with other versions of justice put forward by authors such as Mahowald? Justice expressed simply in libertarian versions is similarly ruled out by justice as virtue, for it is necessarily inclusive of the common good, rather than isolating individual choice within market domains. Yet justice as virtue would also enquire about the extent to which legal justice is also expressive of the common good; Aquinas went so far as to suggest that where the practice of positive law was against the common good, it was permissible to resist this legislation.[54] He was also prepared to admit that positive laws change, depending on cultural constraints and conditions. Mahowald is particularly concerned with rights for all women, regardless of economic status, in terms of equality of access to perceived genetic goods, that is, diagnosis of genetic conditions and availability of abortions. But what if the legal boundaries are themselves insufficient to contain the discrimination against those affected by genetic disease? Given that a high percentage of doctors refuse to carry out late terminations of pregnancies, how far should such practice itself be challenged, at least in those instances where genetic disease is not fatal and the baby has the prospect of a reasonable quality of life? Justice also demands a serious look at the relative costs of the use of reproductive technologies, and at how far these costs are pulling resources away from other, more serious or life-threatening medical conditions. Such costs include not simply those of the development of the technologies themselves, through major research budgets, but also the routinisation of counselling where it is not necessarily required or desired.

Prudential decision-making includes memory of the past, and a recognition that, given the patriarchal and sexist morass in which much medicine has been practised in the past, it is very unlikely that changes will take place overnight. Evelyn Fox Keller points to the way the language of genetics has itself promoted a mythology of control, reaching beyond its basis in scientific discovery.[55] Given this reality, it becomes difficult to find ways forward in the debate, except in as much as problems and cases need to be

---

[54] See Aquinas, *Summa Theologiae*, 1a2ae q. 96.6.   [55] Keller, *Secrets of Life*.

seen in the context of wider social and political pressures. Prudence is about taking counsel, so there is a clear requirement to take advice from as many different sources as possible. This is sometimes expressed in what has become known as evidenced-based policy-making, but this concept can in some cases give the impression that evidence is restricted to that arising out of the 'hard' sciences, or even from statistical results and surveys. Of course, being in touch with scientific research on such areas is an important ingredient in any debate. There is little point in making statements about the damaging effects of IVF, PGD or surrogacy on women's identity or on family life without the hard evidence to support such a claim. Prudence as circumspection is cognisant of both the scientific possibilities that are on offer and are likely to be on offer, and the likely impact these may have on women's lives.

Prudence as caution is necessary in order to penetrate into the heart of the claims about what might or might not be 'good' for women, and is liable to be sceptical of any claims that are not based on accurate knowledge arising out of women's experience. The precautionary principle states that an action is justified only where risks are low, but, of course, for new technologies such certainty can never be achieved. How far are medical experts justified in exploiting the 'desperation' of women, in order to carry out what must inevitably be experimental procedures? While a case can be made for the use of PGD in limited circumstances, other new technologies, such as human cloning, are not justifiable in terms of the likely impact on women's lives and the welfare of the child and family relationships. Prudence as foresight is difficult, in as much as some of the early projections for women (for example, the liberation possible through use of artificial wombs) were quite simply mistaken. However, it is worth noting that, at one time, cloning was thought to be out of bounds in biology, so it might be prudent to suggest that while we can never say never, there are some concepts that are more likely to be actualised than others, and it is these that need to be given particular attention. Foresight implies that some measure of predictability is possible, and, given such future scenarios, considers what might be desirable. Feminists have become highly critical of technophilia, especially to the extent that it serves to promote techno-logical 'solutions' to social and political problems. A prudential way of approaching the issue would be similarly critical of any assumptions about technology as capable of offering the most immediate response to a particular problem, before other means have been tried, or without con-sidering the wider social and political implications of such technology. How far are the new genetic technologies part of a wider package of developments that move human identity away from anything that might be considered human? A posthuman or even transhuman future seems like a golden age for those committed to a form of technologism, but for most ordinary actors it looks very bleak indeed, as it elevates technological advance regardless of more basic concerns about the common good.[56] In addition, posthumanity, at least in some versions, seems to deny the reality of mortality, so that we begin to cross the line identified by Maura Ryan when she asks, 'How do we draw the line between those genetic vulnerabilities that justice or compassion demand we alter if we can, and the shared, inescapable realities of human finitude that we must finally accept?'[57]

Prudence is not simply individual, but reaches out to family relationships, and then beyond these to social and political relationships as well.[58] Given the breadth of the possible applications of prudence, it makes sense within the context of the tension encountered in feminist analysis between, on the one hand, individual freedom of choice and, on the other, responsibility to others and the wider community. What might the common good mean in these circumstances, given that all forms of prudence are orientated to the common good? Maura Ryan similarly believes that the common good includes the creation of social conditions that offer everyone the possibility of meeting basic human needs, so that genetic knowledge must be situated in the light of this broader aim for humanity.[59] In addition, the common good implies that we must think carefully about the impact on future generations, so that there is social accountability for the genetic changes that are made. As I see it, the common good is an attempt to articulate the requirement to balance the needs of a local community with national and international goods. It makes little sense, for example, to exploit poor women in less developed nations of the world for their genetic goods, however 'voluntary' that action seems to be in practice. Such actions reinforce the domination and oppression by the richer nations of those in poorer communities. For even though the practice of international adoption has now been accepted and recognised, gamete or embryo donation involves a deliberate action that will impact on the child, who will have no right or means to trace his or her genetic identity where gametes or embryos

---

[56] Space does not permit a full discussion of these issues here. However, for a further discussion, see Graham, *Representations of the Post/human*.

[57] Ryan, 'Feminist theologies', p. 99.   [58] Aquinas, *Summa Theologiae*, 2a2ae q. 47.11.

[59] M. A. Ryan, 'Feminist Theologies and the New Genetics', in Junker-Kenny and Cahill (eds.), *The Ethics of Genetic Engineering*, pp. 93–101.

come from overseas.[60] The mushrooming of compulsory forms of genetic screening for Down syndrome is arguably not serving the common good in its promotion of ableism and the assumption that women will want to terminate the pregnancy if the tests are positive. In fact, the 'success' of such screening programmes is measured by the termination rates following diagnosis (see chapter 4 above).

CONCLUSIONS

I have discussed a wide range of different feminist debates about the new reproductive technologies. While there has been a general trend among feminist writers away from positive appraisal in terms of choices for women to more cautious estimates, overall there is still considerable diversity in opinion. All feminist writers have as a priority what might be considered the best possible option for women, but there is a difference of opinion over how that might be achieved. The advantages of the new technologies for women are that they open up the possibility of reproductive choices where once women had either to remain childless or to accept the risks associated with familial genetic disease. Feminists recognise that women are most likely to be the primary care-givers for those children born with a serious illness, so a balance needs to be struck between the needs of the mothers and the impact of any social pressure to 'screen out' particular genetic conditions as unacceptable. Many feminists will argue, correctly, that much more support should be given to parents of affected children, and fathers should be encouraged to take more responsibility for childcare. There has been a move among some feminist writers to develop what has come to be broadly called an ethic of care, based either on caring as biological or socially constructed, or on some combination of the two. An ethic of care has not, thus far, been applied consistently to problems associated with the new reproductive technologies, although I have suggested that there are elements within it that are worth incorporating, especially in terms of outlining an ethic of counselling practice.

As an alternative to care-related models, other feminists draw on themes of justice, which have traditionally been more favoured by men. However, it is entirely possible to apply egalitarian forms of justice in thinking

---

[60] The relative importance of genetic identity needs to be qualified in the life of the child; for example, the strong antagonism against donor methods seems to presuppose forms of genetic essentialism, though studies on the welfare of the child would support the view that it is beneficial for such children to know as much as they can about their origins, including their biological origins. I will come back to this issue again in the Postscript.

through issues about women, gender and genetics, and it raises new issues about political expediency in a way that commonly escapes the analysis arising out of models of care. The difficulty with some versions of justice is that they do not challenge what may or may not be available legally; that is, they assume that egalitarianism within the law is the goal, rather than questioning as a matter of principle whether a law is leading to desirable goals or not. For example, according to this model there would be no problem with the use of genetic therapy as long as it could be made available to all who wished to have access to it. The questions surrounding the abuse of information by employers or insurance companies as a means to suppress the poorer members of society further need to be taken very seriously indeed.

A balance between individual choice and social goals expressed in autokoenomy is a useful synthesis, although, of course, one must ask whether all autonomous choices are as free as they seem, and consider where there might be clashes between the demands of one over the other, or even between those of one community over another community. Feminist theologians have drawn on these debates and have similarly found themselves caught between those arguments that support greater choice for women and those socio-political critiques that challenge the development of the new technologies at the expense of women's interests or family life. I have argued that a feminist version of natural-law theory is helpful in as much as it recognises, more than traditional versions do, the flexibility inherent in natural law, and the difficulties in interpretation of its meaning in given historical contexts. Traditions of prudence and charity, alongside temperance, are suggestive of a more holistic approach to the issues – one that seeks to recognise the importance of relationships in the family, but is also realistic about the historical and cultural factors that can make a decision seem good and desirable. Defining what that good might be is a challenge that is continually posed in the context of the debates surrounding the new reproductive technologies. In order to elaborate on what this might mean, I suggest that we need to consider the issues on an even broader canvas, and include not simply impacts on the human community but also wider issues about the impacts of genetics on the environment. In this sense decision-making takes place in a broadly ecological context, recognising human situatedness as integral to the community of creation. It is to this aspect that I will turn in the chapter that follows.

CHAPTER 9

Genetics and environmental concern

I argued in the previous chapter that a Christian concept of justice relating to genetic technologies necessarily includes concern for the underprivileged. I propose here that justice also needs to be thought of in ecological rather than narrowly anthropocentric categories. This does not mean that animals, for example, are now the underprivileged that the Christian gospel speaks about, as Andrew Linzey suggests.[1] Instead, I propose that we need to broaden the remit of our moral consideration so that it includes animals and plants as well as ecosystems. On the basis of belief in God as Creator, all of creation has value in and of itself. However, such a theocentric view can still allow for distinctions between humanity and the non-human world. A focus on virtue ethics might even suggest that it is impossible to give moral consideration to those outside the human community. I will argue here that looking for human character attributes elsewhere in the non-human world is not very helpful in defining human relationships with the natural world. The distinctiveness of all aspects of creation needs to be preserved, along with an awareness of common genetic and biological origin. Concepts such as 'covenant' and 'friendship' are particularly helpful in setting the stage for a consideration of the limits or otherwise of genetic intervention outside the human community.[2] The main purpose of this chapter is to consider those attitudes to non-humans that are relevant in the light of the development of genetic technologies that are permissible in non-humans compared with those taking place in humans.

How far might we be able to identify with the non-human world? Certainly, ever since Darwin, humanity's common biological and genetic

---

[1] Andrew Linzey attempts to find theological support for this idea through the priority for the poor given in the Gospel accounts. For him, animals are the new poor; they, like children, must be treated with the greatest care as they are dependent on humans. A. Linzey, 'Animal Rights', in Clarke and Linzey (eds.), *Dictionary of Ethics*, pp. 29–33; also Linzey, 'The Moral Priority of the Weak'.

[2] The discussion of genetic intervention in the non-human world is necessarily brief, given that the central concern of this book has been ethical issues in human genetics.

ancestry with the plant and animal world has come to be accepted almost as a given.[3] Such common ancestry might encourage us to move away from defining moral value narrowly in terms of human interest alone. Indeed, Alasdair MacIntyre's more recent work suggests that we need to take our biological rootedness into account more fully in coming to moral decisions. He admits that 'I now judge that I was in error in supposing an ethics independent of biology to be possible'. This is because our development into the form of life that we lead, namely the life of virtues, is also a development that 'has as its starting point our animal condition'.[4] Does this mean that our virtues arise simply through biological evolutionary processes, as some sociobiologists have suggested?

Holmes Rolston argues forcefully that this is not the case; rather, human values, such as the virtue of altruism, have distinct cultural origins, even if, in some sense, non-human animals closest to us, such as apes, have premoral tendencies, or in some cases what can be described as mutually beneficial reciprocity.[5] Sociobiologists have tried to find purely naturalistic explanations for ethical behaviour in humans, suggesting, for example, that this might work indirectly through the survival advantage of social cohesiveness that morality brings. But what can this biological survival advantage say about the content or *norms* of such behaviour? With Rolston we can say:

Perhaps ethics starts with a picture of ourselves as natural animals, perhaps it socializes us, but it becomes increasingly clear, when we grow sophisticated at critiquing our origins and natures with norms that are not there in our genetics, that ethics demands and generates novel powers of both analysis and feeling. (p. 247)

It seems to me that such an analysis serves a number of purposes. First, it prevents a naïve view of the origin of values in the human community. The emergence of ethics cannot be related simply to our genetic origins. Secondly, it serves to caution us against finding egalitarian value in humanity and nature; human beings are distinct from the natural world, even if they share common biological roots. Finally, it warns against seeking after human values in the non-human world. Rolston comments succinctly on this latter aspect. He suggests that

---

[3] Stephen Clark points to the fact that this has been accepted, often without due philosophical reflection on the assumptions being made in the process. See Clark, *Biology and Christian Ethics*, pp. 32–3.

[4] MacIntyre, *Dependent Rational Animals*, p. x.   [5] Rolston, *Genes, Genesis and God*, pp. 243–4.

Sometimes it is fruitful to extrapolate, but often it is not. Statisticians know that it is risky to extrapolate very far. We have to ask what is the relevant domain of the regularity. Failing an adequate answer we will extrapolate 'altruism' or 'selfishness' and get absurdity. There is the problem of knowing when to stop, before science transposes to poetry (or nonsense), fact to fiction, illumination to confusion. (p. 279)

We are, in so doing, moving illegitimately from one domain to another; that is, we are making a category mistake.

Given this contrast between human and non-human species, it is worth asking in what legitimate sense we might come to think of ourselves as part of the natural world. Moreover, how might this shape our attitudes towards genetic intervention? Extending rights to animals, while of practical use-fulness, assumes ethical commensurability with humans, which is not very helpful. I will argue below that the themes of covenant and friendship do, however, lend themselves to such an extension, not so much on the basis of ecology as on the basis of a theocentric approach to creation.

THE COVENANT COMMUNITY OF NATURE

How far might the idea of community be considered in an ecological sense? That is, can community in any way apply to non-human species? Many of those who argue in favour of an extension of the community idea to non-human species, or, more radically, for a relocation of the focus of community away from human beings towards the biological entities as a whole, do so on the basis of ecology.

Ecology, through its portrayal of interdependence and interrelationship, offers a way of perceiving science that is rather different from the mechanistic alternative. More specifically, the ideal of ecosystem offers the paradigm of balance, interrelationship and equilibrium. Yet such a view of ecology is naïve and misinformed, since current understanding of ecology shows that ecological systems are fragile, subject to disturbance, inclusive of humans and rarely at equilibrium.[6] Of course, more radical versions of eco-philosophy take their cues from the Gaia hypothesis of James Lovelock, but this, too, is based on a misapprehension of scientific concepts.[7] I suggest that seeking to find evidence in nature for the idealised versions of community is a false premise. Rather, a virtue ethic, by its primary focus on what it means to be human, can then go on to ask *how* human

---

[6] Deane-Drummond, *The Ethics of Nature*, pp. 36–8.
[7] Deane-Drummond, 'Gaia as Science Made Myth'.

interrelationships with the natural world can redefine the concept of community. My criticism of the use of ecology to support community concepts, therefore, does not mean that community ideas are irrelevant; rather, it poses the question: how far can we think of ourselves as both members of a human community and an integral part of the community of life? Indeed, contemporary ecological science would allow such an extension to take place, since it is now recognised that humanity forms an integral part of environmental systems; the one cannot be considered without the other.[8]

I intend here to explore a little more closely ways in which the theological idea of *covenant* can extend to the non-human community and the implications of this for ethical issues in genetics. Andrew Linzey has discussed extending the theological idea of covenant to animals.[9] It is specifically the Noahic covenant that God makes with all living creatures that provides the source for theological interpretation. Linzey has worked with the Jewish theologian Dan Cohn-Sherbok, who considers the Jewish interpretation of this covenant (Hebrew, *berit*). The idea of covenant is central to Jewish self-understanding, though the authors note that the specific inclusion of animals is rarely given proper weight.[10] More precisely, the Noahic covenant of Genesis 9 states:

Then God said to Noah and to his sons with him, 'Behold, I establish my covenant with you and your descendants after you, and with every living creature that is with you, the birds, the cattle, and every beast of the earth with you, as many as came out of the ark.' (verses 8–10)[11]

This passage makes it abundantly clear that the covenant is not just with animals; rather, it includes *all* living things. Linzey focuses instead on the rights of animals, and limits the rights to animals on the basis that only animals can be 'ensouled', and, more important perhaps, only *mammals* have flesh, blood and spirit.[12] However, Linzey's emphasis on the Noahic covenant is suggestive of a broader environmental ethic.[13]

---

[8] Park, *The Environment*.
[9] The idea is a recurrent theme in Linzey's work, from his *Christianity and the Rights of Animals*; *Animal Theology*; and Linzey and Cohn-Sherbok, *After Noah*.
[10] Linzey and Cohn-Sherbok, *After Noah*, p. 22.
[11] Bible quotations are taken from the Revised Standard Version.
[12] Deane-Drummond, *The Ethics of Nature*, pp. 54–85. Whether animals have souls or not is the subject of some discussion: Linzey, *Christianity and the Rights of Animals*, pp. 36, 84–6. However, Linzey is not as far from the Christian tradition as he sometimes implies. As Margaret Atkins points out, there are elements in the Roman Catholic tradition that do hint at the possibility that animals have souls. See M. Atkins, 'Could There Be Squirrels in Heaven?'
[13] Northcott, *Christianity and Environmental Ethics*, pp. 146–7.

Robert Murray's excellent book, *The Cosmic Covenant*, takes this idea further from the perspective of current biblical scholarship. He sets the Noahic covenant in the context of the creation account *per se*, namely the story of creation as the ordering action of God in the face of the tendency to cosmic disorder. Such an ordering is expressed liturgically through the rituals and laws of the Jewish community. He points out that the covenant with Noah binds humans and all creatures together in a partnership between God and God's creatures. It is, nonetheless, difficult to find evidence from the Noahic covenant *alone* that animals are covenant partners with *humans*, though this is hinted at in the book of Job:

> At destruction and famine you shall laugh,
>   And shall not fear the beasts of the earth.
> For you shall be in league with the stones of the field,
>   And the beasts of the field shall be at peace with you.
>
>   (5.22–3)

The righteous person will live free from fear with other creatures, 'as if he were on terms of a solemn treaty or pact with them' (pp. 102–3). More significant still, in the present context, is that the vision of peace with the animals portrayed in Isaiah 11 speaks of the ideal king as one who has the virtues of wisdom, justice and peace (p. 103). The vision of peace with and from animals, where animals apparently change their normal characteristics – lions eat straw, and so on – is eschatological and messianic. Other biblical texts point to the righteous person as one who is characterised by *sedeq*, which includes the idea of personal knowledge, so that Proverbs 12.10a could be rendered, 'A just person feels for the nature of his animals.' In Proverbs 12.10b the capacity for tenderness and compassion, *rahāmim*, becomes its opposite, namely cruelty. It is these attitudes of justice, combined with tenderness and compassion, that are important in defining human relationships with animals.

Northcott draws on Murray's understanding of covenant to develop his own version of ecological community. He is particularly concerned to point to biblical texts, such as those in Jeremiah, where the breakdown of true worship and righteousness leads to correlative ecological devastation.[14] For him,

---

[14] Northcott, *The Environment and Christian Ethics*, pp. 170–1. He has taken up the theme of the link between human disobedience and ecological devastation in subsequent work; see M. Northcott, '"Behold I have set the land before you" (Deut. 1.8): Christian Ethics, GM Foods, and the Culture of Modern Farming', in Deane-Drummond and Szerszynksi (eds.), *Re-Ordering Nature*, pp. 85–106.

The Hebrew connection between the worship of the God of justice, the justice and wisdom of human society and its leaders and the goodness of the land should not be dismissed merely as a primitive myth, for it expresses a fundamental theological and ecological truth. Human life and society are intricately bound up with the life and community of ecosystems and the biosphere.[15]

While I concur that human life is bound up in an intimate way with ecological communities, Northcott's assumption that ecosystems are both naturally stable and in equilibrium is open to doubt. I suggest that Murray's portrayal of the early biblical myth of 'raw' nature being in a state of chaos comes much closer to the contemporary understanding of ecology. Northcott points to the early Sumerian myths of origin, where 'reality is fundamentally chaotic, and order only attainable through violence' (p. 174). He likens this to the Darwinian theory of evolution, where human and non-human lives are portrayed as violent, aggressive and competitive. Against this he sets the 'harmony' of the created order in Genesis, and other scientific studies, such as primatology, which point to co-operation, mutuality and altruism, rather than to competition and conflict. I have already discussed the problems associated with moving from a comparison of the natural world to a mandate for human ethics. More specifically, it is clearly unjustifiable to use the language of violence in Darwin's theory as a way of encouraging human violence, or the language of ecology (or primatology for that matter) to justify human co-operation. The fact that ecologists or evolutionary scientists have found elements of the chaotic in the natural world does not constitute a threat. On the contrary, in the process of creation God's word imposes a boundary (*gĕbul*) and divine ordering or rules (*huqqot*) on the chaotic elements of creation in which the covenant community can emerge.[16] Moreover, it is in the context of cosmic disorder that the cosmic order is referred to in terms of a covenant.[17]

It is in the light of the idea of cosmic covenant set in the context of chaos understood as flux that all members of the ecological community could be said to render praise to God. Richard Bauckham has pointed to biblical texts and early Christian traditions that speak of all creation giving praise to God. Even though the passages are metaphorical, they suggest that all creatures bring glory to God by being themselves.[18] Bauckham rejects the idea of Philip Sherrard and others that humanity is somehow 'the priest' of

[15] M. Northcott, *Christianity and Environmental Ethics*, p. 173.
[16] Murray, *The Cosmic Covenant*, pp. 1–5.   [17] Ibid., p. 14.
[18] Bauckham, 'Joining Creation's Praise'.

creation, for in the book of Revelation there is only one 'humanoid' creature that gives praise to God, so that 'there is no anthropocentrism in heaven'.[19]

The cosmic covenant has ethical significance for the way humans treat the natural world. For Northcott, the idea that the land is a vital part of the covenant community leads to an ethic of love as against one of manipulation and control.[20] It also finds expression in the idea of the Sabbath of the land, reminding the Jewish people that the land is gift, rather than theirs by right (pp. 188–9).[21] For Northcott, it is above all the creative and redeeming love of God that is the primary ethical category; human virtues are situated in the context of the primacy of a love ethic.[22] Yet the subject of his most intensive concern is the human relationship with the land as such, and, once the land is seen as a commodity in world trade, the intimate connection with the land that we see in primitive cultures is lost (pp. 282ff.). For him, 'the realisation of the virtues is, though, only possible in the context of stable relationships of nurture and care, and of stable communities which are orientated towards both moral and spiritual fulfilment' (p. 316). While he seems to be talking here of human communities, the binding of the life and worship of the ideal community with that of the land might suggest that the land is somehow necessary for the expression of such virtues. Northcott does not seem to be making this point here, however; rather, he suggests that 'processes of modernity which are destroying nature are also destroying human moral virtue' (p. 319). In looking for alternative sources for morality he turns once more to the concept of community, especially that of the church. It is essential for him that we stop 'the technological altering of the natural and the human environment'; genetic engineering is therefore ruled out of court, not because it is wrong in itself, but because it is wedded to unjust systems and organisations (pp. 69, 222, 319).[23]

I suggest that the idea of a cosmic covenant has implications for an ethic that is focused on the virtues. Not only do virtues become more ecological, as Northcott suggests, but also the practice of the virtues makes sense in the

---

[19] Ibid. See also Sherrard, *The Rape of Man and Nature*. He has developed this idea further in the cosmic context in *Human Image*.

[20] Northcott, *Christianity and Environmental Ethics*, pp. 187–8.

[21] Ibid., pp. 188–9. I discussed the significance of the idea of the Sabbath for issues in genetics in an earlier chapter. Northcott's focus here is more environmental than theological; the Sabbath has ecological significance in giving the land a rest from potentially environmentally destructive practices.

[22] He briefly describes the virtues of justice, temperance, prudence, fidelity, courage, hope and peaceableness in terms of their significance for revised ecological practice. Northcott, *Christianity and Environmental Ethics*, pp. 314–16.

[23] In '"Behold I have set the land before you"', Northcott rejects the idea that genetic engineering raises new concerns for ethics; rather, it is part of an ongoing intensification of agriculture. I will return to a discussion of this later in this chapter.

context of our self-understanding as *situated* in a cosmic covenant. This does not, however, point back to an idealist community of people and land, in the manner that Northcott indicates; rather, it points forward to a renewed awareness of humanity as *participants* in the natural world. Indeed, the vision of Isaiah implies such an eschatological approach to renewed human relationships with the earth. The forms such participatory action should take are suggested less by looking at stable systems of ecological ordering than by realising that the whole of life is God's gift.

Stephen Clark's interpretation of covenant is of interest in this respect. While, for Northcott, covenant implies justice, especially justice for the land in relation to human communities, Clark prefers to talk of covenant as encouraging a view of other creatures as neighbours.[24] Like Northcott, Clark rejects instrumentalist approaches to the natural world, preferring the idea that all things exist for their own sake, because God creates them as good. Even though the vision of the covenant with all creatures looks ahead to a future ideal, this does not mean that it has no relevance for how we act now. Indeed, we can find examples of companionship between humans and primates that speak of the possibility of friendly association between ourselves and other species. Thus, while Northcott finds evidence for co-operative behaviour in primates, Clark sees such studies as indicative that inter-specific relationships point to forms of relating that are not just based on sharing a common language. More importantly, 'Our ethical relationship to creatures that we can be friends with, will be different from that to those we cannot, but it does not follow that we should think of the latter only as unfriends, or enemies, or mere material' (p. 292).

Another interesting idea is that, according to Clark, animals 'chose' to be domesticated in order to ensure their survival and better medical care compared with their wild counterparts (p. 293). This does not mean choice in the sense of individual volition, but part of a social contract with humans. The human side of the bargain is broken by numerous practices against animal welfare. Domestic animals have a claim on human ties and responsibilities that is different from that of wild animals. In defence of this, Clark comments: 'The truth is that we do not feel ourselves obliged to defend even all human beings against assault' (p. 297). The practical ethical implications of the covenant with all creatures are that

we should live as non-violently as we can manage, building up our friendships and respecting the limits that are needed to allow each kind its place. Let us live

---

[24] Clark, *Biology and Christian Ethics*, p. 283.

according to those rules that will allow as many creatures as possible, of as many kinds, their best chance of living a satisfactory life according to their kind. Let us acknowledge our particular duties of care and forbearance to those creatures who have been part of our society for millennia. (p. 299)

The covenant God made granted all things 'their space'. Clark does not say how the cosmic covenant can intersect with the special option of care for domestic animals. He does, however, discuss how our interests can be enlarged beyond narrowly anthropocentric concern. Industrial society moves us further away from 'caste loyalties, whilst separating us still more from the beasts (except such domestic artefacts as we still allow)'.[25] Against this trend we can see that boundaries between human and non-human are not as clear-cut as many have supposed. Our ethics depends on sentiment and personal attachment, as well as on rational arguments about what creatures like us should do. For 'we may also be forced to realise that our lives and loves depend upon the living earth, made up of many million creatures and kinds of creatures whom we cannot afford to treat as worthless' (p. 165). The fact that other creatures are unlike us does not preclude a sense of friendship with them. But how should we understand the nature of our friendship with all creatures? This seems to me to be a critical outcome of understanding humanity as embedded in a cosmic covenant with all living creatures.

FRIENDSHIP IN THE CONTEXT OF A COSMIC COVENANT COMMUNITY

According to Stephen Clark, the roots of philosophical humanism arose with the Stoics, who had an elitist view of humanity, especially of those who were wise. The vast mass of suffering humanity was, like women, morally incapable. Yet some respect is owed to human beings because of the fact of their humanness. Other animals, by contrast, are owed nothing; pigs are simply 'walking larders, with a soul to keep them fresh in place of salt' (p. 155). Anyone who expressed sympathy for 'brute beasts' was out of line, no better than a brute himself. Such was the strength of this dogma that it took hold in the writings of Augustine, Thomas Aquinas, Spinoza and Kant.[26] How might a virtue ethic that builds on the writing of Thomas

---

[25] Clark, *The Political Animal*, p. 165.
[26] Andrew Linzey writes scathingly of this tradition. See Linzey, *The Status of Animals in the Christian Tradition*; *Christianity and the Rights of Animals*, pp. 36–8; *Animal Theology*, pp. 12–19.

Aquinas disentangle itself from the hostile attitude to animals that he seems to espouse?

First of all, it is clear that, while Aquinas does write in a negative way about animals, it is not necessary to accept this part of his teaching, any more than it is necessary to accept similar attitudes found in Aristotle, Kant, Augustine or Spinoza. In fact, many authors have found in Spinoza an inspiration for pantheistic conceptions of the natural world.[27] Secondly, there are strands in Aquinas' thought that point to the ontological unity that human beings have with all creatures, even beginning with life itself. In this sense his views could be said to be consistent with evolutionary ideas about creation.[28] Thirdly, I suggest that consideration of his ideal of friendship is particularly instructive, as it suggests a way of understanding the concept of covenant community discussed above.

Paul Wadell's discussion of Aquinas in *Friendship and the Moral Life* (pp. 120–41) is particularly significant.[29] He situates his discussion in a more general treatment of the notion of friendship in the Christian tradition. Friendship is integral to a virtue ethic, since it asks 'Who should I become?' as much as 'What should I do?' As I have argued earlier, moral concern needs to go beyond thinking about difficult cases in genetics, or quandaries, to reflect on the kinds of qualities we need to effect such change. But there are other considerations that need to be faced in posing the notion of friendship as integral to moral concern. Certainly, a superficial consideration of our treatment of other animals might imply that it is the notion of universal love, *agapē*, that needs to be inclusive of other members of other species, rather than friendship love. How can friendships, as implying preferential love, be preferable to *agapē*, or Christian love understood as charity (pp. 70–119)?

Wadell comments on Søren Kierkegaard's contrasting notions of friendship, which, he suggests, is based on attraction and is fickle and preferential, and *agapē*, which is based on God's command and is faithful, inclusive and generous (pp. 75–82). Wadell argues that such a narrow view of friendship is mistaken, for Kierkegaard presumes that all friendships share these characteristics; moreover, friendship is not necessarily narrow in its concern. Instead, friendship makes the broader kind of love expressed in *agapē* possible, for 'friendship born from and seeking the kingdom, may be

---

[27] For discussion see S. Clark, 'Pantheism', in Cooper and Palmer (eds.), *Spirit of the Environment*, pp. 42–56.

[28] Barad, *Aquinas on Animals*.

[29] For a detailed study of the relationship between love and friendship, see Carmichael, *Friendship*.

exactly the kind of love which enables us ultimately to be friends of the world. In that case we do not leave preferential love behind. We extend its domain' (p. 73). Moreover, Wadell goes on to suggest that we cannot learn the kind of love needed for *agapē* apart from Christian friendships. *Agapē* is like the 'ever widening scope of friendship whose members are trying to be like God. With agape we come, like God, to make friends with the world' (p. 74). According to Aristotle, friendship is possible only between those who share a common concern for the good. Augustine developed this idea by saying that there could be true friendship only where there is agreement on 'divine things' (p. 101). Furthermore, the true nature of Christian love is in grateful response to the sense of God's love experienced as grace, rather than out of a sense of duty (p. 113).

However, it is in Aquinas' understanding of charity as 'certain friendship with God' that the notion of friendship becomes theocentric rather than limited to the human community.[30] Aquinas states that 'charity is beyond the resources of nature ... we have it neither by nature, nor as acquired, but as infused by the Holy Spirit'.[31] The final perfection or beatitude in God is friendship understood as the friendship life of the Trinity. Charity, understood as friendship with God, thus begins in grace and is our vocation in relationship with God. It is through such grace that broken human nature is healed. Thus Aquinas is aware of the sinfulness of humanity, so that such friendship is grace-laden rather than dependent on our own merit. Such grace allows kinship between God and humanity, and it is through grace that we find a kinship with each other in which peace resides. Aristotle did not consider that it was possible to be friends with the gods, as human beings are too dissimilar from them. Aquinas rejects this view as applied to the Christian life, and suggests instead that, while we never have a friendship with God like that with other human beings, it is still *analogous* to human relationships (2a2ae q. 23.1). Friendship with God, on the other hand, begins in grace, but issues in charity; thus 'charity, and all the virtues born from charity, are nothing more than grace expressed in activity, for they accomplish day by day the transformation of our self unto God which grace enables and always intends'. Furthermore, charity is more than this, for 'when Thomas speaks of charity as our active participation in the Divine Friendship, he discloses what for him is the task and fullness of the Christian moral life'.[32] The final beatitude is everlasting friendship with God.

---

[30] For discussion in Wadell, see *Friendship*, pp. 120–41.
[31] Aquinas, *Summa Theologiae*, 2a2ae q. 24.2.   [32] Wadell, *Friendship*, p. 127.

What are the specific elements of friendship, and how can this be applied to friendship with God?[33] The first is *benevolence*, that is, an active working for the well-being of others; their good becomes our good. As applied to charity, we seek God's good for the sake of God; friends of God will want what God wills as God wills it. The second is *mutuality*, or reciprocity, so that each knows the well-wishing of the other. Self is transfigured through such friendship with God, for the focus on the good of charity is to be changed by it. Thus, 'in charity we take on the form of God, we are formed in the Spirit, qualified by God's friendship; that is how we are remade and that is why charity is our happiness, the most fulsome development of ourselves' (p. 137). The third mark of friendship is that each becomes *another self*, so that to love God in charity leads to a 'similitude' of being with God. Such 'similitude' does not lead to a loss of identity; on the contrary, it is the means of becoming fully ourselves. In one sense we become more like God in loving what God loves, but in another sense we become less like God in becoming ourselves; so friendship achieves not so much identity as 'differentiation fostered by a love for the most genuine good' (p. 139).

Given that friendship with God is core to understanding the goal of the moral life, what implications might this have for all human relationships? Wadell suggests that all friendships pose an element of threat, as well as a sense of gift (p. 154). The risk of becoming a friend means a risk in loss of self. This is especially true when a stranger becomes our friend, a process that is possible only through hospitality. Making strangers into friends takes the form of a call, a summons to respond to the other as other, so that 'in order to be moral we must let their otherness be' (p. 150). It is the hunger for communion that allows the gift to triumph over threat in making friends.

I suggest that a sense of gift needs to prevail over threat if we are to make friends of our enemies, as those uniquely loved by God: this, then, is the widening arc of friendship infused by charity. Furthermore, as God loves all creatures, they too can be drawn into the circle of our friendship. Just as our friendship with God is analogous to human friendships, so friendship with other non-human beings is analogous, but not identical, to human friendships. Much traditional Roman Catholic theology has tended to exclude the possibility of friendship with creatures. Bernard Häring, for example, claims that 'nothing irrational is capable of the beautifying friendship with God which is the bond of Christian love of neighbour'.[34] But this is based on the tradition in Aquinas that, admittedly, is hostile to

---

[33] For discussion, see Wadell, *Friendship*, pp. 132–7.   [34] Häring, *Law of Christ*, p. 362.

animals as 'brute beasts'. Once we reject this claim and focus instead on our common evolutionary and genetic lineage with all creatures, the possibility of friendship becomes evident.

Why choose the notion of friendship in relating to animals, rather than that of neighbourliness? The notion of neighbour has the advantage of implying closeness without identity. I suggest, however, that to act as neighbour puts rather less ethical demand on humanity than does the notion of friendship. Ruth Page uses a term that is, perhaps, intermediate between neighbourliness and friendship, namely companionship.[35] She also suggests that friendship would make 'impossible demands', but I would argue that it depends on what is *meant* by friendship.[36] However, she resists distinguishing human beings from other creatures in arguing for an extension of image-bearing to those species other than humans.[37] The notion of friendship can, by contrast, allow for difference in function, which is perhaps lacking in the notion of companionship. It is also fair to suggest that in practical terms friendship will be most easily realised towards those creatures that are significant in the human community. Neighbourliness seems to imply a lack of reciprocity, which might be truer of some creatures than of others. The elements of friendship discussed earlier are relevant here. Benevolence, wishing well for the other, needs to characterise our friendship with all creatures. Of course, how far *mutuality* might exist between ourselves and other species often seems to depend on how close they are, in evolutionary terms, to humankind. The close affinity many have with primates is well known.[38] A farmer need not feel mutually related to the animals in his care, but he will feel obliged to wish them well. Yet the extent of our natural affections with creatures is not rational. As Stephen Clark wryly admits:

I am fonder of most cats than most dogs; and although I regret the decapitated mice that I sometimes find on the stairs I eat my meals with no less relish because of them. Most people find it difficult to feel much sympathy for rats, and whereas snails have a certain charm, slugs are frankly revolting.[39]

Yet rationality is not the key to friendship, since

---

[35] Page, *God and the Web of Creation*, pp. 154–5. She also uses companionship to describe God's relationship with creatures.

[36] Page, *God and the Web of Creation*, p. 156.

[37] Page, 'The Human Genome and the Image of God', in Deane-Drummond (ed.), *Brave New World?*, pp. 68–86.

[38] See Clark, *Biology and Christian Ethics*, p. 291.   [39] Clark, *The Moral Status of Animals*, p. 90.

our natural affections engage our interest in their object, and create in us the hope of some reciprocated affection. The wholly 'rational' man would not feel such movements of the heart where his reason did not affirm that possibility, but the 'rational' man is probably hardly human. (p. 100)

The extent to which any sense of reciprocity will be felt with different creatures thus depends partly on personal preference, though it seems likely that this aspect will be most keenly experienced with those animals closest to humankind. This does not mean, however, that those creatures that are incapable of any reciprocity should be excluded from our circle of friendship, though it might indicate a certain priority in moral concern. I suggest that those creatures at the furthest limit of our circle of friendship would be more appropriately described as neighbours, or companions, than as friends. Where we draw that line between friendship and neighbourliness – in other words, *how* we decide which creatures are closest to the human community – would be a task of practical wisdom or prudence. Killing or genetically engineering a dog or a sheep is morally more significant than killing or genetically engineering an earthworm. The third aspect of friendship, namely allowing the other to be itself, is also significant. For it is in letting creatures be themselves that their true worth is identified, rather than in forcing them to be 'like' humans.

What other characteristics of friendship are relevant in the context of non-humans? The first is recognition: that we recognise the claim that the other has on ourselves. It is paying attention to the creatures of the world through close observation and a sense of empathy for the other as other. Page suggests that this paying attention can also arise out of a sense of companionship, though we might want to ask why companionship would motivate us sufficiently to pay attention to the other.[40] As Sallie McFague asks:

What justification is there for limiting the subject–subjects model to human beings, drawing a line in the sand at our own species, with all other species and the rest of nature outside the circle? On the basis of Christianity's own basic model, seeing God and others as subjects – as valuable in themselves for themselves, and not just as for me or against me – should we not also love nature this way?[41]

---

[40] Page, *God and the Web of Creation*, p. 157. Page's understanding of 'close companionship' becomes virtually indistinguishable from friendship. It seems to me clearer to use the notion of friendship, while admitting that prudence may well draw the line between neighbourliness and friendship in different places, depending on societal influences and personal conscience.

[41] McFague, *Super, Natural Christians*, p. 167.

While it seems to me that McFague is correct to recognise the possibility of otherness, however, to apply this in a general, non-specific sense to nature as a whole seems to me to be unrealistic. We become friends, not with nature in an idealistic form, but with the creatures in the natural world.

This leads to another characteristic of friendship, namely respect. Respect is born from patience, giving the time needed to pay attention to the goodness in the other. Patience is particularly relevant in the context of friendship with non-humans, as it is not always easy to see the goodness in the other. Are there ways in which we might be able to become friends with slugs, as creatures made by God, or do our natural affections bar such a development? Moreover, friendship implies an element of choice. So we may choose not to be friends with all created things, such as deadly viruses; but in one sense they are still our neighbours, because we have to live alongside these creatures.[42] Following on from recognition and respect, a third characteristic of friendship is response, a moving out of self towards another. Sallie McFague suggests that the reason why we love the earth is not necessarily ethical; rather, 'We can certainly hope that our actions will have an effect, but Christians do not love the earth in order to save the planet. We should love nature for the same reason that we love God and our neighbour: because it is valuable in itself and deserves our love.'[43] However, this seems to me to be a truncated view, possibly related to McFague's attempt to relate to nature as a whole, since she suggests in the same paragraph that 'global outcomes can lead to despair'. But if friendship just means that I have affection for you, but do nothing to work towards your welfare, then what kind of friendship does this betray? It seems to be something more related to my own need for affection, than to service of the other. Rather, friendship is set in the context of a covenant between God and all creatures of the earth, so it is these creatures that require our attention.

CHARITY, WISDOM AND GENETIC TECHNOLOGIES

I have argued so far that the context in which moral consideration of non-humans needs to take place is that of friendship set in a cosmic covenant between God and all creatures. Moreover, friendship itself gives us some clear pointers to how we are to conduct ourselves in relation to non-humans.

---

[42] This assumes that humans will not actively work to eliminate some creatures, which, of course, it can do in exceptional circumstances, as in the smallpox virus.

[43] McFague, *Super, Natural Christians*, p. 177.

In consideration of the genetic manipulation of other creatures, we need to ask ourselves, first, can these creatures be considered as being within a circle of friendship, and in what sense is this or that action really expressing our friendship, understood as charity? Biotechnological interventions in the natural world are commonly predicated on the basis of consequentialist analysis of risk and benefit. Such an analysis has not proved satisfactory, even for those following such as view, not least because of the uncertainty associated with such predictions. Yet, as Banner points out, locating ethical analysis in such uncertainty is a way of narrowing moral concern to scientific reasoning. Instead, 'contestability of decisions about the application of genetic knowledge in the empirical realm, and in particular in the realm of uncertain futures, betrays an albeit unconscious (or at least undeclared) commitment to a highly questionable moral framework'.[44] While Banner was directing his remarks specifically to the British Medical Association's report on genetic engineering of humans, the same could be said of other reports on genetic intervention in the non-human realm.[45] As I mentioned in chapter 2, Banner prefers ethics to take its bearings from Christian dogmatics. I have suggested here that friendship set in the context of covenant is a way of embedding discussion about issues in genetics in a social framework. But whereas the Sabbath in Banner's definition seems to give no clear guidance as to how to act, the concept of friendship allows for human participation and engagement with creaturely beings.[46] In friendship, we could, in theory, come up with a list of rules for protecting animals and other creatures from wanton human cruelty.[47] Although the idea of friendship does not preclude such a list, we would be more likely to ask: how far does this express the nature of friendship, and which elements of friendship are relevant in this case?

I have argued throughout this book that the virtues, especially prudence, justice and wisdom, are essential components in developing an understanding

---

[44] Banner, *Christian Ethics*, p. 211.

[45] See the Nuffield Report, *Genetically Modified Crops*. In coming to conclusions about ethical concerns over how far genetic engineering could be said to be 'unnatural', they suggest that 'it is the deleterious consequences of our farming techniques to our environment and human health, not their "unnatural" character, that should preoccupy us' (p. 123). See BMA, *The Impact of Genetic Modification*. A similar attitude is found here, where 'the BMA accepts that there are potential benefits of GMOs and foods, but believes that it is most important that a comprehensive cost-benefit and health impact assessment, comparing genetic modification with other agriculture techniques, is implemented' (p. 3).

[46] A more appropriate definition of the Sabbath would be to consider it in the context of relationships, as I do below.

[47] Banner's principles for our treatment of animals are to be commended in the sense that they at least set the boundaries for legal human activity. See Banner, *Christian Ethics*, pp. 204–24.

of the ethics of genetics. In what sense does wisdom relate to charity and, through charity, to friendship? The clue to understanding the relationship between Christian community and the wider society comes from consideration of moral virtues as in one sense acquired through teaching and in another sense infused by the grace of God. For Aquinas, the work of prudence or practical wisdom guides human conduct in practical matters relating to the common good in society.[48] However, by grace humanity can receive infused moral virtues as gift, including, particularly, wisdom and charity. The gift of wisdom differs from faith, for 'faith assents to divine truth for itself, the gift of wisdom judges things according to divine truth. Hence the gift of wisdom presupposes faith, since a man judges well what he already knows.' It is in piety and worship of God that faith becomes manifest, which leads Thomas to conclude that 'piety makes wisdom manifest too, and because of that we can say that piety is wisdom, and for the same reason also is fear. If a man fears and worships God he shows he has the right judgment about divine things.'[49] Wisdom is, then, rightness in judging according to divine norms, and 'this sympathy, or connaturality with divine things, results from charity which unites us to God'. Yet while wisdom could be said to be intimately connected with charity, it is not one of the three theological virtues, so there remains a distinction between them: 'wisdom which is the gift does have its cause in the will, namely charity, but essentially it lies in the intellect, of which the act is to judge aright, as we have said' (2a2ae q. 45.2). As T. C. O'Brien notes:

Every human situation, whether of trying to evaluate the meaning of things or of trying to shape a specific course of action, involves judgement; the kind of judgment critical to salvation is one that is infused with the love of charity, that is a *verbum spirans amorem*. Wisdom informed by charity is, however, simply the most eminent form that the experience of grace takes. These two stand for all of the Gifts of knowing and action that cover the conditions of the Christian life.[50]

In consideration of animals

Given that it is impossible to separate the gift of wisdom from charity, and that charity is friendship to God, and, as I have argued, implies a form of friendship with all created things, what are the possible practical

[48] Hall, *Narrative and the Natural Law*, p. 81.   [49] Aquinas, *Summa Theologiae*, 2a2ae, q. 45.1.
[50] T. C. O'Brien, 'Appendix 3: The Sending and Presence of the Person', in Aquinas, *Summa Theologiae*, VII: *Father, Son and Holy Ghost*, p. 264.

consequences for moral decision-making about genetic engineering outside the human realm? In the first place, the kind of judgment that needs to be made in order to express wisdom is one that sees at least some creatures as friends; in this, we look not just to our own self-interest, but also to the interest of creatures as such. Of course, genetic selection might include deliberate breeding as well as direct genetic intervention; the difference lies both in the speed of what can be accomplished and in the possibility of more drastic changes in the creatures themselves. Joyce D'Silva remarks: 'Genetic selection has given us crippled chickens, painfully lame cows, turkeys unable to breed, pigs and chickens that die from heart failure in their infancy – no wonder the concerned welfarist takes a decidedly cautious view of a new technology which can create in a year what may have taken the selective breeders decades to achieve.'[51] The case against the type of factory farming that leads to cruelty towards animals seems relatively clear-cut; this is not the way one would treat enemies, never mind friends.

What about examples of transgenic manipulation of animals, where genes are moved from one species to the next? In this context, all genetic modifications are 'germline', rather than 'somatic'; the ethical restraints on human genetic manipulation, which I raised in earlier chapters, simply do not exist for animals, or for plants for that matter. The motivation for such change comes from favoured consequences, namely disease resistance, increased productivity, production of pharmaceuticals in milk or eggs, and provision of organs for transplant into humans. In other words, ethical justification is mostly based on instrumental use of animals for human benefit. Even in the case of disease resistance, the diseases in question are endemic to factory methods of farming, so that 'the same boring, frustrating and stressful rearing conditions continue, simply propped up by the microinjection rather than the hyperdermic or spray'.[52] The move towards increased productivity has 'brought untold misery to millions of farm animals and poultry'; the use of human growth-hormone genes in the Beltsville pigs is a well-known example. Other experiments, to increase muscle development in lambs and calves, have also failed, at the cost of considerable suffering to the animals concerned. It goes without saying that, on the basis of wisdom understood as situated in charitable friendship with creatures, all such developments need to be vigorously resisted.

---

[51] J. D'Silva, 'Campaigning Against Transgenic Technology', in Holland and Johnson (eds.), *Animal Biotechnology and Ethics*, p. 93.
[52] Ibid., p. 95.

The development of pharmaceutical products through transgenic manipulation of animals often seems, on the surface, to be benign in its impact on the animals themselves. When Dolly the sheep was cloned, it was the transgenic sheep Polly that was the most valued as far as the farm industry was concerned, for Polly was both a clone and also had her genes manipulated so that they contained human blood-clotting proteins, Factor IX. Cloning was done in the interest of making transgenic modifications easier; if cloning could be perfected, it would provide a way of passing on the transgenic qualities from one generation to the next. Publicity at the time made quite sure that Dolly was portrayed as being kept in good, clean and airy conditions. Although more serious readers were aware that 276 attempts were made before Dolly arrived, and that these 'failures' included animals with a range of abnormalities, these aspects tended to be side-stepped in more popular presentations of the discussion. Given the context of friendship in which I have situated ethical decision-making, it is obvious that as far as the sheep are concerned, it is not in their interests to clone or conduct multiple transgenic modifications through cloning. Moreover, the question can be raised about whether such use of farm animals is really necessary. Although key products for particularly severe medical conditions, including emphysema and cystic fibrosis, are being developed from it, why not use plant-tissue culture instead to achieve similar results?[53] Of course, it can hardly be said to be in the interest of plants to engineer them to produce pharmaceuticals, though I suggest that tissue culture does not have the same sense of an identity as an 'other' as do, for example, recognised plant and animal species. Even human tissue can be cultured in a laboratory, but there is no sense that by manipulating such tissue we are manipulating human beings. The model of wisdom in the context of charity and friendship, then, allows for limited use of genetic engineering in tissue culture, but is much more hesitant about the use of animals.[54]

Creating transgenic animals for organ transplants is also highly ambiguous for animal welfare. Experiments on primates are highly restricted in the United Kingdom, and are unlikely to become a possible source for xenotransplantation.[55] Donor animals are more likely to be pigs kept in sterile conditions using specific pathogen-free methods to ensure no disease. The entire uterus is removed into a sterile 'bubble', the sow is

---

[53] In some cases this may not be technically possible from a scientific perspective, because of differences in, for example, animal and plant biochemistry. However, technical difficulties need not limit the search for alternatives, where these are realistically thought to be possibilities.

[54] I will return to broader issues in relation to the ethics of agriculture as such in the section below.

[55] This conclusion is published in what is known as *The Kennedy Report*.

slaughtered, and the piglets are reared in sterile conditions.[56] Human affinity with primates is enough to prevent widespread experimentation, but not so for pigs. Has our sense of friendship with animals narrowed so much that responsibility towards them registers only when they seem more like ourselves? Joyce D'Silva concludes: 'We can only regret that the technological progress and power of the human species has [*sic*] apparently not been matched by any evolution of compassion or of appreciation of the "sacredness" and uniqueness of the animals with whom we happen to share our planet' (p. 101).

It is hardly surprising, then, that animal-rights campaigners such as Andrew Linzey liken all genetic engineering to animal slavery.[57] However, while one may doubt the wisdom of the examples discussed above, I suggest that there is no good reason why, in *some* circumstances, limited genetic engineering might not serve the creatures' interests. Limited application of genetic technology through somatic gene therapy of animals that are suffering various diseases, assuming that this is not brought about through inhumane conditions, might be permissible. Alternatively, there may be situations where it is possible to remove a harmful gene through manipulation of the germline (the most common form of genetic manipulation of animals). It is unlikely that any transgenic manipulations could be justified, for in what conceivable way could this express charity as friendship? The sad fact is that, because animals are not viewed through the eyes of friendship, genetic technology has been directed towards the manipulation of animals for short-term human profits, often in disregard of the suffering caused. Of course, from the perspective of genetics, boundaries between species are far more fluid, so 'any genome is much more like a loose-leaf folder than a carefully stitched volume. Any DNA, in principle, can turn up or be inserted anywhere', so that any individual organism is a 'construct', lacking a 'natural essence'.[58] However, some sense of respect for the identity of the other becomes clear once we start imagining scenarios where 'pure beef' is produced in a self-propagating muscular tissue, engineered from animals and excluding the possibility of pain suffered; there are simply no sense organs to feel such pain.[59] Such 'repugnant' artefacts remind us that 'Once we abandon any sense that there are valuable forms of being, what counts except intensity of feeling? And amongst such feelings is the pleasure of control.'[60]

---

[56] D'Silva, 'Campaigning Against Transgenic Technology', p. 98.
[57] Linzey, *Animal Theology*, pp. 138–55.   [58] Clark, *Biology and Christian Ethics*, p. 234.
[59] Ibid., pp. 264–5.
[60] Ibid., p. 265. See also S. Clark, 'Making Up Animals; The View From Science Fiction', in Holland and Johnson (eds.), *Animal Biotechnology and Ethics*, pp. 209–24.

An important question here is how far clinical trials can be permitted to draw on experiments with animals. Somatic gene therapy, for example, regularly uses primates in order to test out a dosage protocol prior to its administration in humans.[61] Few would want such drugs to be used on humans without prior testing, and would see a rush to clinical trials as irresponsible rather than prudent. However, this raises the question of how far and in what circumstances animals can ever be used instrumentally for human benefit. My suggestion in this context is that gene-therapy experiments require, ideally, prior testing on tissue culture, where this is possible. In addition, a clear rationale needs to be provided for *why* it is necessary to use primate studies, or studies on other sentient animals. Often these tests do not provide a guarantee of success in humans. The notion of friendship can, I suggest, act as a brake on such developments, so that, where possible, other means are sought in order to conduct preliminary trials. In addition, while the level of friendship for other humans is of a different order compared with that for animals, those creatures that are neighbours would be more appropriately sacrificed for testing pharmacogenetic drugs or gene-therapy protocols for clinical safety.

In addition, as more genetic diseases in humans are identified, there will be an increased temptation to model these diseases in animals using transgenic technology. One such attempt was a mouse designed to replicate Lesh-Nyhan's disease in humans. The latter leads to devastating neurological and behavioural symptoms. In the case described, the mouse models were asymptomatic, but there will be a drive, as a matter of logic, to produce animals with the symptoms, as they would have a higher fidelity to the course of the disease.[62] Bernard Rollin believes that the use of such animals in this way would be counter to the social ethic for the treatment of animals, and I would wish to reinforce this and suggest that it represents a dehumanising attitude towards other creatures. In other words, however attractive such live models might seem, to use animals in this way would be unethical and show a lack of compassion for animals.

Genetic engineering of animals also has to be set in the context of the advent of high-technology agriculture. Rollin suggests that the ancient contract with animals, where animals were given the respect they deserved according to their own *telos*, changed drastically in the mid-twentieth

---

[61] See chapter 6 above, on genetic therapies.

[62] B. E. Rollin, 'Biotechnology and Animals: Ethical Issues in Genetic Engineering and Cloning', in Burley and Harris (eds.), *Genethics*, pp. 70–81, esp. pp. 78–9.

century.[63] However, he rejects the notion of 'Divine purpose', added to the concept of *telos*, as a 'conceptual barnacle' (p. 162). Yet the fact that reference to divine purpose is made does not mean, as Rollin seems to conclude, that all ideas about *telos* for the sake of animals themselves are discounted simply in favour of 'Divine purpose'. Rather, it seems to me that divine purpose gives an *additional* motivation for seeking the ultimate good of the creatures; their *telos* is joined with ours. *Telos* refers not just to the immediate survival interests, but also to concern for the psychological welfare of animals as well. However, Rollin goes on to suggest that we might be justified in changing the *telos* of an animal, as analogous to the common practice of domestication of animals. By the same notion it would not, according to his view, be wrong to alter a chicken's *telos* so that it no longer minded being kept in cramped conditions (p. 166). He admits that this might be 'jarring', but the best outcome to expect, given the difficulty of changing conditions. Moreover, set in a wider context of other species, some genetic modifications might be detrimental to the *telos* of other species. Set in the context of a discussion of wisdom and friendship I have outlined above, it is clear that, while this view is inclusive of the idea of *telos*, it is possible to distinguish between the kind of gradual domestication of animals to human husbandry, which existed under a social contract, and the alteration of an animal's *telos* to accommodate factory conditions. For we would not wish such a change on our friends. Just as we would not wish to change the mental capacities of children so that they were not aware of being born into oppressive regimes, to incite such changes in animals is, I suggest, a failure to respect the other as other, even if it leads to a temporary amelioration of suffering. It amounts to a failure of virtue, a failure to recognise that the commercial interests of factory farming have overshadowed other interests.

In consideration of agriculture

Paul Thomson argues that the dominant ethic of agriculture is productionist; increase in yield is the primary goal in agricultural development.[64] It is, furthermore, combined with utilitarian economics expressed as the drive to lower the cost of food. These attitudes inform scientific research, so that 'what it means to be a good agricultural scientist, to be worthy of

---

[63] B. E. Rollin, 'On Telos and Genetic Engineering', in Holland and Johnson (eds.), *Animal Biotechnology and Ethics*, pp. 156–71.

[64] Thomson, *The Spirit of the Soil*.

tenure, promotion, recognition and rewards, is to achieve scientific findings that can be applied to the production of food' (p. 64). From my own
experience as a scientist working in agricultural research, it is true that the
perceived goals were deemed ethical in so far as they seemed to benefit
yields *as such*. There was less questioning whether such increased yields
were really necessary; for example, research in barley and wheat yield
continued even after scientists became aware that there were 'wheat moun-
tains' in Europe. Thompson, writing in 1995, considered that recombinant
DNA technology was not widely used in the farming or the food industry
(p. 33). He seems to be a little out of touch in this respect. Michael
Northcott believes that the social consequences of genetic engineering
need to be more taken into account:

In the current government and corporate framing of agriculture in the European
Union, in North America and in much of the South, GMOs seem set merely to
enhance existing deleterious tendencies in agriculture, making food ever more
heavily subsidised, and chemically laden, at the expense of the taxpayer and at the
risk of the health of the food consumer.[65]

He argues that, by attempting to increase yields still further, production
of GMO crops will exacerbate problems that exist in rural societies,
damaging indigenous subsistence agriculture in the southern hemisphere.
He admits that, in theory, genetic engineering could be used to promote
'sustainable, low energy, low-waste, low-pollution, labour-intensive traditional mixed farming', but this would be 'more fantasy than reality' because
of the control exercised over global agriculture by seed corporations.
However, this is a pessimistic view of the chances that global corporations
might change their policy as a result of public pressure. Large corporations are
often 'greener' than smaller companies, as they can afford to be so.
Moreover, a recent report admits that any positive gains from genetic
engineering have not been directed to serving the needs of the poorer
communities of the world. It argues that research should turn its attention
towards sustainable production of tropical and sub-tropical food staples,
taking into account the needs of poor farmers and rural communities.[66]
The lack of adequate safety regulations in poorer communities over the
release of GM crops is also an issue that needs to be taken into account.

More surprising is Northcott's affirmation of the ideal of stewardship
as the principal governing human relationship with the land.[67] It is

---

[65] Northcott, "'Behold I have set the land before you'".
[66] Nuffield Report, *Genetically Modified Crops*, pp. 67–71.
[67] Northcott, "'Behold I have set the land before you'".

surprising, as he has appeared to argue against the use of this term in his earlier work, where he suggests that stewardship has 'become associated with instrumental attitudes to nature which are linked with environmental exploitation and it may be that association of stewardship with absolute property rights and land ownership patterns in Western civilisation resulted in its mutation into a metaphor of human control and mastery over nature'.[68] The problem is that, while stewardship can be put into a theocentric model of the relationship between God, humanity and the land, it still gives priority to human action and decision-making. Yet it is the focus on ethics as exclusively based in human consciousness that is the object of Northcott's critique. The concept of friendship with the created order, on the other hand, reminds us to treat the natural world as 'other' than ourselves, while still admitting that attitudes to the environment are rooted in who we are as persons, as much as in how this is expressed in action.

In Northcott's later work he seems to put ethical priority on how far actions can be said to have good *outcomes* for the ecological community, which includes the human community, rather than for the individual life forms therein. He rejects the idea that genetic engineering raises new ethical issues; rather, they are part and parcel of a distorted relationship to agriculture. However, we need to ask ourselves whether it really would be beneficial to develop genetic engineering of crops directed towards sustainable agriculture; in other words, is genetic engineering contributing to the overall good or *telos* of the individual plant species, in the context of the social community in which it is placed? There may be some changes in the characteristics of crops that could never be justified, even if they seem at first sight to be of benefit to the poorer communities. Transgenic engineering inevitably brings about a loss of diversity, since the sections of genetic material involved are now shared with other species. An ethic of wisdom in the context of love and friendship would challenge the idea that genetic changes are acceptable as long as they contribute to an idealised traditional agriculture. For the very concept of transgenic engineering breaks something of the covenant with created beings. Such a covenant need not imply that there should be a total ban on all genetic engineering; rather, each case should be set in the context of seeking wisdom, wisdom that is inclusive of the needs of all the different relationships in which humanity is called to live. Such a vocation does not mean fixity in forms of being, in the way Aquinas suggests. His views were wedded to a medieval cosmology of a

---

[68] Northcott, *Christianity and Environmental Ethics*, p. 180.

Chain of Being. However, in the light of the dynamic sense of ecology as in a continual sense of flux and change, human participation in this change should be directed to the good of all aspects of the community in which it is set.

Of course, where there are clashes of interests, discernment becomes difficult. How do we decide when an action in genetic engineering seems in consequentialist terms to be beneficial, not just for the few, but for poorer communities? In these cases I suggest that we need to draw on the principle of wisdom, which is more than the bland precautionary principle advocated in secular literature. The latter is defined as 'a strategy for dealing with environmental risk and uncertainty, which guides us to act cautiously and embark on a systematic programme of research to improve our understanding of the costs and benefits of particular actions'.[69] Rather, wisdom, aligned with prudence, includes the ability to discern the right course of action in order to express a particular virtue, including especially the virtues of charity and justice. Such discernment includes a sense of clear perception of reality, and also memory of the past and shrewdness about the future. Has our experience of genetic engineering of crops given us reason to reject even claims that it could be used to benefit the Third World by changes to tropical and staple crops? The powerful attraction of evil is the way it is portrayed, hence the need for unity of the virtues. There may, under *gnōmē*, be some important exceptions to the more general principle that genetic engineering has not worked for the global good. Examples include the use of cystatin genes in protecting banana and potato plants from the infestations of nematodes, usually controlled by heavy applications of toxic nematocides.[70] Wisdom, as necessary for the expression of all the virtues, is the starting point for ethical consideration; but, as I have emphasised throughout this book, it does not preclude other virtues, such as justice, charity, hope, peaceableness, temperance and fortitude. If the virtue of wisdom is fostered by friendship and rooted in the friendship with God, what might be the limits of our genetic interventions? More importantly, what does the desire to make these changes say about the kind of people we are becoming? The issue of human freedom is developed in the remarks that follow in the Postscript.

---

[69] BMA Report, *The Impact of Genetic Modification*, p. 17.
[70] For further discussion of this aspect, see C. Deane-Drummond, 'Genetic Interventions in Nature: Perspectives from a Christian Ethics of Wisdom', in Edwards and Worthing (eds.), *Biodiversity and Ecology*, pp. 30–44.

Postscript: Concluding remarks

The tour of ethical issues in genetics with which this book grapples reveals the importance of coming to an adequate understanding of what freedom means and of the theological challenge that this poses to anthropology in a secular context. I have argued for a recovery of the virtues, in particular the cardinal virtues of prudence, justice, fortitude and temperance alongside the theological virtues of faith, hope and charity. In addition, I have suggested that the theological principles that act like a sounding-board for this discussion need to refer to wisdom, understood as both learned and a gift of the Holy Spirit. But a broader, overarching issue that encompasses even these discussions is how to express these virtues and receive these gifts. I will suggest in these concluding remarks that the milieu in which such an anthropology is rooted depends on developing an understanding of human freedom, one that is theologically informed, and also provides a counter-culture to those forms of freedom that seem to dominate the secular debate, namely those arising out of rational democratic liberalism.

Liberalist politics assumes a view of the human that is detached from commitments, but it is doubtful whether such detachment is either desirable or possible. Paul Ricoeur argues against liberalist politics on the grounds that it offers too thin a view of the human self; instead, we need to draw deeply on tradition, especially the tradition of *phronēsis* or practical wisdom.[1] The theory of rational liberalism portrays a particular vision of the good in terms of freedom, so that a particular account of what that good might be becomes impossible in the name of that freedom, which puts great emphasis on individual rights understood in terms of procedural justice.[2] What might be an alternative understanding of both freedom and

---

[1] Ricoeur, *Oneself as Another*, p. 280. I am grateful to Jackie Stewart for directing my attention to the significance of *phronēsis* in Ricoeur's work, and to the challenge he brings to liberalism: J. Stewart, 'Ricoeur, Public Ethics and Religion'.

[2] See, for example, Walzer, *Spheres of Justice*.

the human person that seeks to provide a richer understanding of human decision-making, more rooted in tradition, but also open to the future?

Karl Rahner's development of the concept of freedom and the human person is helpful in this context. Rahner suggests that freedom is not so much an 'object' as something continuously given by God as humanity reaches towards self-transcendence.[3] Freedom is directed towards 'the horizon of this absolute transcendence'. Yet it is not possible to go straight to the goal of transcendence; rather, it is expressed indirectly through categorical freedom in the finite sphere. Underlying this view was Rahner's belief that we come to a 'fundamental option' or choice, to say 'yes' or 'no' to this horizon. However, it would be a mistake to think that God offers this horizon only to the human person; rather, God is also deeply involved with concrete decision-making through divinising grace (VI, p. 183). Freedom thus becomes a form of self-realisation, since it is through such choices that humanity becomes itself; but this freedom is fired by love, a love that allows self-forgetfulness. Thus Rahner argues that the most basic ethos for a Christian is love, rather than respecting objective norms imposed by God on reality (VI, p. 188). Even amid this, he insists that because the absolute reality of God is mystery, and because the history of humankind is under a shadow of sin and guilt, the goal of absolute certainty is impossible in the human exercise of freedom (VI, pp. 191–5). At the same time he is ready to admit the need to develop some formal principles. He also brings in a Christological dimension through his notion of freedom as liberated, so that sin can be thought of as a lack of openness to the love of God and as self-assertion in the world, while 'the freedom of man is liberated into immediacy to God's own freedom of being' (VI, p. 196). Because this takes freedom beyond simply an empirical aspect or 'datum' of human life, it is resistant to those forms of empirical psychology that treat freedom as simply the relationships between different material phenomena.[4]

The strength of Rahner's position is that it serves to integrate a transcendental element into freedom, while recognising the importance of grounding that freedom in everyday concrete experiences. He also points to the freedom of God in terms of mystery, which challenges any notion of fixed understanding of human action and behaviour. He develops his ideas on freedom in relation to the varied human practices that express the human capacity for changing self, whether through environmental, biological, genetic, psychological, social or political means.[5] He sees the

---

[3] Rahner, *Theological Investigations*, VI, p. 179.   [4] Rahner, *Foundations of Christian Faith*, pp. 35–6.
[5] Rahner, *Theological Investigations*, IX, pp. 205–24.

approaching changes not so much as a heaven or hell, but as a scenario where 'man is one whose freedom is laid upon him as a burden' (IX, p. 212). Whereas, in the past, such self-manipulation was limited to contemplative knowledge, the possibilities that now exist reach out to other spheres of being, including the genetic and biological spheres. Rahner resists any sense of fixity of human nature. He suggests that, since evil will lead ultimately to non-being, humanity cannot do what it may not do, and what it can do it ought to do without hesitation (IX, p. 216). Such a suggestion might seem to give a *carte blanche* for all genetic manipulations, and Paul Ramsey has criticised him heavily on this account.[6] However, this criticism seems to be based on Rahner's somewhat naïve belief that, where the 'experiment' with humanity is acting out of freedom, then, if mistakes are made, these will prove unfruitful. Rahner believes, for example, that moralists may resist self-manipulation as being counter to human essence, but such instances do not represent a state of sin before God. Rather:

Objectively they belong to the same category as those instances where subhuman, 'innocent' nature permits itself to produce monstrous, aberrant things leading into biological and other culs-de-sac. Even aberrant categorical self-manipulation, seeming to spring from a really transcendental freedom *vis à vis* God, can be an ultimately harmless experiment on the part of nature, experimenting and slowly trying to bring forth what the genuine future holds in promise.[7]

Yet this idea is somewhat optimistic, since Rahner seems to assume that, where being is possible, this is related to the good, even if it is not expressing 'man's free essence as such' (IX, p. 217). It is not clear how this could be the case where it is supposedly springing from a transcendental freedom; in other words, he seems to have separated transcendental freedom from human freedom in a way that is unconvincing. In addition, when he comes to consider what is permissible in terms of the technologies available at the time, he leaves open the possibility of experimentation with human genetic material; but when it comes to use of donor gametes he adopts a more conservative approach that seems at first sight to be somewhat inconsistent with his more theoretical treatment of freedom (IX, pp. 234–7).[8] His concerns include donor anonymity and extramarital

---

[6] Ramsey, *Fabricated Man*, pp. 139–42.   [7] Rahner, *Theological Investigations*, IX, p. 217.
[8] He does, nonetheless, leave open the possibility that, since there may be doubt about whether a human being comes into existence at conception, the possibility needs to be entertained that the reasons for conducting biological research on embryos may outweigh the ethical objections in this case. However, he sits on the fence here, arguing that we cannot 'decide the issue one way or another' (p. 236).

relationships, but also seem to be related to a mistaken projection about the development of state eugenic control of 'sperm banks'.[9]

I suggest that, in order to work out more fully what freedom might mean, and especially how it can come to be expressed in the context of the Christian community and in public discourse, we need to recover the tradition of practical wisdom alongside wisdom as such. Rahner includes in his discussion the notion of charity and faith, through his concept of the fundamental option and of freedom as rooted in and springing from love. However, he is vague about how such freedom might be expressed, other than speaking of its becoming an integral part of what it means to be human. Wisdom, like transcendental and categorical freedoms, includes theological and anthropological components. However, because wisdom is concerned primarily with relationships, and ultimately with the relationship with God and creatures, it offers a way of emphasising the social and incorporating knowledge from science while at the same time offering a critique of its practices. Rahner is correct, in my view, to challenge notions of fixity in human nature; but then the question still remains regarding where to draw the line in such changes. I am less convinced by his idea that biological outcomes will, in effect, rule out all immoral practices, and in other writing Rahner seems to negate this suggestion as well. Of course, there will be some restraints that are built in, as it were, to the natural processes. The practical difficulty of human cloning is a case in point. But this does not mean that this restraint is sufficient; what is needed is a clearer account of where the limits might be placed, and whether such a development is consistent with the expression of human integrity and goodness understood in terms of the public good as well as the individual good.

If the practice of eugenics still casts a shadow, it is surely this: that we cannot be too complacent about endorsing techniques where they are used

---

[9] He was, of course, writing at a time when egg donation and embryo donation were not available. His objections to AID on the basis of eugenics are consistent with his views on human freedom. See Rahner, *Theological Investigations*, IX, pp. 236–7. He also objects on the basis of (a) a 'faith instinct' that rejects such procedures; (b) human nature as being given as a fundamental constitution of human freedom; (c) a driving force in gamete donation being a fear of human destiny; and (d) severance of marriage intimacy and procreation. One could reply to all these objections by arguing, first, that 'faith instinct' does not inevitably object to IVF or AID. Secondly, the success of gamete donation is equally subject to contingency, and so subject to divine permission, so that no person need feel that he or she was pre-planned or 'designed' in the manner that his objection implies. Thirdly, the driving force in gamete donation is not so much fear of destiny (though it certainly will involve pain associated with failure in childbearing) as the love of the couple for each other and their desire for children. Fourthly, while couples do have to come to terms with the separation of their procreative acts and childbearing, this does not inevitably lead to the loss of intimacy that Rahner assumes will be the case. See also below and chapter 8 for further discussion. Rahner, *Theological Investigations*, IX, pp. 238–48.

to manipulate the social and political spheres. In addition, what can appear as a good can sometimes disguise more problematic issues that are left concealed because the arguments are presented in terms of technique alone. The method becomes an end in itself, without a clear-sighted sense of what the implications might be in the future. This memory of the past allows a cautionary note to come to mind in any consideration of what might be possible or permissible. This does not lead to stagnation, however; rather, prudence, or practical wisdom, also allows for foresight, for viewing how such-and-such an action might serve to express divine providence. At the same time it is clear that circumspection involves knowledge of what really is the case. How are we to come to such knowledge? I suggest that knowing about the direction of science practice, and about the kinds of proposals that are on offer, as well as having a modicum of knowledge about what takes place, are necessary in order to arrive at responsible decisions. This calls for a reliance on the expertise and honesty of others who deliver such information.

Aquinas was prepared to go beyond a purely objective calculus and to speak in terms of science as a 'gift'. Unlike wisdom, however, the gift of science is concerned only with human or created things.[10] Science, for Aquinas, was broader than the contemporary concept, for it included theological knowledge; but, rather as it is today, it was also about knowledge in a detached sense: 'hence the knowing of what one ought to believe is the gift of science. But as relating to the realities themselves through being united with them, this is for the gift of wisdom. Accordingly the gift of wisdom corresponds more to charity which conjures man's mind to God.' In addition, he was ready to admit that *some* knowledge of God could come through created things, and this is connected with the office of science. However, science as such does not lead to a capacity to judge aright, for this requires a relationship with God as expressed in wisdom; so, 'when we judge created things in the light of divine things, this belongs to wisdom, rather than science' (2a2ae q. 9.2). This is clarified still further by Aquinas' resistance to naming any beatitude with the gift of science. For him, real happiness could come only from contemplating God, rather than from creaturely being, so that creaturely goods do not arouse spiritual joy except in so far as they are recognised as being charged with divine good. In this way 'spiritual peace and the resulting joy correspond directly to the gift of wisdom' (2a2ae q. 9.4).

---

[10] Aquinas, *Summa Theologiae*, 2a2ae q. 9.2.

Wisdom, in other words, inculcates a mindset different from that initiated by science; it is one that, as gift, admits to relationship with God, though in wisdom as learned it is a trait that is acquired by the human community through communal life in the family and through education. Prudence is more concerned with how to live out such wisdom in practical contexts, in the difficult and often ambiguous situations in which we find ourselves today. Genetic screening and testing bring with them particular ethical issues around consent, the use of knowledge and the commercialisation of genomic knowledge. Hilary Rose gives a fascinating account of the way Iceland was targeted by a particular Icelandic entrepreneur who managed to manoeuvre the political will of the welfare state, venture capital, health management and the insurance industry in setting up a Heath Sector Database (HSD).[11] This database promised much: to monitor genetic profiles and genealogies in order to provide more efficient healthcare and use of appropriate drug doses. Rose raised the importance of the link into previous health records; in other words, the dangers did not arise simply out of the commodification of genetic knowledge, but out of its use of previously existing health records. It is clear that this is a good example of political imprudence. The Health Sector Database Bill was rushed through the legislative bodies without proper consultation, and without including a proper account of the need to protect patients' interests. In addition, the bill favoured the use of the information by a monopoly company, even naming the company who had made the initial approaches for such a development. Those who were under eighteen were forced to be subject to parental choice, and vulnerable groups were not taken into account. Furthermore, the records of the dead were included in the database, even if this was against the wishes of the immediate family. There were other political misdemeanours as well: for example, the National Bioethics Committee, which had resisted the bill, was replaced less than a year after the bill became law. Rose's study also raises the difference in gendered responses to the HSD. Whereas the men she interviewed were more likely to be interested in viewing the database as just another resource, women were much more likely to be concerned about the impact that this would have on their family life. Many distrusted the commercial aims of the private company that set up the database. Yet one reason why the database became a subject for political discussion was its market-led approach to genomics. In countries such as Britain, where

[11] H. Rose, 'The Commodification of Virtual Reality: The Icelandic Health Sector Debate', in Goodman et al. (eds.), *Genetic Nature/Culture*, pp. 77–92.

the state also has some control over health provision, innovations such as this could be incorporated without even going through a democratic process. While I have suggested above that liberalism as an absolute value for decision-making presupposes a narrow notion of the good, in this case the absence of discussion precludes what that public good might entail. It becomes left to what Rose describes as Britain's 'highly secretive political culture, which it is so painfully trying to move beyond' (p. 89).

The political aspects of the debate come out even more strongly when it comes to the discourse on gene patenting. In many of these cases the patent rights of a company seem to be guided by the individual or corporate right in a way that often fails to take into proper account the remits of distributive justice, or what would be directed towards a public account of the good. Political issues are also close to a discussion of the gendered nature of genetic technologies, for intervention in genetics usually affects the lives of women more than men. The political frame comes into play in an equally obvious way once the discussion is enlarged to include ethical issues relating to the genetic manipulation of animals and other creatures. Rahner has called politics 'the innermost part of the factory' of the self-manipulation of humanity, for it is here that different aspects of practice are co-ordinated and given legitimacy.[12] As such, this serves to emphasise even more strongly the requirement for political prudence, distributive justice and an orientation towards the public good in political decision-making.

Familial prudence is more obvious in those contexts where families are engaged in particular decisions about their future and the future of their offspring. This applies to cases of, for example, genetic counselling for the avoidance of particular diseases, and to the use of reproductive technologies in general. Such decisions are never straightforward, but in such circumstances there is a need for a willingness to listen to the concerns of those involved in facing the practical outcomes of those decisions. Some feminists have argued for a more dialogical approach that both respects the autonomy of the individual, and situates the discourse in the context of community life. Balancing these different goods is a task of some delicacy and sensitivity. It is therefore inappropriate in the extreme for Rahner to condemn such practices as donor conception as equivalent to either adultery or rape.[13] Such blanket condemnation is unhelpful and judgmental. In

---

[12] Rahner, *Theological Investigations*, IX, p. 209.
[13] Rahner even uses the language of rape to describe donor conception: 'Genetic manipulation of this sort is no more "human", merely because it produces a human being, than a case of rape'; see Rahner, *Theological Investigations*, IX, p. 246. Oliver O'Donovan takes a similar view, describing AID as

the first place, he assumes, wrongly, that heterologous artificial insemination by donor (AID) was being propagated as a means to control through eugenic goals the human population towards specific ends. In addition, the idea that the marriage bond is compromised through the introduction of the third party assumes that the child arises from an act of betrayal, which it does not. More worryingly, it seems to restrict personal identity to genetic essentialism, failing to take into account the strong influence both of gestation and of subsequent environmental influences in shaping human personality. Further, what needs to be taken into account is not just the intention of the parents, but also the welfare of the child and the good of society as a whole. In other words, although the commercialisation of gametes in a market economy would be unacceptable, where such possibilities were carefully considered under the auspices of a general practitioner, then a theological ethic could permit such practice where it was seen to be working for the ultimate good of a family unit.[14] In addition, the secrecy surrounding such practices must be resisted, for such a culture

analogous to rape or adultery, rather than as something more positive. While he is correct to point to the incongruity in the legal situation of parenthood regarding surrogate and donor relationships, his assumption that donor insemination will be a disruptive factor in a marriage is evidence of an essentialist view of marriage, procreation and parenthood. See O'Donovan, *Begotten or Made?*, pp. 31–48. The legal difficulties arising out of such cases are discussed in more detail in Kaplan, *The Limits and Lies of Genetic Research*, pp. 151–68. He also makes the observation that while there have been instances of sperm donors claiming their parental rights, where the paternity of the child has been discovered, he knows of no case where egg donors have claimed such rights (p. 159). The difference reflects the important difference in the experience of egg donation and sperm donation, the former giving the mother a biological connection with the child that is impossible in the case of sperm donation. O'Donovan argues that this is an unacceptable 'making' of a child, with a biological mother and a genetic mother and father, rather than 'begetting' from two parents. He raises the issue of who might have parental rights or 'ownership' in such arrangements. Against this view I would argue that it is obvious that where a donor has freely given her eggs, there is no ambiguity about her identity as parent; rather, she is the genetic mother, not the parent, of that child. Motherhood begins from the moment of implantation, where that mother intends that child, and that child is to be received as a gift, not as something that she rightfully 'owns'. O'Donovan's language of ownership seems to be a rhetorical device to win over sympathy for his conservative view. There is certainly no controversy in law regarding who is the natural mother of the child in egg-donor relationships. There is little evidence to suggest that children born from such arrangements suffer psychologically as a result; rather, it is the secrecy that surrounds such transactions that is damaging for family relationships. Surrogacy and other contract arrangements bring their own complications, the more so where a 'surrogate' mother is the gestational and genetic mother of the child. In such cases, surrogacy seems an inappropriate label; rather, the surrogate is the mother of the child, and is prepared to give up that child to aid a childless couple. Is this an act of altruism, or an inappropriate abandonment by the mother of her child? I would, in this case, suggest that the latter often applies, especially where there are financial inducements. However, each case would need to be considered in context. It is not an area that lends itself to rule-based ethics, for such measurements are too crude in view of the ethical complexities involved.

[14] While the more liberal position to reproductive ethics suggested here is less common among Roman Catholic theologians, it remains the subject for discussion among Roman Catholic and Jewish theologians. See, Mackler, *Introduction to Jewish and Catholic Bioethics*, pp. 156–89.

reflects the sense of shame that those who are infertile experience. Instead, society should show more compassion, and welcome a child as gift whatever his or her specific genetic origins. Nonetheless, a child is never a 'parental right', and the social pressure towards genetically identical children can lead to promotion of highly unethical practices, such as human reproductive cloning. Fortunately, in this case the high risks attached to the procedure put a brake on its approval in most jurisdictions.

Controversies relating to genetics are likely to become much more intense as the hope of eliminating disease through other means is pursued, as in, for example, the use of inherited genetic modification. In these cases I have resisted its use in principle, except for a cautious introduction of gene repair for serious single-gene defects.[15] The possibility of widespread use of this technique for eugenic purposes is highly unlikely where it involves the simple repair of a lethal gene, for such genes are rare in the population, and other techniques, such as pre-implantation genetic diagnosis (PGD), are currently used. Of course, the latter raises its own ethical issues about whether those who are 'screened out' of a population experience themselves in an even sharper way as being rejected by society. In this context feminist interpretations of ethics that include caring are helpful, though, equally, caring is fostered by classical approaches through the virtue of charity. In addition, while the concept of caring can sometimes be used in such a way as to stereotype the role of women in society, charity that is connected to love of God and that works to enable wisdom and prudence resists the notion of conformity to type. Caring is, in other words, the task of the whole community, not just of women in that community. The social consequences of introducing additional capacities through inheritable genetic modification (IGM) would be more problematic, raising important issues connected with social justice.

Is 'therapeutic' cloning an option for those suffering deleterious disease? A prudential decision in this case lies in the area of individual prudence, through consent, but also includes political prudence. In the United States, the exemplar of a highly liberal democratic society, it might seem incongruous that embryonic stem-cell research failed to win federal support for funds, except for those cell lines that are already established. The compromise position took into account the strong political lobby for affirming the high status of the human embryo. I have resisted giving the embryo a fully personal status, while wanting to affirm the human worth of early embryos and afford them human dignity

---

[15] By 'serious' I mean those likely to be lethal in childhood or early adulthood.

from the moment of implantation.[16] This is earlier than the standard fourteen-day limit embedded in current law, but draws back from the most conservative position, which ascribes personhood from the moment of conception. Bearing this in mind, would it be a prudent decision to help save a life of someone who is dying by creating embryos and using the stem cells that could then be genetically modified prior to treatment? I would resist this route, especially where there are sources of stem cells from spare IVF embryos, on the understanding that these embryos are not deliberately created as surplus to requirements. For a number of reasons, many of such embryos are seldom suitable for implantation and so are unlikely to be viable (note for present purposes viability implies the strong likelihood of implantation), while proving effective as sources of stem cells. In addition, such techniques raise issues of distributive justice in allocation of healthcare resources. These questions lend themselves to the application of political prudence.

How, one might ask, might those engaged in public policy-making, familial counselling or medical practice hold on to a sense of vision for the public good that is presupposed in a recovery of prudence and justice? Such a recovery depends on the gift of fortitude, where fortitude means the ability to hold fast to the public good in spite of personal suffering. Ethical issues in human genetics stretch human reasoning to its limits and beyond, constantly raising questions in a new light and presenting new practical

---

[16] This happens about six days after the egg is fertilised. A similar position is taken by John Bryant and John Searle in their *Life in Our Hands*, pp. 55–9. The traditional Roman Catholic view is arguably a conservative one, naming ensoulment as taking place from conception onwards. See discussion in Jones, *The Soul of the Embryo*, published as the present volume went to press. The incarnation of Christ is an affirmation of the *material created order as such*, not a reification of the moment when sperm and egg unite, which is implied by Jones's linking of the moment of conception with Christ's incarnation. While I would agree with him, and with others such as Robert Song and Brent Waters, in the need to protect vulnerable life, the notion that eschatology includes all conceptuses as well as embryos from early miscarriages, and presumably all conceptuses from whatever source at all, 'natural' or otherwise, strikes me as being as unconvincing as it is irrational, especially for those not convinced by the arguments in support of the equivalent moral status of conceptuses and persons. Robert Song's view fares better when he argues that potentiality is equivalent to personhood, thus not naming the embryo as personal in the absolute sense. This position is far more reasonable compared with Jones's more absolute stance that the conceptus *is* a person. Christians must be respectful of alternative views in this difficult area of ethics in a way that is not always evident. In other words, there needs to be an admission that this is an area for discussion and debate. The very possibility of identical twins, or, in rare cases, of the fusion of two embryos into one (see Porter, 'Individuality, Personal Identity'), counters the view that individual personhood begins at conception. Hence, in the last analysis, I fail to be convinced by arguments for a highly conservative stance, even though I would argue for the value of early human life – not, however, deriving its value from its personal status (i.e. seeing it as a human being), but rather deriving it from its status as *being human*, and thus not a material object to be treated as a commodity. See also Song, 'To Be Willing to Kill What For All One Knows is a Person is to be Willing to Kill a Person', in Waters and Cole-Turner (eds.), *God and the Embryo*, pp. 98–107.

challenges. Who would have suspected, even a few years ago, that scientists would be able to generate sperm or egg cells from early embryonic stem cells? Given the complexities involved, how can we have any certainty about what shape the public good might take? Prudential decision-making includes an admission that there can never be absolute certainty, and in this sense always needs to be open to revision as new insights come to light. However, where there are pressures that militate against the virtue of justice understood in a prudential way, then those involved in such decision-making need to practise the accompanying virtue of fortitude.

Fortitude might seem very old-fashioned in the light of popular naturalistic readings of ethics, such as that promoted by E. O. Wilson. According to his position, the overriding motivation for human action is self-interest, and this serves to inform even those seemingly altruistic acts between neighbours.[17] His rationale for moving beyond one's kin to act in generous ways is still based on self-interested benefits. Other theoretical models in evolutionary psychology include concepts such as 'tit for tat', or reciprocal altruism. While such models may account in a limited way for some tendencies in human behaviour, they are highly unsatisfactory as a basis for ethics, removing, in effect, the notion of freedom and growth in the virtues and resistance to the vices that is integral to the position argued for in this book. In addition, temperance takes this further in that it is not simply about outward action, in the realm of justice, but also about inner attitudes of self-restraint, the mirror-image of absorbed self-interestedness. Temperance, in particular, qualifies those desires that are related to animal behaviour, such as the desires for food and sexual gratification. This is not to deny the worth of such desires, but to situate them in an appropriate context. In this context chastity is the most basic form of temperance, but it is also associated with humility, gentleness and *studiositas*. The latter is the natural striving for knowledge, and as such is a good. However, it can degenerate into an indulgence called *curiositas*, which is inappropriate rather than appropriate, for it is used for self-interested reasons. It is just this kind of indulgence to serve self that Wilson seems to be advocating in his arguments for environmental concern. Aquinas was more troubled by *curiositas* expressed in magic, but, where technique becomes an obsession, detached from the good of others, the concept would also be applicable there too. According to Josef Pieper, *curiositas* is a 'roaming unrest of the spirit', arising out of a sadness that has not sufficiently come to terms with its own humanity, and developing when humanity shakes off its nobility of

---

[17] Wilson, *Biophilia*.

being, losing its capacity to live with itself.[18] Yet Pieper suggests that humanity should move towards a kind of asceticism of cognition, so he can claim boldly that 'it is in such an asceticism of cognition alone that he may preserve or regain that which actually constitutes man's vital existence: the perception of the reality of God and his creation, and the possibility of shaping himself and the world according to his truth, which reveals itself only in silence' (p. 122).

Is such a view realistic? I suggest that it is, but it may be that the utopias offered in the new genetics cannot be resisted. Perhaps we can learn more lessons from the way human intervention in non-human species has gone awry, and this will foster a deeper awareness of the need for temperance understood in this sense. This is not intended to suggest that genetic change in humans is automatically harmful, but rather that, where such practices take over the human psyche and become means for *curiositas*, then they need to be resisted. While temperance supplies the inner will for prudence and justice to be exercised, there is a reciprocal relationship between the virtues, for knowing what might be temperance or intemperance is an activity of prudence.

Above all, it is worth emphasising that, as far as Aquinas was concerned, foresight was the dominant component of prudence, for such foresight, which he also called prevision, could reckon to judge in accordance with human providence, understood as a 'looking ahead to something distant to which present occurrences are to be adapted'.[19] Such a vision for the future is needed if we are to welcome those aspects of genetic science and technology that work for the good of individuals, communities, societies and the wider ecological network in which human society is situated. Of course, where there is a clash of interests, political prudence takes precedence. Yet such political prudence needs to find ways of incorporating the interests, not just of human species, but of the wider creaturely matrix in which human society is necessarily embedded. It is also clear that those areas of genetic practice that appear on the horizon of human manipulation are, in the first place, tested and tried on animal species, and very often on primate species as well. We need, in such a context, to consider the gift of prudence in as much as it gives foresight about the wisdom of some of these developments, even prior to their application to humans. It is an ethic, in other words, that takes into account the intrinsic value of all creaturely being, while recognising that there is an unavoidable hierarchy in what might be permissible, depending on the evolutionary status and ecological

---

[18] Pieper, *Fortitude and Temperance*, pp. 120–1.   [19] Aquinas, 2a2ae q. 49.6.

significance of a given species. If genetics has, on the one hand, challenged boundaries between species, it has, on the other, highlighted how remarkably small genetic differences can lead to significant changes at the phenotypic and behavioural level. It is important to point both to the existing power of genetic knowledge and to its ignorance in terms of specific regulatory processes. Such ignorance should foster a sense of *studiositas*, which has an eye not just on profit margins, but on the good of the community as a whole.

Finally, for the Christian community at least, the virtues of prudence, justice, fortitude and temperance as learned and as infused by God's grace are enlarged upon and developed in the context of the life and liturgy of that community. In other words, it makes no sense to speak of such virtues without association with the theological virtues of faith, hope and charity, and the intellectual virtue of wisdom, which comes both as learned and as gift of the Holy Spirit. Human genetics raises highly emotional and sensitive issues about life at all stages of development, from the moment of conception through to the last days of one who is suffering from a lethal genetic disease. Tremendous resilience and compassion are called for in such circumstances, and it would be easy to make premature judgments or to fail to act. I have argued in this book that rule-based or consequentialist approaches are insufficient in navigating the complexities in such decision-making. It is easy, in the face of anxiety or uncertainty, to fall back on a rule-based approach, seemingly to limit any possible damage. However, I would argue that such a position is not in tune with the vocation of humanity to live in transcendental freedom and transcendental wisdom and transcendental love. In addition, just as transcendental freedom can be expressed only through categorical concrete existence, so divine wisdom finds its expression in human wisdom, more specifically as related to the wisdom of God incarnate as divine Logos.[20] Can humanity be described as in one sense a co-creator or co-redeemer through such activities? I would hesitate to use such labels, as they would, I suggest, threaten to undermine temperance, though I would not automatically assume that such labels would lead to hubris. Instead, perhaps the human being is better thought of as the one who seeks through contemplation and deliberation to act and to serve in accordance with divine wisdom and thus in one sense to reflect, at least partially, divine intentions. It is not surprising that Aquinas associates

[20] C. Deane-Drummond, 'The Logos as Sophia: The Starting Point for a Sophianic Theology of Creation', in Peacocke and Clayton (eds.), *In Whom We Live and Move and Have Our Being*, pp. 233–45.

wisdom with peacemaking, for wisdom at its fullest will always seek to make for peace and that which builds up the common life. Such an ideal is, I suggest, an important aspect to remember when dealing with those areas of genetic technologies that raise controversial and difficult choices. I will give the last word to Josef Pieper, who appreciated more than most the mystical dimension in Aquinas, which served to qualify any interpretation of him in rationalistic terms. In a sense, genetics also gives us pause for thought in the face of such reality:

In the work of St Thomas all ways of creaturely knowing have been followed to the very end – to the boundary of mystery. And the more intently we pursue these ways of knowledge, the more is revealed to us – of the darkness but also of the reality of mystery.[21]

---

[21] Aquinas also believed that all things were creatively thought by the Creator and thus that they bore the stamp of truth in everything that is real. See Pieper, *The Silence of St Thomas*, pp. 44, 59.

Bibliography

Ackermann, D., and R. B. Storm (eds.), *Liberating Faith Practices: Feminist Practical Theologies in Context* (Leuven: Uitgeverij Peeters, 1998).

Adams, M. B., *The Wellborn Science: Eugenics in Germany, France, Brazil and Russia* (Oxford: Oxford University Press, 1990).

Almond, B., and M. Parker (eds.), *Ethical Issues in the New Genetics: Are Genes Us?* (Aldershot: Ashgate, 2003).

Arras, J., and N. K. Rhoden (eds.), *Ethical Issues in Modern Medicine*, 3rd edn (Mountain View, CA: Mayfield Publishing Co., 1989).

Ashley, B., and K. O'Rourke, *Health Care Ethics; A Theological Analysis*, 2nd edn (St Louis: Catholic Health Association of the United States, 1982).

Atkins, M., 'Could There Be Squirrels in Heaven?', *Theology in Green* 4 (1992), pp. 17–28.

Baker, T., and J. Simon, *Embracing Risk: The Changing Culture of Insurance and Responsibility* (Chicago: University of Chicago Press, 2002).

Banner, M., *Christian Ethics and Contemporary Moral Problems* (Cambridge: Cambridge University Press, 1999).

(chairman), *Report of the Committee to Consider the Ethical Implications of Emerging Technologies in the Breeding of Farm Animals* (London: HMSO, 1995).

Barad, J., *Aquinas on the Nature and Treatment of Animals* (San Francisco: International Scholars Publications, 1995).

Bauckham, R., 'Joining Creation's Praise', *Ecotheology* 7/1 (2002), pp. 45–59.

Beauchamp, T. L., and J. F. Childress, *Principles of Biomedical Ethics*, 5th edn (New York: Oxford University Press, 2001).

Beauvoir, S. de, *The Second Sex*, trans. and ed. H. M. Parshley (1952; Harmondsworth: Penguin, 1972).

Beck, U., *Risk Society: Towards a New Modernity*, trans. M. Ritter (London: Sage, 1992).

Benjamin, C., 'Indigenous Peoples Barred from DNA Sampling Conference', *GeneWATCH* 10 (February 1997), pp. 5, 18.

Berry, R. J., *The Care of Creation: Focusing Concern and Action* (Leicester: Inter-Varsity Press, 2000).

Biggar, N., *Hastening that Waits: Karl Barth's Ethics* (Oxford: Oxford University Press, 1995).

Biggar, N., and R. Black, *The Revival of Natural Law: Philosophical, Theological and Ethical Responses to the Finnis-Grisez School* (Aldershot: Ashgate, 2000).

Birke, L., and S. West (eds.), Brighton Womens Science Group, *Alice through the Microscope: The Power of Science over Women's Lives* (London: Virago, 1980).

Bonthron, D., D. FitzPatrick, M. Porteous and A. Trainer, *Clinical Genetics: A Case-Based Approach* (London: W. B. Saunders, 1998).

Bostanci, A., 'Blood Test Flags Agent in Death of Penn Subject', *Science* 295 (25 January 2002), pp. 604b–605b.

Bostrom, N., 'Human Genetic Enhancement: A Transhumanist Perspective', *The Journal of Value Inquiry* 37/4 (2003), pp. 493–506, <http://www.nickbostrum.com>.

British Medical Association, *The Impact of Genetic Modification on Agriculture, Food and Health: An Interim Statement* (London: BMA, 1999).

Bryant, J., and J. Searle, *Life in Our Hands: A Christian Perspective on Genetics and Cloning* (Leicester: IVP, 2004).

Burley, J., and J. Harris, *A Companion to Genethics* (Oxford: Blackwell, 2002).

Cahill, L. S., *Sex, Gender and Christian Ethics* (Cambridge: Cambridge University Press, 1996).

Camenisch, P. F. (ed.), *Theology and Medicine: Religious Methods and Resources in Bioethics* (Dordrecht: Kluwer Academic Publishers, 1994).

Caputo, J. D., *Heidegger and Aquinas: An Essay on Overcoming Metaphysics* (New York: Fordham University Press, 1982).

Carlson, E. A., *The Unfit: The History of a Bad Idea* (Cold Spring Harbor: Cold Spring Habor Laboratory Press, 2001).

Carmichael, L., *Friendship: Interpreting Christian Love* (London: Continuum, 2004).

Cates, D., *Choosing to Feel: Virtue, Feeling and Compassion for Friends* (Notre Dame: University of Notre Dame Press, 1997).

Cates, D. F., and P. Lauritzen (eds.), *Medicine and the Ethics of Care* (Washington: Georgetown University Press, 2001).

Cessario, R., *An Introduction to Moral Theology* (Washington: Catholic University of America Press, 2002).

Chadwick, R. (ed.), *Ethics, Reproduction and Genetic Control* (London: Routledge, 1992).

Chapman, A., *Unprecedented Choices: Religious Ethics at the Frontiers of Genetic Science* (Minneapolis: Fortress Press, 1999).

Chapman, A. (ed.), *Perspectives on Gene Patenting: Religion, Science and Industry in Dialogue* (Washington: AAAS, 1999).

Chapman, A., and M. S. Frankel (eds.), *Designing Our Descendents: The Promises and Perils of Genetic Modification* (Baltimore and London: Johns Hopkins University Press, 2003).

Chesterton, G. K., *Eugenics and Other Evils* (London: Cassell, 1922).

Clark, S., *Biology and Christian Ethics* (Cambridge: Cambridge University Press, 2000).

The Moral Status of Animals (Oxford: Oxford University Press, 1977).

The Political Animal; Biology, Ethics and Politics (London: Routledge, 1999).

Clarke, A., *Genetic Counselling: Practices and Principles* (London: Routledge, 1994).

Clarke, A. (ed.), *The Genetic Testing of Children* (Oxford: Bio Scientific, 1998).

Clarke, P. B., and A. Linzey (eds.), *Dictionary of Ethics, Theology and Society* (London: Routledge, 1996).

Cleminson, R., *Anarchism, Science and Sex: Eugenics in Eastern Spain 1900–1937* (Bern: Peter Lang, 2000).

Cole-Turner, R., *The New Genesis; Theology and the Genetic Revolution* (Louisville: Westminster John Knox Press, 1993).

'Religion and Gene Patenting', *Science* 270 (6 October 1995), p. 52.

Cole-Turner, R. (ed.), *Design and Destiny: Religious Voices on Human Germ Line Modification* (Massachusetts: MIT Press, in press).

Connor, M., and M. Ferguson Smith, *Essential Medical Genetics*, 5th edn (Oxford: Blackwell Science, 1997).

Cooper, D. E., and J. A. Palmer (eds.), *Spirit of the Environment: Religion, Value and Environmental Concern* (London: Routledge, 1998).

Cooper, M., 'Regenerative Medicine: Stem Cells and the Science of Monstrosity', *Journal of Medical Ethics, Medical Humanities Edition*, 30/1 (June 2004), pp. 12–22.

Coors, M., *The Matrix: Charting an Ethics of Inheritable Genetic Modification* (Lanham: Rowman and Littlefield, 2003).

Cornish, W., and D. Llewelyn, *Intellectual Property: Patents, Copyright, Trade Marks and Allied Rights*, 5th edn (London: Sweet and Maxwell, 2003).

Correa, C. M., *Intellectual Property Rights, the WTO and Developing Countries*, (London: Zed Books, 2000).

Crisp, R. (ed.), *How Should One Live? Essays on the Virtues* (Oxford: Clarendon Press: 1996).

Crisp, R., and M. Slote (eds.), *Virtue Ethics* (Oxford: Oxford University Press: 1997).

Crystal, R. G., 'Fooling Mother Nature: Correcting Defective Genes at the mRNA Level Shows Promise for the Treatment of Cystic Fibrosis', *Nature Biotechnology* 20 (January 2002), pp. 32–3.

Curran, C. E., *Politics, Medicine and Christian Ethics: A Dialogue with Paul Ramsey* (Philadelphia: Fortress Press, 1973).

Darwell, S. (ed.), *Virtue Ethics* (Oxford: Blackwell, 2002).

Darwin, C., *The Descent of Man, and Selection in Relation to Sex* (1871; repr. Princeton: Princeton University Press, 1981).

'Letters to the Editor', *Nature* 3 (27 April 1871), pp. 502–3.

Deane-Drummond, C., *Biology and Theology Today; Exploring the Boundaries* (London: SCM Press, 2001).

'Come to the Banquet: Seeking Wisdom in a Genetically Engineered Earth', *Ecotheology* 9 (2000), pp. 27–37.

Creation through Wisdom: Theology and the New Biology (Edinburgh: T. & T. Clark, 2000).

The Ethics of Nature (Oxford: Blackwell, 2004).

'Gaia as Science Made Myth: Implications for Environmental Ethics', *Studies in Christian Ethics* 9/2 (1996), pp. 1–15.

Theology and Biotechnology: Implications for a New Science (London: Geoffrey Chapman, 1997).

Deane-Drummond, C. (ed.), *Brave New World? Theology, Ethics and the Human Genome* (London: Continuum/T. & T. Clark, 2003).

Deane-Drummond, C., and B. Szerszynski (eds.), *Re-Ordering Nature: Theology, Society and the New Genetics* (London: Continuuum/T. & T. Clark, 2003).

Deech, R., 'The Ethics of Embryo Selection', paper presented to a conference entitled 'The Meaning of the Person: Consciousness, Genetics and Evolutionary Biology', Ian Ramsey Centre, St Anne's College (12 July 2002).

Deneulin, S., M. Nebel and N. Sagovsky (eds.), *Capabilities and Justice: Towards Structural Transformation* (Dordrecht: Kluwer, forthcoming).

Dennis, C., 'Deaf by Design', *Nature* 431 (21 October 2004), pp. 894–6.

Department of Health, *Our Inheritance, Our Future: Realising the Potential of Genetics in the NHS* (London: HMSO, 2003), also available at <http://www.doh.gov.uk/genetics/whitepaper.htm>.

Dequeker, E., and J. J. Cassiman, 'Genetic Testing and Quality Control in Diagnostic Laboratories', *Nature Genetics* 25 (2000), pp. 259–60.

Du Bose, E. R., R. P. Hamel and L. J. O'Connell (eds.), *A Matter of Principles: Ferment in US Bioethics* (Valley Forge: Trinity Press International, 1994).

Dugdale, R. L. *'The Jukes': A Study in Crime, Pauperism, Disease and Heredity* (New York: G. P. Putnam's Sons, 1877).

Dupré, A., *Human Nature and the Limits of Science*, (Oxford: Oxford University Press, 2002).

Dyson, A., *Ethics and the New Reproductive Technologies: On Listening to Feminism*, Contact Pastoral Monograph 1 (London: *Contact: Interdisciplinary Journal of Pastoral Studies*, 1991).

Dyson, A., and J. Harris (eds.), *Ethics and Biotechnology* (London: Routledge, 1994).

Editorial, 'Toward Tailored Cancer Therapy', *Science* 304 (4 June 2004), p. 1409i.

Edwards, D., *Jesus the Wisdom of God; An Ecological Theology* (Homebush: St Paul's, 1995).

Edwards, D., and M. Worthing (eds.), *Biodiversity and Ecology: An Interdisciplinary Challenge* (Adelaide: ATF Press, 2004).

Edwards, R. G. (ed.), *Preconception and Preimplantation Genetic Diagnosis of Human Genetic Disease* (Cambridge: Cambridge University Press, 1993).

Evans, J. H., *Playing God: Human Genetic Engineering and the Rationalisation of Public Bioethical Debate* (London and Chicago: University of Chicago Press, 2002).

Fletcher, J., *Humanhood* (Buffalo: Prometheus Books, 1979).

Fletcher, J. F., *The Ethics of Genetic Control: Ending Reproductive Roulette* (Garden City: Anchor Press, 1974).

Fox Keller, E., *Secrets of Life, Secrets of Death: Essays on Language, Gender and Science* (London and New York: Routledge, 1992).

Friedmann, T., 'Principles for Human Gene Therapy Studies', *Science* 287 (24 March 2000), pp. 2163–5.

Fukuyama, F., *Our Posthuman Future* (London: Profile, 2002).

Fulford, K. W. M., G. Gillett and J. Martin Soskice, *Medicine and Moral Reasoning* (Cambridge: Cambridge University Press, 1994).

Galton, F., 'Experiments in Pangenesis, by breeding from rabbits of a pure variety, into whose circulation blood taken from other varieties had previously been largely transfused', *Proceedings of the Royal Society (Biology)* 19 (1871), pp. 393–404.

Hereditary Genius, 2nd edn (London: Macmillan, 1892).

'Hereditary Talent and Character', *Macmillan's Magazine* 12 (1865), pp. 157–66, 318–27.

Inquiries into Human Faculty and its Development (London: J. M. Dent, 1883).

'Letters to the Editor', *Nature* 4 (4 May 1871), pp. 5–6.

Sociological Papers (London: Macmillan and Co., 1905).

Gee, H., 'Flores, God and Cryptozoology', <http://www.nature.com/news/2004/041025/full/041025–2.html>, accessed 1 November 2004.

Gelb, S., 'Social Deviancy and the Discovery of the Moron', *Disability, Handicap and Society* 2 (1987), pp. 247–58.

Genetics Commissioning Advisory Group (GenCAG), *Pre-Implantation Genetic Diagnosis (PGD) – Guiding Principles for Commissioners for NHS Services* (London: Department of Health, September 2002).

George, R. (ed.), *Natural Law Theory: Contemporary Essays* (Oxford: Clarendon Press, 1992).

Gibbons, A., 'Tracking the Evolutionary History of a "Warrior" Gene', *Science* 304 (7 May 2004), pp. 818–19.

Giddens, A., *Modernity and Self-Identity: Self and Society in the Late Modern Age* (Cambridge: Polity, 1991).

Gill, R., 'Review: *Unprecedented Choices: Religious Ethics at the Frontiers of Genetic Science* by Audrey Chapman (Fortress Press: Minneapolis, 1999)', *Zygon* 39/3 (2004), pp. 713–15.

Gill, R. (ed.), *Cambridge Companion to Christian Ethics* (Cambridge: Cambridge University Press, 2001).

Gilligan, C., *In a Different Voice* (Cambridge, MA: Harvard University Press, 1982).

Goddard, H., *The Kallikak Family: A Study in the Heredity of Feeblemindedness* (New York: Macmillan, 1912).

Goodman, A. H., D. Heath and M. S. Lindee (eds.), *Genetic Nature/Culture: Anthropology and Science Beyond the Two-Culture Divide* (Berkeley: University of California Press, 2003).

Gould, P., 'Key Genes May Not Create Down Syndrome', *Nature* (21 October 2004), published online, <http://www.nature.com/news/041018/full/041018–14.html, accessed 1 November 2004.

Graham, E., *Representations of the Post/human: Monsters, Aliens and Others in Popular Culture* (Manchester: Manchester University Press, 2002).

Grantén, E., *Patterns of Care: Relating Altruism in Sociobiology and the Christian Tradition of Agape* (Lund: Lund University Studies in Ethics and Theology, 2003).

Guo, H., M. Kerberg, M. Long, J. P. Jones III, B. Sullenger, and A. M. Lambowitz, 'Group II Introns Designed to Insert into Therapeutically Relevant DNA Target Sites in Human Cells', *Science* 289 (21 July 2000), pp. 452–7.

Gustafson, J. *Ethics from a Theocentric Perspective, I: Theology and Ethics* (Chicago: University of Chicago Press, 1981).

Ethics from a Theocentric Perspective: II: Ethics and Theology (Chicago: University of Chicago Press, 1984).

A Sense of the Divine; The Natural Environment from a Theocentric Perspective (Edinburgh: T. & T. Clark, 1994).

Habermas, J., *The Future of Human Nature* (Cambridge: Polity, 2003).

Hall, D. J., *Imaging God; Dominion as Stewardship* (Grand Rapids: Eerdmans, 1986).

Hall, P., *Narrative and the Natural Law: An Interpretation of Thomistic Ethics* (Notre Dame: University of Notre Dame Press, 1994).

Hanson, M. J., 'Religious Voices in Biotechnology: The Case of Gene Patenting', *The Hastings Center Report* 27 (November/December 1997), S10–11.

Häring, B., *The Ethics of Manipulation* (New York: Seabury Press, 1975).

Law of Christ, I (Cork: Mercier Press, 1960).

Harper, P. S., and A. J. Clarke (eds.), *Genetics, Society and Clinical Practice* (Oxford: Bios Scientific Publishers, 1997).

Harris, J., *Clones, Genes and Immortality: Ethics and the Genetic Revolution* (Oxford: Oxford University Press, 1998).

Harris, J., and S. Holm (eds.), *The Future of Human Reproduction: Ethics, Choice and Regulation* (Oxford: Clarendon Press, 1998).

Hauerwas, S., *A Community of Character: Towards a Constructive Christian Social Ethic* (Notre Dame: University of Notre Dame Press, 1981).

Suffering Presence: Theological Reflections on Medicine, the Mentally Handicapped and the Church (Notre Dame: University of Notre Dame Press, 1986).

Häyry, M., 'There is a Difference Between Selecting a Deaf Embryo and Deafening a Hearing Child', *Journal of Medical Ethics* 30/5 (October 2004), pp. 510–12.

Hefner, P., *The Human Factor: Evolution, Culture and Religion* (Minneapolis: Fortress Press, 1993).

Technology and Human Becoming (Minneapolis: Fortress Press, 2003).

Heller, M. A., and R. S. Eisenberg, 'Can Patents Deter Innovation? The Anticommons in Biomedical Research', *Science* 280 (1 May 1998), pp. 698–701.

Hettinger, N., 'Patenting Life: Biotechnology, Intellectual Property and Environmental Ethics', *Environmental Affairs* 22 (1995), pp. 269–86.

Heyman, B., and M. Henrikson, *Risk, Age and Pregnancy: A Case Study of Prenatal Genetic Screening and Testing* (Basingstoke: Palgrave, 2001).

Holland, A., and A. Johnson (eds.), *Animal Biotechnology and Ethics* (London: Chapman and Hall, 1997).

Hollenbach, D., *The Common Good and Christian Ethics* (Cambridge: Cambridge University Press, 2002).

Hopkin, M., 'Mother's Genetics Could Influence Sexual Orientation', <http://www.nature.com/news/2004/041011/full/041011–5.html> (12 October 2004), accessed 1 November 2004.

House of Lords Select Committee on Science and Technology, Report (March 2001).

Hui, E. C., *At the Beginning of Life: Dilemmas in Theological Bioethics* (Leicester: Inter-Varsity Press, 2002).

Human Genetics Commission (HGC), *Inside Information: Balancing Interests in the Use of Personal Genetic Data* (HGC, May 2002), <http://www.hgc.gov.uk/insideinformation/index.htm>, accessed 29 August 2003.

 Public Attitudes to Human Genetic Information: People's Panel Quantitative Study, October–December 2000 (HGC, 2000), <http://www.hgc.gov.uk/business_publications.htm>.

Human Genome Organisation, HUGO Ethics Committee, *Statement on Benefit Sharing* (London: HUGO, 9 April 2000).

 HUGO Ethics Committee, *Statement on Human Genomic Databases* (London: HUGO, December 2002).

 HUGO IP Statement on Patenting of DNA Sequences in Particular Response to the European Biotechnology Directive (London: HUGO, April 2000).

 HUGO Statement on the Patenting of DNA Sequences (London: HUGO, January 1995).

Hunt, K. K., and S. A. Vorburger, 'Hurdles and Hopes for Cancer Treatment', *Science* 297 (19 July 2002), pp. 415–16.

Hursthouse, R., *On Virtue Ethics* (Oxford: Oxford University Press, 1999).

Jagger, A. M., *Feminist Politics and Human Nature* (Totawa, NJ: Rowman and Allanheld, 1983).

Jones, D., *The Soul of the Embryo: An Inquiry into the Status of the Human Embryo in Christian Tradition* (London: Continuum, 2004).

Jones, L. G., *Transformed Judgment: Towards a Trinitarian Account of the Moral Life* (Notre Dame: University of Notre Dame Press, 1990).

Junker-Kenny M. (ed.), *Designing Life? Genetics, Procreation and Ethics* (Aldershot: Ashgate, 1999).

Junker-Kenny, M., and L. Sowle Cahill (eds.), *The Ethics of Genetic Engineering*, Concilium (London: SCM Press, 1998).

Kaiser, J., 'Side Effects Sideline Hemophilia Trial', *Science* 304 (4 June 2004), pp. 1423–5.

Kaplan, J. M., *The Limits and Lies of Human Genetic Research: Dangers for Social Policy* (London: Routledge, 2000).

Keenan, J., 'What is Morally New in Genetic Manipulation?', *Human Gene Therapy* 1 (1990), pp. 289–98.

Kelves, D. J., *A History of Patenting Life in the United States with Comparative Attention to Europe and Canada* (Luxembourg: European Commission, 2002).

Kennedy, I., *A Report by the Advisory Group on the Ethics of Xenotransplantation of Animal Tissues into Humans* (London: Department of Health, HMSO, 1997).

Kerr, F. (ed.), *Contemplating Aquinas: On the Varieties of Interpretation* (London: SCM Press, 2003).

King, M., and S. Ruggles, 'American Immigration, Fertility, and Race Suicide at the Turn of the Century', *Journal of Interdisciplinary History* 20 (1990), pp. 347–69.

Kingston, H. M., *ABC of Clinical Genetics*, 3rd edn (London: BMJ Books, 2002).

Kotva, J. J., *The Christian Case for Virtue Ethics* (Washington: Georgetown University Press, 1996).

Kuliev, A. M., K. Greendale, V. B. Penchaszadeh and N. Paul (eds.), *Provision of Genetic Services: An International Perspective* (New York: Birth Defects Foundation, 1992).

Land, R. D., and C. B. Mitchell, 'Brave New Biopatents', *First Things: A Monthly Journal of Religion and Public Life* 63 (May 1996), p. 21.

'Patenting Life: No', *First Things: A Monthly Journal of Religion and Public Life* 63 (May 1996), pp. 20–2.

Lavery, S. A., R. Aurell, C. Turner, C. Castellu, A. Veiga, P. N. Barri, and R. M. Winston, 'Preimplantation Genetic Diagnosis: Patients' Experiences and Attitudes', *Human Reproduction* 17 (May 2002), pp. 2464–7.

Lewens, T., 'What is Genethics? Commentary on "Companion to Genethics" by Justine Burley and John Harris (2002)', *Journal of Medical Ethics* 30/3 (June 2004), pp. 326–8.

Lewis, C. S., *The Abolition of Man* (Glasgow: The University Press: 1943).

Linzey, A., *Animal Theology* (London: SCM Press, 1994).

Christianity and the Rights of Animals (London: SPCK, 1987).

'The Moral Priority of the Weak', *Theology in Green* 5/2 (1995), pp. 3–21.

The Status of Animals in the Christian Tradition (Birmingham: Woodbrooke College, 1985).

Linzey, A., and D. Cohn-Sherbok, *After Noah: Animals and the Liberation of Theology* (London: Mowbray, 1997).

McFague, S., *Super, Natural Christians: How We Should Love Nature* (London: SCM Press, 1997).

McGibben, B., *Enough: Genetic Engineering and the End of Human Nature* (London: Bloomsbury, 2003).

McGrath, A., *A Scientific Theology, II: Reality* (London: Continuum, 2002).

MacIntyre, A., *After Virtue: A Study in Moral Theory*, 2nd edn (London: Duckworth, 1985).

Dependent Rational Animals: Why Human Beings Need the Virtues (London: Duckworth, 1999).

Mackler, A. L., *Introduction to Jewish and Catholic Bioethics* (Washington: Georgetown University Press, 2003).

McNeil, M., I. Varco and S. Yearley (eds.), *The New Reproductive Technologies* (Basingstoke and London: Macmillan, 1990).

Mahowald, M., *Genes, Women, Equality* (Oxford: Oxford University Press, 2000).

Malakoff, D., 'The Calculus of Making Stem Cells a Campaign Issue', *Science* 305 (6 August 2004), p. 760.

Marshall, E., 'FDA Halts All Gene Therapy Trials at Penn', *Science* 287 (28 January 2000), pp. 565b–567b.

'Gene Therapy's Web of Corporate Connections', *Science* 288 (12 May 2000), pp. 954–5.

'Panel Reviews Risk of Germ Line Changes', *Science* 294 (14 December 2001), pp. 2268b–2269b.

May, C., *A Global Political Economy of Intellectual Property Rights: The New Enclosure?* (London: Routledge, 2000).

Meilaender, G., 'The Thinning of Bioethical Discourse', *Medical Humanities Review* 16/2 (2002), pp. 71–5.

Messer, N., 'Health Care Resource Allocation and the "Recovery of Virtue"', *Studies in Christian Ethics* 18/1 (forthcoming).

Moltmann, J., *The Future of Creation*, trans. M. Kohl (London: SCM Press, 1978).

Muers, R., 'Pushing the Limit: Theology and the Responsibility to Future Generations', *Studies in Christian Ethics* 16/2 (2004), pp. 36–51.

Muller, H. J., *A Decade of Progress in Eugenics* (Baltimore: Williams and Wilkins, 1934).

Out of the Night: A Biologist's View of the Future (New York: Vanguard Press, 1935).

Murray, R., *The Cosmic Covenant* (London: Sheed and Ward, 1992).

Noddings, N., *Caring: A Feminine Approach to Ethics and Moral Education* (Berkeley: University of California Press, 1984).

Northcott, M., *Christianity and Environmental Ethics* (Cambridge: Cambridge University Press, 1996).

Nuffield Report, *Genetically Modified Crops: The Ethical and Social Issues* (London: Nuffield Council on Bioethics, 1999).

O'Donovan, O., *Begotten or Made?* (Oxford: Clarendon Press, 1984).

Resurrection and Moral Order: An Outline for Evangelical Ethics (Leicester: Inter-Varsity Press, 1986).

O'Neill, J., 'Property in Science and the Market', *The Monist* 73 (October 1990), pp. 601–20.

O'Neill, O., *Towards Justice and Virtue: A Constructive Account of Practical Reasoning* (Cambridge: Cambridge University Press, 1996).

Okin, S. M., *Justice, Gender and the Family* (New York: Basic Books, 1989).

Opinion on Ethical Aspects of Patenting Inventions Involving Human Stem Cells (Luxembourg: European Union, 2002).

Organisation for Economic Cooperation and Development (OECD), *Genetic Testing: Policy Issues for the New Millennium* (Paris: OECD, 2000).

Page, R., *God and the Web of Creation* (London: SCM Press, 1996).

Parfit, D., *Reasons and Persons* (New York: New York University Press, 1984).

Park, C., *The Environment: Principles and Applications*, 2nd edn (London: Routledge, 2001).

Paul VI, Pope, *Humanae Vitae* (London: Catholic Truth Society, 1986).

Paul, D. B., *Controlling Human Heredity: 1865 to the Present* (New Jersey: Humanities Press, 1995).

Peacocke, A., and P. Clayton (eds.), *In Whom We Live and Move and Have Our Being: Reflections on Panentheism in an Age of Science* (New York: Eerdmans, 2003).

Pearson, K. *The Life, Letters and Labours of Francis Galton*, IIIA (Cambridge: Cambridge University Press, 1930).

Penchaszadeh, V. B., 'Reproductive Health and Genetic Testing in the Third World', *Clinical Obstetrics and Gynecology* 36/3 (1993), pp. 490–3.

Pennisi, E., 'Genome Comparisons Hold Clues to Human Evolution', *Science* 302 (12 December 2003), pp. 1876–7.

'Searching for the Genome's Second Code', *Science* 306 (22 October 2004), pp. 632–5.

Pernick, M. N., *The Black Stork: Eugenics and the Death of 'Defective' Babies in American Medicine and Motion Pictures since 1915* (Oxford and New York: Oxford University Press, 1996).

Peters, T., 'Patenting Life: Yes', *First Things: A Monthly Journal of Religion and Public Life* 63 (May 1996), pp. 18–20.

Playing God: Genetic Determinism and Human Freedom (London: Routledge, 1998).

Science and Theology: The New Consonance (Boulder: Westview Press, 1998).

Peters, T. (ed.), *Genetics; Issues of Social Justice*, (Cleveland: Pilgrim Press, 1998).

Peterson, J., *Genetic Turning Points: The Ethics of Human Genetic Intervention* (Grand Rapids: Eerdmans, 2001).

Pieper, J., *Fortitude and Temperance*, trans. D. F. Coogan (London: Faber and Faber: 1955).

The Four Cardinal Virtues (Notre Dame: University of Notre Dame Press, 1966).

Prudence, trans. R. and C. Winston (London: Faber and Faber, 1959).

The Silence of St Thomas, trans. D. O'Connor (London: Faber and Faber, 1957).

Polkinghorne, J., *Belief in God in an Age of Science* (New Haven and London: Yale University Press, 1998).

Science and Christian Belief: Reflections of a Bottom Up Thinker (London: SPCK, 1994).

Polkinghorne, J. (ed.), *The Work of Love: Creation as Kenosis* (London: SPCK, 2001).

Porter, J., 'Individuality, Personal Identity, and the Moral Status of the Preembryo: A Response to Mark Johnson', *Theological Studies* 56 (December 1995), pp. 763–70.

Moral Action and Christian Ethics (Cambridge: Cambridge University Press, 1996).

The Recovery of Virtue (London: SPCK, 1994).

Post, S. G., L. G. Underwood, J. P. Schloss and W. B. Hurlbut (eds.), *Altruism and Altruistic Love: Science, Philosophy and Religion in Dialogue* (Oxford: Oxford University Press, 2002).

Poulton, E. B., S. Schönland and A. E. Shipley, *Essays upon Heredity and Kindred Biological Problems*, 2 vols. (Oxford: Clarendon Press, 1891).

Public Health Genetics Unit, 'Brief UK Policy Update', in *Human Genetic Databases and the Protection of Medical Information*, <http://www.medschl. cam.ac.uk/phgu/info_database/ELSI/genet-database.asp>, accessed 21 August 2003.

Rahner, K., *Foundations of Christian Faith*, trans. W. V. Dych (London: Darton, Longman and Todd, 1978).

Theological Investigations, VII: Concerning Vatican Council II, trans. K. H. and B. Kniger (London: Darton, Longman and Todd, 1969).

Theological Investigations, IX: Writings of 1965–7, trans. G. Harrison (London: Darton, Longman and Todd, 1972).

Ramsey, P., *Basic Christian Ethics*, (1950; Louisville: Westminster John Knox Press, 1993).

'A Christian Approach to the Question of Sexual Relations Outside Marriage', *The Journal of Religion* 45 (1965), pp. 100–18.

Fabricated Man: The Ethics of Genetic Control (New Haven and London: Yale University Press, 1970).

'Shall We Reproduce? I. The Medical Ethics of In-Vitro Fertilization', *Journal of the American Medical Association* 220 (5 June 1972), pp. 1346–50.

'Shall We Reproduce? II. Rejoinders and Future Forecast', *Journal of the American Medical Association* 220 (12 June 1972), pp. 1480–5.

Rawls, J., *A Theory of Justice* (Cambridge, MA: Harvard University Press, 1971).

Reich, W. T. (ed.), *Encyclopaedia of Bioethics*, rev. edn, IV (New York: Simon and Schuster Macmillan, 1995).

Resnik, D., *Owning the Genome: A Moral Analysis of DNA Patenting* (Albany: State University of New York Press, 2004).

Ricoeur, P., *Oneself as Another* (Chicago and London: University of Chicago Press, 1992).

Rolston III, H., *Genes, Genesis and God: Values and Their Origins in Natural and Human History* (Cambridge: Cambridge University Press, 1999).

Roslansky, J. D. (ed.), *Genetics and the Future of Man* (Amsterdam: North Holland Publishing Co., 1966).

Ruddick, S., *Maternal Thinking* (New York: Ballantine Books, 1989).

Service, R. F., 'Recruiting Genes, Proteins, for a Revolution in Diagnostics', *Science* 300 (11 April 2003), pp. 236–9.

Shannon, T. A., *Made in Whose Image? Engineering and Christian Ethics* (New York: Humanity Books, 2000).

Shannon, T. A., and L. Cahill, *Religion and Artificial Reproduction: An Inquiry into the Vatican 'Instruction on Respect for Human Life in its Origin and the Dignity of Human Reproduction'*, (New York: Crossroad, 1988).

Shannon, T. A., and J. T. Walter (eds.), *The New Genetic Medicine: Theological and Ethical Reflections* (London: Sheed and Ward; Lanham: Rowman and Littlefield, 2003).

Sharpe, V., 'Justice and Care: The Implications of the Kohlberg–Gilligan Debate for Medical Ethics', *Theoretical Medicine* 13 (1992), pp. 295–318.

Sherrard, P., *Human Image: World Image: The Death and Resurrection of Sacred Cosmology* (Ipswich: Golgonooza Press, 1992).

The Rape of Man and Nature: An Inquiry into the Origins and Consequences of Modern Science (Ipswich: Golgonooza Press, 1987).

Sherwin, S., *No Longer Patient: Feminist Ethics and Health Care* (Philadelphia: Temple University Press, 1992).

Shildrick, M. B., *Leaky Bodies and Boundaries: Feminism, Postmodernism and Bioethics* (London: Routledge, 1997).

Shiva, V., *Biopiracy: The Plunder of Nature and Knowledge* (Dartington: Green Books, 1998).

'Life on a Threatened Planet. Inaugural Address', paper given to 'Life on a Threatened Planet: Genetic Controversy and Environmental Ethics' advanced workshop (Center for Theology and Natural Sciences, Berkeley, 4 June 2002).

Smith, C. H. (ed.), *Alfred Russel Wallace: An Anthology of his Shorter Writings* (Oxford: Oxford University Press, 1991).

Smith, D. H., and C. B. Cohen, *A Christian Response to the New Genetics: Religious, Ethical and Social Issues* (Lanham: Rowman and Littlefield, 2003).

Soloway, R. A., *Demography and Degeneration: Eugenics and the Declining Birthrate in Twentieth Century Britain*, 2nd edn (Chapel Hill: University of North Carolina Press, 1995).

Song, R. *Human Genetics: Fabricating the Future* (London: Darton, Longman and Todd, 2002).

Spink, J., and D. Geddes, 'Gene Therapy Progress and Prospects: Bringing Gene Therapy into Medical Practice: The Evolution of International Ethics and the Regulatory Environment', *Gene Therapy* 11/22 (23 September 2004), pp. 1611–16.

Stanworth, M. (ed.), *Reproductive Technologies, Gender, Motherhood and Medicine* (Minneapolis: University of Minnesota Press, 1987).

Statman, D. (ed.), *Virtue Ethics: A Critical Reader* (Edinburgh: Edinburgh University Press, 1997).

Steinberg, D., *Bodies in Glass: Genetics, Eugenics, Embryo Ethics* (Manchester: Manchester University Press, 1997).

Stephan, N. L., *The Hour of Eugenics: Race, Gender and Nation in Latin America* (Ithaca and London: Cornell University Press, 1991).

Stewart, J., 'Ricoeur, Public Ethics and Religion', paper presented to the Association of Teachers in Moral Theology, Leeds (6 November 2004).

Stone, D., *Breeding Superman: Nietzsche, Race and Eugenics in Edwardian and Interwar Britain* (Liverpool: Liverpool University Press, 2002).

Szerszynski, B., 'Risk and Trust: The Perfomative Dimension', *Environmental Values* 8/2 (1999), pp. 239–52.

Taubes, G., 'The Strange Case of Chimeraplasty', *Science* 298 (13 December 2002), pp. 2116–20.

Testa, G., and J. Harris, 'Ethical Aspects of ES Cell-Derived Gametes', *Science* 305 (17 September 2004), p. 1719.

Thomas Aquinas, *Summa Theologiae*, VII: *Father, Son and Holy Ghost*, 1a, trans. T. C. O'Brien (London: Blackfriars, 1976).

XXIII: *On Virtue*, 1a2ae, trans. W. D. Hughes (London: Blackfriars, 1969).

XXVIII: *Law and Political Theory*, 1a2ae, trans. T. Gilby (London: Blackfriars, 1966).

XXXII: *Consequences of Faith*, 2a2ae, trans. T. Gilby (London: Blackfriars, 1975).

XXXIII: *Hope*, 2a2ae, trans. W. J. Hill (London: Blackfriars, 1969).

XXXV: *Consequences of Charity*, 2a2ae, trans. T. R. Heath (London: Blackfriars, 1972).

XXXVI: *Prudence*, 2a2ae, trans. T. Gilby (London: Blackfriars, 1974).

XXXVII: *Justice*, 2a2ae, trans. T. Gilby (London: Blackfriars, 1974).

Somme théologique: La Prudence, 2a2ae questions 47–56, traduction francaise par T. H. Deman. Editions de la 'Revue des jeunes' (Paris: Desclée, 1949).

Thomson, P., *The Spirit of the Soil: Agriculture and Environmental Ethics* (London: Routledge, 1997).

Tong, R., *Feminist Approaches to Bioethics* (Boulder: Westview Press; London: HarperCollins, 1997).

Towns, C. R., and D. G. Jones, 'Stem Cells, Embryos and the Environment: A Context for Both Science and Ethics', *Journal of Medical Ethics* 30/4 (August 2004), pp. 410–13.

Traina, C., *Feminist Ethics and Natural Law: The End of Anathemas* (Washington: Georgetown University Press, 1999).

UK Biobank, 'Ethics and Consultation', <http://www.biobank.ac.uk/ethics.htm>, accessed 21 August 2003.

'Protocol for the UK Biobank: A Study of Genes, Environment and Health' (February 2002), <http://www.biobank.ac.uk/status.htm>, accessed 27 August 2003.

'What's New? <http://www.biobank.ac.uk/whatsnew.htm>, accessed 27 August 2003.

United Nations Development Programme (UNDP), *Human Development Report 2001: Making New Technologies Work for Human Development* (Oxford: Oxford University Press, 2001).

United Nations Educational, Scientific and Cultural Organisation (UNESCO), *International Declaration on Human Genetic Data* (Paris: UNESCO, October 2003).

Universal Declaration on the Human Genome and Human Rights (Paris: UNESCO, 11 November 1997).

Vacek, E. C., 'Catholic Natural Law and Reproductive Ethics', *Journal of Medicine and Philosophy* 17 (1992), pp. 339–43.

Van Overwalle, G., *Study on the Patenting of Inventions Related to Human Stem Cell Research*, Report from the European Group on Ethics in Science and New Technologies (Luxembourg: European Commission, 2001).

Vardy, P., *Being Human: Fulfilling Genetic and Spiritual Potential* (London: Daton, Longman and Todd, 2003).

Wadell, P., *Friendship and the Moral Life* (Notre Dame: University of Notre Dame Press, 1989).

Walzer, M., *Spheres of Justice: A Defence of Pluralism and Equality* (New York: Basic Books, 1983).

Ward, L. (ed.), *Considered Choices? The New Genetics, Prenatal Testing and People with Learning Disabilities* (Kidderminster: British Institute of Learning Disabilities, 2001).

Waters, B., and R. Cole-Turner (eds.), *God and the Embryo: Religious Voices on Stem Cells and Cloning* (Washington: Georgetown University Press, 2003).

Watson, J., *Passion for DNA: Genes, Genomes and Society* (Oxford: Oxford University Press, 2001).

Wellcome Trust, Medical Research Council and Department of Health, Press release, 4 April 2003, 'New CEO Announces His Vision for UK Biobank at Parliamentary Event', <http://wellcome.ac.uk/en/1/awtprerel0403n289.html>, accessed 27 August 2003.

Westberg, D., *Right Practical Reason* (Oxford: Clarendon Press, 2002).

Westermann, C., *Genesis 1–11*, trans. J. Scullion (Minneapolis: Fortress Press, 1987).

White House, 'Joint Statement by President Clinton and Prime Minister Tony Blair of the UK' (14 March 2000), <http://usinfo.state.gov/topical/global/biotech/00031401.htm>.

Willard, H. F., 'Artificial Chromosomes Coming to Life', *Science* 290 (17 November 2000), pp. 1308–9.

Wilson, E. O., *Biophilia* (Cambridge, MA: Harvard University Press, 1984).

On Human Nature, (Cambridge MA: Harvard University Press, 1978).

Wolf, S. M. (ed.), *Feminism and Bioethics: Beyond Reproduction* (Oxford: Oxford University Press, 1996).

World Trade Organisation (WTO), *Declaration on the TRIPS Agreement and Public Health*, Doha (14 November 2001).

Zanjani, E. D., and W. French Anderson, 'Prospects for In Utero Human Gene Therapy', *Science* 285 (24 September 1999), pp. 2084–8.

Index